THE COST OF WAR
British Policy on French War Debts, 1918–1932

For Susan, Sarah and Paul

The Cost of War

British Policy on French War Debts, 1918–1932

Arthur Turner

sussex
ACADEMIC
PRESS

BRIGHTON • PORTLAND

2 4 6 8 10 9 7 5 3 1

First published 1998 in Great Britain by
SUSSEX ACADEMIC PRESS
Box 2950
Brighton BN2 5SP

and in the United States of America by
SUSSEX ACADEMIC PRESS
5804 N.E. Hassalo St.
Portland, Oregon 97213-3644

British Library Cataloguing in Publication Data
A CIP catalogue record for this book is available from the British Library.

Library of Congress Cataloging-in-Publication Data

Turner, Arthur (Arthur S.)
The cost of war : British policy on French war debts, 1918–1932 / Arthur Turner.
p.   cm.
Includes bibliographical references and index.
ISBN 1–898723–37–0 (hc : alk. paper)
1. Debts, External—France.   2. World War, 1914–1918—Finance—France.
3.   Loans, British—France.   I. Title.
HJ8646. T87   1998
336.3´435´0944—dc21   98-27762
CIP

Printed by Bookcraft, Midsomer Norton, Bath
This book is printed on acid-free paper

Contents

———

Acknowledgements

———

I wish to acknowledge the assistance which I have received during the research for this book from archivists and other staff at the following: the Bank of England archives; Birmingham University Library; The British Library; The British Library of Political and Economic Science; Cambridge University Library; Churchill College archives, Cambridge; the Record Office, House of Lords; the Public Record Office.

I am extremely grateful to Professor George Peden of Stirling University who offered some perceptive and valuable comments on an early draft, though it scarcely needs to be said that responsibility for the finished product rests with the author alone. I also wish to thank the British Academy and the Carnegie Trust for their financial assistance.

Above all I owe a great debt to my family, and especially to my wife Susan whose unfailing support and encouragement have sustained me throughout the preparation of this study.

The Cost of War

British Policy on French War Debts, 1918–1932

Introduction

Georges Clemenceau is reputed to have said, during a conversation with Lloyd George in June 1921, 'Within an hour after the Armistice I had the impression that you had become once again the enemies of France', to which the other supposedly replied: 'Has that not always been the traditional policy of my country?'[1] This exhange – whether apocryphal or not – gives a fairly accurate impression of the wretched state of Anglo–French relations in the years immediately following the First World War. As soon as the overriding objective of defeating the common enemy had been achieved, Britain and France seemed to revert as if by instinct to the chronic rivalry that had characterised their relationship for centuries. Serious disagreements emerged in the course of the Paris peacemaking, and these foreshadowed a succession of bitter quarrels which at times strained the Entente almost to breaking point. Conflicting ambitions and interests in the Near and Middle East were one source of dissension. Differences also developed over policy towards Soviet Russia. Most serious of all, however, were the disputes that arose about implementation of the Treaty of Versailles, disputes rooted in Britain's failure to satisfy French demands for security and in the existence of fundamentally different strategies for dealing with a defeated Germany. The question of reparations proved to be especially contentious, provoking a whole series of crises in Anglo–French relations, the gravest of which occurred when – in flat defiance of British wishes – French and Belgian troops were sent into the Ruhr in January 1923 because of a default on reparation payments. In addition, there was persistent friction throughout the 1920s over the related matter of French war debts. Indeed, the acrimonious history of Anglo–French debt negotiations during this period offers solid evidence for the wisdom of the maxim 'Neither a borrower nor a lender be'.

This last aspect of Anglo–French relations has not received the attention from historians that it warrants. The war debt issue was a highly emotive one which aroused strong feelings – in official circles as well as amongst the public – on both sides of the Channel. It constituted an important piece in the intricate jigsaw of inter-state financial obligations bequeathed by the war. It greatly complicated the difficult task of producing a satisfactory and viable reparation settlement. More generally, it made its own special contribution to the prevailing mistrust that hampered co-operation between London and Paris during the 1920s. Yet despite this, comparatively little has been written on the subject, though it has figured as a minor theme in a number of the monographs that have been published in recent years on reparations and on European economic and financial recon-struction after the First World War.[2] Some useful information is to be found in the French historian Denise Artaud's massive two-volume history of inter-allied debts.[3] As a general study, however, this inevitably devotes only a limited amount of space to the specific topic of French obligations to Britain. Moreover, the book is not available in translation. There is undoubtedly room, therefore, for the comprehensive analysis of British policy on French indebtedness to Britain which this present work is intended to provide.

There is one point which it is perhaps worth emphasising at the outset. To readers accustomed to the enormous scale of current British public expenditure, many of the sums which appear in this study will seem small beer indeed. Equally, it may not always be easy to appreciate the passionate haggling taking place over what seem like trifling amounts by the standard of the 1990s. What has to be borne in mind, therefore, is that this is simply a reflection of the extent to which inflation has eroded the value of the pound since the end of the First World War. In order to convey some idea of how matters appeared to contem-porary policymakers, it might be pointed out that total British government expenditure for the financial year 1921–2, for instance, was only £1.136bn.[4] This was not much more than twice the value of the outstanding French war debt which, with accrued interest, stood at well over £500m at that time.[5]

1

Origins of the War Debts

I

When the French found it necessary to seek financial assistance from Britain (as well as the United States) during the First World War, little serious consideration was given by either side as to how, or to what extent, the vast sums that were being borrowed would eventually be repaid.[1] At a time when the Allies were engaged in a life-and-death struggle, such details understandably seemed relatively unimportant when compared with the overriding need to keep the war effort going. Certainly each of the various loan agreements set out in detail the terms and manner of repayment.[2] While the legal obligations were clear, however, what was less so was how rigorously they would be enforced. Because of the special circumstances in which the debts had been contracted, it was from the outset highly improbable that accounts would ever be settled on a purely book-keeping basis.

Other factors – economic, political and even emotional – were bound to intrude themselves into the negotiating process. When peace came, was it likely that Britain would insist that her main wartime Ally should pay what she owed to the last penny, or would the debt be partially cancelled in recognition of her appalling sacrifices? Would the French be willing or able to meet their obligations in full, or even to any significant extent, after the exertions of the war? Would it necessarily serve British interests to demand substantial payments when to do so would not only produce friction, but might also drive down the value of the franc, thereby giving a competitive advantage to French exports? These and similar considerations were almost certain to come into play and to offer ample scope for differences and misunderstandings.

Such proved to be the case. During the 1920s the war debt question was a constant irritant in Anglo-French relations, with each side accusing the other of bad faith and selfishness. As will be seen, the British became increasingly indignant at the French delay in negotiating a funding agreement, arguing that because of this delay the British taxpayer and British industry were bearing financial burdens which ought to be borne by their French counterparts. For their part, the French believed that the British failed to take sufficient account of the special character of the debts, the terrible losses that France had suffered during the war and the magnitude of her postwar financial difficulties.

II

The debts which France owed Britain were only one strand in a complex network of inter-allied indebtedness. The First World War imposed a huge financial burden on each of the countries taking part.[3] It has been estimated that the total direct cost to all the belligerents was about $210bn, with the Allied and Associated Powers spending some two-and-a-half times more to win the war than the Central Powers did to lose it.[4] According to one official estimate, Britain alone spent over £7bn, excluding loans to Allies – an amount equivalent to thirty-eight times annual peacetime expenditure in the immediate pre-war years.[5] The methods used to pay for the war varied somewhat from country to country. Despite differences of detail, however, there was a common pattern. Nowhere was any attempt made to finance the bulk of war expenditure through taxation. Although the costs were met to a limited extent by increasing existing taxes and introducing new ones, such as the levies on war profits in Britain and France, there was a far greater reliance on deficit financing. Thus Britain met only a quarter or so of her war expenditure from taxation,[6] while France – without any effective system of income tax until the closing stages of the war – managed a smaller proportion still: one estimate puts the figure as low as 2 per cent.[7] Vast sums were raised from domestic borrowing – the French government, for instance, obtaining advances totalling almost 19bn francs from the Bank of France and more than 35bn francs from the sale of short-term National Defence Bills (*Bons de la Défence Nationale*).[8] In almost every case, it also proved necessary to borrow abroad. Of the Allied and Associated Powers, only the United States was able to finance its war effort from its own resources. The rest – Britain, France, Italy, Russia and the smaller states such as Greece, Romania and Serbia – were all obliged to seek foreign credits for imports of food, armaments and other essential war materials.

In the period before America's entry into the war in April 1917, Britain acted as principal banker to the Continental Allies. The British government provided them with a number of substantial loans, and more generally played a key role in bolstering allied credit and facilitating allied purchases in the United States.[9] The Allies, and Britain and France in particular, bought vast quantities of American foodstuffs, cotton, petroleum, copper, pig-iron, steel, munitions and many other items.[10] In order to obtain sufficient dollars for such purchases, Britain found it necessary to borrow large amounts on the American market, to liquidate or pledge as collateral British holdings of American securities (both public and private), to ship gold from the Bank of England to New York, and to organise similar gold shipments by her Allies, including £53.5m worth from France. The whole operation placed an enormous strain on British resources and on the British and European exchanges, and by the summer of 1915 the pound sterling had slipped from its pre-war rate of $4.86 to a disturbing low of $4.50. In October of that year, therefore, a joint Anglo-French loan of $500m was raised in New York in order to 'peg' the pound at $4.765. The franc was also pegged at the same time.[11]

After the Americans joined the war the main responsibility for funding the allied war effort inevitably shifted to them, with the United States Treasury undertaking to make available the necessary funds for purchases in America.[12] Despite pressure from London, however, what the Americans were not prepared to do was to provide resources for use elsewhere. The British government was therefore obliged to continue furnishing the Allies with credits for such purposes – albeit with growing reluctance because of its own financial problems – until the end of hostilities and, indeed, beyond. By the spring of 1919 Britain had advanced a total of more than £1,650m to her Allies, while she herself had borrowed in excess of $4bn (around £840m) from the American government.[13]

Of Britain's debtors, France came second only to Russia in the amount owed. It was inevitable that France would need to borrow from abroad on a massive scale in order to finance the importation of a whole range of essential war materials which she could not provide for herself. This need was accentuated, however, by the fact that for almost the whole of the war some of the country's most prosperous and heavily industrialised regions were under enemy occupation or formed part of the battle zone. The effect of this was to disrupt economic activity and further increase French dependence on imports and the foreign credits to pay for them.[14] The fact that the greater part of her pig-iron production was in German hands and many of her mines destroyed meant that France had to buy iron, steel and coal in Britain, as well as woollen cloth, chemicals and a wide variety of other manufactured goods for which sterling credits were advanced. There were also purchases on an even bigger scale from America. As a result of these transactions, by the time fighting ceased France had borrowed a total of some $4.2bn from Britain and the United States.[15] Further debts were then contracted during the period of postwar reconstruction, with the credits in this case coming almost entirely from the United States. While borrowing from the British and Americans, France herself had by the end of the war lent the equivalent of some $1.5bn to Russia, Belgium, Serbia and a number of other states.[16]

III

The debts which France owed to Britain fell into three categories. First, there were obligations arising from a wartime advance from the Bank of England to the

Bank of France. In the spring of 1916 the French became concerned about the weakness of their currency relative to sterling and sought British help to support it.[17] A meeting was accordingly held on 28 March at which Lord Cunliffe, the Governor of the Bank of England, Georges Pallain, his French counterpart, Alexandre Ribot, the French Minister of Finance, and Reginald McKenna, the Chancellor of the Exchequer, discussed what measures ought to be adopted. Pallain, who had originally suggested an advance of only £24m, now pressed for £160m. McKenna thought this was too much, however, and on 25 April Cunliffe and Pallain signed a formal agreement providing the Bank of France with a continuous credit of £60m, to be used for the sole purpose of strengthening the franc against sterling.[18] The credit was renewable until six months after the end of the war and interest was set at 6 per cent or 1 per cent above Bank rate, whichever was higher. It was covered by a deposit of gold to the value of one-third of the advance, that is to say £20m. This was to remain earmarked to the Bank of France and to be returned in proportionate instalments as the debt was paid off.[19]

In the course of the next few years, these terms were modified in a number of ways. Article 4 of an agreement reached at Calais on 24 August 1916 – the main feature of which was a loan of £150m to the French government – extended the period during which the inter-bank credit could be renewed until two years after the end of the war.[20] Then, in January 1917, the amount was raised to £72m (with an accompanying increase in the deposit of gold to £24m), before being reduced to £65m in November 1918 when a partial repayment was effected with half the proceeds from a French government loan floated on the London market.[21] There was a further modification in the spring of 1923. By that time Montagu Norman, who had succeeded Cunliffe as Governor of the Bank of England some three years earlier, had become convinced that the French would not be able to repay the sum of £55m still outstanding by the appointed deadline of 31 August 1923. He also anticipated problems for the City if payments were made in accordance with such a timetable. He therefore responded favourably to a request from Pallain and his successor at the Bank of France, Georges Robineau, for a new schedule of payments. Norman's initial intention was that the debt should be discharged by means of eleven annual instalments of £5m.[22] But this suggestion did not find favour with Otto Niemeyer,[23] the Controller of Finance at the Treasury, who was consulted: Niemeyer's preference was for a repayment period of only seven years.[24] In the event, the agreement which Norman eventually concluded with Robineau on 12 April 1923 provided for the first payment to be made by by 30 November 1926 and the last one by 30 November 1931. Niemeyer also indicated to Norman that he would like to see changes in the existing arrangements concerning the gold deposited by the Bank of France. If possible, he wanted £10m of it to be purchased immediately. At the very least, however, he felt that all of it should be kept in London until the debt had been wholly paid off. Norman pressed this line during talks with French representatives on 7 and

8 March, but in the end had to settle for a compromise whereby none of the gold was to be returned before November 1928.[25] This aspect of the 1923 agreement rankled for a long time at the Bank of France: Emile Moreau, who replaced Robineau as Governor in the summer of 1926, felt particularly strongly about it.

There was also great resentment over another condition imposed by Norman. In a letter of 21 March, Norman informed Robineau that from 1 September 1923 the Bank of England would set aside 1 per cent of the value of the credit, and from 1 June 1928 until 31 May 1931 1.5 per cent of its value. The money thus accumulated was to be placed in a special Suspense Account and given to the Bank of France upon completion of the final payment. This rebate would be automatically cancelled, however, if France failed in any way to carry out the terms of the 1923 agreement.[26] In addition, Norman stipulated that the amount in question must not be used 'directly or indirectly otherwise than for the sole benefit of the Bank of France'[27] – a stipulation designed to prevent any financial benefit going to the French Treasury. When negotiations were set in motion in 1926 to further modify the terms of the agreement, this provision, along with that relating to return of the gold, was to present serious difficulties.

Strictly speaking, the whole matter of the Bank of England's wartime credit to the Bank of France was one between the banks alone and not connected with the question of inter-government debts. However, since the French Treasury were under an obligation to reimburse the Bank of France whenever repayments were made, they insisted that the two issues did have a bearing on each other and ought to be considered together. As will be seen, the British Treasury were prepared to give a sympathetic hearing to this argument – much to the annoyance of Norman.

The second sort of debt was that incurred when the French government raised money on the London market through the sale of bonds, or *rentes*. These bonds were issued as an integral part of French national war loan operations. They were purchased mainly by private investors and financial institutions, although some were also taken up – albeit with the utmost reluctance – by the Treasury. During the war there were four major operations of this type yielding a total of £54.5m: the first – raising £22m – in November 1915, and the rest in October 1916 (£16m), November 1917 (£2.5m) and November 1918 (£14m).[28] The outcome of the last flotation was far from satisfactory. According to one Treasury official, indeed, it was a 'fiasco', for which the French held the Bank of England to blame.[29] Because it raised less than £11m from the public, instead of the sum of £14m underwritten by the Treasury, the latter had no alternative but to make up the shortfall of £3,610,935; and in that way the British government acquired an unwanted direct interest in the market loans. It was to prove a costly and irksome business. Unfortunately for investors, including the Treasury, although the bonds provided France with sterling, they were expressed in francs. Nor was any guarantee provided against fluctuations in the exchange rate. As a result, the 1926 *de facto* stabilisation of the franc at around 122 to the pound, only one-fifth of its pre-war rate, was to wipe more than £40m off the value of the holdings, a development which naturally aroused a great deal of indignation and demands for compensation.[30]

The third and most substantial element of French indebtedness – and the one which will be the main subject of this study – was a consequence of direct wartime advances from the British to the French government. French attempts to raise money on the London market were not entirely successful: they found the terms increasingly onerous and the amounts which could be obtained too small. The British government therefore stepped in with Treasury loans – a development which had the considerable advantage, from London's standpoint, of making it easier to exercise control over French purchases.[31] The first of these loans was negotiated in Paris on 5 February 1915 during an inter-allied financial conference attended by the Chancellor of the Exchequer, David Lloyd George, and the French and Russian finance ministers, Alexandre Ribot and Peter Bark.[32] Another participant in the conference was John Maynard Keynes. At the outbreak of war Keynes had been an economics fellow at King's College, Cambridge. In January 1915, however, he had been appointed to a position in the Treasury as assistant to Sir George Paish, the special adviser to Lloyd George, and it was in this capacity that he attended the meeting in Paris. Some three months later he became a member of the Treasury's First Division, chiefly concerned with the financial direction of the war, and in February 1917 he was put in charge of a new department – the so-called 'A' division – to deal with all questions of external finance. Throughout this period, Keynes made a major contribution to the development of the inter-allied finance and purchasing system, being prominently involved *inter alia* with the negotiation of credits to France.[33]

The loan agreement negotiated in Paris was followed by a whole series of similar ones, the last of which was signed by the then Chancellor of the Exchequer, Austen Chamberlain, and the French Finance Minister, Louis-Lucien Klotz, in March 1919.[34] The loans totalled £446,226,000 and were advanced against the deposit of short-term (mainly one year) French Treasury bills, expressed in sterling. Interest rates varied, being set at the prevailing market rate. Bills covering some £58m of the total debt were to be renewed as they matured for a period of up to two years after the conclusion of peace – a date which was later defined more precisely as being that of the Treaty of Sèvres, 10 August 1920. All the rest were renewable until three years after the conclusion of peace, as stipulated in the Calais agreement of 1916.[35] In other words, it was expected that arrangements would be made to fund the debt by August 1923 at the latest. It was further expected that the French government would proceed by raising a sterling loan on the London market. In the event, however, neither of these expectations was fulfilled.

The advances were used to some extent to finance French imports from the British Empire and neutral countries. For the most part, though, they were spent in Britain – mainly to pay for coal, woollen goods, special steels, munitions and other items provided by government supply departments, as well as the cost of transporting them by rail and sea.[36] At the time, the amounts charged for these goods and services were not challenged. In later years, however, they were to be the subject of heated controversy. The official British position was that prices had invariably been fixed on a non-profit basis, with specially reduced rates being applied to freight charges and to a whole range of commodities, including coal, oil and wool.[37] According to the French, however, there had been a substantial element of overcharging – an accusation which Raymond Poincaré did not hesitate to make in the most explicit and insulting terms in his forceful reply to the Balfour Note of 1 August 1922.[38]

Another feature of the wartime debt agreements which was to cause a great deal of discord at a later date was the British insistence that France should deposit gold in London. By article 2 of the Calais agreement of 1916 – which, as we have seen, provided the French government with a loan of £150m – the Bank of France undertook to place gold to the value of £50m at the disposal of the British Treasury. A further £3.5m worth was deposited in connection with a subsequent credit, making a total of £53.5m.[39] This arrangement was partly to provide security for French borrowing; but the gold was also put to practical use. Along with stocks obtained in similar circumstances from Russia (£60m) and Italy (£22.2m), it was shipped to the United States to assist in purchasing supplies there and in supporting the dollar exchanges.[40] It was originally intended that the gold should be treated as a non-interest bearing loan. As a gesture of good will, however, the British government offered to pay interest from the date when it was actually exported to America, an offer immediately accepted by the French Minister of Finance, Ribot.[41]

From the outset, the British authorities had reservations about the arrangements reached over the gold, with Treasury officials expressing some anxiety about problems which might arise if the French did eventually ask for its return. Thus Keynes would have preferred to see the gold purhased outright rather than having it on loan. In a memorandum of 10 March 1917, he warned about possible difficulties and misunderstandings. The present position, he maintained, was based on calculated ambiguity. Britain had so far undertaken to return to France and her other major Allies as much as £156m in gold at various times after the war. These commitments had been assumed in the hope that there was an element of 'mutual humbugging' involved, that most of the gold would never have to be returned, and that the whole matter could be settled by a purely bookkeeping exercise in which the value of the gold was simply deducted from the amount owed by the Allies. It was by no means certain, however, that things would in practice work out in quite such a convenient way, and Keynes foresaw an embarrassing situation in which France and the others might actually try to recover all the gold they had deposited in London.[42]

His forebodings proved to be amply justified, for in the postwar period there was to be persistent friction about the £53.5m of French gold. The issue came to a head in January 1923, at the time of the Paris conference on reparations, when the French alleged that the gold had been sent to the United States without their knowledge – an allegation which the British vigorously denied. (The truth appears to be that the French had in fact been informed about the gold being shipped off, but the Poincaré government took alarm at the outcry caused by the public revelation of this fact and was afraid to acknowledge that it knew what had happened). There was also a dispute over actual ownership of the gold. The Bank of France continued to include it in its reserves under the heading 'gold held abroad'. Moreover, the French authorities and government always assumed that it would be handed back at some point.[43] This was not an assumption shared by the Bank of England or the British Treasury who were extremely reluctant to see the gold returned and sought to prevent that from happening by imposing conditions which they thought France would not be able to fulfil.[44] The matter was further complicated by the terms of a supplementary agreement reached on 13 December 1919 between Basil Blackett,[45] who occupied the important new post of Controller of Finance at the Treasury, and Joseph Avenol, the French Financial Delegate in London. Article 7 of this agreement stipulated that the French government was not to ask for the return of the gold 'until the moment arrives when the whole of the French debt to the British government is liquidated'.[46] On the face of it this was unambiguous enough. But the French later refused to accept that this particular aspect of the agreement was binding, on the grounds that Avenol had entered a reserve about it at the time and it had not been ratified by the French government. Since this provision was void, they contended, the relevant clauses of the 1916 Calais agreement remained in force and France was therefore entitled to recover all her gold as soon as she repaid the £150m borrowed under that agreement. Such arguments, as might be expected, left the British distinctly unimpressed.

IV

In the latter stages of the war the British government, headed by Lloyd George, became increasingly anxious to scale down and even terminate its financial assistance to France and the other Allies. This was mainly because it wished to minimise its own borrowing from the United States and was convinced that such borrowing was only necessary because of Britain's obligation to lend to her Allies. During the twelve month period following America's entry into the war in April 1916 Britain borrowed the dollar equivalent of £500m from the United States and lent virtually the same amount (£505m) to her Allies. It seemed to the current Chancellor of the Exchequer, Andrew Bonar Law, that this was an 'absurd' and needlessly complicated state of affairs.[47] In March 1918, therefore, he put to the United States Secretary of the Treasury, William Gibbs McAdoo, a proposal designed to simplify matters and obviate the need for further British borrowing: in future Britain would pay cash for the goods which she bought in the United States, if Washington in turn agreed to meet all the credit requirements of the rest of the Allies, including those needed for expenditure in Britain. France, Italy and the others would henceforward be allowed to pay for items obtained in Britain with dollars rather than sterling. These dollars could then be used for British purchases in America.[48] In other words, under the suggested new arrangements Britain would be relieved of having either to lend to the European Allies or to borrow from the United States. While clearly advantageous to Britain, however, what was being proposed had a number of drawbacks for the Americans. They would be receiving as security for the credits which they provided French and Italian Treasury notes instead of British. Their government supply departments would find it difficult to exercise the same degree of control as they had done so far over British purchases in the United States. There was also the unwelcome prospect of enormous sums of American money being spent in Great Britain by France and Italy. Not surprisingly, therefore, Bonar Law's proposal was rejected (in a note of 12 June to the Chancellor of the Exchequer),[49] with the result that Britain was obliged to continue the same pattern of borrowing and lending until the end of the war. The British were bitterly disappointed at this outcome and later claimed that they had incurred debts to the Americans unnecessarily and solely because of the need to lend to their Allies. This claim was used in a way calculated to make Britain's debtors feel a greater moral obligation to pay their debts. As might be expected, therefore, it was indignantly rejected by the French. To what extent it was valid is a complex matter which will be discussed later, in connection with the controversy arising out of the Balfour Note.

With the cessation of fighting in November 1918, the question arose whether British financial help to Fance should stop immediately or continue into the period of postwar reconstruction.[50] Here the British and French governments had very different views and interests. On the British side, there was some feeling – as expressed in a Foreign Office memorandum of October 1918 – that the existing arrangements over financial and economic support tended to 'breed irresponsibility' on the part of the recipients.[51] It was also felt to be neither necessary nor possible for Britain to provide France with the additional large-scale advances which she sought. The United States, it was thought, was far better placed to afford assistance. Moreover, France could help herself by allowing her currency to drift downwards instead of wasting resources on trying to maintain it at an artificially high level. Nor was she without foreign exchange. During 1918 the French government had furnished francs for the upkeep of American forces in France, and in return the United States had placed at its disposal an equivalent amount of dollars. Partly as a result of this, at the end of November 1918 France had undrawn credits in the United States amounting to $435m.[52] To the British Treasury, it seemed that the availability of these substantial dollar

balances removed any urgent need for British credits.[53] In any case, quite irrespective of French needs, the Treasury took the view that Britain's own financial
difficulties precluded the possibility of further assistance to France. In the
months following the armistice, the Treasury had to contend with worries about
sterling and the balance of payments. They faced continuing uncertainty over
whether America would provide the credits required by Britain herself, as
Congress exerted growing pressure for the imposition of tighter controls on
lending to the Allies.[54] They were also increasingly anxious about the state of
domestic finances. There was a budget deficit of £1.6bn for the year ending 31
March 1919 and the national debt had grown to alarming proportions.[55] Between
31 March 1914 and 31 March 1919, the latter had soared from £650m to £7,435m
and it was estimated that it would cost up to £472m merely to service it in the
year ahead.[56] Confronted by such acute financial problems of their own, the
Treasury were understandably determined to shed the burden of providing
credits to France at the earliest opportunity. From November 1918 onwards, their
intentions were made clear to the French Finance Minister, Klotz. The latter,
however, continued to insist on the necessity of further credits for the purchase
of imports and for supporting the franc.

On 28 November 1918, and again on 18 December, Bonar Law wrote to Klotz
suggesting that the time had come when France could afford to dispense with
British credits.[57] Klotz remained unconvinced, but on 3 January 1919 the French
government was formally notified that there would be no more.[58] In response to
a French request for tripartite talks between Britain, France and the United
States, a meeting was then held in Paris on 19 February. This was attended by
Keynes, representing the British Treasury, Alexandre de Célier, the Director of
the *Mouvement Général des Fonds* in the French Ministry of Finance, and two
senior officials of the United States Treasury who were serving as financial
experts with the American peace conference delegation, Norman Davis and
Albert Strauss. The talks centred on two main issues: the international value of
the franc and the attitude of the United States towards further financial help for
Britain.[59] So far as the franc was concerned, Keynes set out the familiar British
Treasury line that it was overvalued. It was, he argued, French insistence on
maintaining the franc at an unrealistic level which made it dependent on British
and American support. On the second point – whether Britain could count on
continued American help if she herself continued to provide credits to France –
the British and French representatives seemed to be talking at cross purposes.
The French government believed that the main reason Britain was anxious to be
rid of her financial responsibilities to France was fear that the support which she
herself had been receiving from the United States would be withdrawn, thus
leaving Britain in desperate financial circumstances.[60] It followed that if the
British government received satisfactory assurances on that score, it would then
be prepared to offer further credits. However logical, this analysis was based on
a misunderstanding of the true British position. To be sure, the British Treasury

did have doubts about Washington's willingness to continue making advances after the armistice. But the real key to their thinking was not this particular concern, but rather their profound aversion to the idea of piling up further obligations to the United States. Even if the Americans were prepared to go on lending, the British Treasury were not prepared to go on borrowing – certainly not for the purpose of making it possible to help France.[61] In any case, the point was academic, for the Americans had already made it clear that they were unwilling to continue providing Britain with substantial financial aid: in late December 1918 the British financial representative in Washington, Sir Samuel Hardman Lever, had been informed that the United States Treasury were unable to advance the $500m credit he had been instructed to seek.[62]

The February talks ended without agreement. Following representations from France and the United States, however, the British government agreed to take part in a further tripartite meeting in Paris. In the meantime, France was to continue receiving financial help from Britain.

These decisions were taken at a Cabinet meeting of 25 February 1919, at which ministers considered a statement from Keynes indicating that the French were asking for a credit of £100m from Britain, as well as $650m from the United States, partly to pay for goods supplied and partly to support the franc. Keynes pointed out that French difficulties stemmed to some extent from their attempts to maintain the franc at 26 to the pound: if it were allowed free play it would drop as low as 50. The general feeling appeared to be that France ought to be given some assistance, although doubts were expressed about the British capacity to contribute much. Lloyd George thought that the Americans should be pressed to play a major role. Churchill, the Secretary of State for War, said that a British credit must only be used for making purchases in Britain. This prompted a warning from Austen Chamberlain, who had replaced Bonar Law as Chancellor of the Exchequer the previous month, that even that might entail additional expenditure on imported raw materials. Bonar Law, now the Lord Privy Seal, weighed in with the clinching argument that France must not be allowed to go bankrupt. The Cabinet then approved an advance of £2m which had already been promised to France and agreed that Chamberlain should go to Paris to discuss matters with the French and Americans the following week.[63]

On 7 and 8 March Chamberlain duly held talks in Paris with Klotz and Colonel Edward House, President Wilson's personal adviser. Chamberlain was in determined mood, making no attempt to disguise his extreme reluctance to meet the French request for funds.[64] He made it clear to Klotz that Britain's own financial resources were stretched to the limit in a way that ruled out any further assistance to France. Certainly there could be no question of continuing British support for the franc at its current highly artificial level.[65] Since Chamberlain had already decided to cease supporting the pound – a decision put into effect on 20 March[66] – his refusal to help to prop up the franc was hardly surprising.

The fact remained, however, that the French position was desperate: existing credits were already exhausted. On 13 March, therefore, following a personal appeal from Klotz, Chamberlain grudgingly signed an agreement providing France with a final credit of £30m, of which £4m was to be made available immediately.[67] Within a matter of weeks, this agreement was in tatters. At Chamberlain's insistence, it stipulated that the promised funds would only be released if the French govenment agreed to sell to Britain £21m worth of the gold deposited at the Bank of England under the 1916 Calais agreement. It was this stipulation which caused a hitch. The French failed to fulfil it and the agreement therefore lapsed.

The first indication of difficulties ahead came on 28 March when Edwin Montagu, formerly Financial Secretary to the Treasury and Minister of Munitions and now the minister in charge of general Treasury matters at the Paris peace conference, reported to Chamberlain that he had received a visit from Edouard Rothschild, a Regent of the Bank of France.[68] The unwelcome news brought by Rothschild was that the Bank of France was opposed to the sale of any of the gold deposited in London and was therefore not prepared to agree to the arrangement reached between Klotz and Chamberlain. France still needed credits, however, and Rothschild suggested that the British Treasury should lend her some small amounts to pay for absolutely essential imports. Montagu's reaction was scathing. He wrote to Chamberlain:

> The situation strikes me as undesirable because we are the victims of gross misman-
> agement of this distressed country. Klotz was told in November that he could
> expect no more money. He was given money till February. You then listened to a
> cri de coeur from him and agreed to an arrangement which will put at his disposal
> another £27 million. You did this on the understanding that this is the last, the end,
> and final. He then dare not come to you again, but sends the Bank of France to
> make pathetic appeals for more or for alternative plans.[69]

Chamberlain was no less indignant.[70] As a man who attached the utmost importance to honourable behaviour, he was outraged by what he regarded as a gross breach of faith on the part of the French government. Klotz had assured him that his government would use all its influence with the Bank of France to secure its assent to the sale of the gold deposited in London. Indeed, Klotz's assurance was all the more binding since he had consulted the Prime Minister, Georges Clemenceau, before giving it. Chamberlain could not believe that the French government lacked the power to go through with the agreement if it chose to exert sufficient pressure on the Bank of France. He was therefore determined to hold the French to their part of the bargain and withdraw the offer of a credit if they failed to do so. As he told Montagu, Britain was hard-pressed to meet her own financial needs, and it seemed to him impossible to 'admit in the midst of our own difficulties that the resources of the British Treasury are more available to the French Government than the resources of French institutions'.[71]

This unpleasant episode was to have an equally unpleasant sequel some years later. In 1924 Klotz published his memoirs, *De La Guerre à La Paix*, in which he made a number of serious allegations about the conduct of both Chamberlain and Keynes. He described the latter's behaviour as 'atrocious' and accused him of having pronounced Germanophile and Bolshevik tendencies, as well as suffering from megalomania. According to Klotz, Chamberlain had been merely a cypher in the spring of 1919. The true Chancellor of the Exchequer had been Keynes, and it was he who had been instrumental in the decision to cut off financial support for France in February 1919 – a decision which, Klotz alleged, had precipitated a disastrous fall in the value of the franc.[72] Keynes dismissed Klotz's allegations in a devastating review article in *The Times*.[73] Klotz replied and Chamberlain felt obliged to join in the debate. The result was a bitter public controversy, conducted through the correspondence columns of the *The Times*, in which charges of distorting the truth were mingled with a liberal dose of personal abuse from both sides.[74]

The disagreeable manner in which British financial assistance to France came to an abrupt end in the summer of 1919 – it was formally terminated on 9 July[75] – provided a foretaste of the unedifying squabbles that were to develop over repayment of French war debts in the mid-1920s. Yet in the years immediately after the war the question caused relatively little friction in Anglo-French relations. Why this was so will become apparent in the next chapter.

2

The Immediate Postwar Years, 1918–1922

I

The wartime loan agreements between the British and French governments allowed France a period of three years from the conclusion of peace in which to make arrangements for repaying her debts. In the event, however, this deadline of August 1923 – three years from the Treaty of Sèvres – passed without the French having made any real effort to meet it. Indeed, there were to be no serious negotiations about a funding agreement until the spring of 1925, and even then the first tentative proposals put forward by the French government were dismissed as completely unacceptable. Significant progress was made in August of that year when the then Chancellor of the Exchequer, Churchill, and his French opposite number, Joseph Caillaux, reached a provisional agreement. But once again there were further frustrating delays before a definitive settlement was eventually concluded, more than seven years after the cessation of hostilities, on 12 July 1926.

The three-year breathing-space allotted to France was a maximum. It was understood and expected that in the meantime she would take steps to redeem at least some of her obligations by raising loans on the London market, with assistance from the British authorities, whenever circumstances permitted. Conditions for doing so seemed reasonably favourable in the summer of 1922, as shown by successful flotations for the Seine Department and the French railways. The fact that the French government made no move, therefore, caused intense disappointment at the British Treasury where it was felt there were legitimate grounds for complaint that not even a token effort had been made, 'if only as evidence of an intention on the part of France to do her best to meet her obligations'.[1]

There was growing dissatisfaction, too, over the French failure to make any interest payments. What happened was that as the different blocks of loan certificates matured and were renewed, new bills were accepted, with interest added to them at current Bank rate. No cash was received, the result being that the cost of servicing the debt – estimated at around £16m annually – fell entirely on the British taxpayer.[2] Initially, the British government regarded this situation with a certain degree of tolerance. Given the chaotic state of their finances in the period immediately following the war, it was recognised that it was probably beyond the capacity of the French to pay even the interest on their debts.[3] In any case, the French behaviour was no different from that of any of the other allied debtors, Britain included. In September 1919 the United States Treasury announced their willingness to forego interest payments from allied debtors for a period of three years.[4] The Lloyd George government, which had encouraged the Americans to take this step, adopted a similar policy. Until October 1922, therefore, there was a general *de facto* moratorium on inter-allied debt interest payments. While this remained in force Britain suffered no special disadvantage. The position was radically changed, however, when it expired.

In March 1922 the decision was taken that Britain would resume interest payments in cash to the United States from 15 October onwards, and provision was made for the forthcoming Budget to include a sum of £55m for that purpose.[5] This inevitably brought to the fore the question of whether she in turn should demand payments from her own debtors. The issue needed to be resolved quickly. The April Budget statement would have to contain some reference to it. It would also be necessary to give debtors adequate warning of British intentions. Strictly speaking, only two of them, Romania and Italy, were entitled to such consideration – both having received an undertaking in June 1921 that they would be given six months' notice. On political grounds, however, the Chancellor of the Exchequer, Austen Chamberlain, thought that it would be advisable to extend this concession to the rest of the debtors. Thus on 31 March 1922 the French and other governments concerned were formally notified that Britain reserved the right to demand cash payments for interest falling due on or after 1 October of that year.[6]

By sending this formal notification, the British government kept open the option of seeking interest payments from France in the near future. Whether that option ought to be exercised, though, was the subject of much discussion at the Treasury. The policy debate there revealed a strong feeling that the French were grossly abusing Britain's unwillingness to press her legitimate demands. This was balanced, however, by a realistic appreciation of the difficulties involved in actually getting them to pay. In a note dated 14 September 1922, Otto Niemeyer, the Deputy Controller of Finance, advised the Chancellor that there was not the slightest chance of securing cash from either France or Italy over the next few months.[7] Reviewing the position in March of the following year, another Treasury official, Frederick Phillips (an Assistant Secretary), arrived at an equally pessimistic conclusion.[8]

In the end, the arguments against pressing for cash payments prevailed and no request was sent.[9] The amount owed by France therefore continued to grow, as outstanding interest was automatically added to the original debt of £453m:

by January 1923 the total had risen to £541m and by March to £598m.[10] Viewed from the British standpoint, this was a thoroughly unsatisfactory state of affairs. From 15 October 1922 Britain was paying interest in full to the United States, while receiving nothing at all from France. The position became worse still following the negotiation of the 1923 Anglo-American war debt agreement, under which Britain was to pay annuities equivalent to £33m from June of that year.

Not surprisingly, the French government's continuing failure to pay even the interest on their debt generated great resentment in British official circles, where it was felt that France and the rest of the Allies were not taking their obligations seriously enough.[11] This was reinforced by a growing conviction that Britain was not obtaining what was due to her largely because of French financial misman-agement. Klotz and his successors at the Ministry of Finance – Frédéric François-Marsal (January 1920 to January 1921), Paul Doumer (January 1921 to January 1922) and Charles de Lasteyrie (January 1922 to March 1923) – commanded little respect amongst British policymakers, their budgetary measures being regarded as derisory and wholly inadequate for the scale of the problems facing France.[12] In this respect, unflattering comparisons were invari-ably made with the tight fiscal and monetary policies currently being pursued by the British government. The conventional wisdom was that Britain was taking the right steps to get her finances in order, even though this meant painful cuts in government spending and a level of taxation which most expert opinion considered near to the limits of acceptability. All the indications were that France was not making a comparable effort. Her political leaders, it was thought, shrank from telling their electorate the harsh truth that greater sacrifices were needed, preferring instead to rely on anticipated reparation receipts from Germany to solve their difficulties. Such a view of the repective merits of British and French policies was no doubt complacent and not entirely fair to France. It was, however, commonplace amongst British ministers and officials. They were convinced that the French taxpayer was bearing a much lighter burden than his British coun-terpart,[13] and this helps to explain why they tended to react with scepticism as well as irritation to claims that France could not afford to pay the interest on her war debts because of the state of her public finances.

There were other reasons why such claims were treated with a degree of scep-ticism. While it was accepted that France did indeed face serious financial problems, it did not go unnoticed that she was nevertheless able to spend large amounts of money on non-essential items like foreign loans to friends and allies in eastern Europe and elsewhere.[14] As was pointed out at a Cabinet meeting of 2 June 1920, such expenditure hardly seemed consistent with French jeremiads about their financial weakness.[15] This observation was prompted by reports from Budapest that France proposed to lend Hungary 260m francs, the equivalent of more than £3.5m. The loan to Hungary was the first of many over the next few years. In the course of 1923 the French parliament sanctioned credits amounting to 800m francs (£11m) – principally for the purchase of war material – to Romania, Yugoslavia and Poland, with the last-named receiving half of that total 'to assist her to preserve and ensure her economic and military development'.[16] Further loans were made available to Belgium (400m francs), Greece (over 300m francs) and Morocco (150m francs).[17] The British reaction to this policy was overwhelmingly hostile. In the case of the Polish credit, the intense criticism which it aroused doubtless owed something to the fact that the Poles were deeply unpopular in many quarters: Lloyd George was not alone in viewing them as a volatile and quarrelsome people whose excessive territorial ambitions had caused difficulties at the Paris peace conference and, more recently, led to war with Soviet Russia. But there was also, as with the other credits, real indignation that the French should be lending substantial sums abroad while at the same time refusing to pay interest on the money owed to Britain. Nor were such sentiments confined to official circles. The aggrieved public mood, as reflected in the press, was well summed up by cartoons appearing early in January 1924 in *Punch* and *The New Leader*, both of which portrayed the current French Prime Minister, Poincaré, showering money borrowed from Britain on his country's eastern European allies.[18]

French protestations that they were incapable of paying interest on their war debts were also undermined in British eyes by the knowledge that France found it possible to devote substantial financial resources to her armed forces. This was at a time, moreover, when Britain herself was having to cut back. In the early postwar years, the British government pursued a policy of severe retrenchment in all areas of military spending. The adoption of the so-called Ten Year Rule in August 1919 and the recommendations of a number of economy committees provided the framework for deep cuts in expenditure on the armed services: in 1920 it was reduced from £604m to £292m, and over the next two years it was further reduced to £111m.[19] In France, by contrast, an obsessive preoccupation with national security kept defensive preparations at a high and costly level. As the French Prime Minister, Aristide Briand, made clear at the Washington naval conference in November 1921, France had no intention of embarking on a programme of large-scale disarmament – a stance which infuriated Lloyd George.[20] However understandable, given their deep-rooted fear and distrust of Germany, French insistence on maintaining a big military establishment – including as it did the strongest army and air force in Europe, as well as a powerful fleet of submarines – caused a great deal of adverse comment in Britain. This was not only because the level of French armaments was felt to be unnecessarily high and provocative to Germany, but also because it was regarded as intolerable that France should be spending large amounts on her armed forces while not paying any interest on her war debts.[21]

The offence was compounded in British eyes by the fact that French military strength was seen as potentially dangerous to Britain. During the immediate postwar years, and for that matter throughout the 1920s, France was the only country in a position to pose an immediate threat to the security of the British Isles. She was the dominant military power in Europe and capable of inflicting great damage on a country whose own forces were run down steadily after 1919.[22] Sir Maurice Hankey, the influential Secretary to the Cabinet and to the Committee of Imperial Defence, described the situation graphically when he told his deputy, Tom Jones, that France alone could 'deal us a blow at the heart'.[23]

Two main threats stood out, both clearly identified in various assessments prepared by the Committee of Imperial Defence in the early 1920s. First there was the danger from submarines, the destructive capability of which had been amply demonstrated during the First World War. France had a sizeable fleet of such vessels, and her geographical position and possession of strategically situated colonial bases meant that she was well placed, should a conflict arise, to menace vital routes through the Channel and the Mediterranean.[24] The second potential danger lay in French air superiority. At the end of the war the R.A.F. could muster 3,000 first-line aircraft, with 20,000 in reserve. Yet within two years of the armistice it had been pruned so drastically that its entire strength barely sufficed to provide tactical support for the army and navy. French air power, by contrast, was substantially maintained into peacetime, with the result that during the 1920s France had an air force which was the largest in the world and certainly much stronger than the British.[25] What particularly worried the Air Staff was the steady growth in the size and capablity of the French bomber force – hardly surprising, considering their attachment to the strategic doctrine that the bomber would play a decisive role in future warfare.[26] In March 1922 the then Secretary of State for Air, F. E. Guest, presented the Cabinet with an alarming picture of Britain's relative weaknes in bombers[27], and his warnings were echoed by the Balfour and Salisbury committees, two sub-committees of the Committee of Imperial Defence set up in 1922 and 1923 repectively to examine the adequacy of British air defences. Both of these were impressed by evidence from Sir Hugh Trenchard, the Chief of the Air Staff, about the scale of bombing raids that France was judged to be capable of launching against London and other parts of the south-east, and both recommended an expansion of Britain's own forces. Their recommendations were later adopted by the government, albeit not implemented in full.[28]

Although there was a great deal of nervous speculation in the early 1920s about a potential military threat from France, few British observers – whether politicians or military planners – believed that war between the two countries was in fact a serious possibility. On the other hand, as Balfour pointed out, the eventuality – which he said would be 'a world calamity' – could not be ruled out completely. It was therefore thought prudent to increase the strength of the air force along the lines suggested by the Salisbury committee.[29] This decision was taken with great reluctance, since heavy taxation was regarded as a major cause of Britain's current recession and the government was accordingly anxious to reduce military expenditure to the lowest possible level. To the British government, therefore, French policy appeared to be doubly unhelpful. In the first place, France was seen to be spending on her armed forces unnecessarily large sums of money, at least some of which might have been used instead to meet the interest charges on her war debts, currently being borne by the British taxpayer. Secondly, by doing so, she was obliging Britain herself to spend more on her air force at a time when economy was a prime objective: in August 1922 Austen Chamberlain (then Lord Privy Seal) complained to colleagues about French air power 'putting us to a great deal of expense'.[30] It scarcely needs to be said that such a critical reaction to French policy, whilst understandable, was purely emotional and divorced from political reality. The British might well feel that their interests were being disregarded and that France had her priorities in the wrong order. But it was utterly inconceivable that the French would ever share the view that repayment of debts owed to Britain should take precedence over expenditure on national security.

II

Although increasingly exasperated by the French failure to pay interest on their war debts, the Lloyd George government was nevertheless slow to exert any pressure on Paris to begin negotiations on a funding agreement. Indeed, it was not until the despatch of the Balfour Note on 1 August 1922 that France, along with the rest of Britain's debtors, received a formal request to make arrangements for settling her debts.

There were a number of reasons for this initial lack of urgency, quite apart from the fact that there were many other important and pressing matters competing for the government's attention in the aftermath of the war. Straightforward technical considerations played a part. It was the case, for example, that the wartime loan agreements entitled France to a period of three years from the end of the war in which to negotiate a settlement. Thus there could be no legitimate grounds for complaint if the French chose not take action before the appointed deadline. However unco-operative their behaviour might appear to be, it could not be said that they were in breach of their treaty obligations. A further complication arose from the fact that the French Treasury certificates deposited against the British debts, unlike those for debts contracted from the United States, did not bear an explicit statement that the debtor could be required to convert short-term obligations into long-term ones on demand. Austen Chamberlain, the Chancellor of the Exchequer, seems to have attached considerable weight to this point, as he told his Cabinet colleagues in December 1920 when explaining some of the difficulties involved in sending France a demand to fund her debts.[31]

More important than such technicalities, however, was the existence of an element of genuine sympathy for an ally who had recently fought alongside

Britain in a great common cause and suffered dreadful losses in the process. Unlike the Americans, the British never looked upon war debts as ordinary commercial obligations. It was always recognised that they had been contracted in circumstances which gave them a special character and that France's own principal contribution to the joint war effort had been made in blood rather than treasure.[32] For four years France had been the main battleground. Ten of her most prosperous departments had been ravaged by war. She had lost more than one-and-a-half million men. Sympathy for such hardships was bound to exercise a softening influence on British policy – at least to begin with, before exposure to the constant refrain of 'nous avons beaucoup souffert' caused it to wear somewhat thin. It was in this spirit of sympathy that Lloyd George assured the French Prime Minister, Alexandre Millerand, at the second Hythe conference of 20 June 1920, that 'France need not be anxious about our insistence on our full rights when she had difficulties in her devastated regions'.[33]

But even if Lloyd George and his colleagues had wished to play the role of harsh creditors, the inescapable fact they had to face was that France needed time to recover before she could begin to contemplate paying off her debts. In the immediate postwar period, the French lacked not only the will – something which they continued to lack – but also the means, to repay foreign creditors. France had emerged from the war exhausted and impoverished. The bulk of her 45bn francs of overseas investments had been either liquidated or, like those in Russia, rendered worthless.[34] She was now a debtor rather than a creditor nation, burdened with enormous foreign and domestic debts. The franc stood at only 50 per cent of its prewar value in 1919 and was to fall further still over the next few years. Agricultural and industrial production were only a fraction of what they had been before 1914, as were exports. At the same time, money had to be found for a massive programme of reconstruction in the devastated areas.[35] In such unpromising circumstances, it is hardly surprising that French leaders showed themselves to be less concerned with paying off old loans than with securing new ones to support a weak currency and to purchase food and raw materials from abroad. In 1920, for instance, France needed to borrow hundreds of millions of dollars to pay for imports of cotton, copper, oil and essential foodstuffs – and this at a tme when it was extremely difficult to obtain credits in either New York or London.[36]

So far as foreign debt repayment was concerned, the French faced two basic problems, neither of which they were capable of solving in the immediate postwar years.[37] First, there was the problem of transfer across the exchanges. This was aggravated by the persistent weakness of the franc after it was 'unpegged' in March 1919, the effect of which was to increase the real burden of repayment.[38] Gold shipments on a big enough scale were out of the question. Payment by goods and services was equally impracticable, given the shattered state of the economy, the need for industry to restock and the existence of an adverse trade balance. By the end of the war French industrial production was between 30 per cent and 40 per cent below its prewar level. Nor did it recover to that level until 1924.[39] Furthermore, in each of the years between 1919 and 1923 there was a hefty, if diminishing, deficit on the balance of trade: 24.058m francs in 1919; 22.536m francs in 1920; 2.083m francs in 1921; 2.6m in 1922; and 2.238m in 1923.[40]

The second basic problem involved in debt repayment was that of generating a big enough budget surplus; and this, too, was beyond the French governments of the time. During the early 1920s, a succession of finance ministers, starting with Klotz, made repeated attempts to balance the budget. All failed.[41] The French historian Jacques Néré gives them credit for at least making making a valiant effort.[42] But this is a view shared by few others who have studied the question, and it is hard to disagree with the majority's somewhat less charitable verdict on the performance of Klotz and his successors. Their financial proposals were inadequate to begin with and were invariably mutilated by Parliament. As a result, there was a substantial budget deficit in every year between 1918 and 1926. Expenditure was grossly inflated by a number of costly items: high military spending; pensions for disabled veterans, war widows and orphans; the cost of re-integrating Alsace-Lorraine and administering the Saarland; and provision for reconstruction of the devastated regions.[43] There was also the crippling cost of servicing the national debt. During the years 1919 to 1922, that charge alone absorbed between 44 and 57 per cent of what was termed the 'ordinary' budget.[44]

At no stage was any serious attempt made to meet all this expenditure from taxation. To demand the sacrifices necessary to do so, indeed, would have been politically disastrous in view of the almost universal expectation amongst the French electorate that Germany would be made to pick up the bill for reconstruction. The lack of any real will to balance the books was reflected in the very structure of the budget system. During the war it had been the practice to draw a distinction between 'ordinary' and 'extraordinary' expenditure, the latter relating to military costs. This practice was carried over into peacetime and in 1920 a third category of budget was added, one devoted to expenditure supposedly recoverable from Germany. Only in the case of the 'ordinary' budget was even a token effort made to meet spending from tax revenue. Other types of expenditure were financed almost entirely through large-scale borrowing and, in particular, through the sale of *Bons de la Défence Nationale*. These short-term bonds, which had played a major part in funding the French war effort, continued to be sold in peacetime – until 1927 in fact – and in June 1922 the total value of outstanding bonds reached a peak of 63.8bn francs.[45] The existence of such a gigantic floating debt, allied to persistent uncertainty over whether there would be sufficient demand for new issues of the bonds, not only added greatly to the burden of annual interest charges but also posed a constant threat to the country's financial stability.[46]

Given the disorganised state of French national finances in the immediate postwar years, there was obviously little prospect of early negotiations for a war debt settlement. In addition to the money which France owed Britain, there was also to be taken into account the even larger amount due to the United States. It was unthinkable that the French should settle with one creditor without also settling with the other, and the combined weight of debts was manifestly beyond their capacity to pay in the near future. There was no question of outright repudiation of their obligations, if only because France was looking to Britain and the United States – and to the latter especially – to provide financial assistance to aid her recovery. On the other hand, the French attitude was certainly characterised by an extreme reluctance to fund the debts that had been contracted and start making payments. The French argued, with considerable justification, that their country's desperate economic and financial plight ruled out any possibility of repayment for some years to come. It was also made clear that they were not prepared to begin negotiations on a war debt settlement until they had first recovered from Germany enough reparation money to meet the costs incurred in restoring the devastated regions.[47]

Beneath the French resistance to an early settlement there lay a more fundamental objection to having to pay at any time. This rested on a passionate conviction, equally evident in official circles and amongst the general public, that it was wrong to expect France to pay back what she had been forced to borrow when her very survival was at stake. To the French, the credits they had received during the war were different in kind from normal commercial obligations. They represented a contribution to the common war effort by Britain and the United States. France had made her own special contribution. She had sacrificed a far higher proportion of her manpower than the other two countries, and her territory and productive resources had been devastated in a way that theirs had not. It therefore seemed a matter of elementary justice that she should be treated with sympathetic consideration and that the debts owing to her foreign creditors should be substantially reduced or even cancelled. British and American industry, it was pointed out, had benefitted from the wartime orders France had placed for equipment and materials of all description. There were even hints – later to become more explicit in Poincare's robust rejoinder of 1 September 1922 to the Balfour Note – of British overcharging and profiteering. One particularly emotive line of argument was that it was monstrous that France should have to pay back money used to buy foreign uniforms in which French soldiers had laid down their lives. In the early 1920s such sentiments and arguments were not yet voiced openly, but they were to be found in briefing papers prepared at the Ministry of Finance. One such paper, dated 22 October 1921 and sent to the Foreign Ministry, roundly declared that France owed nothing at all:

> Le gouvernement français est fondé en équité à prétendre qu'il ne doit rien, sous aucune forme, à aucun titre; cette thèse, qui répond au sentiment profond, sinon complètement exprimé du peuple français, ne manquera pas d'être ratifier par l'histoire.[48]

III

In the immediate postwar years the French contention that they were not yet in a position to begin repaying their debts was not seriously challenged in British official circles. Hence Lloyd George's observation to the French Finance Minister, François-Marsal, in June 1920 that 'with France devastated, it was inconceivable that Great Britain could exercise pressure [for payment] on her'.[49] It is true that Lloyd George for one was apt to suggest, on the not infrequent occasions when he was irritated with France, that she could well afford to pay something. It is also true that there was a great deal of critical and disparaging comment, not least from the Treasury, about the French government's handling of national finances and about the low level of French taxation compared to British taxation[50] – a disparity which was felt to place British industry at an unfair disadvantage. There was, moreover, considerable indignation about French lending to foreign countries and about continuing high levels of French military expenditure, with questions inevitably being raised about how these two aspects of policy could be reconciled with the repeated claim that France was too impoverished to pay anything to her creditors. Even so, notwithstanding periodic grumbling and a widespread feeling that France was not tackling her financial difficlties with sufficient determination, it was grudgingly accepted in British official circles that she must be allowed a respite before starting to pay off her debts. The Treasury regarded it as axiomatic that she was for the time being incapable of paying the interest charges alone. Indeed, they were sometimes doubtful even about the longer-term prospects for repayment.

Besides this recognition of French financial difficulties, there were other reasons why the Lloyd George government delayed exerting pressure for the conclusion of a debt agreement. Not the least of these was concern about the effect that such action might have on the value of the franc and, in consequence, on British exports. In the spring of 1920, the feverish postwar boom which Britain had been experiencing since the previous summer came to an abrupt end. This marked the onset of a dramatic slump in economic activity which saw industrial production fall by more than 18 per cent and employment by nearly 15 per cent in the course of the following year. By the end of 1921, unemployment had risen to around 22 per cent of the insured workforce. Nor were there signs of an impending recovery. Various explanations, including excessively high taxation, were offered for the recession. One of the most popular, however, was that British industry was finding it hard to export to the Continent because of the low value of the French and other European currencies compared to sterling; and those who subscribed to this view, including several members of the Cabinet, argued that to press France and the rest of Britain's debtors to negotiate a funding agreement would only aggravate matters by depressing their exchanges still further.

Yet another factor was the belief of some ministers, amongst them Lloyd

George, Austen Chamberlain and the influential Secretary of State for War, Churchill, that French indebtedness to Britain gave the latter useful leverage – especially when it came to resolving differences over reparation payments. In the early 1920s the British and French governments clashed repeatedly over reparations. More specifically, they became embroiled in recurring disputes over how to respond to German defaults, with the British generally favouring a less coercive approach. In this context, it was thought – mistakenly as it turned out – that Britain's position as a major creditor of France would perhaps make it possible to exercise a restraining influence on her. The argument was quite simple. If France sought to take a tough line on reparations, then Britain could retaliate by taking an equally tough line on French war debts. Conversely, France might be offerd lenient terms for a debt settlement as an inducement to moderate her stance over reparations.[51] As will be seen later, this was essentially the tactic tried in December 1922 when the so-called Bonar Law Plan was put forward in an (unsuccessful) bid to dissuade France from sending troops into the Ruhr. Since it was obvious that the debts would cease to be of use as a bargaining weapon once an agreement had been reached on funding them, on those grounds at least there was a case for deferring such an agreement.

But the most important reason for the Lloyd George government's lack of urgency in pressing for a debt agreement with France was the priority it accorded to achieving a wider settlement embracing not only all elements of inter-allied indebtedness but also reparations. From 1918 onwards the oficial view in London was that the existence of huge inter-governmental debts arising out of the war caused serious instability on the exchanges, undermined confidence and represented a major obstacle to financial and economic recovery in Europe. One of the principal aims of British foreign policy in the early postwar years, therefore, was to secure the cancellation, or at the very least a substantial reduction, of such debts.[52] As Blackett, the Controller of Finance at the Treasury, put it in a memorandum of 2 February 1920:

> Our idea has always been that ultimate repayment by the continental Governments of Europe of their debts to the United Kingdom and the United States of America was in fact out of the question, that the existence of this mass of external indebtedness lay like a dead weight upon the credit of continental Europe and made reconstruction even slower and more painful than it needed to be, and that the statesmanlike thing to be done was for the United Kingdom and the United States of America to make a 'beau geste' by offering to wipe out the whole of such indebtedness by a stroke of the pen.[53]

Clearly, as Blackett indicated, such a policy would only be feasible with the full co-operation of the biggest creditor, the United States. From the outset, however, the American government categorically rejected all attempts to involve it in producing an all-round agreement, refusing to accept any link between reparations and war debts, and insisting that the latter must be paid in full – like any other commercial obligations – and that the only acceptable way to proceed was for each debtor to negotiate separately with Washington.

Despite persistent discouragement from the Americans, London continued to seek a comprehensive settlement throughout the early 1920s; and it was not until after the negotiation of the Anglo-American debt agreement in early 1923 that the quest was eventually abandoned with undisguised reluctance. It is in this broader context that the British approach to an Anglo-French debt settlement must be viewed. The Lloyd George government's overriding objective was a global solution to the problem of war debts and reparations. It followed from this that a bilateral agreement with France was regarded as being of secondary importance, something that would limit the government's room for manoeuvre and impede rather than facilitate its efforts to attain the greater goal. As Austen Chamberlain told Avenol, the French Financial Delegate in London, in September 1919, he and his colleagues feared that a preliminary accord between the debtor countries would prejudice wider-ranging discussions on war debts which, whilst not likely to be fruitful at that time, might become so later if American attitudes were to change.[54] Lloyd George made the same point at the second Hythe conference of June 1920 when explaining to Millerand why he would prefer not to discuss the French war debt to Britain at that stage:

> In principle, it was much better to wipe out inter-Allied debts than for the Allies to go on paying each other for forty years. Italy to France and France to Great Britain, and all of them to the United States of America. He rather thought that such an agreement might be reached. If, however, Great Britain, for example, were to give up her loan rights, when the time came to discuss the matter with America the United States would say that we had already given up our rights to France and that they could not have anything to do with it. Hence he would rather postpone the question.[55]

Between the end of the war and 1923, then, British policy on French war debts was conducted at every stage with one eye on the United States. The main concern of the Lloyd George government was to persuade American opinion that inter-allied debts should be cancelled or reduced. As a result, such questions as whether or not a settlement should be concluded with the French, and if so on what terms, were considered largely in relation to the probable reaction from Washington. It is important to emphasise in this connection how far British policy on French war debts was influenced in particular by the United States' stance on Britain's own debt obligations. For, no matter what the Americans might say to the contrary, to the British at least the two matters were indissolubly linked. Put at its simplest, the extent of British generosity to France was governed in considerable measure by what concessions America was prepared to make to Britain.

IV

In the event, British endeavours to win American backing for a policy of all-round cancellation were a complete failure. As early as November 1918, the Chancellor of the Exchequer, Bonar Law, along with the French Finance Minister, Klotz, suggested the adoption of such a policy to a senior American Treasury official, Oscar T. Crosby, only to meet with a sharp rebuff.[56] At the Paris peace conference the United States representatives refused to even discuss the question of war debts, and from that time onwards neither the Wilson administration nor the Republican administration of Warren G. Harding, which succeeded it in March 1921, was prepared to countenance the possibility that inter-allied debts should be wholly or partially written off. It was claimed that the strength of Congressional and public feeling against any concessions tied the government's hands and forced it to take a less lenient line than it would have wished. There was undoubtedly some truth in that. It seems clear, however, that the policymakers themselves – including both Presidents and successive Secretaries of the Treasury, McAdoo, Carter Glass, David Houston and Andrew Mellon – were personally less sympathetic to any reduction in debt obligations than they were generally prepared to admit.[57]

The Americans' uncompromising attitude became abundantly clear in the course of difficult and lengthy talks between the British and United States Treasuries. These talks, conducted mainly by Blackett and the American Treasury's representative in Europe, Albert Rathbone, began in October 1919. They were essentially a dialogue of the deaf, with the two sides working on different assumptions and pursuing different objectives. The British, as has been seen, started from the premise that there was no realistic possibility of debts being collected from the countries of continental Europe and that they should therefore be cancelled. They suggested as much to the Americans and sought to get them to initiate the proposal on the grounds that they, as debtors to nobody, would be free from suspicion of acting out of self-interest. The United States Treasury were reported to be 'horrified' at the mere mention of such a plan.[58] They did not share the British conviction that the existence of war debts was hampering European recovery. Nor did they accept that the Continental debtors were unable to meet their obligations, arguing that they could perfectly well do so if they increased taxation, curtailed expenditure – especially on armaments – and negotiated a sensible arrangement about reparation payments. So far as the American authorities were concerned, general debt cancellation, along the lines advocated by Britain, was simply not open to discussion. There were only two topics that they were prepared to talk about: postponement of interest payments and the conversion of existing demand obligations into long-term ones.

When Blackett proposed all-round cancellation in December 1919, the response was completely negative.[59] Despite this, with what the French historian

Denise Artaud calls 'astonishing obstinacy', the Chancellor, Austen Chamberlain, took up the idea again in a letter of 7 February 1920 to Russell C. Leffingwell, an Assistant Secretary of the United States Treasury.[60] At the same time Blackett, too, raised the subject with both Leffingwell and Rathbone. The result in every case was a rejection in terms which came close to being insulting, and on 21 May Chamberlain informed Rathbone that he had decided that the Treasury talks should be suspended.[61]

Lloyd George was the next to try his hand at persuasion. He had already, in April 1919, fruitlessly sent the American President a copy of a plan for financial reconstruction devised by Keynes which envisaged, amongst other things, the wiping out of most inter-allied debts by means of payment with reparation bonds.[62] On 5 August 1920, as authorised by the Cabinet, he addressed a further personal letter to Wilson on the 'knotty problem of Inter-Allied indebtedness'.[63] He was prompted to do so mainly by lack of progress in the Blackett-Rathbone discussions, but also by his recent meeting at Hythe with the French Prime Minister, Millerand. At that meeting the two leaders had agreed on the importance of reaching a settlement which would – in the words of their joint statement – 'embrace the whole body of the international liabilities which have been left as a legacy of the War' and at the same time ensure a parallel liquidation of inter-allied debts and reparations.[64] In his letter to Wilson, Lloyd George sought to demonstrate the essential interconnection between these two elements. He had managed to convince his French colleague, he said, that it was necessary to fix a figure for reparations which was within Germany's capacity to pay. But Millerand had pointed out that France could not possibly accept less than her full entitlement under the Treaty of Versailles unless there was a corresponding reduction in her own debt obligations. The British government regarded this position as 'eminently fair'. On the other hand, it felt unable to remit any of the debt owed by France except as part and parcel of an all-round settlement. A one-sided arrangement at Britain's expense would never be tolerated by public opinion. It would also embitter relations between the British and American people, 'with calamitous results to the future of the world'. The French government had therefore been informed that Britain would accept any equitable scheme for the cancellation or reduction of inter-allied debts, but that such a scheme must be one that applied all round.[65]

Wilson was annoyed at this blatant attempt to make a moderate reparation settlement conditional upon an abatement of allied debts to the United States. He made no immediate reply. He delayed for so long, indeed, that the British ambassador in Washington, Sir Auckland Geddes, was asked to make discreet inquiries as to whether the letter had been received and read.[66] When an answer was eventually sent on 3 November 1920, Wilson's message was unequivocal:

It is highly improbable that either the Congress or popular opinion in this country will ever permit a cancellation of any part of the debt of the British Government to the United States in order to induce the British Government to remit, in whole or in part, the debt to Great Britain of France or any other of the Allied Governments, or that it [sic] will consent to a cancellation or reduction in the debts of any of the Allied Governments as an inducement towards a practical settlement of the reparation claims.[67]

V

Washington's unbending opposition to the idea of a general cancellation or reduction of war debt obligations presented the Lloyd George government with a serious tactical dilemma. Broadly speaking, there were three main policy options available to it, each of which enjoyed a measure of support amongst policymakers and each of which had a direct bearing on the French debt question. The first was to continue to work for all-round cancellation in the hope that American opinion would eventually become more favourable to such a solution. In the meantime, there would be no bilateral settlements with either the French or the Americans. The second option was for Britain to negotiate a separate funding agreement with the United States and begin to pay off her own debts, while at the same time unilaterally cancelling the obligations owed by France and Britain's other debtors both as a gesture of goodwill and as an act of enlightened self-interest. The third option was to settle with the Americans, if such a move proved unavoidable, but in that case to demand an element of repayment by France.

None of these courses was without serious drawbacks, and for almost three years after the end of the war the Lloyd George government was unable to make a clear choice between them. As a recent study by Anne Orde has emphasised, indeed, its whole approach to the question of war debts was characterised by chronic muddle and vacillation.[68] Some of those involved in the formulation of policy were themselves uneasily aware of this. In a memorandum submitted to the Cabinet in February 1920, Auckland Geddes, the President of the Board of Trade (shortly to become ambassador to Washington), referred to a worrying tendency within the government for everybody to 'oscillate from one extreme to another' in forming an opinion on the matter.[69] Churchill (Secretary of State for War until 1921 and then Secretary of State for the Colonies) similarly expressed concern about the lack of a firm and consistent policy.[70]

In fairness, it must be said that the decisions to be made by Lloyd George and his colleagues were difficult and complex. There were many imponderables. It was simply not possible, for example, to predict with accuracy the economic consequences which would flow from the adoption of any one of the three main policy options outlined above – although it is certainly somewhat surprising that the two departments with the necessary interest and expertise, the Treasury and the Board of Trade, did not undertake a more systematic and thorough analysis of the subject than they appear to have done. How would the exchanges be affected in each case? Would it be more beneficial to the British economy if the war debts owing to Britain were unilaterally cancelled or if they were paid in full? Such questions were obviously of vital importance when it came to determining policy, but they were not susceptible of any clear-cut answers. There were two main schools of thought on the subject. According to one of these, compelling France to fulfil her obligations would have a detrimental effect on the British economy, the argument being that it would cause the franc to depreciate, thereby hitting British exports to France and boosting the competitiveness of French manufacturers.[71] The contrary view was that British industry suffered from being more heavily taxed than its French counterpart and that one way to even out this imbalance would be to make France pay her debts.[72] Both these arguments were advanced in Cabinet discussions, but there was no consensus within the government about which one was likely to be correct.

Another imponderable was the attitude of the Americans. With the benefit of hindsight, it can be seen that there was not the slightest chance that they would alter their stance and drop their opposition to a policy of debt cancellation. At the time, however, it was not quite so obvious. It is true that the signs were not promising. Reports from the British embassy in Washington offered scant encouragement: from 1920 to 1923 the consistently depressing message from the ambassador was that it was pointless to expect a change of heart. Foreign Ofice officials were inclined to agree with Geddes' assessment. So, too, were those members of the Cabinet – like Sir Alfred Mond (First Commissioner of Works and later Minister of Health) and Lord Inverforth (Minister of Munitions) – who had the opportunity to test American opinion at first hand during visits to the United States. On the other hand, there were at least some straws to grasp at for those who were less pessimistic in their reading of the situation. A number of leading figures in American banking, including Paul Warburg of Kuhn Loeb, Thomas Lamont of J. P. Morgan, and the Governor of the Federal Reserve Bank of New York, Benjamin Strong, were known to favour a more generous approach towards their country's debtors; and early in 1920 President Wilson's influential personal adviser, House, was reported as believing that America's current economic difficulties, especially over exports, would eventually oblige the administration to reassess its position on war debts.[73] However insubstantial, such indications that there might be a shift in American opinion were sufficient to prevent British hopes from being completely extinguished. There was, in any case, much wishful thinking about the possible evolution of American policy, fed by the widespread conviction that it was so manifestly damaging and misguided that it must sooner or later be modified.

The persistence of illusions about Washington's future intentions had the effect of complicating and prolonging discussion within the Lloyd George government on whether to conclude an early debt settlement with the United States or to put off doing so for as long as possible. The government was simply unable to make up its mind on the matter. Typical of its dithering was an incident in December 1920 when the Cabinet agreed that Lord Chalmers, a former Joint Permanent Secretary at the Treasury, should be sent to conduct negotiations on funding arrangements, only for the decision to be rescinded soon afterwards.[74] The arguments for and against a strategy of playing for time were evenly balanced. On one side, it was urged that procrastination would only serve to harden American opinion and ultimately result in harsher terms. It might also permit other debtors to step in first and secure preferential treatment – a risk highlighted by the French government's decision in July 1922 to despatch to Washington a mission headed by a senior Treasury official, Jean Parmentier.[75] Although the Parmentier mission turned out to be a fiasco, for a time it did raise fears in London that the French were seeking to steal a march on Britain.[76] Another argument against delay was that the Americans might lose patience and put the debts on the market as negotiable bonds, something to be avoided at all cost since it would rule out once and for all any prospects of cancellation or reduction, Quite apart from this, there was concern about the damage that might be inflicted on Britain's credit and prestige by a continuing refusal to comply with America's request to fund the obligations. On the other side, the weightiest arguments for delay were that an early bilateral settlement with the United States would entail considerable financial sacrifices for Britain and, in addition, gravely prejudice the achievement of the government's central objective of a comprehensive agreement on all inter-allied debts and reparations. It would serve no useful purpose to examine in greater detail here the way in which the debate on this particular question developed during the immediate postwar years. Of more direct relevance to this study is the parallel debate which took place on a closely related issue: whether, if a funding agreement were negotiated with the United States, Britain should insist on obtaining equivalent or proportionate payments from France and the rest of her debtors. The issue involved important political as well as financial and economic considerations, all of which were fully discussed when the Treasury proposed that Britain, while meeting her own obligations to the Americans, should cancel unilaterally all the war debts owed to her.

 ·   The author of this radical proposal was Blackett. He put it forward for the first time in December 1919 and then repeated it in a memorandum of 2 February 1920 which was prepared after consultation with the Permanent Secretary of the Treasury, Sir Warren Fisher, and later submitted to the Cabinet.[77] From both its content and tone, it is clear that this memorandum was esentially the product of Blackett's frustration at the failure of all his recent efforts to reach a satisfactory accommodation with the Americans. During the war, when serving under Lever on the special Treasury mission to the United States, Blackett had experienced substantial difficulties over collaboration with the American Treasury.[78] These were on a minor scale, however, compared to the problems he encountered in the course of his discussions with Rathbone from the autumn of 1919 onwards.[79] As has been seen, it proved impossible to find any common ground.

Rathbone and his colleagues were totally out of sympathy with the British preference for dealing with inter-allied debts and reparations within the framework
of one general settlement. They were even less sympathetic to the suggestion of
all-round cancellation. What they favoured was a preliminary agreement
between the United States and Britain on the basis of payment in full of the
amount owed. The two countries would then make a joint approach to their
European debtors with a view to negotiating similar agreements with them. The
British Treasury were not averse in principle to the idea of an Anglo-American
common front. There was, after all, much to be said for the closest possible co-
operation with the country whose financial and economic assistance was deemed
essential to European recovery. The trouble was that such co-operation appeared
to be available only on terms which were considered unacceptable and humiliating. At one stage in the negotiation, the Americans sought to obtain from all
their debtors, including Britain, what Blackett regarded as a begging letter stating
that their requests for postponement of interest payments were based on inability
to pay. It emerged, moreover, that they wished to make the prospective debt
agreements conditional upon acceptance of their views on a number of
contentious issues.

In his memorandum of 2 February Blackett complained bitterly about the attitude of the Americans. They had shown, he felt, little appreciation of the
damaging effects of war debts or of the need to cancel them. They had also put
forward 'irrelevant and unfair' demands, and generally abused their position as
creditors to make Britain abandon her own policies and accept theirs. The time
had come, therefore, to consider whether it was desirable to continue with this
'one-sided cooperation' or to adopt instead a dignified and independent line.
Given Britain's position as a debtor of the United States, it was not possible for
the British government to propose officially a plan for cancellation of all inter-
allied debts. What it could do, however, was to indicate that it was prepared to
wipe out unconditionally the debts due to Britain from her European Allies
(except for Russia). That was what he now proposed.

Blackett acknowledged that the adoption of this policy might give rise to a
number of difficulties, but did not think that these would be insuperable. Besides
the relatively minor problem of soothing French and Italian sensitivity over
receiving such a gift – something which could be dealt with by careful presentation – he foresaw two risks: a possible adverse effect on the sterling exchange and
the danger of jeopardising co-operation with the United States. Blackett devoted
relatively little attention to this latter point, arguing that co-operation with the
Americans was already far from satisfactory. In assessing the financial and
economic consequences of his proposal, he was extremely optimistic, whilst
conceding that it was 'extraordinarily difficult' to gauge exactly how the
exchanges would move. A lot would depend on how Washington reacted. There
was a chance that the Americans might follow suit and remit all the allied debts
owed to them, including Britain's. That was the best possible outcome. There

were, however, two alternative possibilities: either they could continue to insist that all debts must be paid, or they could cancel them all except Britain's. Even in this last case, which was obviously the least favourable from the British point of view, the position need not be completely gloomy. The burden of repaying the dollar equivalent of £850m to the United States would certainly be a heavy one. Providing Britain was given sufficient time, however, the task would not be beyond her. Furthermore, there might well be important compensations in the shape of a much improved export performance – resulting from a fall in the value of sterling – in American, French and Italian markets. In an orgy of wishful thinking, doubtless born of real or imagined humiliations at the hands of the United States Treasury, Blackett even envisaged a situation where the American government might eventually become so alarmed by the scale of British imports that it would be driven as a matter of self defence 'to beg us to accept as a favour the wiping out of our debt to it'. In the meantime, whatever the Americans decided to do, Britain would surely have earned the gratitude of the whole world for adopting a realistic approach and for giving new hope to Europe by 'clearing away, as far as we were able, the useless obstruction of a vast mass of paper indebtedness between governments'.[80]

Blackett's memorandum was put before the Cabinet, along with a brief covering note from the Chancellor of the Exchequer on 6 February.[81] According to Anne Orde, although Chamberlain was willing to submit the proposal for consideration, he was not convinced by it.[82] This is a surprising assertion. No evidence is offered to support it. Nor does the covering note itself provide any hint of doubt or lack of conviction. Like Blackett, Chamberlain stressed the futility of waiting for the Americans to agree to all-round cancellation. He followed him, too, in playing down the risks and sacrifices involved in the policy now being recommended: 'If our Allies could pay us and if the United States did not follow our example, we should be the losers. But will our Allies ever be able to pay us and would America permanently refuse to follow our example if we had acted spontaneously?'[83]

The Treasury's initiative received strong backing in some quarters. The reaction from the Foreign Office was particularly enthusiastic, although officials there could not refrain from suggesting that it might be useful to link up the question of debt remission with such matters as territorial differences with the French and Italians in Africa[84] – something which would have completely altered the character of Blackett's proposal and robbed it of much of its intended dramatic impact. Foreign Office officials welcomed the idea of a generous act of debt cancellation by Britain and surmised – correctly – that it would be supported by the Foreign Secretary, Curzon, on the grounds that there was no other policy which would have 'so good an effect on our foreign relations for a generation to come', and that it would give the British government 'the incontestable moral leadership of the world'.[85] Amidst the general satisfaction, however, there was concern about the likely effect on opinion in the United States. Thus the head of the department's American section, Rowland Sperling, thought that it would be prudent to consult with the British embassy in Washington before going ahead:

> Strictly speaking, it is no concern of the United States if we like to write off the Allies' debts to His Majesty's Government, but if, as I understand, we want to shame the United States into following our example and write off our debt to them, the most careful stage management will be required.[86]

On 24 February 1920, the *chargé d'affaires* in Washington, Ronald Lindsay, was accordingly asked for his views. When he replied on 26 February, he came out strongly against making any move of the sort being contemplated until the approaching presidential elections were out of the way. He had been 'considerably impressed', he reported, by the views expressed to him recently by Davis and Leffingwell of the United States Treasury, both of whom had told him that public opinion would be adversely affected by the mere mention of the word cancellation. He agreed with their assessment. There was, moreover, a danger that the American government would interpret London's action as an invitation to pursue a similar policy itself, would consequently be offended and perhaps take a harder line over postponement of interest payments on Britain's debts.[87]

Meanwhile, the Blackett plan had already run into vehement opposition from elements within the Cabinet. In a memorandum of 12 February, the President of the Board of Trade, Auckland Geddes, raised strong objections to what was being proposed. He had no quarrel with a policy of cancelling all inter-allied indebtednes, including that of Britain to the United States. But there was no guarantee that the course now being recommended by the Treasury would lead to that end. It was in fact a 'gamble' and the matter was 'too serious to be settled in such a way'. Like Lindsay, Geddes believed that it was not a good time, with the presidential electons not far off, to announce a new policy on war debts. If, as seemed probable, the Americans felt that an attempt was being made to force their hand, they would resent it. They might then cancel all the allied debts due to them except for the British. The French, in particular, would derive considerable benefit from this, mainly at Britain's expense. What Geddes visualised and feared was a situation where France was relieved of having to repay either Britain or the United States, while Britain herself remained burdened with her American debt – a debt 'assumed mainly on account of French needs and not of our own'. Were that to happen, in ten years' time France could be in a far stronger economic position than Britain, especially since her reparation receipts might turn out to be more than was currently expected and since her industrialists had not been 'drained by war taxation as our business people have been'.[88]

The reservations expressed by Geddes, and even more so the warning noises from Lindsay, seem to have had their desired effect, for on 4 March 1920 the latter was abruptly informed that it had been decided not to proceed with Blackett's plan: he was to mention the subject to no one.[89] By mid-May, however,

the proposal was again being pushed by the Treasury. In the intervening period
there had occurred a sharp debate on the subject amongst Cabinet ministers, in
the course of which the staunchest support for the Treasury line came from
Curzon. In a memorandum of 17 April, the Foreign Secretary endorsed their
view that the economic and financial benefits of retaining Britain's claims on her
European debtors were highly dubious.[90] It was impossible to say whether France
or Italy would ever be able to repay the principal: all that was certain was that if
Britain held them to their obligations – instead of taking a step which would 'go
far towards clearing away the mass of paper now jamming the European
economic machine' – the effect would be to reduce the chances of their recovery
and increase the risk of political upheavals. Nor would payment of the debts be
to the advantage of British exports, since the French and Italians could only pay
by improving their trade balance with Britain. In any case, Britain had a vital
interest in the prosperity of France and Italy, and in the economic revival of
Europe as a whole. Something on a really big scale was needed to give the necessary impetus, and the only measure which Curzon could think of which was both
comprehensive enough and within the realms of practical politics was cancellation of the war debts owed to Britain. On political grounds, too, Curzon felt that
there was an overwhelming case for cancellation. Despite finishing on the
winning side, the French and Italians had emerged from the war greatly impoverished and, indeed, not much better placed financially than the Germans, who
had little or no external debt. They were in a sullen and disappointed mood, and
would react with great bitterness if Britain insisted on repayment. Britain herself
would forfeit her traditional reputation for fairness. If, on the other hand, she
agreed to write off what was due to her, she would 'obtain the moral leadership
of the world at a stroke'. Moreover, such a gesture would immediately improve
the international climate and be of incalculable benefit to the morale of Europe,
which was in desperate need of some such psychological boost.

In one respect at least, Curzon went further than the Treasury had intended.
Although he argued that it was important not to make the proposed concession
in an 'atmosphere of bargaining', that did not prevent him from suggesting, with
scant regard for consistency, that certain counter-concessions might be sought.
It will be recalled that Foreign Office oficials had already hinted at the desirability
of linking up the question of cancellation with a settlement of various territorial
differences with the French and Italians. Curzon had something else in mind.
What he suggested was that the debtors might be required to provide 'suitable
guarantees for a wise policy of financial reconstruction': it might be arranged, for
example, that the wiping out of debts must proceed *pari passu* with increases in
direct taxation by France and Italy. Another possibility was that those two countries could be presented with a solemn warning that in future no anti-British
actions would be tolerated in any area of policy.

Curzon dealt with two further aspects of the matter, the first of which was the
likely effect upon American opinion. Here he was reasonably optimistic. Initially,

he thought, the British gesture would probably cause intense irritation in Washington. In the longer term, however, it might perhaps prick the Americans' conscience and persuade them to follow suit 'before a year was out'. His other, and final, concern was with the best way of presenting the proposed concession to Parliament and the British public. He doubted whether it would be wise to explain all the reasons behind it: Parliament could not be told, for instance, that France and Italy were bankrupt in any case, so that Britain would only be writing off a bad debt. There was one central fact, however, which would have to be made public sooner or later, namely that the best the British taxpayer could hope for was to get a quarter of the debt paid in a quarter of a century:

> It seems possible that this depressing fact, coupled with the general economic arguments for remission, and with an appeal on the ground that a beau geste showing high constructive imagination is justly required of Great Britain in the interests of impoverished Europe, would make the proposal palatable to the country.

It would help the necessary process of education, Curzon felt, if private briefings were given to the City, to newspaper editors and to responsible trade unionists, leaving it to them to assist in winning over the public.[91]

In marked contrast to Curzon, two other ministers – Churchill and Sir Robert Horne, who had just succeeded Geddes at the Board of Trade – were fiercely opposed to the Treasury's proposal. Churchill's opposition was based on three main grounds. In the first place, he was far from convinced that a policy of unilaterally wiping out the debts owed to Britain would produce a generous response from Washington. A more effective way of securing a cancellation of Britain's own debts, he maintained, would be to declare publicly that Britain was ready to write off all the amounts due to her if the Americans would agree to deal with her obligations to them in a similar fashion. Having adopted that position, the government should refuse to budge from it, regardless of any outcry in the United States. There was no need to fear anti-British feeling or propaganda there: American opinion would simmer down once the presidential elections were out of the way, and a Republican victory might well lead to improved relations. Secondly, Churchill was certain that the British public would never tolerate the kind of one-sided concession that was now being considered:

> It would, I am sure, call forth a violent outbreak of anger in this country if it were known that while we are taxing ourselves more than double as much as the French, we are nevertheless forgiving them their debt, and at the same time allowing the United States, which has already pillaged us of twelve hundred millions of our securities, to continue to extract from us payment to the uttermost farthing of a debt contracted in a common cause.[92]

Thirdly, Churchill argued that it would be a serious tactical error to renounce British claims on France until an acceptable settlement had been reached over reparations. Britain wanted a reparation settlement which was 'moderate and reasonable'. Before agreeing to that, however, the French would doubtless demand some remission of their war debts as a *quid pro quo*. By surrendering its power to grant such a concession at this stage, the British government would needlessly deprive itself of 'the means of effecting a good arrangement for Germany'.[93]

As might be expected, the objections raised by the President of the Board of Trade centred on the economic implications of what was being proposed. The arguments which Horne deployed – in a telling memorandum of 1 May 1920 – were broadly in line with those put forward by his predecessor, Geddes, but were developed much more fully. He began by questioning the assumption that France and Italy would never be in a position to meet their obligations. He accepted that they were unable to pay for the time being, but it seemed to him premature to treat the sums due from them as bad debts, especially when the amounts involved were substantial – more than 13 per cent of the total Britain had loaned to foreign governments during the war. To cancel the European debts would have a serious effect on Britain's financial position, while at the same time alleviating that of the French and Italians who were already less heavily burdened with war debts. If the Americans reacted by agreeing to remit all debts owed to them, Britain would undoubtedly benefit. But Horne thought that such an outcome was highly unlikely. It was more probable, he believed, that they would continue to insist on repayment, in which case the main effect of the British gesture to her European debtors would simply be to enable them to pay the United States what they could not otherwise have done. From the economic standpoint, Horne was deeply sceptical about the Treasury claim that Britain's export trade would be stimulated if the French and Italian debts were written off. On the contrary, what he feared was that a reduction in the already relatively light financial burden borne by France – 'our most powerful economic rival' – would increase the competition which it faced. Nor did he accept another argument put forward to support the Treasury's case, namely that the European Allies needed the incentive of relief from their debts to encourage them to adopt the stringent financial measures necessary for their recovery, and that British commerce would benefit indirectly from that recovery. Whatever advantage Britain might derive in this way could not conceivably be commensurate with the sacrifices she would be making. In any case, it was by no means certain that the debtor countries would be prepared to tighten their belts or that it would be politically possible to demand a guarantee on that score of the sort suggested by Curzon. After subjecting the Treasury proposal to close scrutiny, Horne's general conclusion was that it would be unwise to go ahead with it until more information was available about such important matters as Germany's capacity to pay reparations and future American policy.[94]

Despite the powerful resistance offered by both Horne and Churchill, the Treasury were reluctant to abandon their plan. In May 1920, they made another effort to obtain Cabinet approval for it.[95] They were stung into action by anger at what Chamberlain called the 'intolerable pretensions of the United States Government' and, more specifically, by the receipt of an American draft agreement – which Rathbone handed to Blackett on 30 April – dealing with postponement of interest payments and conversion of the British debt into long-term obligations.[96] The American intention was that once Britain had accepted the draft terms the two countries should together ask their French and Italian debtors to negotiate an agreement along the same lines. The British had no fundamental objection to this method of proceeding. There were, however, various items in the draft to which they took great exception. The proposal concerning resumption of interest payments, for example, was seen to give preferential treatment to France and Italy as compared to Britain. It was stipulated that interest should be paid as soon as the exchange value of the currencies of any two debtor and creditor countries reached par. Given that sterling was much stronger than either the franc or the lira, what this provision meant in practice was that Britain was almost certain to begin making payments at an earlier date than the others. Another objectionable feature was an attempt to make the funding terms on offer conditional upon arrangements being reached over reparations and tariffs which were satisfactory to the United States Treasury. When Chamberlain read this particular section of the text, he told Rathbone that he could never insult the French by presenting such a demand to them, nor could he ever 'consent to sell his country into bondage by accepting it. He would rather pay if he could, or default if he could not'.[97]

The draft agreement of 30 April 1920 confirmed both Blackett and Chamberlain in their already strong belief that it was useless to expect America to show breadth of vision or generosity over war debts and that it was up to Britain to give a lead in statesmanship. In a memorandum of 11 May, Blackett accordingly argued in favour of a policy of renouncing all the war debts due to Britain, while at the same time making arrangements for payment in full of current and back interest on Britain's own debts to the United States. Such a policy, he admitted, would inevitably involve a measure of sacrifice; but that seemed to him preferable to accepting a position of subservience to the Americans in return for quite negligible advantages. Chamberlain strongly supported Blackett's proposal and intended to press the Cabinet to adopt it when it met on 19 May.[98] He was prevented from doing so, however, by the intervention of the Prime Minister. Lloyd George was at that time engaged in discussions with Millerand at Hythe and therefore unable to attend the Cabinet meeting, which was chaired in his absence by Bonar Law. His views were nevertheless made known through a statement informing those present that he had fully considered the paper circulated by the Chancellor of the Exchequer but did not approve the adoption 'at the present time' of the policy which it recommended. Chamberlain thereupon indicated that he did not propose to trouble the Cabinet with the matter. That was not, however, before Churchill had managed to make his own reservations clear, urging that any undertaking to forego repayment by the French should be provisional and 'contingent on the United States granting a similar release to us'.[99]

During the next few months, the Treasury proposal that Britain should offer to write off the money owed by her European debtors was in abeyance. In accordance with decisions taken by the Cabinet on 19 and 21 May, attention was focused instead on negotiations for a funding agreement with the United States.[100] When these failed to make progress, however, the proposal was once again revived, almost as an act of desperation.

The decisive influence on Treasury thinking, as before, was the uncompromising attitude of the Americans. As long as there remained a faint possibility of obtaining concessions from them, there was perhaps something to be said for retaining Britain's position as a creditor of the French and Italians for use as a bargaining counter in negotiations with Washington. Such a policy only made sense if the Americans were willing to bargain, however, and there was nothing to indicate that they were, or that they were likely to become so. In June 1920 the Secretary of the Treasury, Houston, coldly informed London that it was idle to hope that Congress would ever be prepared to cancel or reduce the British debt; and in November President Wilson conveyed the same disappointing message when replying to Lloyd George's personal letter of 5 August.[101] The assessments provided by the British embassy in Washington were equally discouraging. Throughout the summer and autumn of 1920, Geddes reported that the only way to prevent a dangerous hardening of American opinion was to conclude a funding agreement as soon as possible. Unless that was done, he warned, there was a real possibility that the Brtish debt might be put on the market. Chamberlain was worried by the ambassador's warnings and by late November was again urging his colleagues to adopt the twofold strategy which he and Blackett had unsuccessfully advocated in February and May: a prompt settlement with the United States and cancellation of the debts owed to Britain.[102]

He put the case for the first part of this strategy in a memorandum of 30 November. He had, he said, received an account of the American government's attitude through a private but authoritative source. From this it was clear that there was no chance of any relaxation of the line that it had taken so far. If it chose to do so, it could demand immediate payment of the full debt. In Chamberlain's judgement, such a demand would be so absurd that non-compliance would not be harmful to Britain's credit and honour. Refusal to pay outstanding interest, on the other hand, would. As of 5 November 1920 the interest due on the British debt stood at $314,583,000. While it was within Britain's capacity to pay that amount, considerable sacrifices would be called for: large quantities of gold would have to be shipped to the United States, the convertability of sterling would need to be suspended, and the whole operation would 'seriously cripple our resources'. Chamberlain naturally wished to prevent that from happening.

The problem was that Congress had empowered the American government to grant a postponement of interest payment only as part of an arrangement for the conversion of demand obligations into long-term ones. In other words, the only way to avoid having to pay interest was to negotiate a funding agreement; and that was what Chamberlain recommended. A settlement along the lines proposed by Rathbone should be accepted – with the important proviso that any resulting bonds should be held by the United States Treasury and not made available to the public. However unpalatable such a course might seem, Chamberlain took the view that it was unavoidable, given the position taken up by the Americans:

> The American Government and people are living in a different continent – I might say in a different world. It is useless and worse than useless to criticise their insularity, blindness and selfishness, and it is not compatible with our dignity to appear as suitors pressing for a consideration which is not willingly given.[103]

Prompted by a particularly disturbing telegram from Geddes, on 3 December Chamberlain produced a supplementary note, this time dealing not only with the necessity of an early settlement with the United States, but also with the other aspect of his proposed strategy – cancellation of the war debts owed to Britain as a *'beau geste'*.[104] Chamberlain argued that British exports were being badly affected because Europe could not buy for want of credit. It would be possible for Britain to free the Allies' credit by remitting their war debts. These debts were in any case of little worth. In the state of exhaustion to which Europe had been reduced, they could not be paid. Even interest could not be collected for some time – and then only at the cost of 'a permanently debased exchange, lessened purchasing power and increased commercial competition wherever the products of our Allies compete with ours'. But not only would it be 'bad business' to refuse to cancel the debts: there would also be a political price to pay. It would scarcely help to promote good relations with France and Italy if every French and Italian taxpayer was to be told – as was bound to happen – that his taxes were high because the British government demanded its pound of flesh. For a combination of political and economic reasons, therefore, Chamberlain wanted Britain to make a generous gesture: to fulfil her obligations to the United States, but at the same time 'do the right and wise thing towards our Continental Allies'.[105]

Once again Chamberlain failed to persuade his colleagues that it made sense to write off the debts due to Britain, although they did prove to be more receptive to the case for settling with the Americans. The two matters were discussed at a Cabinet meeting of 17 December 1920 when ministers had before them the memoranda prepared by Chamberlain and a telegram from Geddes of 15 December discounting any possibility that the newly-elected President, Harding, would offer more lenient terms.[106] Chamberlain informed the Cabinet that the United States Treasury had the right to insist on a conversion of the

British sight debt into long-term bonds whenever they requested. They had made such a request and Britain was thus failing to fulfil her obligations. The telegram from Geddes clearly indicated that the incoming administration had no intention of treating Britain any more favourably than its predecessor and was likely to demand both a funding agreement and payment of back interest amounting to some £80m. The Minister of Munitions, Lord Inverforth, who was just back from a visit to the United States, and Sir Alfred Mond, the First Commissioner of Works, strongly endorsed Chamberlain's statement. There was some inclination to resist the Americans' demands, coupled with a feeling that their behaviour was selfish and would recoil on them. The Cabinet as a whole, however, reluctantly accepted that there was no real alternative to compliance and it was decided to invite Lord Chalmers to head a debt funding mission.[107]

Chamberlain was less successful in winning support for his recommendation that the European debts should be cancelled. One minister – probably Churchill – suggested that if America insisted on being paid 'we should at once pass on to France our demand for an equivalent payment, or at least for a proportionate payment of their debt to us'. In the discussion which ensued, a number of objections were raised against this course: it was pointed out, for example, that it might further depress the Continental exchanges and thus hamper British exports. No decision was reached and the question was adjourned for further discussion.[108]

In the event, this was to be the last time that unilateral cancellation of the debts owed to Britain was given serious consideration at government level. On three separate occasions Chamberlain had sought to win Cabinet approval for it. Each attempt had failed because of the powerful opposition which it aroused and which even the combined advocacy of the Treasury and Foreign Office was insufficient to overcome. Critics had felt anxious about the likelihood of a hostile reaction from the United States. There had also been considerable scepticism about whether the proposed policy would actually produce the economic and financial benefits for Britain that its proponents claimed, with the Board of Trade arguing that, on the contrary, it was Britain's commercial rivals – above all France – who stood to gain most. Another important factor had been the feeling that public opinion would almost certainly be incensed at the prospect of further demands on the British taxpayer. This consideration had counted a great deal with both Churchill and Lloyd George, and it continued to do so in the following months. Indeed, hostility to the Treasury's proposal from two such influential and persuasive ministers was undoubtedly a major reason for its failure to gain acceptance.

VI

By the close of 1920, then, the Lloyd George goverment had effectively rejected the idea of unconditional renunciation of French and other war debts. Most ministers felt that there could be no justification for sacrifices by Britain alone. During 1921 and the early part of 1922, this feeling showed no sign of abating. If anything, indeed, it grew stronger, fuelled by concern about the country's failure to pull out of recession and irritation at mounting American pressure on London for negotiation of a debt settlement. The British remained reluctant debt collectors. No change had taken place in the official line that war debts were a serious obstacle to revival of the international economy and that the best policy for all concerned would be to wipe them out or reduce them to the lowest possible level. At the same time, there was a growing determination that Britain's desire to achieve that objective should not be exploited and that any concesssions by her must be reciprocated by others – especially the United States.

Throughout 1921 British policymakers continued to hanker after a multilateral settlement involving not only inter-allied indebtedness but also reparations. The argument for including the latter element was given added force by the onset of a major crisis over the Germans' unsuccessful attempts to make the payments required of them. Whether through deliberate intent or lack of the necessary resources, from the outset Germany repeatedly failed to meet her financial obligations under the Treaty of Versailles.[109] On 27 April 1921, in accordance with that treaty, the Reparation Commission set her total liability at 132bn gold marks, the equivalent of £6.6bn, and the following month the London conference devised a schedule of payments in cash and kind by which the debt was to be discharged over a period of 36 years. Under the London Schedule of Payments, 1bn gold marks were to be paid by 31 August 1921. The German government, which only accepted these terms under the threat of force, managed to meet the target. But the foreign exchange operations needed to transfer such a sum encouraged speculation and caused a sharp drop in the international value of the mark. Other currencies suffered associated disturbances, with the pound sinking from $4 to $3.57, and the franc from $8.78 to $7.64, between 21 May and 30 July.[110] From September the fall of the mark accelerated in anticipation of the substantial foreign exchange purchases Germany would require for instalments due in November 1921 and the first two months of 1922.[111] The Germans sought to obtain loans from abroad in order to alleviate their difficulties. On 28 September Carl Bergmann, formerly Germany's delegate on the Reparation Commission, set off for the United States to try to raise credits there, and at the end of November Walther Rathenau, the Minister of Reconstruction, travelled to London for talks with British bankers, bearing a letter from Rudolf Havenstein, the President of the Reichsbank, asking Norman about the prospects for financial aid from the City. Both missions proved fruitless, however, and on 14 December the German government, headed by Josef Wirth, was obliged to ask the Reparation Commission for a moratorium on the payments scheduled for January and February 1922.[112]

This request produced divergent reactions from the British and the French. In London it was received with considerable sympathy, not least because it was believed to be in Britain's own interest that Germany should be given a breathing-space. During his visit there in the first week of December 1921 Rathenau had meetings with many prominent figures, including Norman, senior Treasury officials, Horne, who had replaced Chamberlain as Chancellor of the Exchequer the previous March, and Lloyd George. The gloomy message which he conveyed to all was that Germany was on the verge of financial chaos which could only be averted by an immediate moratorium on reparation payments. Those to whom he spoke needed little persuading of the gravity of the situation and had themselves already reached a similar conclusion about the remedies which needed to be applied. Some, indeed, believed that Germany needed even greater relief than Berlin had sought – according to Blackett, 'a considerable breathing-space – say two years at least without payment other than deliveries in kind'.[113] As early as 16 November, the Treasury sent the Cabinet a memorandum urging the necessity both of a moratorium to enable Germany to put her finances in order and of a revision of the existing schedule of payments. It was not in British interests, the Treasury stated, to see the financial collapse of Germany, involving as it would an enormous loss in the purchasing power of the whole of central Europe.[114] The Chancellor developed this argument in a paper circulated to the Cabinet on 28 November and at meetings of the Cabinet Finance Committee in early December, emphasising the damaging effects which a German default in January would have on Britain's financial and commercial position.[115] Norman, too, argued the case for a moratorium of at least six months' duration. In his judgement, however, even that would not suffice to provide a satisfactory solution to the current crisis. The only way to restore confidence on a long-term basis was to work out a general settlement dealing with reparations and inter-allied indebtedness as a whole.[116] As he explained to Benjamin Strong, it defied common sense to treat the two items separately:

> We are as it were in jeopardy today of making a temporary European adjustment of the Reparation payments which adjustment may last long enough to allow the inter-Allied debts to be settled next spring or summer in a totally different and separate question. Such a possibility is too ridiculous. Having, let us suppose, steadied the Exchanges by some Reparation adjustment, we are immediately to see them unsteadied by Inter-Allied Debt payments?[117]

Unlike the British, the French were not disposed to agree to a moratorium. They took the view that the Germans could pay if they made the effort, were deliberately exaggerating the magnitude of the crisis and were themselves principally responsible for whatever difficulties they did have because they were unwilling to raise the taxes necessary to meet their obligations. In any case, France faced severe financial problems of her own, including a substantial budget deficit, massive floating debts and a huge bill for reconstruction.[118] For dealing with these, her reparation receipts were considered essential. What influenced the French attitude above all, however, was the fear that once payments were suspended they would never be resumed.

It was in the context of this basic disagreement about how to respond to Berlin's request for relief that Britain's position as a creditor of France came into play in late 1921. In London, it was fully recognised that nothing could be achieved without French acquiescence. There was, though, less certainty over how that might be obtained. One obvious possibility was to make use of their indebtedness as a means of exerting pressure on the French. Alternatively, they might be offered some form of financial inducement to co-operate, either through a reduction in their war debt or a reapportionment of reparation receipts to their advantage – or a combination of both. For his part, Norman preferred the former, more forceful, approach. If France tried to block a moratorium, he suggested, Britain should simply hand over to the German government French and Italian war debt bills of an amount equivalent to the reparation payments due in the next quarter. Germany would then be able to discharge her obligations with these bills and France would have no alternative but to accept them.[119] Clearly the implementation of such a scheme would have been deeply humiliating to France and extremely damaging to Anglo-French relations. These considerations were evidently of no great concern to Norman, an inveterate Francophobe. But his cavalier attitude was shared by few others within the ranks of British policymakers. Amongst ministers and senior officials there was in fact a general wish – particularly strong at the Foreign Office – to keep on as good terms as possible with Britain's most important partner in Europe, and for that reason alone the provocative and undiplomatic methods favoured by Norman had little apppeal.[120] More attractive was the idea of winning French consent to a moratorium by providing them with compensation for the financial losses which such a measure would cause them. It was to this policy that the Lloyd George government turned its attention – or such of it as could be spared from Irish affairs and the Washington naval conference in November and December 1921.

The French Prime Minister, Briand, was due to travel to London for talks with Lloyd George in mid-December. The main purpose of his visit was to bring about a much-needed improvement in Anglo-French relations and, more specifically, to discuss matters relating to security. But the British also hoped that the discussions might lay the foundations for a broad understanding on reparations and war debts which would resolve the growing crisis in Germany. It was arranged that a preliminary 'personal and informal' meeting should take place between British ministers and the French Minister for the Liberated Regions, Louis Loucheur, who apparently inspired more trust than his colleague Paul Doumer, the Minister of Finance.[121] By the time Loucheur arrived in London on 8 December, he already had in mind a scheme on reparations and war debts which was probably influenced by ideas recently formulated by Jacques Seydoux, the Assistant Director of Commercial Affairs at the Quai d'Orsay, and Alexandre

Aron, the Secretary-General of the French Delegation to the Reparation Commission.[122] A central feature of Loucheur's scheme was that there should be a substantial reduction in Germany's reparation burden. This was to be accompanied by measures designed to cushion France from any resultant financial sacrifice: cancellation of war debts and a revision – in a manner favourable to France and disadvantageous to Britain – of the allocation of reparation receipts agreed to at the Spa conference of July 1920.[123] Such a programme did not differ in its essentials from plans which were currently being mooted in British official circles, so it is hardly surprising that Loucheur's talks at Chequers with Lloyd George and Horne proceeded reasonably smoothly. It is not possible to discover exactly what was said. British accounts of the meeting are fragmentary and vague.[124] Nor are they entirely consistent with that provided by Loucheur himself in his *Carnets secrets*.[125] It seems clear, however, that the conversation revealed a broad measure of agreement about the need to deal with reparations and war debts together and to ensure that any scaling down of the former should be linked to reduction or cancellation of the latter. The possibility of a significant reduction in Britain's share of reparations was also touched upon, though there is some doubt about who raised the matter. No fundamental differences arose. Certainly the British felt sufficiently encouraged by the outcome to decide to sound out American opinion on the prospects for an early meeting between Lloyd George, Briand and Harding to discuss a solution to the German crisis and the state of the world economy.

The attitude of the Americans was crucial, for during his talk with Loucheur on 8 December Lloyd George was adamant that everything under consideration hinged on the willingness of the United States to play its part in a general cancellation of war debts. For various reasons the British seem to have convinced themselves at this stage that there was a reasonable chance of American co-operation to that end. Anglo-American relations were undoubtedly in a healthier state than they had been for some time. The successful conclusion of negotiations between the British government and Sinn Fein in early December made a major contribution to easing tensions between London and Washington. Moreover, there was considerable satisfaction in both capitals at the progress being made in the early stages of the Washington naval conference. The British and American delegations, led respectively by Balfour and Secretary of State Charles Evans Hughes, had quickly established a good working relationship, and hopes were already high that the conference would produce satisfactory results. Some British observers believed that these promising developments might well improve the chances of reaching agreement in other areas, including war debts. Thus Hankey, who was at the conference, reported to Lloyd George on 29 November:

> All the Americans and big politicians whom I talk to tell me that if only the conference succeeds they have great hopes that the better atmosphere created among nations may lead to a settlement of many other outstanding questions. I have an

idea that in their minds they have the question of the debt.[126]

More than that, there was a strong feeling within the Cabinet that Britain's efforts to accommodate American wishes over both naval disarmament and Ireland deserved some sort of gesture in return.[127]

Such expectations were soon dashed, for cautious British feelers about reparations and war debts met with the customary cold reception from the Americans. On 12 December 1921, at the request of the Chancellor of the Exchequer, Norman telegraphed Strong to ask him about the possibility of an early meeting between the British and French premiers and President Harding. The purpose of this meeting would be to determine 'more or less unofficially but in principle' the broad lines to be followed when the time came to summon a general economic conference, and in the meantime to establish the necessity of a short moratorium on German reparation payments.[128] On the same day, the British delegation at the Washington conference was instructed to find out whether there was any chance of Lloyd George, Briand and Loucheur receiving a presidential invitation to go to the United States to discuss the growing crisis in Germany and the economic condition of Europe as a whole.[129] Speculation about a likely initiative by the British government appeared in the press on 13 December, however, and made it impossible for the matter to be taken any further. On 16 December Horne explained the current position to the Cabinet. When arrangements had been made for Briand's visit, he said, it had been hoped that it would present the opportunity for a meeting of British, French and American representatives to discuss in general terms inter-allied debts and other important outstanding questions. It would then have been possible, in the event of America being prepared to do likewise, for Britain to have cancelled the debts owed to her – and perhaps also to have foregone her reparation claims. Such a policy would have enabled France to obtain enough from reparations to cover the cost of restoring her devastated regions. Loucheur had indicated his willingness to consider favourably proposals of this character. However, as a result of tentative enquiries in 'responsible quarters', it was now certain that any suggestion to the United States government that it should take part in the sort of discussions being contemplated would be given a 'very hostile reception'. It remained the view of the great majority of Americans that war debts ought to be paid. That being the case, Horne concluded, the European Allies must now try to deal with the problem of reparations on their own and in a more limited way than they would have liked.[130]

As a result of the Americans' unresponsive attitude, therefore, when Briand and Loucheur arrived in London on 19 December, Lloyd George felt unable to offer them any substantial concessions on reparations or war debts. If the United States had been prepared to co-operate, he told Briand, it would have been a different matter. But with unemployment in Britain standing at two milllion and with the economy showing no signs of an improvement, it was impossible for the British government to take responsibility for a unilateral cancellation of debts.

Nor would public opinion tolerate the sacrifices entailed in such a policy.[131]

VII

The next important development in the evolution of British policy on French war debts was the sending of the so-called Balfour Note on 1 August 1922 requesting France and the rest of Britain's debtors to take steps to negotiate a funding agreement. This followed several months of confused and inconclusive debate about inter-allied debts. The collapse in December 1921 of British and French efforts to bring about a cancellation of war debts and a reduction of reparations in one general settlement had left the Lloyd George government uncertain as to what course to take. Even after this latest rebuff from Washington, it still refused to abandon all hope that the Harding administration might yet change its mind. This was reflected in the proposal which Lloyd George put to Louis Barthou at the Genoa conference of April 1922: Britain would be prepared to surrender both its share of reparations and all claims on its debtors – provided the Americans agreed to cancel the debts owed to them.[132] Increasingly, however, London was forced to recognise that any policy predicated on American willingness to make such a sweeping concession was completely unrealistic. An alternative strategy for dealing with the problem of debts would thus need to be found. There was not a great deal of choice. In practice, the only alternative to waiting for a shift in American policy which would make a comprehensive settlement possible was for Britain herself to conclude a funding agreement with the United States. In the first half of 1922, therefore, Lloyd George and his colleagues returned again and again to two basic questions: should Britain negotiate a bilateral debt agreement with America and, if so, what line should she then take towards her own debtors? The Cabinet was deeply divided on both these issues, and it was not until late July 1922 that a coherent policy at last emerged when it was decided to send the Balfour Note.

This decision was taken largely in response to growing American pressure for a debt settlement. As far back as December 1920, the Cabinet had agreed that a debt funding mission, led by Lord Chalmers, should be sent to Washington – only to drop the idea less than two months later.[133] Thereafter most ministers remained extremely reluctant to sanction negotiations. On 10 May 1921 the Cabinet decided that for the time being there should be no approach to the Americans about Britain's debt, a decision which prompted Austen Chamberlain to ask for his dissent to be recorded;[134] and at a Cabinet meeting of 16 December 1921 the view was forcefully expressed that the time was not yet ripe for putting any definite proposals to the United States and that it would be a profound mistake to begin making any payments 'except under the greatest pressure'.[135] Throughout 1921, then, British policy was to play for time in the hope that there might be a change in Washington's stance. But such a change was in fact out of the question. President Harding, who took office in March 1921, Andrew Mellon, the Secretary of the Treasury, and Herbert Hoover, the Secretary of Commerce, were all convinced that their country's current recession was the result of excessive taxation, and their resultant commitment to cutting taxes left little scope for generosity to America's debtors. The mood was even tougher in Congress, which on 9 February 1922 took a major step towards getting negotiations with the debtor countries started by passing an act for the establishment of the five-man World War Foreign Debt Commision (WDC).[136] This commission, which was chaired by Mellon, instructed the Department of State to request the governments concerned to send negotiators, and notes to that effect were duly despatched in April 1922 – the note to Britain being transmitted to the Foreign Office by the American ambassador, George Harvey, on 24 April.[137]

This development placed the British government in an acutely embarrassing position. It was clear that the Americans were now in earnest. They had never disguised their impatience and displeasure at the failure of the European debtors to submit any proposals for paying their debts. But they had hitherto desisted from making any formal demands. The fact that they had now done so made it far more difficult for the British to continue with their delaying tactics. As Austen Chamberlain and his successor as Chancellor, Horne, repeatedly pointed out to their colleagues, Britain's debts were in the form of demand obligations. It followed that a refusal to respond to the request contained in the American note would be tantamount to repudiation and therefore highly damaging to Britain's reputation and credit. By giving notice in March 1922 of its intention to make interest payments from the following October, the British government had created a little more room for manoeuvre. Even so, the pressure to fund the debts was now greater than it had ever been. At the same time, the incentive to do so was less. The WDC's freedom to conduct negotiations with foreign debtors was severely limited by tight legislative constraints: payment was to be completed within a maximum period of 25 years and the rate of interest was to be at least 4.25 per cent. In the absence of any discretionary powers for the WDC, there was no reason to believe that Britain could 'earn' more favourable terms by showing a willingness to settle as soon as possible.

Under the circumstances, it is hardly surprising that British reactions to the American note of 24 April were mixed, with a sharp difference of opinion developing between the Foreign Office and the Treasury. Officials at the Treasury wanted to postpone negotiations until after the Congressional elections of November 1922 were out of the way, and they saw no reason why the Americans should not be kept waiting. In early June, Blackett told the Permanent Under-Secretary at the Foreign Office, Eyre Crowe, that to send a mission to negotiate now would be equivalent to unconditional acceptance of the whole debt. That would be contrary to the present policy of the Cabinet which was to oppose committing Britain to paying in full and so losing the possiblity of using such payment as a lever for inducing the United States to deal comprehensively with inter-allied indebtedness as a whole.[138] Crowe himself thought that there was some force in this argument; but others in the Foreign Office, including the head of the American section, Sperling, were completely opposed to the Treasury's approach. They believed that negotiations should begin as a matter of urgency and that delay would only damage British interests.

Their attitude was influenced by several factors. First, they were motivated by a natural desire not to undermine the recent encouraging improvement in Anglo-American relations. Secondly, they were subjected to continuing pressure for prompt action from the United States government and its representatives in London: the note transmitted by Harvey on 24 April was soon followed up by another asking for information about the names of the British representatives who were to be sent and the likely date of their arrival; and on 6 June the Foreign Office received a telephone call from Averel Harriman of the American embassy saying that the State Department was pressing for an answer.[139] Finally, there can be little doubt that Sperling and his colleagues attached great weight to the advice being offered by the British embassy in Washington. Certainly they felt that Geddes was a 'much more trustworthy authority' than the Treasury on the state of American opinion.[140] Since his appointment as ambassador some two years previously, Geddes had consistently argued for a debt settlement with the United States at the earliest opportunity. In his view, the American government's formal request for negotiations made the case for such a policy even more compelling. From mid-May 1922 he repeatedly warned about the consequences of failing to act promptly. American feelings about the debts were hardening all the time, he informed London, and the situation was likely to get even worse.[141] There was also the danger that France might secure a tactical advantage over Britain by taking the lead in starting negotiations. On 17 May, Geddes reported speculation in the American press that the Harding government had been notified that France was ready to send a special mission to discuss debts, and this was confirmed on 6 June when the Secretary of State announced that a French commission headed by Parmentier would shortly be travelling to the United States.[142]

Foreign Office officials were much impressed by Geddes' warnings, sharing his concern about French manoeuvring and the reported stiffening of American attitudes.[143] They were therefore disturbed by the Treasury line that there was no need for haste. On 18 May Sperling wrote to Blackett asking him whether the Treasury still adhered to the view that negotiations ought to be postponed until after November. Blackett's reply was uncompromising: the department's opinion was unchanged. According to Blackett, prompt funding was unlikely to achieve any material improvement in the terms offered because the American government's power to make concessions was strictly limited by law. In some respects, moreover, the existing demand obligations were more convenient for Britain than long-term bonds with fixed interest and sinking fund provisions. For these reasons the Treasury still wished to delay the appointment of a delegation to go to Washington. Not surprisingly, this reply did nothing to satisfy Sperling who, in a minute of 24 May, asked for a decision on whether the Foreign Office was prepared to commit itself to the Treasury line.[144] In an attempt to resolve differences between the two departments and establish a common position, discussions took place in early June between Blackett and Crowe and between Horne and Balfour, then acting Foreign Secretary because of Curzon's indisposition through phlebitis (between 25 May and 8 August).[145] Although these exchanges evidently gave the Foreign Office a better understanding of the Treasury's viewpoint, differences persisted.

Within the Cabinet, too, there was a sharp division of opinion about how to respond to the United States' invitation to negotiate. Ministers were unable to agree on the merits or otherwise of an early funding agreement. More contentious still was the related question of whether Britain should follow the United States' example and present her own debtors with a demand for repayment. Both these issues were the subject of passionate debate at a series of Cabinet meetings held between May and August 1922, with Horne and his predecessor as Chancellor, Austen Chamberlain, adopting a position which left them increasingly isolated. At these sessions Lloyd George – irritated with the French because of Poincaré's obstructive attitude towards the recent unsuccessful conference on European reconstruction at Genoa – was not in a charitable mood. On 23 May he told the Cabinet that there could be no question of unilateral concessions by Britain. It was impossible to go to the country, burdened as it was with a national debt of £8bn and an unemployment figure of two million, and

> announce that we were going to forgive the debts owing to us by France, Italy, Germany and so forth, while at the same time we were to pay our debt of £1000 million to the United States. The position would be quite different if the United States were prepared to forgive us our debts as we forgave those of our debtors.[146]

In subsequent Cabinet discussions Lloyd George continued to take a firm line, arguing that it was a matter of basic justice that France and the other debtors should help to ease the burden being carried by the long-suffering British taxpayer. This view received strong backing from Churchill and most other ministers: only Horne and Chamberlain challenged it.

On 16 June the Cabinet considered the whole question of inter-allied debts. The starting point for the discussion was a memorandum of 8 June by the Chancellor of the Exchequer arguing that negotiations with Washington should be started without delay.[147] The meeting opened with a statement of the case for funding the American debt. Although the minutes do not indicate who the speaker was, it seems highly probable that it was Horne himself since the views put forward were almost identical to those expounded in his paper. The Cabinet was reminded that Britain was under a definite obligation to convert the existing demand obligations into long-term bonds if requested to do so by the United

States Secretary of the Treasury. Such a request had now been made. It was generally agreed that the United States would not offer any relaxation of repayment terms to Great Britain: if anything American opinion was tending to harden. There was therefore nothing to be gained by delaying the opening of negotiations. Indeed, delay would cause difficulties. It was maintained that Britain's main interest was in reaching a settlement in Europe, and this could not be effected until satisfactory arrangements had been made for dealing with reparations. France would only consent to such arrangements when she knew what she had to pay to Britain and the United States. A policy requiring France and Britain's other debtors to fund their debts would increase French reluctance to make any concessions over reparations to Germany, 'with the result that the latter country would go bankrupt and European revival would be indefinitely postponed'. There was no chance that America would assist in bringing about a European settlement until she had reached an agreement on debts with Britain, who was rightly regarded as her only solvent debtor. Thus any delay in dealing with the British debt to the United States would further postpone European reconstruction. If the debt were funded, it would probably be impossible to prevent it being placed on the market. Despite that, no matter how 'unconscionable' the attitude of the Americans was thought to be, it would be incompatible with national honour and credit to refuse to pay, and inconceivable that Britain would ever place herself in the humiliating position of being a defaulter to the United States.[148]

From another quarter it was urged that Britain should insist that in no circumstances would she be given less favourable treatment than America's other European debtors. In this context, it was thought highly desirable that Europe should present a common front to the United States and that the Americans should not be allowed to settle with their debtors individually. The suggestion was then made that a note should be drafted and despatched to France and the other debtors 'setting out the nature of the demand made by the United States, the seriousness of the economic and financial situation in Great Britain, the extent of British taxation compared with that of other Powers, and the necessity, in these circumstances, of exacting from her European debtors repayment on the lines of the American demand'. The note would have to be carefully worded and would indicate the British view that American policy was wrong and that it was 'unreasonable and inequitable' for the United States to try to deal separately with its debtors. It would also emphasise that, much as it regretted having to request payments, the British government was left with no alternative because of American demands. Another note should be prepared for sending to the United States saying that Britain would not be in a position to put forward definite proposals until she had completed discussions with her own debtors. It was felt to be important to bring home to America that she would be making herself the 'tax-gatherer and rent-collector of the civilised world'.

Finally, it was pointed out that public opinion would be extremely critical of of any proposals which obliged the British taxpayer to pay the American debt while obtaining litle or nothing from Britain's debtors. British taxation was twice the French level, and unemployment in Britain much worse than in France or any of the other debtor countries:

> It was most mortifying for Great Britain to have to forego her European debts while at the same time to be 'lectured' by M. Poincaré, who had the temerity to suggest that our unemployment problem was mainly attributable to a mistaken monetary policy and the way in which we handled the question of the export of raw materials.[149]

The Cabinet eventually agreed that the acting Foreign Secretary, Balfour, should draft two notes along the lines suggested for consideration at a later date. It also decided that, as far as possible, there should be no reference to inter-allied debts when Poincaré paid his scheduled visit to London for talks on reparations on 19 June.[150] As a result, the topic was barely touched upon during the French Prime Minister's conversations with Lloyd George – the latter merely saying that Britain could not renounce her claims unless the United States did likewise, and that there was no possibility of that happening in the current year.[151] On 30 June the Cabinet provisionally approved a draft note to the allied debtors prepared by Balfour.[152] The matter was further discussed at a Cabinet meeting of 7 July, at which it was agreed that the draft should be examined by Balfour, Horne and Geddes (who had returned to London for consultation in late June), with discretion being allowed them to soften any passages thought to reflect badly on the American people, and that it should contain a hint that the allied debtors should meet the British government in conference to discuss the funding of allied debts to Britain and the possibility of cancellation. At the same time, the Cabinet agreed that the American ambassador should be informed that a British delegation would be arriving in Washington in early September.[153] This represented an abrupt change from the previous decision of 16 June to inform the United States that the British government was not yet ready to begin negotiations. The reason for this shift is not absolutely clear. It seems likely, however, that it was a response to some encouraging indications about the Harding administration's attitude from the United States ambassador, Harvey, and the American Chief Justice, Wliiam Howard Taft: the latter, while lunching with Lloyd George, Bonar Law, Churchill and Horne on 5 July, hinted that modification of the law governing the WDC was not out of the question.[154]

At the Cabinet meeting of 7 July no objections were raised to the despatch of the Balfour Note to Britain's debtors. But that did not mean that the policy commanded unanimous support from ministers. On the contrary, both Horne and Austen Chamberlain had serious misgivings. When the matter was discussed on that particular occasion, however, Chamberlain was not present. As a result, Horne felt isolated and chose not to voice his reservations. It was to be a different matter when the question again came before the Cabinet on 25 July, with both men speaking out strongly against what was being proposed. Developments in the intervening period had only strengthened their opposition. A German request for a moratorium on reparation payments on 12 July, followed by a rapid fall in the value of the mark, made it appear a particularly inopportune time to press France and the other debtors to meet their obligations. Moreover, it seems reasonable to assume that Horne's own doubts had been reinforced by the fierce resistance to sending the Balfour Note expressed in the meantime by one of his most senior advisers, Blackett. As Blackett told Keynes at the time, he fought a dogged rearguard action lasting almost four weeks against the Note.[155]

In a paper written for the Chancellor on 12 July, Blackett declared that the Cabinet's decisions of 7 July were 'so fraught with evil consequences that I venture to appeal to you for its reconsideration before it is too late'.[156] His central complaint was that the policy was 'fundamentally insincere'. By this he meant that it was impossible to carry it out. There were, Blackett argued, only two possible courses for the British government to follow: either it could fund and pay Britain's debt to the United States and reserve an absolutely free hand for dealing with claims on Europe, or it could say – as had been done so far – that it could not deal with the British debt in isolation from the whole question of inter-governmental indebtedness. The Cabinet was now professing to take a third course, namely to negotiate a funding agreement with America and collect from Europe just enough to meet the resultant payments. Blackett dismissed the idea that this was feasible as 'completely erroneous', arguing that the consequence of attempting such a policy would be to saddle Germany with an impossibly heavy reparation burden. On the assumption that the British debt to America were funded at 4.25 per cent over 25 years, the dollar equivalent of £57m would need to be paid annually. If the bill were presented to France, Italy and the other debtors, they would certainly insist that Germany must bear the cost. France, for her part, would never accept a reparation settlement which did not provide her with sufficient to cover not only her payments to Britain and the United States but also the 80bn francs – around £1.5bn – which she had already spent on her devastated areas. It was probable, indeed, that the French budget could never be balanced if she received less. Taking all these considerations into account, Blackett calculated that the end result of the Balfour Note policy would be to leave Germany to pay an amount which was far in excess of her capacity: a capital sum of at least £2.75bn and annual payments of £184m or £139m, depending on whether they were spread over 25 or 50 years. This being the case, how could the draft despatch to the allied debtors be reconciled with Britain's policy of persuading France to agree to a big reduction in the total demanded from Germany? There was, it seemed to Blackett, a much better option available to the British government:

A sincere policy of funding our debt to the United States of America preparatory to a settlement with Europe designed to rescue Europe from chaos might well bring the United States of America in to our help. An insincere policy will have the reverse effect. And if we really mean to try to save Europe and are merely ventilating our preliminary grumble before doing so, is it worth while to begin by pillorying American selfishness?[157]

By the time the Cabinet met to discuss the projected despatch on 25 July, therefore, a certain amount of opposition to it had aready begun to build up. This was reflected in the emotional debate which ensued. After joint scrutiny by Balfour, Horne and Geddes, the original draft had been somewhat modified, a penultimate sentence having been added which was intended to stress the extent of British generosity. But this did nothing to satisfy critics. When Balfour claimed that the Cabinet had at one stage been unanimous in approving the policy in the draft despatch – although conceding that there had subsequently been a certain 'wavering' – Horne immediately objected that he for one had never favoured it. He still believed that it was 'profoundly wrong', his principal concern being that it would antagonise the Americans. It was worthwhile, he thought, attempting to placate them. They could make things extremely difficult for Britain, if they chose to do so, by commercialising the debt in a way which might ruin British credit. On the other hand, a policy of 'meeting the American demand according to its tenour' might secure a lower interest rate and longer repayment period than permitted by the law establishing the WDC. It might also be possible to ensure that any bonds which were given would be held by the United States Treasury instead of being placed on the market. Turning to Europe, Horne argued that the French retort to a British demand for repayment of war debts would be to exact as much as possible from Germany. The committee of bankers set up by the Reparation Commission to consider the conditions under which a reparation loan might be raised had recently reported that Germany could pay £125m per annum at most. Yet France would need to obtain £259m annually in order to meet British and American claims. 'In effect, Germany would become the sole debtor, and her position would be made much worse.' There would be a further drop in the value of the mark, with Germany following Austria on the road to bankruptcy.[158]

Austen Chamberlain echoed Horne's warnings about the likely effect of the Balfour Note policy on both American and European opinion. He confessed that for some time he had not seen eye to eye with his colleagues on inter-allied debts. While fully sharing their feelings about the 'selfishness' and 'insolence' of the United States' official attitude, he disagreed about what should be done in the light of that attitude. Since America had already rejected British proposals for a general remission of debts, Chamberlain believed that it was incompatible with Britain's dignity and status to 'ask again, and as a favour, what had been refused when advanced in the interests of world peace'. Even if the Americans could be persuaded to renounce their claims on Britain, the money thus saved would be 'spent over and over again in our subsequent loss of credit'. To send the Balfour Note, Chamberlain argued, would have a disastrous effect upon relations with the United States. In order to support this contention, he cited the views of the British ambassador to Washington, but Geddes, who had been invited to attend the Cabinet meeting, immediately interjected to say that his position was being misrepresented. Despite this intervention, Chamberlain continued to insist that there would be an outcry in the United States which would undo all Balfour's good work at the Washington naval conference. As for the French and Italians, they 'would feel, with added bitterness, what we felt in regard to the United States. France would point to her devastated regions and hold us up to obloquy'. Nor would the note produce any tangible financial gains for Britain, given that current Cabinet policy was not to ask debtors to pay anything in the immediate future. On all counts, therefore, Chamberlain believed that to send the note would be a great mistake:

> We would be regarded as gibbeting the United States before the world. They might deserve that, but it was a mad policy to pursue: it would destroy our good relations with the United States, and would increase the dislike (already considerable) felt for England in France and Italy.[159]

The views put forward with such conviction by Chamberlain and Horne obtained scant support from other ministers – the only hint of backing coming from Mond, the Minister of Health, who intervened briefly to express anxiety about the effect that sending the proposed note to Britain's debtors might have on the franc and the lira.[160] Admittedly, the contribution from Geddes was ambiguous to say the least. When invited by Lloyd George to give an assessment of the effect publication of the note would have on American public opinion, the ambassador at first said that nothing ought to be done to irritate American opinion and that he was unwilling to see a note sent which pilloried the United States government. Yet he then added that he did not think it helped to be unduly lenient to America. 'He thought it better to hit back and hit hard at once.'[161] What his listeners were meant to infer from this confused and contradictory statement is difficult to know. The rest of those who spoke were all unequivocally in favour of the note being sent. Balfour emphasised that France was being asked to pay considerably less than she owed, while H. A. L. Fisher, the President of the Board of Education, suggested that 'the result would bring relief to France'[162] – without offering any explanation as to why the note should have that effect.

By far the most forceful supporters of the note were Lloyd George and Churchill, the latter reminding his colleagues that the Cabinet had already discussed the matter twice and approved the proposed course of action by 'an overwhelming majority'. Churchill described the Balfour Note as a 'righteous and a proper document, enunciating a policy of wisdom, firmness and broad justice'. The government, he argued, had a duty to send it and thereby safeguard the interests of the British people who ought not to be asked to surrender all that was owing to them while being compelled to pay all that they owed. Unlike Chamberlain and Horne, he was not particularly worried about a hostile reaction from either the European debtors or the Americans. The Europeans would realise that the note was really directed at the United States and that they were not in fact being called upon to pay. As far as the Americans were concerned, Churchill dismissed as illusory the idea that they would 'put the pincers in the fire and begin to tease and torture us'. After some momentary irritation, they would be driven to examine their consciences about the policy they had followed so far.[163] Lloyd George, who concluded the discussion, fully agreed with these views. Even more than Churchill's statement, his gave vent to pent-up resentment towards the United States. In the case of Lloyd George, there was an additional element of animus against France. While conceding that the French and Italians might be a little angry at the note, Lloyd George insisted that it was time for Britain to assert herself:

We were enduring a most burdensome taxation. In other countries taxes were less high and they were not, in fact, all being collected. We were expected to bear this unexampled burden and also to pay all our debts . . . Why should we be apologetic to the United States? All we could gain by cringeing would be perhaps some ten or fifteen millions. It was not worth bartering our self-respect and suing *in forma pauperis*. They had taken advantage of our complications in the War to try to capture our International Shipping position and were actually trading with South America while using our ships to convey their troops to France . . . They had done their best to wrest our Naval supremacy . . . Today they were trying to wrest our financial and commercial supremacy. They were claiming £850,000,000 for goods that were bought in the States for the Allies and from the sale of which huge profits were made by their manufacturers. They were claiming also £100,000 of deferred interest . . . That was an ignoble attitude, but in spite of it he did not think the British Empire ought to lower its self-respect . . . With regard to France, she was one of the richest countries in Europe, and he was not sure that we should not obtain something from France. We could point to the large number of Air Squadrons she was building – a policy if which [sic.] persisted in would force us to do the same. Europe owed us £3,300,000,000. We were offering to forgive this if the United States were prepared to forgive us £950,000,000. Our policy should be put forward as an attempt to wipe out international indebtedness in order to give the world a fresh start. The Americans were ignorant of some of the great facts of the War. They had no idea of the magnitude of the war effort of the Allies . . . The publication of this document, and the controversy to which it would give rise, would have important educational results on American opinion. He would have a paragraph stating quite unequivocally that we were prepared to forgive the whole of the debt of the Allies and of Germany to us.[164]

Following this diatribe, the Cabinet approved the draft despatch – with Chamberlain and Horne asking for their dissent to be recorded – and on 1 August 1922, in accordance with a decision taken by the Cabinet Finance Committee on the previous day, the Balfour Note was duly sent to France and the rest of Britain's debtors.[165]

3

The Balfour Note and the London
Conference of August 1922

I

The despatch of the Balfour Note marked the beginning of a new phase in British policy on French war debts and, indeed, on war debts generally. Until then Britain had, as the Note somewhat sanctimoniously put it, 'silently abstained' from making any demands upon her debtors either for a funding agreement or for payment of interest. It is true that in March 1922 the Lloyd George government had served notice that it reserved the right to start collecting interest payments from the following October. But this had been very much a formality, and no decision had as yet been taken to actually exercise that right. At that stage there was no wish to negotiate a series of bilateral settlements with each of Britain's debtors. Instead, the government's attention was focused, as it had been throughout the period since the end of the war, on seeking a comprehensive agreement on all elements of inter-allied indebtedness. The Balfour Note did not signify the final abandonment of this objective: that was not to come until the negotiation of the Anglo-American war debt agreement several months later. Nevertheless, it did mean a significant change of emphasis in existing policy. While continuing to declare its preference for an all-round solution, for the first time the British government clearly and publicly asserted its own rights as a creditor.

The Note – which was aimed principally at the Americans and, to a lesser extent, the French – was concerned to emphasise the generosity of British policy on war debts and the extreme reluctance with which the government was now approaching its debtors.[1] It pointed out that Britain was a net creditor by a substantial margin: whereas she owed the United States the dollar equivalent of some £850m (plus accrued interest since 1919), this represented only a quarter of the amount due to her from reparations and war debts combined – a total of £3.4bn exclusive of interest, made up of £1.45bn from Germany, £650m from

Russia and £1.3bn from the rest of the ex-Allies. Despite this, the Note said, Britain had so far been prepared to remit all the loans owing to her, as well as her share of reparations, provided such a policy 'formed part of a satisfactory international settlement'. Such a stance had been rendered untenable, however, by America's recent request that Britain should fund her debts. The British government was loath to forsake its policy of all-round cancellation, for it continued to believe that war debts should not be treated as ordinary commercial obligations. On the other hand, it could not accept as right that 'one partner in the common enterprise should recover all that she has lent, and that another, while recovering nothing, should be required to pay all that she has borrowed'. That would not only be contrary to every principle of natural justice. It would also be completely unacceptable to the British people, who were already suffering from an unparalleled burden of taxation and severe unemployment. The British government therefore felt compelled to ask the debtor countries to take whatever steps they could to repay what they owed. The amount to be paid depended on what Britain was required to pay the Americans. Under no circumstances, however, would Britain seek to obtain from war debts and reparations combined more than was necessary to meet her own obligations to the United States.[2]

This principle or formula was to exercise a major influence on British policy on war debts, the French included, over the next few years. In practice, successive governments showed that they were prepared to modify it as circumstances required. Thus as early as January 1923 Lloyd George's successor, Bonar Law, in a last-ditch effort to avert a military occupation of the Ruhr by France, put forward a complex set of proposals on reparations and war debts which envisaged British concessions beyond those implied in the Balfour Note principle. In the ensuing years, moreover, there was a growing recognition that strict fulfilment of the principle might not be feasible. From June 1923 Britain began making annual debt payments of over £33m to the United States. As against that, with the exception of small amounts from Germany, she herself received nothing at all from her debtors until 1926, when funding agreements were concluded with the French and Italians. During the period 1923–26, therefore, a substantial gap developed between outgoings and receipts. Nor was there any real expectation in British official circles that this 'deficit' would ever be made good – especially since the sums which France and Italy were scheduled to pay in the years immediately following 1926 were fixed at a very low level.[3] Nevertheless, despite the practical difficulties involved in its implementation, the principle enunciated in the Balfour Note served as a guideline for British policy from 1922 onwards. More than that, it was actually embodied in clauses contained in both the Anglo-French and Anglo-Italian settlements.

On the face of it, the principle represented a clear statement of policy: that it was Britain's intention to secure from her ex-Allies and Germany enough to cover her own payments to the United States. But what did this mean in practical terms? How was the total burden to be apportioned between the individual debtors, and what sort of sums would each be liable to pay? On these crucial questions the Balfour Note offered no guidance. The information needed to make detailed calculations was not, of course, available in August 1922. In the first place, it was not yet known how much Britain would have to pay the United States: only after negotiations for an Anglo-American debt settlement were effectively concluded in early 1923 did it emerge that the annuities would be the dollar equivalent of £33m for the first ten years, rising to an average of £38m thereafter.[4] On the other side of the equation, at the time the Balfour Note was sent the scale of German reparation payments was still as uncertain as ever. It was not until the Dawes Plan came into force two years later that it became clear what Britain was supposed to obtain from that source.

Quite apart from the initial absence of such information, there were other reasons why it was impossible to say in August 1922 – or, indeed, for some time afterwards – precisely how much France and the other debtors would each have to pay if the Balfour Note principle were put into effect. As became plain when the British and French began to make their respective calculations, the arithmetic was largely dependent on conjecture and subjective notions of fairness. The French were naturally anxious to minimise their own obligation and chose to interpret the principle in a way which would further that objective. From the outset, therefore, they insisted that the total to be provided by Britain's ex-allied debtors should be calculated by deducting the full nominal value of British reparation receipts from the amount to be paid by Britain to the United States. The figure thus arrived at must then be distributed between all the individual debtor countries – including Russia – in strict proportion to the nominal debt of each. Unless this procedure were adopted, they argued, France would be treated unfairly: in effect, she would be penalised for the default of others.

Not surprisingly, the British took a different line. In their view, it was highly improbable that Germany's creditors would ever receive the whole of whatever sum Berlin agreed to pay. For that reason they were not prepared to accept more than 50 per cent of the face value of Britain's share of reparations as a prudent basis for calculation. Nor did they agree with the French view that each of the allied debtors should bear a share of the common burden which was proportionate to what they owed.[5] Such an approach was seen as unrealistic. Given the Bolshevik government's consistent repudiation since early 1918 of all pre-revolutionary foreign debts, Russia's obligations to Britain were understandably regarded as worthless. Nor were those of the smaller Allies such as Belgium, Romania, Serbia and Greece expected to yield much. Under these circumstances, it was seen as inevitable that it would fall to France and Italy to contribute nearly all of the money needed to bridge the gap between Britain's Dawes receipts and her payments to the United States. From the French standpoint, that was bad enough. To make matters even worse, the British insisted that France was capable of paying a great deal more than Italy, and must indeed do so – regardless of the fact that her debt to Britain was not much bigger.[6]

II

These differences over the concrete financial implications of the Balfour Note principle, although present from the beginning, were not to become fully apparent until serious negotiations for an Anglo-French war debt settlement got under way from early 1925 onwards. Yet the Note as a whole made an immediate and dramatic impact on Britain's relations not only with France but also with America. As Austen Chamberlain and Horne had warned, it met with an over-whelmingly hostile reception in the United States.[7] The Americans were acutely sensitive about their image in Europe as a grasping 'Uncle Shylock' and rightly saw the Note as an attack on their policy. It was true that it had not been addressed to them. On the other hand, as the Washington correspondent of *The Times* pointed out, it was clearly designed to 'hit the United States by ricochet'.[8] The references made to American conduct were not overtly critical: on the contrary, they were said to have behaved with 'the utmost courtesy' and 'in the exercise of their undoubted rights' in asking Britain to settle her debts. Reading between the lines, however, it was impossible to miss the implied reproaches. No amount of polite language could disguise the intended underlying message that America's blinkered and selfish position on war debts was the only major obstacle to a sensible policy of all-round cancellation. Those who had favoured sending the Note, like Churchill and Lloyd George, had argued that it would produce only short-lived irritation in the United States and would have a valuable educative effect on American opinion. Their judgement turned out to be wrong on both counts. In the event, the Note led to an appreciable hardening in Washington's attitude – as reflected in a strongly worded statement issued by the United States Treasury on 3 August[9] – and within a matter of months Britain was obliged to negotiate a debt setlement which made few concessions.

In France, too, the Balfour Note aroused intense anger.[10] Indeed, it would be no exaggeration to say that it brought an abrupt end to a period in which Britain and France had adopted broadly similar positions on the subject of war debts. There had never been any question of a concerted policy between the two coun-tries, for that would only have been possible on the unthinkable basis of joint repudiation of their obligations to the United States. Nevertheless, it was undoubtedly the case that between the end of the war and August 1922 British and French war debt policies had to a considerable extent coincided. Nor is this really surprising. Both countries were large-scale debtors to the United States as a result of wartime borrowing. Both were also substantial creditors, but without any realistic prospect of recovering much of the money that they had lent to Russia, Italy, Belgium and the smaller Allies. In addition, both had financial claims on Germany which were of doubtful value. Under such unpromising circumstances, Britain and France clearly had a common interest in promoting some sort of general solution to the problem of war debts and reparations –

whether through straightforward all-round cancellation or through what was euphemistically referred to as a 'just apportionment' or 'pooling' of war costs, the end result of which would be to transfer most of the burden to America. As long as they both continued to pursue this objective, the basic conflict of interest between Britain as creditor and France as debtor tended to be obscured. By sending the Balfour Note, what the British government had done was to bring it fully into the open.

For the French, the revelation that they might after all have to repay their debts came as a rude shock for which they were not really prepared.[11] It seems a fair assumption that they would have reacted badly to a request to negotiate funding arrangements whenever it was sent and however it was worded. It must be said, though, that the timing of the Balfour Note was unfortunate to say the least, coming as it did shortly after France had received a similar message from the United States, less than three weeks after Germany had requested a moratorium on reparation payments, and on the eve of an inter-allied conference convened to discuss that request.

The timing was not, of course, entirely of British choosing, being determined principally by the need to react to American pressure on London for a debt settlement.[12] Responsibility for how the Note was worded, on the other hand, rested squarely on the British government, and there can be no doubt that at least one passage which it was decided to include did cause unnecessary offence. It was claimed that British debts to the United States had been 'incurred for others, not for ourselves', and that the American government had insisted, 'in substance if not in form', that it was not prepared to lend to France and the other Allies except on British security. The French regarded this latter claim as both insulting and factually incorrect. André Tardieu, the man who had been responsible for negotiating France's wartime loans from the United States government, publicly rejected it in an article in the *Echo National* of 3 August, and on 12 August the French financial attaché in London, Avenol, lodged a strong protest about it with the British Treasury.[13]

The controversy took a fresh turn on 24 August when the American Secretary of the Treasury, Mellon, issued a statement flatly contradicting the suggestion contained in the Balfour Note that in some way Britain had been made to underwrite the credits which the United States had advanced to the other Allies.[14] The challenge was taken up, and on the following day a counter-statement, described as coming from 'an authoritative source', was released to the press setting out the official British case and referring to an earlier statement made in the Commons on 20 October 1921 by the Chancellor of the Exchequer, Horne, who had asserted: 'If we had not had to meet any calls for assistance from our Allies, it would have been unnecessary for us to ask asistance from the United States Government.'[15] This, in turn, prompted a further note from Avenol in which the British claim – dismissed as *'une légende'* – was rebutted in detail.[16] Although irritated, the Treasury wished to avoid becoming involved in a wrangle over 'this so delicate question', and it was therefore decided not to reply.[17]

That was not the end of the affair, however, for the dispute was to flare up again in the spring of 1923 when the American ambasador in London, Harvey, publicly repeated Mellon's earlier assertion at the end of February.[18] As in the previous August, the British government again refused to retreat. Speaking about the relevant passage in the House of Lords on 8 March, Balfour declared: 'I am unable myself to find in these words anything which is either misleading or obscure.[19]' There the matter rested – at least until the time of the Anglo-French war debt settlement of July 1926, when further comments by Mellon provoked angry exchanges between the British and American Treasuries.

The subject was clearly one which stirred strong feelings on the part of all concerned, with the British taking one view and the French and Americans holding to another. The facts are difficult to disentangle from the claims and counter-claims. On the narrow point of whether Britain did actually guarantee the loans contracted in the United States by France and the other Allies, the British were undoubtedly mistaken. Indeed, their marked tendency to disregard this particular aspect of the argument is in itself a strong indication that they themselves recognised that they were on weak ground. There remains, however, a broader and more complicated question. Was it true, as the British implied in the Balfour Note and openly stated on many other occasions, that Britain would not have found it necessary to borrow from the American government if she herself had not needed to lend to her Allies?[20]

It is easy to see why this belief took root. In the period between the United States' entry into the war in April 1917 and the cessation of hostilities, Britain borrowed from America the dollar equivalent of £876m. Over the same period, she lent to the Allies a sum of £897m.[21] The fact that there was such a close approximation between these two sets of figures seemed to provide at the very least strong circumstantial evidence that Britain was only borrowing because she had to lend. Certainly that was the inference drawn by many people in Britain – not only by members of the general public, whose sketchy knowledge about the technical details is understandable, but also by successive Chancellors of the Exchequer and other senior ministers, as well as Treasury experts and representatives of industry.[22] Yet the truth was less straightforward than was usually assumed. It is clear that even if Britain had not lent a penny, she would still have required dollars for unavoidable purchases of food and munitions in the United States. On the other hand, it might well have been possible to obtain the necessary currency without having to borrow it. If the Americans had been been willing to let France and Italy pay for British goods and services with dollars instead of sterling, those dollars could then have been used to finance Britain's own requirements in the United States. As was shown in chapter one, however, when such an arrangement was proposed by Bonar Law in the spring of 1918, Washington rejected it. What could legitimately be argued, then – and often was – was that a more co-operative attitude about wartime finance on the part of the

Americans would have left Britain with a much smaller debt to repay. But that was not the argument put forward in the Balfour Note. There it was suggested that Britain would not have had to borrow at all but for having to lend to her Allies, and such a suggestion was simply not consistent with the facts.

While this tendentious claim was in itself enough to cause great resentment on the part of the French, it was by no means the only feature of the Note which they disliked. The Prime Minister, Poincaré, gave vent to his indignation, not least about the timing of the Note, in the course of one of his customary weekend speeches at Bar-le-Duc on 21 August.[23] By that time the inter-allied conference called to discuss Germany's request for a moratorium on reparation payments had already met in London (between 7 and 12 of August). As will be seen, it was an ill-humoured affair. The proceedings were dominated by a fundamental disagreement between the British and French delegations, and they ended in acrimonious failure. Poincaré's disappointment and frustration at this outcome doubtless helps to account for what the British ambasssador in Paris, Lord Hardinge, termed the 'bitter and disappointed' tone of his speech.[24]

His official reply of 1 September was in a similar vein. Lloyd George aptly conveyed its flavour when he wrote in *The Truth About Reparations and War Debts* that Poincaré's

> petulant and ill-conditioned letter was an assertion that France would pay no debts until the reparations had been paid in full; that we had been slack and ineffective in our war effort; and that we had been guilty of sharp practice in our price estimates for the munitions and other goods we had supplied to France.[25]

The note began in a deceptively conciliatory fashion, expressing agreement with the British government's belief in the necessity of dealing with reparations and war debts at a conference attended by all the states concerned.[26] For the rest, however, it consisted of a trenchant assertion of French financial interests, interlaced with barbed innuendoes about British policy and lack of integrity. It was stoutly maintained that there was a strong moral argument for cancelling all inter-allied debts because they had been contracted in a common cause. It was made clear, moreover, that there could be no question of any settlement of French debts until Germany had reimbursed France for all the money which she had already had to spend on restoring her devastated regions. That obligation must have priority over all others: once it had been discharged the French government 'would not be opposed to the consideration of a general settlement of international debts'. Finally, it was emphasised that when the time did come to consider the French debt to Britain, certain factors would first have to be taken into account. Not the least of these was the necessity of drawing a distinction between the war debts owed by France to the United States and those owed by her to Britain. Part of the debt oustanding to the United States had been contracted after the armistice in order to purchase surplus American stocks.

Since these stocks had subsequently been sold for the benefit of the French Treasury, the debts incurred in the course of such transactions were regarded as straightforward commercial ones in a way that the British were not. As for the remainder of the American debt, that too was held to be different in nature from its British counterpart, on the rather curious grounds that the United States and Britain had fought the war for completely different reasons: whereas the former had supposedly entered the conflict in order to defend 'the principles which lie at the basis of civilisation', the latter had been fighting to 'safeguard not only her independence and her territory, but also the life, the property and the means of existence of her nationals'. American involvement in the war, in other words, had been less self-interested.

Another factor which would have to be taken into account, the note stated, was that the amount that France was said to owe Britain was pitched too high. According to Poincaré, where foodstuffs and materials had been interchanged, the relevant British and French authorities had adopted different costing methods. The Department of the British Quatermaster General had debitted for all deliveries at the maximum price and then added a further charge to cover departmental expenses incurred while the supplies were in Britain. The French Ministry of the Interior, by contrast, when charging for consignments to the British army, had invariably used the specially low rate, the *tarif intérieur*, paid by one French service to another. It followed that any debt settlement between Britain and France would have to be preceded by 'a minute examination [of accounts], in order to fix the amount of the debt at an equitable figure, established on identical bases'.[27]

As might be expected, given such comments, the publication of Poincaré's note made a highly unfavourable impression on British opinion. Even those who felt that there was some justification for the views which it expressed, nevertheless deprecated its tone.[28] The reaction in official circles was one of outrage. When the Cabinet discussed the matter on 7 September, it was informed of the view of Sir John Bradbury – who was in Paris serving as the British representative on the Reparation Commission – that the note was a diversionary tactic designed to distract attention from the real issues involved in the current crisis over reparations. According to the official record, members of the Cabinet were particularly upset by

> the offensive tone of the second part of the French Note in which undue emphasis was laid upon various accounting matters between the French and British Governments including a suggestion that France had been overcharged by the British Government for consignments of foodstuffs and materials supplied during the war by the addition of overhead charges and export duties.[29]

Although united in their indignation, however, ministers were divided about how to respond. Curzon, who had by this time recoverd sufficiently from his prolonged illness to resume his duties at the Foreign Office, argued that the most dignified course would be to pass over the allegations in silence – a view which was reported to command considerable support within the Cabinet.[30] On the other hand, it was feared that this might lead outside observers, and the Americans in particular, to infer that there was some substance in them. One suggestion was that two notes should be sent: one replying in general terms, the other providing a detailed examination of the accounting matters raised by Poincaré. In the end it was decided that the Treasury should prepare a draft reply for submission to the Foreign Secretary.[31]

The draft accordingly prepared by the Treasury pulled no punches. It pointed to the fact that Britain, as well as France, had suffered grievous and costly losses during the war: losses in ships and cargoes alone were said to have totalled £745m. It dismissed as inequitable any suggestion that Britain should pay twice over for any alleviations granted to Germany, by both renouncing her own share of reparations and remitting all the allied debts due to her. It also strenuously rejected Poincaré's contention that France was under a greater obligation to repay the United States, especially since Britain had fought longer and sacrificed more to achieve victory. The British debt, it insisted, must be treated on an equal footing with the American.[32]

On 8 September, as arranged, the Treasury draft was sent for consideration by the Foreign Office. Feeling there was strongly opposed to being drawn into a bitter dispute over Poincaré's note. The two officials with special responsibility for policy on reparations and war debts, Gerald Villiers (Head of the Western Department) and Miles Lampson (Central Department), both took this view, albeit with some difference of emphasis. The latter, sticking closely to the line taken by Curzon at the Cabinet meeting of 7 September, argued that the wisest course would be not to reply at all, on the grounds that to do so would only give rise to a lengthy and fruitless correspondence and would embitter Anglo-French relations. Villiers, who described Poincaré's note as an 'outrage', likewise thought that it would be best not to reply. At the same time, he was concerned about the effect that this might have on French public opinion. 'Is it advisable and is it wise', he minuted on 11 September, 'to leave France under the impression that there are no insults that we will not swallow, and that we cannot refute the charges of extortion brought against us?' If a reply were to be sent, Villiers added, then it should not be 'a milk and honey note like the present Treasury draft, but something of a more stinging nature'.[33]

A more senior official, the Assistant Under-Secretary, Sir William Tyrrell, maintained that it would be a serious mistake to respond to Poincaré's note, and Curzon emphatically agreed.[34] In the case of both men, the key to their thinking lay in the threatening situation that had developed in the Near East following the recent military successes of the Turkish nationalists under Mustapha Kemal. A Turkish advance launched a few weeks earlier, in mid-August, had driven the Greeks from Anatolia and left the small allied forces in the area surrounding

Constantinople dangerously exposed to attack. At this critical juncture, therefore, it was deemed esential for Britain and France to present a united front. For some time the two countries' policies towards Turkey and her attempts to overturn the Treaty of Sèvres had seriously diverged.[35] On 14 September, however, Poincaré was persuaded to join in sending a warning to Mustapha Kemal against attempting to enter the zone occupied by the Allies. Even so, it remained extremely doubtful whether the French would continue to co-operate, and in this delicate situation Tyrrell and Curzon were anxious not to prejudice the chances of their doing so by getting embroiled in a wrangle over Poincaré's note.[36] As a result, when Curzon submitted a draft reply to the Cabinet on 17 September – a much stiffer one than the original Treasury version – he strongly advised that it should not be sent for the time being. Fortunately, a diplomatic escape route presented itself. A note had just been received from Belgium seeking the British government's views on a proposal from France to hold an inter-allied conference on reparations and war debts. This offered the government an opportunity to write to the French on the subject of the Belgian note, adding that it considered it inexpedient to answer the 'contentious points' raised in Poincaré's letter of 1 September, but also making it clear that silence must not be interpreted as acquiescence in them.[37]

III

The irritable public exchanges which took place between London and Paris on the subject of the Balfour Note, along with evidence of America's deep hostility towards it, served to strengthen the doubts already felt by many people in Britain about the wisdom of sending it in the first place. Disapproval of the Note was voiced in various quarters. The leader of the opposition Liberals, Asquith, was highly critical of it;[38] Keynes subjected it to a scathing attack;[39] and influential sections of the press, including *The Times* and *The Economist*, expressed strong reservations.[40]

From the outset, critics of the Note warned that it was likely to have a number of unfortunate consequences. What happened in the weeks that followed seemed to bear out their worst fears. In the United States there was a further hardening of feeling against any element of debt cancellation. Anglo-American and Anglo-French relations suffered a setback. There was a sharp fall in the international value of the mark, the franc and other Continental currencies. In the second week of August the London conference on reparations met in a rancorous atmosphere and failed to produce an agreement, one consequence of this being an increase in French intransigence towards Germany. Rightly or wrongly, all these developments were seen as a direct consequence – the bitter 'firstfruits' – of the Balfour Note.[41]

The central thrust of the domestic criticism directed at the Note was that it had dealt a heavy blow at hopes of international reconciliation and economic recovery. It was argued that a more generous policy towards France and Britain's other debtors would have produced far better results. By renouncing its claims on the French, which were in any case of little real worth, the British government could have encouraged them to agree to a moderate reparations settlement. That, in turn, would have made possible an international loan for Germany. Even the Americans might have been sufficiently impressed by the British gesture to reconsider their position on war debts. According to this line of argument, in brief, the government had missed a great opportunity to give a statesmanlike lead in dealing with the vicious circle of reparations and war debts which was paralysing Europe. As an editorial in *The Economist* put it, Lloyd George had had in his hand the key to a general economic revival, but had chosen to put it in his pocket instead of using it.[42] Nor was it accepted that the policy set out in the Balfour Note was essential for the protection of the British taxpayer. When defending that policy in the Commons on 3 August, Lloyd George and Horne claimed that the alternative suggested by opponents of the Note – cancellation of the debts owed to Britain, without regard to Britain's own obligations to the United States – would be contrary to the taxpayer's interests.[43] *The Economist* disagreed:

> What is most directly against the British taxpayer's interests is that the present financial tangle, with its potent and deplorable restraints on production, should remain unravelled. If, on the other hand, in return for surrendering credits whose value is a great deal more than dubious, the British taxpayer could obtain a sound reparations settlement, the rebirth of confidence, and the revival of world trade, then he would be greatly the gainer by the bargain.[44]

At a more fundamental level, the Balfour Note was criticised as being inherently flawed – in the words of Keynes, 'bad in principle'.[45] In the first place, it was objected that the sums which France would have to pay were to be determined in accordance with a formula which bore no necessary relation to what she could afford. Capacity to pay, widely regarded as the only sensible criterion, would not be taken into account. Secondly, it was felt to be inequitable that France should be expected to make good any shortfall in British receipts arising from a complete or partial German default on reparation payments. It was this aspect of the Note which drew Keynes' strongest fire. Such an arrangement, he contended, would never be accepted by the French. Nor was it just or workable:

> It is of the essence of the Note that the less Germany pays, the *more* France shall pay; that is to say, the less France is in a position to pay, the more she shall pay. Diplomatically and financially alike, this is topsy turvy. It would never bring us cash; yet it would destroy our diplomatic authority as a moderator between France and Germany . . . There can be no working settlement except on exactly the oppo-

site principle, namely that the less Germany pays, the *less* France shall pay. The amount of France's payment must vary in the same direction as Germany's, not in the opposite direction.[46]

Much of the contemporary critcism of the Balfour Note by Keynes and others has been endorsed by historians. Indeed, it is impossible to find amongst those who have studied the question anyone who has had a favourable word to say about the Note. One historian has described it as 'an international disaster'and 'an abdication of all responsibility for European affairs'.[47] To another, Denise Artaud, the policy which it represented seems 'absurd'.[48] The unanimous verdict appears to be that its timing was inept and its consequences disastrous, in that it reduced the British government's room for manoeuvre, needlessly antagonised the French and Americans, ruined the prospects of agreement at the London conference and gave a further twist to the current reparations crisis.[49]

Not surprisingly, given such views, there is considerable puzzlement as to why the British government decided to send it. Anne Orde concludes that the motives of Lloyd George and his colleagues were hopelessly confused.[50] A similar interpretation is offered by Marc Trachtenberg who sees the key factor as the increasingly emotional state of Lloyd George himself. According to Trachtenberg, his policies at this time were less the product of rational calculation than of strong surges of irritation and resentment: 'The documents of this period record sharp outbursts of anger at France, America and even Germany – a clear indication that Lloyd George was losing his grip on events.'[51] Bruce Kent likewise emphasises Lloyd George's 'provocative behaviour' and 'truculence' towards France. At the same time, he sets the Balfour Note in the context of a broad strategy which was allegedly designed to 'goad Poincaré into violent action' and show him the futility of attempting such a solution to the reparations problem.[52]

The indictment is a long and formidable one. Is it, however, entirely justified? Was the Balfour Note really so pointless, maladroit, unreasonable and damaging as it has invariably been portrayed? Clearly it was far from being a diplomatic masterstroke. Nor did it achieve its main objective of shaming the Americans into a change of policy – of forcing them to 'search their consciences', as Churchill put it. On the other hand, it would be wrong to dismiss it as nothing more than a self-indulgent public grumble about the way in which Britain had been treated by creditors and debtors alike. There was certainly an element of that: the Note served as a vindication before world opinion of the stance that the British government had consistently taken on reparations and war debts since the end of the war. But that was not all that there was to it. Despite its undoubted shortcomings, what the Balfour Note offered was a definite and coherent policy on inter-allied indebtedness after years of inconclusive debate within the Lloyd George government. Although it was generally agreed that all-round cancellation would be the best solution, the attitude of the Americans had rendered that impracticable. Yet in the immediate postwar years there had emerged no alternative policy which could command a general measure of support. Instead, ministers and departments had remained deeply divided about such basic issues as whether or not to settle with the United States before dealing with the European debtors, and whether or not to renounce Britain's own claims as a creditor. If it did nothing else, the Balfour Note at least put an end to this dithering. More than that, it was a serious attempt to produce a strategy which took account both of the legitimate interests of the British taxpayer and of the need to make sacrifices as a contribution to European recovery. It might be objected, with some justice, that the policies which it put forward were not as devoid of self-interest as the British government liked to think. It is by no means self-evident, however, that they were any less generous and statesmanlike than those currently being proposed, for example, by the Americans or the French.

But what of the consequences of the Balfour Note? Were they as disastrous as has often been suggested? Here again it apears that the criticism has been much overstated. While the Note undoubtedly made the Americans angry, there seems no reason to think that it had a material effect on their policy. After 1 August 1922 that remained precisely the same as it had been before: that even partial remission of debts was out of the question, and that all funding agreements must conform to the stringent conditions laid down by Congress in the previous February. According to some critics of the Balfour Note, a more generous British offer to France and the other debtors would have served as a good example to the United States and thus helped to 'revolutionise' American attitudes. Yet there is not a shred of evidence to substantiate such a view. Since 1919 the Lloyd George government had exhausted every conceivable argument in its efforts to persuade Washington to relax its uncompromising stance on war debts. It had failed completely, and there seems no reason to suppose that any action which it might have taken in the summer of 1922 would have produced a different outcome. Indeed, it is worth remembering in this connection that when the idea of a unilateral cancellation of war debts by Britain was contemplated in 1920, one of the main factors that caused the government not to go ahead with it was the warning received from senior United States Treasury officials that any such move would be resented by America as a form of moral blackmail.[53]

Nor can it be taken as axiomatic that the Balfour Note made a significant contribution to the failure of the inter-allied London conference. To believe that it did so is to attach too much importance both to the Note itself and to an apparent change of policy by Poincaré after it was sent. At the end of July 1922, just over a week before the conference was due to meet, the French Cabinet approved a general plan for dealing with reparations, war debts and an international loan for Germany. Although its contents were not divulged to the British government, substantially accurate reports of this plan appeared in the British and French press.[54] It contained two main elements. First, there were proposals for a parallel reduction of reparations and inter-allied indebtedness. Germany's total obligation was to be limited to 50bn gold marks – the amount represented by the A and B series of bonds in the 1921 Schedule of Payments. France was to receive the bulk of this, with priority being accorded to the restoration of her devastated regions, on which some 90bn francs (about £1.8bn) had allegedly already been spent. The C bonds, with a nominal value of 82bn gold marks, were to be used for the purpose of liquidating debts between the Allies. Secondly, Germany was to be subject to elaborate measures of control to ensure that payments were made. There must be radical reform of German finances; definite pledges or *gages* would be demanded, such as direct payment to the Reparations Commission of receipts from German customs dues; and finally, there was the possibility of allied participation in German industrial concerns. The intention was that Poincaré would put this plan forward at the London conference. After the despatch of the Balfour Note, however, it was decided that there was no longer any point in doing so since the positions adopted by the British and French govenments appeared to be so much at variance.[55]

On the face of it, therefore, the Balfour Note would seem to have brought a sudden end to a promising development in French policy and thereby ruined whatever prospects there were of reaching agreement at the London conference. But such a conclusion rests upon two highly dubious assumptions. The first of these is that the plan which Poincaré intended to put forward ever stood a real chance of being accepted. What evidence there is would seem to indicate that this was far from being the case. The key factor was the attitude of the British, and their reaction when they eventually learned of the plan's main features was decidely hostile: at a Cabinet meeting held on 14 August 1922, during the closing stages of the conference, the plan was described as 'ridiculous and insulting'.[56] The clear inference to be drawn from this is that the actual effect of the Balfour Note was not to preclude the adoption of an acceptable scheme at the conference, but rather to alert Poincaré to the futility of proceeding with it. What happened, in other words, was that he was spared an outright rejection of his proposals. From the tactical point of view, therefore, the Note was of considerable benefit to Poincaré. As the British ambassador to Paris, Hardinge, ruefully pointed out, it enabled him to throw the responsibility for the failure of the London conference onto the British government and to claim – with the support of the French, and some sections of the British, press – that he had been compelled to take a tougher line with Germany because his original scheme had been sabotaged.[57] It was for this reason that Lloyd George regretted the fact that the French proposals had not been openly discussed at the conference in a way that would have exposed their deficiencies to public view.[58]

The second dubious assumption is that a more generous British offer than the one contained in the Balfour Note – an offer, say, of complete debt cancellation plus a reduction in Britain's share of reparations – would have diverted Poincaré from a policy of seeking pledges from Germany. What this fails to take account of is why such pledges were sought. The main reason was a basic lack of trust in

German good faith. The French felt that the Germans were not making a serious effort to meet their obligations and that the existing measures of control to make them do so had shown themselves to be completely inadequate. It was this belief that fuelled Poincaré's demand for cast-iron guarantees, and no financial concessions from Britain, however welcome, would have served as an adequate substitute.

IV

Even without the complications introduced by the Balfour Note, reaching agreement at the London conference would have presented severe difficulties. The immediate purpose of the inter-allied conference was to decide how to respond to Germany's request of 12 July 1922 for an extended moratorium on reparation payments. The July instalment had been reluctantly paid on the scheduled date. A further payment was due on 15 August, and it was therefore necessary to come to a decision before then on whether a moratorium should be granted.[59] The main stumbling block was a sharp difference of opinion between the British and French governments on what line to take.

This was by no means the first time that the question of giving Germany a breathing-space had produced such disagreement. In December 1921, when the Wirth government first made a formal application for a suspension of payments, the reaction in London had been much more favourable than that in Paris.[60] This had set the pattern for the whole of the following year, as the British continued to view Germany's desire for some measure of relief more sympathetically than the French. As Bradbury told Blackett in late January 1922, he was 'more than ever convinced that Germany cannot get on her financial legs without a period in which no cash shall be taken for reparations, and only very moderate deliveries in kind. The only other alternative is Reparation crises every six months'.[61]

The crises which Bradbury foresaw had come thick and fast in the first half of 1922, with the Germans constantly claiming that they were unable to meet their obligations under the London Schedule of Payments. In January 1922 the Cannes conference approved a decision by the Reparation Commission to postpone the instalments due in that month and February. It was stipulated instead that there should be cash payments of 31m gold marks (£1.55m) every ten days from 18 January until the provisional postponement expired in mid-March. In addition, the German government was to submit by 28 January a complete programme of cash payments and deliveries in kind for the year 1922, together with a comprehensive scheme for currency and budgetary reform involving such measures as increased taxation, reduced state expenditure on subsidies and other items, a ban on the export of capital, guaranteed autonomy for the Reichsbank and a strict limit on the issue of new notes.[62]

These arrangements were never intended to be more than a stop-gap and in

March, after difficult negotiations between Berlin and the Reparation Commission, another temporary solution was devised prescribing payments totalling 720m gold marks (£36m) in cash and a maximum of 1.45bn gold marks (£72.5m) in kind during 1922. This time Germany was set certain specific financial targets, including a drastic increase of taxation by 60bn paper marks. If these were not achieved by 31 May, the partial moratorium would be suspended and the original schedule of payments would come into force again as from 15 June. Failure to pay would lead to a declaration of default by the Reparation Commission, leaving the allied governments free to take 'such measures as they determined to be necessary'. After initial resistance, at the end of May Berlin indicated its general acceptance of these terms and the partial moratorium was duly confirmed for the remainder of the year.[63]

The respite proved short-lived, however, for within a matter of weeks the Wirth government was seeking further help. Its hopes had been pinned on the issue of an international loan, the proceeds of which would be used partly to stabilise the mark but mainly to redeem the reparation debt. These hopes were soon dashed. On 24 May a committee of experts – the so-called Bankers' Committee, appointed by the Reparation Commission on 4 April and chaired by Léon Delacroix of Belgium[64] – met in Paris to consider the circumstances in which such a loan might be raised. From the outset, however, the French representative, Charles Sergent, found himself at odds with the rest of his colleagues about the wide terms of reference which they wanted the committee to have, and in the end he submitted a separate report. The main conclusion of the majority report, issued on 10 June, was that conditions were unfavourable for a loan and would remain so until there was a significant reduction in Germany's reparation burden.[65] This disappointing verdict precipitated a sharp fall in the value of the mark, a development aggravated by the assassination of the German Foreign Minister, Rathenau, on 24 June: from a level of 1,200 to the pound at the beginning of June, it slumped to 2,400 by the end of the first week in July.[66] Faced by this deteriorating financial situation, on 12 July the German government sent a note to the Reparation Commission asking to be released from all cash payments not only for the remainder of 1922, but until the end of 1924.[67]

The response from Britain was notably sympathetic: on 14 July, without consulting the French, Lloyd George publicly supported Germany's request.[68] The British had long taken the view that a moratorium of two or three years was essential and had positively encouraged the Germans to seek one.[69] More than that, they believed that the scale of payments fixed by the London Schedule was far too high and must be reduced to a more realistic level as a necessary first step towards the restoration of German credit.

The attitude of the French was completely different. They reacted to Germany's request in a suspicious and hostile manner. The Poincaré government, under growing pressure to take a tougher line om reparations from right-wing parliamentary critics, led by Tardieu, was anxious not to appear weak.[70] It had no intention of permitting a suspension of cash payments for more than a few months – and even then subject to strict guarantees.[71] Nor was it prepared to contemplate any reduction in the reparation figure of 132bn gold marks set in May 1921, unless arrangements were made – through a combination of war debt cancellation and redistribution of reparation receipts – to compensate France for any resultant financial loss. At the very least, it was insisted, any new reparation settlement must provide France with enough money to cover the cost both of restoring her devastated regions and paying her allied creditors.

There was thus from the outset a basic disagreement between Britain and France over what to do about Germany's request for a moratorium, a disagreement which was to intensify in the months following July 1922 and strain the Entente almost to breaking point. It arose partly from a straightforward clash of financial interests between the two countries: each government, after all, was naturally concerned to protect its own taxpayers as far as possible from the sacrifices involved in a suspension and reduction of reparation payments. But it was also the product of conflicting assessments both of the nature of the current crisis over reparations and of the best way to solve it.

Central to the French analysis of the situation was the assumption that Germany was principally if not entirely to blame for the difficulties which had arisen over reparation payments. Throughout the second half of 1922 the prevailing belief in French official circles continued to be, as it had been for some time, that the Germans had made no serious effort to fulfil their obligations – whether financial or otherwise – under the Treaty of Versailles. According to Poincaré, indeed, developments in the summer of 1922 clearly showed that they had not the slightest intention of doing so. It was noted with disgust that those tried on war crime charges at Leipzig had been treated with what seemed like ridiculous leniency, while at the same time the French government was receiving disturbing reports from its military representatives in Germany of serious breaches of the Versailles disarmament provisions. Viewed in this context, Germany's reparation policy seemed to French political leaders to be simply one strand in a general pattern of treaty evasion.[72] Poincaré repeatedly argued, when opposing a lengthy moratorium on reparation payments and a reduction in Germany's total liability, that such concessions were unnecessary. Germany was fully able to meet her existing obligations. All that was lacking was the political will. Like most of his countrymen, he believed that the root problem lay in the unwillingness of the Wirth government to take the measures needed to put the national finances on a sound footing. Since the armistice, Poincaré claimed, successive German goverments had 'spent recklessly and without count', and the current one was no different.[73] It was pouring money which could have been used for paying Germany's debts into what was described as 'luxury' expenditure on railways, the merchant marine and a whole range of costly state subsidies.[74] Only a part of this was paid for by taxation: indeed, the level of taxation in Germany was said to be lower than that in many of the allied countries. Much of it was financed through a massive expansion in the money supply – the main cause, as far as Poincaré was concerned, of the unbalanced budget, high rate of inflation and depreciating currency from which Germany was suffering.[75]

Nor was Berlin's behaviour considered to be simply a matter of financial irresponsibility. Reflecting French opinion in general, Poincaré was convinced that the Germans were engaged in a concerted attempt to dupe and defraud the Allies, with the government deliberately stoking up inflation and leading industrialists exporting capital on a massive scale. Germany, he alleged, was 'systematically ruining herself, going into a more or less fraudulent bankruptcy and making unlimited issues of paper money'.[76] It was his conviction on this point that underlay Poincaré's insistence that there could be no suspension of reparation payments without the imposition of a more effective system of allied control on German finances. Experience over the past three years had amply demonstrated that Germany could not be trusted to put her own house in order. It was clear, moreover, that the existing control provisions – agreed in principle at the end of May 1922, but taking a further two months to work out in detail – had failed to achieve their objective. In mid-July the French Finance Minister, de Lasteyrie, complained bitterly that so far control had been nothing but a 'façade'. Poincaré shared to the full his colleague's dissatisfaction with the current arrangements and was adamant that they must be tightened up.

The need to strengthen allied control over German finances assumed added importance in French eyes because it was closely connected with the question of an international loan for Germany. The idea of such an operation, which would make it possible to mobilise the reparation debt, had considerable appeal for Poincaré. Despite the negative verdict of the Bankers' Committee in June, he remained reasonably hopeful that a successful flotation might yet take place in the not too distant future – encouraged in this belief, it appears, by the American banker J. P. Morgan.[77] There was clearly little prospect of that happening, however, so long as potential investors lacked confidence in Germany's financial stability, and one obvious way to increase their confidence was to set up a really effective system of external control. To this end, Poincaré wanted the Guarantee Committee, which was responsible for ensuring that Germany observed her reparation obligations, to be permanently resident in Berlin and given a much greater say in the running of German financial affairs – including the right to participate in the framing of budget estimates, increase taxation and veto items of expenditure.[78]

But stronger financial control was not the only, or even the most important, condition laid down by the French for their consent to the moratorium requested by Berlin. On past performance, it was by no means certain that Germany would submit to whatever procedures were agreed, or that France would be able to count on British support in compelling her to do so. Under these circumstances, it is understandable that the French should have thought it prudent to call for additional guarantees, demanding that the Allies must obtain from Germany valuable state assets which would serve as *gages productifs*.[79] On 27 July 1922 the French government adopted a policy of insisting on such productive pledges as an indispensable counterpart to the granting of any new moratorium to Germany.[80] This policy was confirmed on 3 August, and for the next five months, until French and Belgian troops occupied the Ruhr in January 1923, it was pursued with unswerving determination.

What the French envisaged was first revealed at the London conference of August 1922, when Poincaré put forward a number of proposals designed to yield substantial financial gains for the Allies – the most important being that the Allies should take possession of mines and forests in the Ruhr and the Rhineland.[81] These proposals, with some inessential modifications, were to remain a key element in French policy until the occupation of the Ruhr. As will be seen, they encountered fierce opposition from Britain, as well as resistance of a milder sort from Belgium and Italy. Yet in spite of this, at no stage was the French government prepared to abandon its basic position on the necessity of productive pledges. It refused to compromise, even at the risk of isolation and a breach with Britain, and this raises the question why it attached such importance to the matter.

In the first place, *gages* were regarded as a powerful weapon for ensuring that Germany not only agreed to a satisfactory reparation settlement, but also actually carried it out. It was never the French intention, however, that they should be used purely and simply as a means of exerting pressure on Berlin. Their main purpose, as Poincaré always stressed, was to provide Germany's creditors with readily available money. They were to be pledges 'susceptible of immediate realisation'.[82] The hope was that the profits to be derived from them would help to extricate France from the financial quagmire in which she found herself. According to the French goverment, France had been brought to the brink of financial ruin by Germany's failure to meet her obligations. It was calculated that up to the summer of 1922 more than 80bn francs (50bn gold marks) had been spent on restoring the devastated areas and on war pensions, a figure that would rise to 100bn by the end of the year. Contrary to expectation, none of this expenditure had been met from reparations, not least because the cost of maintaining allied occupation forces in the Rhineland had absorbed most of the limited amounts of money Germany had actually paid. Rather, it had been financed by borrowing – principally through the sale of national defence bonds. The situation, Poincaré said, was 'full of peril' and could not last.[83] Looking ahead to 1923, the French government was faced with the prospect of continuing heavy expenditure on reconstruction. Unless this was paid for out of reparation receipts, there would have to be additional borrowing and higher taxation in France. Yet it was felt to be politically impossible to call upon the French people to make fresh sacrifices while granting an unconditional moratorium to Germany.[84] Hence the crucial importance of productive pledges, both as a source of much-needed cash and as a symbol of the French government's resolve to make Germany honour her commitments. While it was acknowledged that the pledges were unlikely to produce vast amounts – perhaps 500m in paper marks – it was argued that even such a modest sum was better than nothing and would offer some welcome relief to the French taxpayer.[85]

In London, such arguments were dismissed as thoroughly misguided. Indeed, the whole French approach to the question of a suspension of reparation payments was seen as a recipe for disaster. The official British line was that the collapse of the mark and the state of the German budget meant that there was an unanswerable case for what Bradbury termed an 'immediate and generous moratorium'.[86] That being so, there could be no justification for trying to impose conditions of the sort demanded by France. Unlike the French, who were absolutely convinced that the blame for the latest reparation crisis rested squarely with Germany, the British took a less clear-cut view. On the one hand, there was undoubtedly a general belief among ministers and officials alike that financial mismanagement by the German government was at least a contributory factor. On the other, it was also felt that events were to a considerable extent beyond Berlin's control.[87] Certainly this latter was the opinion of Bradbury. Reporting to the Treasury on 4 August 1922, he rejected the French contention that the Germans were guilty of serious negligence and defiance. On the contrary, he was perfectly satisfied that the Wirth government had made, and was continuing to make, 'a genuine effort to carry out, under disheartening conditions, the obligations which it assumed in May 1921'. The trouble was that it had been given an impossible task.[88] Lloyd George inclined to a similar view. As he told Poincaré in June 1922, he was simply not convinced that Germany was shamming and attempting to defraud her creditors. Rather, she was having real difficulty in paying instalments across the exchanges, chiefly because of the current international recession. German exports had slumped to 25 per cent below their pre-war level and until they recovered, as part of a worldwide economic revival, there could be no possibility of reparation payments being made on the scale laid down by the London Schedule.[89]

While disagreeing with the French about the extent of Germany's culpability, the British did share their view on the need to apply more stringent allied control over German finances.[90] Even here, however, there were major differences of opinion. It was common ground that existing procedures were inadequate; but the British had grave doubts about whether the powers of the Guarantee Committee to intervene in the management of German financial and monetary affairs should be increased to the extent proposed by France.[91]

The issue which caused the most serious divergence, however, was the French insistence on seizing productive pledges. Neither the Lloyd George government nor the Bonar Law government, which succeeded it in October 1922, could see any merit in such a policy. On the contrary, both believed that its implementation would have disastrous consequences not only for Germany but also for the

Allies themselves. There was little confidence that the seized assets would yield any worthwhile sums of money – most of which, in any case, would be swallowed up by administrative and military costs.[92] Certainly there would not be sufficient to afford the immediate financial relief sought by France. The Treasury view, as expressed by Blackett, was that it might be possible to obtain a limited amount from the collection of customs dues. Bradbury thought that the Allies would finish up with only 'a little cash'.[93] Lloyd George was more pessimistic still. In his opinion, the most likely outcome was that Germany's creditors would be left with nothing to show for their exertions but tons of useless paper marks to add to the 4bn or more that they already possesed.[94]

The price to be paid for these negligible (and far from certain) financial gains, the British argued, would be a disproportionately heavy one. Germany's credit would be undermined at a stroke. Her capacity to make substantial reparation payments in the future would be fatally prejudiced. German economic activity would be severely disrupted. There would be a further slump in the value of the mark. In short, the bankruptcy of Germany would be completed.[95] Nor would France herself emerge unscathed; for, once it had been realised that the policy of productive pledges was not going to work, French credit would be drastically weakened and the franc would come under intense pressure. In political terms, too, the damage would be enormous, since there was bound to be increased friction between Germany and her creditors – especially if German workers offered resistance and it proved necesary to use military force.[96] The French claimed that the economic measures which they proposed could be carried out by a relatively small team of administrators and civil engineers: troops should not be required, providing the Allies maintained a united front.[97] The British were unconvinced, however, and Lloyd George was not slow to remind Poincaré that at the time of the Spa conference of 1920, when an allied occupation of the Ruhr was under consideration, Foch had advised that such an operation would necessitate the use of seven divisions.[98]

In addition to these objections, which the British government felt able to put openly to the French, there were others of a more sensitive nature. It was feared that French plans for the Ruhr might have adverse effects on Britain's economic interests, with the economic adviser to the British section of the Rhineland High Commission warning in December 1922 of the danger of increased competition for the British coal industry.[99] More important still, concern was felt in some quarters about possible ulterior motives on the part of the French government. There was, in particular, a lurking suspicion that the policy of *gages* was merely a cloak for long-standing French ambitions to establish a position of economic and political dominance in the Rhineland.[100] At the Foreign Office it was not forgotten that Poincaré had been one of the fiercest critics of Clemenceau's compromise over that territory at the Versailles conference, and on 10 August 1922 Miles Lampson minuted:

We may therefore take it as axiomatic that there is a political motive behind the French proposals and that the political motive is to speed up the process of detaching the Rhineland from the Reich and absobing it into France as in Napoleonic days.[101]

For a variety of reasons, then, the British were utterly opposed to the policy of productive pledges advocated by France. Their own strategy for dealing with the reparation crisis ran along completely different lines and was based on the premise that the Allies' only chance of obtaining significant sums at any time lay in the restoration of German credit. That meant the grant of a moratorium – without onerous conditions – on all payments in cash and most payments in kind until at least the end of 1924. It also meant the reduction of Germany's obligations to a figure which the German people themselves, and world opinion in general, believed to be within her capacity to pay. These concessions would help to bring about a marked improvement in Germany's credit, and it might then even be possible to raise an international loan for her.[102]

To British financial experts and political leaders, it seemed self-evident that this was the only approach which stood any chance of success. But it was one which found little favour with Poincaré, whose own thinking was so much at variance with it. The unenviable task facing the British government, therefore, was to persuade the French Prime Minister to follow the programme suggested by London and abandon his own plans which (in British eyes) were bound to end in catastrophe.

From late July 1922 until January 1923, that is precisely what it attempted to do, both at inter-allied conferences in London and Paris and through constant diplomatic exchanges. The message was repeatedly hammered home, notably by Lloyd George and Bonar Law, that a policy of seizing productive pledges was doomed to failure. Strenuous efforts were also made to draw Belgium and Italy into the British camp and so intensify the pressure on France. It soon became apparent, however, that such tactics would not suffice. Poincaré proved characteristically impervious to argument. Nor did the prospect of isolation cause him to change his mind. As early as April 1922, in a notorious speech at Bar-le-Duc, he had made it clear that France was fully prepared to go into the Ruhr on her own.[103] Besides, there was mounting evidence that that would not be necessary. For a time, especially during the London conference of August 1922, it did appear possible that the Belgians and Italians might join Britain in opposing Poincaré's policy. The Belgian Prime Minister, Georges Theunis, and his Foreign Minister, Henri Jaspar, seemed distinctly unhappy at the prospect of being dragged into the Ruhr in the wake of France. Indications that a substantial number of Socialist and Flemish deputies in the Belgian parliament would be fiercely hostile to their country's involvement in any such action further encouraged British hopes – and especially those of Lloyd George – of support from Belgium.[104] But these were illusory, as more realistic observers realised.[105]

At a Cabinet meeting of 10 August Curzon told colleagues that France 'dictated Belgian policy', as well as that of Italy.[106] The British ambassador in Brussels, Sir George Grahame, warned that the Poincaré line enjoyed much sympathy amongst the French-speaking section of the population and that political considerations would compel the Theunis government to back France;[107] and the Chancellor of the Exchequer, Horne, was left in no doubt by Theunis himself that if the French did take independent action his government would have no real choice but to acquiesce in it.[108] As for the Italians, following Benito Mussolini's advent to power in October 1922, their policy on reparations moved steadily closer to that of the French.[109]

V

Unable to persuade Poincaré to alter his stance either by diplomatic manoeuvring or by force of argument, the British goverment was obliged to give serious thought to another tactic: the offer of a financial inducement. This was not a new approach. As has been seen, in December 1921, when the French opposed Germany's first official request for a moratorium on reparation payments, the Lloyd George government had considered the possibility of getting them to change their mind by agreeing – as a *quid pro quo* – to a remission of their war debt obligations and to an increase in their share of reparation receipts at Britain's expense. In the summer of 1922 this idea once again came under active consideration. Circumstances this time, though, were different in two vital respects. First, the earlier plan to make financial concessions to France and other allied debtors had been explicitly conditional on the United States being prepared to adopt a more generous policy on Britain's own obligations: when it became clear that there was no chance of that happening, the plan had immediately been dropped. In August 1922, however, this was no longer the case, and the subject was discussed on the assumption that a gesture by Britain was unlkely to be matched by one from America. It was recognised that the imminence of Congressional elections made it politically impossible for the Harding administration to contemplate any remission of foreign debts. In any case, the Cabinet had already decided that the British debt must be paid and that a negotiating mission should proceed to the United States at some time in the autumn. A second difference was that the crisis over reparations was by August 1922 far more acute than it had been when Berlin sought a moratorium at the end of the previous year. In the intervening period there had been an alarming deterioration in Germany's financial position. Moreover, there was now the real danger of French military action in the Ruhr.

With the stakes so high and the situation so perilous, it is hardly surprising that the British government should have been prepared to pay a certain price to bring about a change in French reparation policy. Nor was Poincaré, for his part, wholly unreceptive to the idea of a financial bargain. Trachtenberg and Schuker have argued that it was only with great reluctance and as a last resort that he decided to send troops into the Ruhr. The argument is a persuasive one, and the evidence does seem to suggest that the French Prime Minister made strenuous efforts to achieve his financial and political objectives by other means. Certainly from late August 1922 onwards he was pressing strongly for the early summoning of an inter-allied conference in Brussels to discuss a parallel reduction of reparations and war debts, while at the same time dropping broad hints – through the Comte de Saint-Aulaire, the French ambassador in London, and Louis Dubois, the French delegate on the Reparation Commission – about the sort of settlement he would regard as acceptable.

While there existed on both sides a basic desire to reach a comprehensive financial agreement, however, working out the actual terms of such an agreement presented formidable difficulties. Matters were complicated by a certain amount of ambivalence and confusion in British thinking about how far they were prepared to go in making financial sacrifices. On the one hand, it was felt to be worth paying a relatively high price to avert an occupation of the Ruhr.[110] On the other, there was considerable resentment at the fact that Britain – when heavily taxed and in the midst of a severe recession – should have to purchase French approval for policies which would be of great benefit to France herself and, indeed, to Europe as a whole.[111] In addition, there was understandable concern, at a time of stringent economy, that the cost of securing this approval should be kept to an absolute minimum. As Bradbury told Bonar Law in December 1922: 'The idea now is to do a deal . . . on inter-allied debts as cheaply as possible.'[112]

These cross-currents of opinion within British official circles were not conducive to the formulation of a coherent policy. There was certainly some support for taking a generous line on war debts and reparations. The Foreign Office was desperately anxious to avoid a break with the French, not least because their co-operation was seen as essential to bring current negotiations with Turkey to a successful conclusion.[113] It therefore favoured a conciliatory policy in financial as well as other matters. At the Treasury, too, it was thought that there was a good case for a generous approach. In a note of 6 December 1922, Niemeyer advised the recently-appointed Chancellor of the Exchequer, Stanley Baldwin, that it would probably be worthwhile on economic grounds – given the depressed state of the British economy and the unemployment level of 1,300,000 – for Britain to make financial sacrifices, if those sacrifices helped to produce a satisfactory general settlement on reparations and war debts and thus improved the prospects of international recovery.

Although such a step would involve 'giving up the lever of our debt claims on the French', there would be a number of compensatory advantages. The British government would be demonstrating its commitment to the reconstruction of Europe. It would be more difficult for the French to precipitate a rupture in the Entente. There was even a possibility that the Americans might be sufficiently impressed to offer more lenient terms for British debt repayment:

> It may make all the difference whether we go there [Washington] in the atmosphere
> of a large minded offer or as one of what America rightly or wrongly regards as a
> horde of vultures.[114]

Blackett agreed with his deputy's analysis. Nor is this really surprising, since it
was he who had two years earlier initiated the Treaury proposal that Britain
should unilaterally cancel the war debts owing to her. The rejection of that
proposal by the Cabinet had produced no fundamental shift in Blackett's position, and on 8 December 1922 he minuted: 'I think that it is up to us to take a
very big line and that by doing so we shall gain eventually both in improved trade
and in better relations with the United States of America in the matter of our
debt.'[115]

Others were more reluctant to make sweeping concessions to France over war
debts and reparations, as well as being less convinced about the advantages to be
derived from such a gesture. These included Bradbury and Lloyd George, both
of whom found it hard to understand why the French should receive a financial
inducement to do what was in their own best interests. Bradbury set out his views
in a memorandum which he prepared for the Chancellor of the Exchequer in
mid-June 1922, when it was already obvious that Berlin would not be long in
seeking a lengthy moratorium on reparation payments. He expressed strong
reservations about the very notion that if France agreed to 'concessions' to
Germany over reparations she ought to be compensated by means of reduced
debt demands from Britain and the United States. This was the prevailing
opinion in France, and – to Bradbury's regret – it had been encouraged in various
inter-allied discussions. But Bradbury himself believed it to be 'wrong in principle and likely to lead to an impasse in practice'. It was based upon the belief
that allied consent to a reduction in the London Schedule of Payments and to a
moratorioum would constitute a 'concession' to Germany. That was not so. The
only object in writing down the German obligations was to set a realistic target.
A bad debt would thus be turned into a good one, and France, who was entitled
to 52 per cent of total receipts, stood to gain more from that than any other
country. In Bradbury's opinion, there was in fact a good case for reducing or even
cancelling the French and other war debts. It was esential to treat that question
on its merits, however, and it must be made clear to France that there could be
no British concessions over war debts until agreement had first been reached on
a sensible reparation settlement:

> I believe that in the present state of French public opinion an attitude of this kind
> on our part will be more likely to result in real business than if we lend ourselves
> to the French attempt to do a hors[e] trade. If we encourage the French to think
> that their stiffness towards Germany is so much more damaging to us than to them-

selves that we shall be willing to buy them off, they will persist in this line in the hope of getting something out of us which (even if we were prepared to give it to them on merits) we shall be prevented from giving them by reason of the attitude of America.

If on the other hand we tell them firmly that a provisional settlement with Germany is an indispensable preliminary to any discussion of inter-allied debts it will not be long now before they become more practical.[116]

This grudging approach to the idea of offering France substantial concessions was not untypical. There was in fact a widespread feeling amongst British policymakers that Britain was being placed in an invidious position and that it should not be incumbent upon her alone to meet the cost of any reduction in Germany's reparation burden.[117] It was accepted that there would have to be an element of financial sacrifice. What was regarded as intolerable was the apparent belief of the French and the other Allies that this should be borne almost entirely by Britain. As the British ambassador to Belgium, Grahame, complained to Theunis in September 1922: 'The [reparation and war debts] settlement would have to be on somebody's back and the general opinion abroad seemed to be that it must be done on that of the already sorely-burdened British taxpayer.'[118]

Both Lloyd George and Bonar Law felt strongly on this point – the former telling the Chancellor of the Exchequer and Treasury officials, at a meeting held on 15 July, that the French had a fixed idea that everybody should surrender their share of reparations except themselves and the Belgians.[119] Bonar Law, for his part, took great exception to the tendency which he noted in France and other Continental countries to assume that Britain could well afford to forego both her reparation and war debt claims. It was not generally appreciated by foreign governments, he told Poincaré, that Britain could not be as generous as she would like to be. If her budget and exchange positions were strong, that was only because of heavy taxation and deflationary policies. The result of these was severe unemployment – much worse than in France and Italy – and the government was having to spend £100m per annum on provision for the unemployed: 'In a sense this was the British war damage.'[120]

In addition to the resentment engendered by the prospect of disproportionate sacrifices by Britain, there were a number of other factors tending to temper British willingness to make financial concessions to France. First, considerable indignation was felt at what were seen as French attempts at blackmail. The British government made no secret of the great importance it attached to securing both an extended moratorium on reparation payments and a new settlement involving smaller claims on Germany. This convinced the French that they were in a strong bargaining position and could demand a high price in return for their co-operation in achieving these objectives. According to Bradbury, indeed, Poincaré became 'obsessed by the notion that Great Britain is so anxious to reduce the German liability that by stone-walling us he can induce us to give up our share of reparations and write off the French debt as the price of his consent to such a reduction'.[121] At the beginning of September 1922 the French Cabinet decided to call for the summoning of a inter-allied conference in Brussels to consider the whole question of war debts and reparations,[122] and over the next few months Britain was subjected to intense pressure to agree to attend. London's reaction to this development was one of deep mistrust, for it was suspected – with good cause – that the main purpose of the French plan was to obtain a remission of their debts.[123] As Bradbury warned his government, it was highly likely that the conference would quickly 'resolve itself into an attempt by France to get inter-allied debt concessions as a bribe for abandoning a policy of coercion [in the Ruhr] which she herself now knows would be suicidal'.[124]

A far more blatant attempt to extort financial concessions occurred in connection with the Turkish question, with the French seeking to capitalise on Britain's obvious desire for a successful outcome to the Lausanne conference. In an interview with Curzon on 11 November 1922, the French ambassador, Saint-Aulaire, dropped a thinly veiled hint about the possibility of a deal linking a settlement on reparations and war debts with one on the Near East. It would be easier to reach agreement over policy towards Turkey, he told the Foreign Secretary, if there was reason to believe that 'in return for a solid front in Constantinople and Lausanne, the French would have a chance of obtaining better terms as regards reparations and the European situation'. The French public took the view that a Turkish settlement was of much greater importance to Britain than to France and 'was disposed, in return for a complaissant attitude in the East, to demand some compensation in the West'. When it became clear that Curzon was not interested, Saint-Aulaire immediately retreated, denying that it had ever been his intention to suggest a bargain. Curzon was unconvinced, however, and outraged by the other's use of diplomatic methods that he considered to be disreputable.[125]

A second factor lessening British willingness to make financial concessions to France was the continuing belief of some ministers and officials that to cancel the French and other allied debts would be to throw away an important bargaining weapon which might otherwise be used in the forthcoming negotiations about a funding agreement with the United States. Those who wanted to retain Britain's claims on her debtors also saw them as providing a valuable means of restraining France, especially in her dealings with Germany. As Bradbury put it: 'if we let France off her debt to us the French would at once turn their attention to worrying Germany again'.[126] At a time when Poincaré appeared poised to take action in the Ruhr, this was not a negligible consideration.

Thirdly, British policy was doubtless influenced to some extent at least by a growing sense of resignation, even fatalism, in face of French intransigence over the question of productive pledges. This mood was certainly evident in the case of Lloyd George, who seems to have concluded as early as August 1922 that Poincaré was absolutely determined to go into the Ruhr and that nothing could be done to dissuade him. Such an outcome, Lloyd George thought, although regrettable, might nevertheles prove salutary if it led to a greater sense of realism on the part of the French people and government. Occupation of the Ruhr, costing a great deal and producing nothing but vast quantities of paper marks, would be a sobering experience:[127] 'If France thought that she could get more, he was convinced that it was necessary to let her be disillusioned in her own way.'[128] Whether such an attitude represented a cynical abdication of responsibility, as some historians have suggested,[129] or whether Lloyd George was simply being realistic about the chances of persuading Poincaré to change his policy, is a moot point. However that may be, it seems reasonable to assume that a growing belief in the inevitability of coercive measures by France made the case for offering her financial concessions appear considerably weaker.

Finally, the general climate of Anglo-French relations at this time was not one which was calculated to encourage a generous gesture of any sort by the British government. In the summer and autumn of 1922 Britain and France were at loggerheads not only over reparations, but over a wide range of other important issues, including Morocco, Tangier and, above all, Turkey. On all these matters, the British held the French responsible for the failure to reach agreement. Even the Foreign Office, which was generally well disposed towards France, took this line, with a memorandum of 9 May 1922 identifying her 'treachery and duplicity' as the main obstacle to a resolution of outstanding differences.[130] French policy was blamed both for the collapse of the recent Genoa conference and for the Soviet-German *rapprochement* at Rapallo. It was thought to be one of the main reasons for the 'repeated postponement of a practical reparations settlement'. More generally, it was seen as a major cause of European instability. The Foreign Office found it

> intolerable that the intransigence of one Power, whose military strength dominates the Continent, and whose aerial and submarine projects are a potential threat to ourselves, should frustrate our efforts to bring Russia back into the economic orbit of Europe, to restore the general, commercial and financial conditions that are vital to the British Empire, and to avoid any return to the European group system that provided the conditions of the last war.[131]

Quite apart from the considerations set out above, it must also be borne in mind that the British government's freedom of action was limited by several constraints, not the least of which was the need to take account of domestic opinion. Lloyd George for one was undoubtedly worried that a policy entailing substantial concessions to France might provoke an adverse reaction from Parliament and the public. His successor, Bonar Law, faced an additional problem. This was the danger that cancellation of the French debt and a reduction of Britain's share of reparations would provide the late Prime Minister and his followers with ammunition to attack the new government for supposedly sacrificing the interests of the British taxpayer.[132] There was some concern, too, about the likely attitude of the business community. Amongst manufacturers there was mounting indignation at France's failure to pay even the interest on her war debts, their complaint being that this placed British industry in a position where it was, in effect, subsidising French competitors. This feeling was exacerbated by the French government's recent adoption of protectionist economic measures. At the beginning of December 1922 the President of the Board of Trade, Philip Lloyd-Greame, drew Bonar Law's attention to the current mood of dissatisfaction on this matter and warned him of the criticism that the government would be bound to encounter from manufacturing interests unless it could secure some reduction in French tariffs in return for any remission of war debts.[133] The Prime Minister was sufficiently impressed by this warning to ask for a paper from the Federation of British Industries (FBI) giving its views on inter-allied debts in general. The FBI duly obliged with a memorandum of 5 December which came out strongly against any idea of unilateral concessions by Britain, concluding:

> They [the FBI] consider, therefore, that the risk involved in cancelling any substantial portion of the debts owed to this country outweighs any possible advantage to be gained, since to cancel these debts would be to throw away our principal bargaining weapon in any future settlement . . .
> Until other countries show some disposition to bear their fair share of the burden no abatement should be made of the legitimate claims of this country.[134]

Opinion in the Dominions was another factor that had to be taken into account, and here the indications were that there was a distinct lack of enthusiasm in some quarters at least at the prospect of financial concessions being made to France. The influential Prime Minister of South Africa, Jan Smuts, made his feelings on the matter unmistakably clear in two highly emotional telegrams which he sent to Bonar Law on 20 November and 13 December 1922. At this time Smuts was suspicious and bitterly critical of French policy both in the Near East and in Europe. It seemed to him, indeed, that the French government was 'out for world power'. It had 'played the most dangerous anti-ally game with Kemal', and its current policy towards Germany could only end in chaos and ruin. Smuts urged Bonar Law to dissociate the British Empire from the line being taken by Poincaré. He also suggested that war debts should be used as a weapon to bring about a change in French policy. No concession should be granted to France as long as she threatened to occupy the Ruhr, and any remission of debts that London might be disposed to make should be conditional upon her 'desisting from isolated coercive measures and agreeing with [her] Allies to a policy of appeasement'.[135]

Finally, a further constraint under which the British government had to operate was the difficulty of reconciling a policy of debt cancellation with the

Balfour Note principle of obtaining enough from reparations and war debts combined to repay the United States. The difficulty should not be exaggerated. At this stage the newly-enunciated principle had not yet hardened into a rigid formula, and Bonar Law was to demonstrate, during the Paris conference of January 1923, that there was scope for a certain amount of flexibility in its application. Nevertheless, there was clearly a limit to how far the government could go in abandoning the position which it had adopted, amidst much publicity and controversy, as recently as the beginning of August. A full-scale retreat would have been politically embarrassing to say the least, and most ministers appear to have accepted that the question of debt cancellation must be considered within the broad framework of the Balfour Note policy.

VI

It was against this generally unpromising background that the Lloyd George and Bonar Law governments made a sustained effort from August 1922 onwards to deflect Poincaré from his avowed aim of seizing state assets in various parts of Germany. As they fully appreciated, there was only one hope of achieving that objective, namely to offer France new arrangements on reparations and war debts which would be sufficiently attractive to render such a policy redundant. In the event, they failed, and the price of their failure was the Franco-Belgian occupation of the Ruhr in January 1923.

It would have been difficult enough for the British to negotiate some kind of financial trade-off with the French if the matter had been one which did not involve others as well. What made the task more formidable still was the need to accommodate the interests not only of Britain and France, but also those of Belgium, Italy and Germany. Negotiations were further bedevilled by the sheer complexity of the numerous sets of proposals and counter-proposals put forward at this time. 1922 has been aptly described as the year of reparation and war debt plans.[136] Bradbury alone was the author of several, and leading French officials such as Jacques Seydoux and Jean Tannery were scarcely less prolific. These plans were invariably full of abstruse technicalities. By their own admission, even some of the experts had difficulty in understanding them,[137] and it is hard to resist the conclusion that most political leaders often found themselves completely out of their depth. A more basic obstacle to the negotiation of a deal, however, was the existence of a wide gulf between British and French perceptions of what would constitute a fair and workable financial settlement. Differences persisted about the amount of reparations that Germany could afford to pay. The two sides were also unable to agree on how the total should be divided out. As for the question of war debts, the British government could never quite bring itself to make the only proposal that would have stood any chance of being acceptable to by France – complete and unconditional cancellation.

Having initially insisted that there could be no scaling down of the figure of 132bn gold marks fixed by the London Schedule of reparation payments, the French were gradually forced to accept that it might be necessary to settle for a significantly lower sum – perhaps 50bn, or even 40bn. They were adamant, however, that such a reduction could not be contemplated unless France were allotted a larger share of the new total than the 52 per cent to which she was entitled under the Spa agreement. In addition, there would have to be acceptance of the principle of priority for the devastated regions – something which the British had consistently refused to recognise. These demands followed logically from the minimum French requirement that their reparation receipts must be sufficient to reimburse them for expenditure on reconstruction, with something left over to help towards repayment of war debts. It was estimated that the equivalent of 30bn gold marks had already been advanced for reconstruction, with more spending for that purpose still to come. Moreover, France was indebted to the United States to the extent of 14bn gold marks. Even on the assumption that the French obligations to Britain were to be completely cancelled, therefore, 52 per cent of a total German liability of 50bn would clearly fall far short of satisfying French needs.

If such calculations seemed incontrovertibly fair and reasonable to the French, however, they were viewed in an altogether different light in London. The official line there was that it was unjust to expect Britain to make a double sacrifice, by both renouncing the debts owing to her and accepting a smaller proportion of reparation payments. Apart from anything else, for her to do so would make it absolutely impossible to fulfil the Balfour Note principle. A reduction of the overall amount due from Germany, it was argued, would affect Britain as well as France. If, in addition, she were to receive a reduced percentage of the total, while at the same time writing off the debts due to her, it was inconceivable that she would ever be able to obtain the equivalent of 20bn gold marks that was needed to repay the United States. As Bradbury pointed out, indeed, assuming that Germany's total obligation were set at 50bn gold marks, the Balfour Note principle could only be met by increasing Britain's share from 22 per cent to 41 per cent.[138]

This basic incompatibility between British and French expectations presented a serious impediment to the negotiation of a comprehensive agreement on reparations and war debts of the sort that perhaps might conceivably have persuaded Poincaré to call off his intended seizure of productive pledges. Developments at the London conference of 7–14 August 1922 provided an early indication of the difficulties that lay ahead. The conference, which was convened to consider the Allies' response to Germany's application of 12 July for a moratorium on all reparation payments in cash until the end of 1924, took place in a sour and strained atmosphere. This was reflected in prickly exchanges between the British and French representatives on such sensitive matters as the relative levels of taxation in their two countries and the amount that France had actually spent on restoring her devastated regions.[139] Poincaré came to London in an aggrieved mood. He was angered by the Balfour Note. He was also upset at recent articles in the British press about French plans for submarine construction and other manifestations of alleged militarism.[140] Nor were the prospects for a successful outcome improved by the personal antipathy that he and Lloyd George so obviously felt for each other:[141] one experienced observer, Paul Cambon, the former ambassador to London, described the proceedings as degenerating into 'une question d'amour-propre entre deux hommes qui se détestent'.[142] But the central problem, the one which dominated the conference and which was ultimately to cause its failure, was a fundamental disagreement on the vexed question of productive pledges.

At the opening session of 7 August Poincaré ruled out a moratorium without productive pledges and put forward a series of proposals for obtaining immediate payments from Germany. He proposed, amongst other things, that existing allied controls on the German import and export licensing system in the occupied territories should be continued; that the Allies should levy duties along a customs line established between the occupied territories and the rest of Germany, and should also collect certain taxes within the occupied territories themselves; that the Reparation Commission should be given a stake – perhaps 60 per cent – in the share capital of some of the chemical and other manufacturing enterprises operating on the Left Bank of the Rhine; and – most important of all – that the Allies should take possession of mines and forests in the Ruhr and the Rhineland.[143] The British reaction to these proposals was overwhelmingly hostile, with Lloyd George voicing the opinion of the entire British delegation when he described them as 'unreal' and 'quite hopeless'.[144] Since the Belgians and Italians also expressed strong reservations, the British negotiators were in a fairly strong position. Their hand was further strengthened when a committee of experts, set up at Lloyd George's prompting to investigate the likely yield from the measures recommended by Poincaré, produced an unfavourable report. That did not mean, however, that they could afford to adopt a purely negative stance, simply criticising and blocking the French proposals. As early as 9 August, there was disturbing talk of a rupture in the Entente, something which the Foreign Office in particular was desperate to avoid, and from the tactical standpoint alone it was essential to be able to demonstrate that Britain had done everything within her power to prevent that from happening. More important still, Poincaré had made it clear that France would go ahead and take pledges on her own account if his proposals were rejected.[145]

Faced with a stalemate and the threat of an early breakdown of the conference, on 9 August Lloyd George decided to call a meeting of the Cabinet. He specifically requested that Curzon, who was still recovering from his attack of phlebitis, should attend if the state of his health permitted. He also asked that the Treasury should prepare a paper setting out some British counter-proposals in order to make it harder for Poincaré to effect a rupture.[146]

When the Cabinet met on 10 August, it was given details of a plan accordingly drafted by Blackett. The overriding issue which confronted ministers was whether or not to break with France if it proved impossible to reach agreement with Poincaré on the basis of that plan. There was a strong feeling, voiced by Austen Chamberlain and Balfour, that under no circumstances should Britain agree to go along with what the French had proposed.[147] As against that, it was recognised that a rupture of the Entente would be calamitous. Curzon, anxious not to forfeit the chances of French co-operation over Turkey, urged that every effort should be made to avoid a breach and to provide Poincaré with a bridge over which he might retreat without loss of prestige. If there were a breach, he warned, it was highly probable that the Belgians and Italians would side with France. Nor would the United States necessarily support Britain. British interests would suffer. France, who was 'threatening to become the military dictator of Europe', had for some time indulged in anti-British activities in various parts of the world. In the event of a rupture, this problem would be greatly magnified and Britain would then 'have to contemplate a hostile France over the whole of the Near East and in Egypt, in Morocco and in Tangier'.[148]

Lloyd George, whilst agreeing on the importance of striving to preserve the Entente, took a less pessimistic view about the consequences of a rupture. He was confident of American backing and not unhopeful that the Italians and Belgians would also take Britain's side. In any case, he was convinced that 'any policy involving the handing over of Europe to the tender mercies of Monsieur Poincaré and the French militarists' would be fatal to the reconstruction of Europe and highly dangerous to the British Empire. There were signs, he thought, that France was seeking to establish a dominant position in Europe – a tendency which must be resisted. To give way in the face of an ultimatum from Poincaré would be seen as a sign that Britain was prepared to yield up control of the Continent to the representatives of French chauvinism, an act of capitulation which would not be tolerated by the British working man or by the business and financial community. The British government should do what it believed to be right and there ought to be no question of 'hauling down the flag because of the threatened military resources of France, backed by the politics of the Quai d'Orsay'.[149]

In the course of a lengthy and complicated debate, one of the topics discussed was the possibility of cancellation of the war debts owed to Britain. This had already been discussed on the previous day at a conference of the four ministers in the British delegation: Lloyd George, Horne, Austen Chamberlain (Lord Privy Seal) and the Secretary of State for War, Sir Laming Worthington-Evans.[150] At the Cabinet meeting it was raised by the Minister of Health, Mond, who asked whether it would not be possible to put forward some proposals based on a remission of inter-allied debts – the idea being that this might help to break the deadlock at the conference. What Mond suggested was that France should be offered a moratorium on all interest payments for the next five years. The

Chancellor of the Exchequer responded by saying that he himself had something like that in mind; but it was essential to avoid giving the impression that Poincaré had achieved a great success in London. The discussion then moved off in a different direction and nothing further was said on the subject. In the end no decision was taken about making an offer on war debts. Instead, the Cabinet simply agreed that it could not accept Poincaré's proposals and approved the draft British counter-proposals. In the event of a final disagreement with the French, Lloyd George was to suggest that the matter should be submitted to the Reparation Commission or the League of Nations.[151]

The question of debt remission was to figure much more prominently in two subsequent Cabinet meetings on 12 and 14 August, after it had become plain that the British counter-proposals stood no chance of being accepted. The latter were based on the premise that Germany should be given a complete respite from all cash payments until the end of 1922. They contained no demand for additional guarantees, and they provided for a form of allied supervision over German mines and forests only in the case of a voluntary default on coal and timber deliveries.[152] In essence, they amounted to an almost total rejection of the measures advocated by Poincaré at the first session of the conference. Not surprisingly, Poincaré's reaction was one of intense disappointment. He was particularly critical of the draft formula on state mines and forests, which he described as 'unacceptable and hypothetical'. During discussions with Lloyd George and Theunis on 11 August, he made some concessions – indicating, for example, that he was prepared to drop his plans for establishing a customs barrier around the occupied territories and for taking a 60 per cent stake in the share capital of chemical factories on the Left Bank of the Rhine. There remained, however, one irreducible demand: immediate action over mines and forests.[153]

When the Cabinet met again on 12 August, therefore, it was to hear from Lloyd George that the British counter-proposals had been badly received and that the conference was still deadlocked.[154] Frustrated at the lack of progress, Austen Chamberlain suggested a different approach, seeking some latitude for himself and his fellow-negotiators to make an offer on war debts. He conceded that there was a limit to what could be done. Because of the stance which the Cabinet had taken over obtaining enough from reparations and war debts to repay America, any concession which could be made at present would probably not be sufficient either to strike the public imagination or to satisfy the allied debtors. Even so, he wanted the negotiators to be empowered to say that the British government was prepared to write off all back interest and any interest falling due during the moratorium granted to Germany.[155] His suggestion obtained little support. Worthington-Evans stressed the difficulty of devising a plan which would carry out the Balfour Note principle and yet afford an opportunity for a bargain with the Allies. Lloyd George pointed out that any offer which might be made was bound to have a bearing not only on the resolution of current differences with France, but also on forthcoming debt negotiations with the US:

It might be the case that we should not obtain a penny from France or Italy, but if we made it clear to the United States that the action of America was responsible for the continuance of chaos in Europe, it would be a negotiating pawn when our representatives went to Washington.[156]

Despite these reservations, in the closing stages of the conference some rather half-hearted attempts were made to avert a final breakdown by holding out the prospect of partial debt cancellation by Britain. As Austen Chamberlain had feared, however, the debtors showed little interest in the somewhat limited concessions that the British negotiators felt able to offer. During the three-and-a-half years since the end of the war the French and Italians had grown accustomed to not repaying the money they had borrowed, and by this stage clearly had little intention of ever doing so. This was reflected in the attitude of the Italian Foreign Minister, Carlo Schanzer. When he was sounded out about the possibility of reducing 'very substantially' Italy's debt to Britain, he showed no enthusiasm whatever for the idea. The impression gained by the British delegates, indeed, was that he was looking for total cancellation.[157] There is no evidence of a similar approach being made to Poincaré. On the last day of the conference, however, at a meeting of the heads of all the delegations, Lloyd George put forward four proposals, one of which related to war debts. These were: that the conference should be adjourned until the return of the allied delegates from the United States; that, in the meantime, the question of German payments should be left to the Reparation Commission; that the guarantees insisted on by the Committee of Guarantees as a condition of the partial moratorium of March 1922 should be put into effect immediately; and that, during the interval, no demands should be made for payment of interest on inter-allied debts.[158] In rejecting the proposals, Poincaré made no effort to deal with them separately or in detail, simply restating the basic French position that a moratorium until the end of 1922 could only be granted in return for new guarantees and pledges.[159]

This rejection of the British proposals was followed by adjournment of the conference on 14 August, without any decision having been reached on Germany's request for a moratorium.[160] On the same day, after receiving a report on the latest developments from Lloyd George, the Cabinet was invited to consider the question of inter-allied indebtedness and, more particularly, its relationship to current difficulties over reparation payments.[161] It was by then, of course, too late to salvage the conference. But the threat of independent French action remained as strong as ever, and a way of averting it had still to be found. It is impossible to tell from the official record what was said by individual ministers, though it seems probable that Austen Chamberlain played a prominent part in the discussion, since some of the arguments and phrases which appear in the minutes echo those used by him at the Cabinet meeting held two days earlier. On the one hand, it was argued that there was a strong case for Britain making a 'fair and reasonable' offer on debt cancellation 'so that it could not be urged against her that she had taken no step in this direction and had allowed the collapse of Germany and the deterioration of the European situation without making any concrete proposals to her debtors'.[162] It was held to be vital that there should be a financial and economic settlement of Europe, and the only way that could be achieved was by raising an international loan equivalent to the capital value of Germany's capacity to pay. The sum fixed by the London Schedule was excessive and, as the Committee of Bankers had made clear, would some day have to be reduced to around £2.5bn. But it was certain that France would not agree to such a figure without a corresponding reduction in war debts. There was therefore much to be said for Britain agreeing to surrender the debts owing to her in exchange for some small cash payments. The Balfour Note had set out the general lines of government policy. The question to be be considered was

> whether we had really examined as fully and as carefully as we might do the whole question of Inter-Allied debts so that we could say sincerely that there was no proposition which we could make to our Allies which if adopted would help to ease the situation. Should France take any extreme step it was most undesirable that she should lay the blame of having had to do so on Great Britain's failure to make a reasonable proposition regarding inter-Allied debts.

Under the circumstances, it was suggested, it might be a good idea to inform the allied delegates to the London conference that proposals were now under consideration by the British government which would be submitted to them when they had returned home.[163]

On the other side of the argument, emphasis was laid upon the grave financial difficulties faced by Britain herself and upon her need to meet American demands for debt repayment. It was pointed out that the United States was pressing for payment of some £1,050m and that the considered view of the Cabinet so far had been that the British response should be to press their own debtors. Any relief granted to France and the others would be at the 'sole expense' of Britain, and an opportunity would be lost of using the outstanding obligations as a pawn in forthcoming negotiations with the Americans. Furthermore, it was clear that no proposition that Britain could now make would be entertained for a moment by her debtors. Indeed, since France and Italy 'had no intention whatever of ever paying anything to Great Britain or America', they would regard a proposal limited to partial cancellation as a retrograde step. Britain would thus have made her best offer for nothing and would be exposed to criticism from all sides: she would be criticised by some for breaking with France 'on a beggarly minimum' and by others for surrendering the main portion of the amount owing to her. There was also the danger that any offer made now would be taken as a starting point in future bargaining. Finally, it was argued that it was not perhaps entirely regrettable that there should be a breach with France at this stage. It was time for the French to face reality and take responsibility for their actions. Britain had adopted the right policy at the London conference, and the best course now might be to make the British proposals known to the public in a simple and easily-understood form: 'Public opinion could not comprehend proposals involving complicated calculations respecting inter-Allied debts.'[164]

What this inconclusive discussion revealed was that there were important members of the government, including the Prime Minister, who were not yet willing to make concessions over war debts on anything like the scale that would be needed to have the slightest influence on French policy. The most that the Cabinet was prepared to concede was a suspension of interest payments for the duration of the moratorium granted to Germany – an offer which Poincaré would have doubtless regarded as derisory. During the next few months, however, there was to be a significant, if grudging, change of attitudes, as the reparation crisis intensified and as it became increasingly apparent that Poincaré – driven by financial necessity and mounting pressure from right-wing parliamentary critics – would almost certainly carry out his threat to seize productive pledges. In the face of this alarming prospect, one of the ways in which the British government sought to dissuade him from doing so was by putting forward a series of proposals on reparations and war debts. A notable feature of this process was a progressive improvement in the terms offered to France and the other allied debtors, a development which reached its culmination in the Bonar Law Plan of January 1923.

4

From the London Conference to the Occupation of the Ruhr, August 1922–January 1923

I

The failure of the London conference left the question of Germany's application for an extended moratorium hanging in the air. As an emergency measure, on 14 August the Repararation Commission informed Berlin that the instalment of 50m gold marks due on the following day was to be temporarily suspended, and shortly afterwards an interim solution was adopted to cover the remainder of the year. The latter was made possible by an initiative from the Belgians who, by virtue of the priority accorded to them, were entitled to all of the cash payments to be received by the Allies in the period up to the beginning of 1923. During the London conference, Theunis had suggested a scheme whereby German three-month bonds might be handed over instead of cash.[1] His suggestion was later taken up and slightly modified by the Reparation Commission, and on 31 August it was decided that Germany should be allowed to meet her cash obligations with six-month Treasury certificates.[2] This provided a breathing-space. But there remained the problem of what to do when this makeshift arrangement expired. From January 1923 Germany would have to resume payment of the sums stipulated in the London Schedule – a task that had already proved beyond her. She would also have to deal with the maturing Treasury certificates held by Belgium. Under these circumstances, it was imperative to negotiate a more permanent arrangement before the end of 1922. It was recognised by all concerned, more-over, that this must be accompanied by a parallel arrangement on inter-allied debts.

Between September 1922 and January 1923, the British and French govern-ments were engaged in constant diplomatic exchanges in an attempt to reach an accommodation on both these matters. It could be argued that in some respects there was a narrowing of the gap that separated their respective views. On the one hand, it was increasingly accepted by the French that the Allies would have to settle for considerably less than 132bn gold marks. On the other, the British gradually came to realise that they would need to make a far more generous offer on war debt remission than the one they had been prepared to consider during the London conference. Nevertheless, substantial differences remained, the most intractable being Poincaré's continuing insistence that there must be no moratorium without pledges. The months following the London conference saw no lessening of British opposition to this policy. In December 1922, indeed, Niemeyer was to be found telling the Chancellor, Baldwin, that the powerful objections which had been raised against it in August applied with even greater force now:

> If you feel that a moratorium must be given to enable Germany ultimately to pay something, it is ridiculous to make her recovery more difficult by sequestrating part of her assets, erecting customs barriers, interfering with trade and confidence etc.[3]

There was another important area of disagreement. For the British, the first priority was to secure a three- or four-year moratorium for Germany: only after that had been settled would it be time to turn to the task of negotiating a long-term agreement on reparations and war debts. The French, by contrast, attached the highest importance to dealing with the latter question without delay. Poincaré made this clear in his reply of 2 September to the Balfour Note, when he stated that the problem of reparations could only be finally solved if it was 'united in some way or other to the problem of inter-Allied debts', and that it seemed to him 'necessary that this question be examined before long under all its forms at a conference to which all the interested States would be summoned'.[4] It was at the instigation of the French that on 13 September the Belgian government formally proposed the convening of such a conference – to meet in Brussels in the autumn – for the purpose of dealing simultaneously with reparations and war debts.[5] The idea was given a cool reception in London. The Treasury took the line that it was too soon yet to attempt a permanent settlement, and on 9 October a belated reply was sent in which the government, while professing its readiness to examine the proposal sympathetically, expressed the view that it would be premature to hold such a conference before the result was known of the British and other allied missions which were shortly to go to the United States to discuss the funding of war debts.[6]

This guarded reaction was not simply a consequence of uncertainty over the outcome of impending negotiations with the Americans. There was understandable concern at the likelihood of being faced by a coalition of allied debtors, headed by France, demanding cancellation of their debts as the price of their consent to a reduction in Germany's reparation burden.[7] Nor did there seem much point in having a conference intended to produce a final reparation settlement when German finances were in a chaotic state: by the end of October 1922 the mark had fallen to around 20,000 to the pound, compared to 5,200 to the pound on 1 September.[8] In a telegram to Bonar Law, dated 23 October, Bradbury argued that to hold the proposed conference now or in the near future could only result in a fiasco. He had information that Poincaré was prepared to come down to a figure of 40bn gold marks for Germany's total liability, in return for Britain's renunciation of her share of reparations and cancellation of European inter-allied debts. But that was still unrealistically high. The sum of 132bn set out in the London Schedule was at least patently absurd and had therefore 'ceased to be, psychologically at any rate, any real incubus'. If the Allies really attempted to recover 40bn, however, 'we should be passing from pure to applied lunacy'. Bradbury was sure that no figure above 25bn would be of any help in restoring German credit. On the other hand, one as low as that would be not only politically impossible for the French but also bad business for the Allies in general, since much more could be obtained if the asset was properly nursed.

> It seems to me, therefore, that a Conference runs the risk either of leading to nothing at all or of causing us to give away claims, which however valueless they may be in themselves are extremely valuable for bargaining purposes when a real general settlement becomes possible . . . and at the same time getting us committed to joining in 'energetic action' against Germany to enforce demands which though reduced are still impossible.[9]

Bradbury's suggested course of action was that the government should try to delay the conference for as long as possible, whilst avoiding a quarrel with France. That was the policy that the government had in fact been following since mid-September and that it was to continue until the end of the year. Not surprisingly, such foot-dragging tactics exasperated the French, and as early as 19 October Saint-Aulaire warned Curzon that France would not tolerate a lengthy postponement of the conference.[10] On the same day, however, the Lloyd George coalition collapsed, and this development provided a legitimate excuse for further British procrastination. On 23 October Bonar Law formed a new Conservative government, retaining Curzon as Foreign Secretary and appointing Baldwin as Chancellor of the Exchequer in place of Horne. He then called an election for 15 November, and until that was out of the way there could be no possibility of a firm British decision on whether to support or take part in the Brussels conference. Another important consequence of the change of government was that the planned debt mission to the United States was once again postponed.

The new Prime Minister was from the outset determined to establish a better relatonship with France, and his dealings with Poincaré were noticeably free of the personal animosity that had characterised the latter's relations with Lloyd George.[11] This was reflected in the atmosphere of the inter-allied London conference of December 1922, which was far less strained than at the proceedings of the previous August. The improvement was so noticeable, indeed, that one of the delegates, Theunis, was prompted to comment on it.[12] Although Bonar Law's style was certainly different from that of his predecessor, however, the policy which he adopted on reparations and war debts was substantially the same. He sympathised with French mistrust of German good faith and was fully prepared to co-operate in applying sanctions against Germany if she failed to make payments which were truly within her capacity. At the same time, he was no less opposed than Lloyd George had been to Poincaré's proposals on productive pledges.[13]

It might have been expected that Curzon, freed from the overpowering dominance of Lloyd George, would have played a major role in the formulation of reparation and war debt policy after October 1922. But that was not the case. Indeed, his involvement could fairly be described as peripheral. Part of the explanation for this lies in his notorious lack of interest in financial matters. It was said of Curzon that the only finances in which he took any interest were his own.[14] Bonar Law, by contrast, as a former businessman and Chancellor of the Exchequer had considerable experience of financial affairs, and the Foreign Secretary appears to have been perfectly content to follow his lead. More important, however, was the Foreign Office's preoccupation at this time with the Near Eastern question. On 20 November the Allies began negotiations with Turkey at the Lausanne conference, and for the next few months Curzon had his hands full with developments there. He was convinced that the key to a successful outcome to the conference was co-operation between Britain and France, and it was only when that seemed to be threatened by Anglo-French differences over reparations and war debts that he reluctantly turned his attention to these other issues. Tyrrell, Eyre Crowe's deputy, was also heavily involved in the Lausanne conference.[15]

With the Foreign Office thus engrossed in negotiations with Turkey, and with the new Bonar Law government inevitably taking time to get its bearings, the influence of Bradbury – already considerable – became greater still. Bradbury's position was somewhat ambiguous. Other countries' representatives on the Reparation Commission, including the French, acted as spokesmen for their governments. The British always claimed that their representative, by contrast, was wholly free from political interference and control. While this was not strictly accurate, it was certainly the case that Bradbury did enjoy a certain measure of freedom to act on his own initiative. Working closely with the Treasury, he played a central role in shaping policy. As a former head of the Treasury and the British delegate on the Reparation Commission since its inception, Bradbury was obviously extremely well-informed on the subject of reparations and war debts. His opinions carried weight.[16] Nor did he hesitate to press them forcefully at the highest level, sometimes to the point of hinting at resignation if the goverment felt unable to endorse the line that he recommended. It was originally intended that he should relinquish his position on the Reparation Commission on 30

November 1922. At the end of September, however, in response to a personal appeal from the Chancellor, Horne, he had agreed to stay on until the end of March in the following year – an episode that can only have strengthened his authority.[17] After the fall of the Lloyd George coalition, he lost little time in proffering advice to Bonar Law and Baldwin, and on 11 November he indicated his wish to visit London to discuss the policy of the new government.[18]

His ensuing conversation with Bonar Law on 22 November brought to a head feelings of unease that had been building up for some time at the Foreign Office.[19] The department was unhappy at Bradbury's habit of making unauthorised policy statements to the press. It resented the fact that he communicated directly with, and received instructions from, the Treasury – rather than going through the Foreign Office, as in the case of other British representatives operating abroad. Above all, it disliked what was seen as his dangerous independence from political control.[20] As Curzon later complained to Bonar Law, in January 1923, Bradbury had been 'a great trial to the Foreign Office, having consistently regarded himself as an independent potentate.'[21] The problem was compounded, it was felt, by a lack of political judgement on Bradbury's part.[22]

In the opinion of one Foreign Office official, Ralph Wigram,[23] this last failing, along with others, was amply illustrated by Bradbury's performance during his meeting with the Prime Minister on 22 November. Bradbury strongly advocated an indefinite postponement of the Brussels conference – at least until the Allies, and Britain and France in particular, had reached some preliminary agreement. The basis of this agreement should be the summoning of a fresh 'bankers' conference' to consider the terms on which an international loan for Germany might be floated. In the meantime, Bradbury saw no prospect of the Germans making an offer on the capitalised value of their reparation liability which would be acceptable to the Allies. When questioned about taking action to compel Germany to make a reasonable offer, he agreed that the French would probably propose vigorous measures in the Rhineland or the Ruhr. Bonar Law asked whether there was not something to be said for giving them their heads on this point, but Bradbury deprecated the use of force on the grounds that it would be contrary to the Treaty of Versailles, and that it would spell the ruin of the franc and thus of Europe – a forecast which the other seemed to find exaggerated. According to Wigram, who attended the meeting, Bradbury concluded with

> a clear indication that he had a policy of his own in these matters which he intended to pursue on the [reparation] commission, that it might not always be that of H[is] M[ajesty's] G[overnment], but that if the Prime Minister thought Sir John's policy was likely to embarrass him, he was ready to resign.[24]

Wigram clearly found the tone of Bradbury's statement offensive, likening it to a 'lecture'. He was even more dismayed by its content. He was concerned that it took no account of what would happen to the franc if strong action was not taken against Germany and France consequently obtained no reparation money at all. Nor was there any reference to the possibiity of a 'communist outbreak' in Germany if the German government continued to avoid paying reparations by depreciating the mark, to the pauperisation of the middle classes. It seemed to Wigram that Bradbury's analysis was unduly favourable to Germany, while paying insufficient attention to the danger of forcing France to act alone and rupturing the Entente by continuing to oppose French policy. Taken as a whole, the views expounded by Bradbury

> only served to intensify and throw into still stronger relief the conviction which I have long held of the extreme danger of allowing a question of the prime political importance of reparation to be dealt with by a few Treasury officials and ex-officials acting in complete independence of the Foreign Office.[25]

There was no doubt an element of inter-departmental jealousy in such complaints,[26] which were echoed by other Foreign Office officials like Lampson and Crowe. But there are indications of some disquiet elsewhere, although the evidence is less conclusive. During his discussion of 22 November with Bradbury, Bonar Law reacted to the other's thinly-veiled threat of resignation by expressing the hope that 'Sir John Bradbury would *in future* [my italics] keep in very close touch with the Government'[27] – the strong implication being that this had not always been the case in the past. As for the Chancellor of the Exchequer, Baldwin, it is possible to detect signs that he too was not entirely satisfied with the line advocated by Bradbury. Thus in early December he asked Niemeyer whether the Treasury had any proposals to make for a comprehensive reparation and war debt settlement which were distinct from those being put forward by Bradbury. Niemeyer's reply was decidedly unhelpful: he found it dificult to answer without knowing more precisely the government's attitude on a number of matters, and especially on whether it was prepared to discuss the question of allied debts to Britain prior to British discussions with the United States. Having entered this caveat, Niemeyer then set out his own position on a reparation and war debt settlement, which was in fact broadly similar to that taken by Bradbury.[28]

II

One of Bradbury's most significant contributions to policymaking was his drafting of a series of schemes for a general settlement of reparations and war debts, the most ambitious of which was the Bonar Law Plan of January 1923.[29] The origins of this plan can be traced back to proposals put to the Reparation Commission on 8 October 1922. Bradbury believed that the collapse of the mark at that time made it essential to give Germany immediate and generous relief from reparation payments.[30] He therefore proposed that all cash payments falling due under the London Schedule in 1923 and 1924 should be met by German Treasury five-year bonds. This arrangement might be extended for two more years if the Reparation Commission considered it necessary. Deliveries in kind were to continue. To prevent this becoming an immediate charge on the German budget, however, the German government was to be paid for them in five-year Treasury bonds guaranteed by the countries taking delivery. There were to be tighter controls on German finances, including a strict limit on the note issue and the imposition upon the Reichsbank of the legal obligation to sell gold at a fixed mark price – the level of which was to be determined by a three-man 'mixed commission' comprising one member appointed by the German government, another by the Reparation Commission, and an American financial expert agreed by the other two. In addition, in order to assist the various governments which had been counting on cash receipts from Germany to help in balancing their budgets, it was proposed that the allied governments should consider the 'grant of indulgence in respect of inter-Allied war indebtedness during the period up to the maturity of the last issued German guaranteed bonds'.[31]

Bradbury was confident that his plan would find favour with France and the other Allies, since it would provide them with a substantial measure of budgetary relief if they were prepared to guarantee and market the German bonds.[32] Such confidence can only be regarded as wholly unrealistic, however, given the extent to which the main features of the plan were incompatible with the French government's general hostility to a moratorium on reparation payments and with its stance on productive pledges. In the event, Bradbury's proposals provoked bitter criticism in France.[33] Louis Barthou, who had recently replaced Dubois as the French delegate on the Reparation Commission, made it clear that they were totally unacceptable to his government, and on 22 October he submitted a set of counter-proposals which were completely different in character, being concerned almost exclusively with the imposition of much tougher financial controls on Germany.[34]

In the weeks following the rejection of his original plan by the Reparation Commission, Bradbury was engaged in preparing an amended version. He did so with some reluctance, for he was still of the opinion that it was premature to attempt a comprehensive reparation and war debt settlement. Nevertheless, the British government was under growing pressure to agree to an early conference in Brussels and Bradbury thought it advisable to have some proposals ready to counter those which Poincaré was expected to unveil there.[35]

On 1 November 1922 the Belgian government repeated its proposal of 13 September for the meeting of a conference to consider the joint questions of reparations and inter-allied debts. The beginning of December was suggested as a suitable date, and the British government was warned that if it delayed acceptance the French intended to take matters into their own hands and convene a conference in Paris. The imminence of the general election (15 November) made it possible to send a non-committal reply.[36] After the election, however, the newly-returned Bonar Law government found it increasingly difficult to continue playing for time. By that stage the pressure for a quick decision was coming mainly from the French rather than the Belgians. On 28 November Saint-Aulaire informed Bonar Law that Poincaré regarded it as essential that the Brussels conference should take place by 15 December at the latest and was anxious that there should be a meeting of allied Prime Ministers before that date.[37] It was accordingly agreed – with little enthusiasm on the British side – to hold a preliminary conference in London on 9 and 10 December.[38]

By the time this conference opened, Bradbury had already completed a rough draft of his new plan. Its underlying purpose, Bonar Law explained to Curzon on 7 December, was to 'express our willingness to cancel all our European debts on condition that our share of the reparation which Germany will pay should be sufficient, in form at least, to make good what we will pay the Americans'.[39] According to Bradbury, if Britain was to cancel all inter-allied debts owing to her, it was essential to fix Germany's reparation liability at a figure well within her capacity to pay – no more than 40 bn gold marks. Otherwise the British government would find itself involved in helping France with 'unremunerative coercive measures which France herself will be better able to afford because she has been relieved of her debt to us'.[40] Under Bradbury's plan, Germany was to be given a moratorium on all payments until January 1927. Thereafter she would begin paying an annuity of 2.5bn gold marks, a figure that would rise gradually to 3.5bn from 1930 to 1939 – unless it was decided by an 'impartial tribunal' that the increase was beyond her capacity. Provision was made for early repayment on favourable terms. As for sanctions, they were to be applied only by unanimous agreement of the allied creditors. Thus far the plan entailed no radical departure from that which Bradbury had submitted to the Reparation Commission in October. The real novelty lay in its treatment of war debts. In October, it had been proposed that there should be no debt repayment by the European Allies during the moratorium granted to Germany. What Bradbury now proposed was an immediate cancellation of all but a small percentage of the debts due to Britain. In return for this concession, France and Italy were to abandon their claims on the gold which they had deposited in London during the war.[41]

As in October, Bradbury was hopeful that his plan would meet with general approval. Its chief merit in his eyes was that it set Germany a target – an estimated present value of 40bn gold marks – which was realistic and consistent with the restoration of German credit. From the British viewpoint, there appeared to be two main advantages. First, there was the prospect of a practicable settlement which would provide Britain with 'a reparation creance of real value instead of claims against two debtors who are rapidly reducing themselves and each other to bankruptcy by scrapping'. Secondly, Britain would be committed to coercive measures only if Germany proved to be really recalcitrant. Bradbury thought that the plan would also have attractions for the French. If (as seemed likely) it helped to restore German credit, there would be plenty of ready money available to them in the near future. They would receive large deliveries in kind over the next three years. They would have the promise of British support for *gages* and sanctions if Germany failed to carry out her obligations. Not least, they would be completely rid of their debt to Britain.[42]

Even Bradbury conceded that there was one problem, though he appeared not to appreciate its full implications. When explaining the plan to Baldwin in late November, he hinted that it might leave Britain in a position where she received less money than was necessary to repay the Americans. Britain, he pointed out, owed the United States £1.039bn, the equivalent of 20bn gold marks. If she cancelled her European debts altogether, therefore, the Balfour Note principle could only be fulfilled on the basis of a 55 per cent British share of the proposed total reparation figure of 40bn. Yet that was not the proportion she was entitled to under Bradbury's plan, which allotted Britain 41 per cent, the same as France. Bradbury offered no suggestion as to how this dilemma might be resolved.[43]

When the draft plan was circulated for comment in late November and early December, a number of reservations were expressed about it. One of those whose views were sought was Keynes who had resigned from the Treasury in June 1919 in disgust at the terms of the Versailles peace settlement but who nevertheless continued to be consulted by the department.[44] Keynes' reaction was that it was a 'most brilliant' document but far too complicated and obscure. He himself, he observed, had had to read it three or four times before he could grasp it fully. He doubted whether Poincaré or de Lasteyrie ever would.[45] In the light of subsequent complaints from many quarters about the sheer incomprehensibilty of the Bonar Law Plan, this comment is highly revealing.[46] Keynes felt that there were two other basic problems. First, he believed that Bradbury's proposals on reparations, although a distinct improvement on the London Schedule, were still too severe. Secondly, he was critical of the treatment to be accorded to France both over remission of war debts and the share of reparation recepts to be allotted to her: 'We have got to be far more generous than this to France if there is to be the remotest possibility of a settlement now.' The proposals would perhaps serve as an opening negotiating position at the Paris conference. Unless an offer 'of far more striking generosity' was made, however, the conference was bound to fail. Keynes declared that he himself was prepared to 'go an enormous way further to meet France as to her share of the plunder' and, with that in mind, set about preparing a scheme of his own.[47]

At the Treasury, there was agreement with Keynes' observations about the undue complexity of Bradbury's proposals, but not about its likely impact on Germany. The general feeling amongst senior officials there was that Germany would be getting off lightly. In a minute of 6 December, indeed, Niemeyer said that his one real worry about Bradbury's plan was the possibility that it might in the long run leave her in a stronger financial position than the Allies.[48] Another issue raised by Niemeyer was whether any attempt should be made to attach conditions to Britain's financial concessions to her debtors. His own tentative conclusion was that it would not be unreasonable to expect modifications in the Rhineland occupation regime, as well as a reduction in French armaments.[49] Blackett, too, argued in favour of political conditions:

> I believe some substitute for the Army of Occupation must be envisaged, at any rate at the end of an earlier period than the original 15 years, if Germany is to be in a position to pay effectively. It would be a pity if we gave up the Allied debts without getting some real settlement of this political question.[50]

Blackett's principal concern, however, was how the French would react. Like Keynes, he was certain that they would not be favourably impressed by the plan and would feel that it was far too advantageous to Britain. They were not yet ready to contemplate a reduction in reparations to the level suggested by Bradbury and would expect to get in return not only complete cancellation of their debts to Britain, but also most of the reduced reparation total. If they obtained only 41 per cent, as proposed, they would be left with little or nothing over after paying off their debts to the United States. Blackett therefore advocated a more generous approach to France. At the very least, he suggested, reparations should continue to be distributed in accordance with the Spa percentages.[51]

III

In response to some of the critical comments made about his plan, and especially about its complexity, Bradbury subsequently introduced a number of modifications to it.[52] That occurred, however, after the abortive London conference had taken place.

When the conference opened on 9 December 1922, Bradbury's scheme still existed only as a rough draft. For that reason alone there could be no question of putting it forward as the basis of an official British proposal. In any case, it was never Bonar Law's intention to make such a proposal at that time. Having agreed to call the conference only with great reluctance and as a sop to the French, he had from the outset very low expectations about its outcome. His main objective was a strictly limited one: not to produce a comprehensive agreement on reparations and war debts, but simply to avoid a clash with the French which might undermine current attempts to negotiate a Near Eastern settlement.[53] Shortly before the conference began, he received an urgent appeal from the Foreign Secretary in Lausanne, begging him to do everything within his power to avert a breach with France. According to Curzon, he was 'fighting a desperate battle' to reach an agreement with the Turks and could not afford to lose any cards. 'I am afraid that if you break with Poincaré in London', he said, 'it will mean the end of my already slender chances here. Poincaré will at once issue orders to Barrère to be disagreeable'.[54] For obvious reasons Bonar Law was unable to meet a request from Curzon for a postponement of the London conference until the middle or latter part of January 1923. The best he could offer was an assurance that he would do his utmost to prevent an open rupture in London. Rather than allow difficulties to come to a head there, he promised, he would arrange for another meeting to be held in Paris ten days or so later.[55]

Like Bonar Law, Poincaré too approached the London conference in the belief that it would achieve little or nothing. Although he already had a clear idea by early December of the proposals which he intended to submit whenever the Brussels conference eventually met, he was not prepared to divulge them before then.[56] Certainly he had no intention of presenting any general scheme on reparations and war debts at the London conference. As far as Poincaré was concerned, the purpose of the conference was merely to make arrangements for Brussels and if possible reach some agreement on the question of *gages*.[57] During discussions with his Finance Minister, de Lasteyrie, he made it clear that he regarded the forthcoming meeting as an essentially futile exercise:

> Let us face facts. We are going to London to ask for a liquidation of inter-allied debts; they will reply that it is impossible. Next we will ask for loans to be floated for Germany; they will reply that it is impossible. Then we shall come back and put into force our own policy.[58]

Given the pessimistic, almost fatalistic, attitude of both prime ministers, and given the wide divergence between their respective standpoints on the future of reparations and war debts, it is hardly surprising that the proceedings in London quickly developed into a stalemate.[59] Poincaré was adamant that there could be no reduction in France's claim on Germany (as part of an overall scaling down of reparations) unless Britain conceded an equivalent remission of the French war debt. He also insisted on the occupation of the Ruhr districts of Bochum and Essen as an essential precondition of any extension of the moratorium on German payments beyond 15 January 1923. On neither of these points was Bonar Law able to agree. He was more than ever convinced that a policy of seizing pledges would end disastrously: at the very least it would damage Germany's ultimate capacity to pay. Nor was he prepared to countenance any reparation settlement which involved unilateral British sacrifices, pointing out that Britain, no less than France, was currently experiencing severe financial difficulties. With unemployment relief alone costing £100m a year, he said, the British government simply could not afford to be as generous as it wished.

Poincaré's stance on the subject of war debts produced an equally cool response. The familiar argument was advanced that it would be unfair to expect France to begin paying off her debts until after Germany had fully reimbursed her for expenditure on reconstruction. This was followed by a specific proposal:

that war debts should be liquidated through the use of some of the C series reparation bonds. France would discharge her obligations to Britain by the transfer of an equivalent amount of the French share of these bonds. If Britain agreed to accept this arrangement and to cancel the bonds that she thus received, France would adopt the same procedure for dealing with the debts owed to her. Not only would this solve the problem of inter-allied debts. It would also bring about a substantial reduction in Germany's nominal liability. Poincaré had planned to lay this scheme before the previous London conference in August, only to change his mind because of the Balfour Note. At that time Lloyd George had ridiculed the idea, dismissing the C series bonds as 'a quite worthless security'. Now Bonar Law raised strong objections to it for similar reasons.[60]

In an attempt to find some common ground with the French, Bonar Law indicated that he was willing to make a concession. If he saw the chance of a complete settlement, he said, he 'would be prepared to run the risk in the end of having to pay an indemnity, that is to say, of paying more to the United States of America than Great Britain would receive from the Allies and Germany'.[61] The significance of this statement, as Theunis immediately pointed out, was that it involved a relaxation of the Balfour Note principle. As such, it was warmly welcomed by the French Prime Minister. The declaration was a vague one, however, and certainly insufficient to produce the desired softening in Poincaré's position.

Throughout the conference the British and French remained consistently at odds. The sole point of agreement between them came when they joined with the rest of the allied representatives in rejecting out of hand a German reparation and stabilisation plan presented on 10 December by the recently-formed Cuno government.[62] This plan apart, the only other detailed proposals were those advanced by the Italians. These envisaged the cancellation of the C series bonds and a consequent reduction of the German debt to the 50bn represented by the A and B series. There was to be a two-year moratorium on cash payments, although deliveries in kind were to continue. Germany was to raise an international loan of between 3bn and 4bn, a part of which was to be used to stabilise the mark and the rest to be divided between the Allies. Specified German revenues were to be pledged as security for the loan. Internal financial reforms were to be controlled by the Reparation Commission and the Committee of Guarantees. Finally, Britain was to write off all the debts owed to her.[63]

By the time this scheme was submitted on the second day of the conference, it was already obvious that there was no real hope of breaking the deadlock that had developed during the two opening sessions. As Bonar Law and Poincaré both conceded, in 'very private conversations', the differences between the British and French positions were so great as to appear irreconcilable.[64] Under these circumstances, Bonar Law's chief concern was to postpone a final breakdown so as to avoid prejudicing Curzon's chances of reaching an agreement with the Turks at Lausanne. He therefore proposed an adjournment and a resumption of talks in Paris on 4 January 1923. Poincaré initially expressed some misgivings about the

effect of an adjournment on French public opinion. He was also worried that the
suggested date would not leave enough time to fit in the Brussels conference
before the expiry of the German moratorium. When Bonar Law indicated that
he was prepared to go to Paris on 2 January, however, he acquiesced.[65]

IV

In the interval between the London and Paris meetings, work went ahead on the
preparation of a comprehensive British plan, with Bradbury continuing to play
a leading role in the process. On 15 December he sent the Chancellor of the
Exchequer a new version of the draft that he had prepared in late November.
This had been criticised as being too intricate. Bradbury therefore aimed to make
the new one simpler. As he told Baldwin:

> In substance (i.e., as regards the amount and incidence in point of time of the finan-
> cial burdens on Germany and sacrifices asked of the respective Allies) there is no
> great variation from my original plan, but I have made considerrable alterations of
> form and machinery, which I hope will make it more easy to grasp.[66]

In view of subsequent complaints from Bergmann that he 'would rather pay reparations than try to understand the Bonar Law Plan',[67] there must be grave doubts
about whether Bradbury was successful in this respect.

By his own account, another factor influencing Bradbury's new draft was the
scheme submitted by Mussolini during the London conference. As we have seen,
this proposed, amongst other things, the cancellation of the London Schedule C
series bonds and the reduction of Germany's total reparation debt to the 50bn
gold marks of the A and B series bonds combined. Taking this proposal as his
starting point, Bradbury then proceeded to modify it in a way which was designed
to limit the burden on Germany during the early years to a level that he considered tolerable. The existing A, B and C bonds were to be replaced by new ones,
divided into two series, and future reparation receipts were to be derived from
the interest paid on these. The first series was to consist of bonds to the value of
50bn gold marks, repayable in 1954 and bearing interest at the rate of 5 per cent
per annum. No interest was to be paid until 1 January 1927 and only 4 per cent
from then until 1 January 1931. The amount of the second series was to be
17.31bn gold marks – a sum equal to the deferred interest on the bonds of the
first series. At the discretion of a specially appointed arbitration board, Germany
might be relieved of the obligation to issue these second series bonds if it was felt
that the payment of interest on them exceeded her capacity.

The main effect of the proposals, then, was that Germany would obtain
complete relief from all cash payments for the first four years and partial relief
for four years thereafter, during which period she would pay a sum of 2bn marks

per annum. The remaining annual payments would vary between 2.5bn and 3.5bn, depending upon what was decided by the arbitration board. Bradbury estimated the present value of the total cash liability as between 39.5bn and 50bn marks. But the calculation was complicated by the provision of a generous discount for anticipated payment of the annuities, the result of which might be a figure of less than 30bn. Deliveries of coal, dye-stuffs, timber and other items were to continue, even during the early years. These were to be subject to new agreed maxima, however, and paid for by each of the receiving powers by means of a set-off against the interest due on the bonds held by it.

With regard to war debts, as in his previous draft, Bradbury proposed the cancellation of all but a small proportion of the obligations outstanding to Britain. There were, however, a number of conditions attached, including the familiar stipulation that the French and Italians must relinquish all claims on the gold deposited in London as security for their wartime loans. France was to transfer to Britain her share of the new German bonds applicable to the settlement of Belgium's war debt, and Italy was likewise to hand over 1.5bn of the first series bonds to which she was entitled. Belgium was to waive her claim to priority. The Italian debt to France was to be written off. An attempt was made to deal with the thorny question of indebtedness to the Americans by suggesting that the second series bonds should be distributed between the various European Allies in proportion to their respective obligations to the United States. Finally, all countries benefiting from a remission of debts owed to Britain were to undertake to support whatever proposals the British government might make for alleviating the reparation burdens of Austria, Hungary and Bulgaria.[68]

As might be expected, Bradbury was convinced that his latest scheme had much to offer both to Germany and to her various creditors. He was, however, considerably less sanguine than on previous occasions that his proposals would meet with the approval of other governments. He predicted that the Germans, for example, would be extremely reluctant to accept them.[69] His forecast proved to be correct. Despite pleas from Bergmann that the Cuno government should adopt the draft plan and put it forward as its own, Berlin eventually decided to reject it as impossible to carry out.[70] As for the French, Italians and Belgians, as will be seen, their reaction to what came to be known as the Bonar Law Plan was one of intense indignation.

Because he was concerned about the likelihood of stiff resistance to his proposals, Bradbury devoted considerable thought to the question of presentation. From a tactical standpoint, he believed that it would be best to communicate them to the countries concerned in advance of the Paris conference, rather than waiting until it met. One advantage of this, he told Niemeyer on 19 December, was that it would help to destroy French illusions about what sacrifices Britain might be willing to make when negotiations were resumed. It would also improve the chances of securing support for the British proposals from Belgium and Italy.[71] In order to further enhance the prospects of obtaining backing from those quarters, Bradbury made sure that his Belgian and Italian colleagues on the Reparation Commision were well briefed on his proposed plan. To them – although not, it appears, to the French representative, Dubois – he confided its general outlines. They were given fairly precise figures for reparations, but on the subject of inter-allied debt concesions Bradbury was less forthcoming: he confined himself to saying that France would probably get between 15bn and 16 bn gold marks net of her debt to Britain.[72] According to Bradbury (reporting to Bonar Law on 21 December), Delacroix – 'an incurable optimist' – expressed the view that this should be good enough: 'Je crois qu'ils [the French] acceptent'.[73] Bradbury attached particular importance to winning over the Belgians. Despite the fact that his scheme involved surrendering their right to priority over reparation receipts, he was reasonably hopeful that they would accept it. He anticipated greater difficulties from the Italians. They would need careful handling. While Mussolini might prove helpful in the early stages of negotiation, when it came down to detailed bargaining he would be 'for sale to the highest bidder'. In Bradbury's judgement, there was something to be said for confidentially disclosing the British proposals in their entirety to Delacroix. The danger, as he fully appreciated, was that the French and Italians would be gravely offended if they found out about it from a leak.[74]

If Bradbury was at best doubtful as to whether his proposals would be accepted, Bonar Law's attitude was bleakly pessimistic.[75] A message which he sent to Curzon in late December gives a fair indication of his mood: 'The outlook for our meeting on the 2nd of January is very black but we must do the best we can and I am trying to have ready a complete scheme of settlement of our own.'[76] His discussions with Poincaré at the London conference had plainly demonstrated the full extent of Anglo-French differences, and further unfruitful exchanges, conducted through Saint-Aulaire between 24 and 28 December 1922, only underlined how difficult it would be to reconcile those differences – not least on the crucial question of pledges. Some members of the British embassy staff in Paris, including Eric Phipps (the minister there), argued that there was still a chance of doing so, provided the British government could build for Poincaré 'a sufficiently golden bridge to return with grace into the embrace of the Entente'.[77] Bonar Law was not convinced, however, believing that mounting domestic pressures would make it almost impossible for the French Premier to retreat from the intransigent position that he had adopted. The strength of public opinion would probably compel him to go into the Ruhr.[78] In any case, his hands were tied by the appalling state of national finances. 'The real truth', Bonar Law told Curzon on 21 December, 'is that French finance is so bad that for them to agree to any arrangement which is possible to Germany would be equivalent to declaring that they are practically bankrupt'.[79] It seemed to Bonar Law that the only thing which could retrieve the situation was intervention by the United States; but he rightly judged that such a development was highly unlikely – especially after the Secretary of State, Hughes, on 18 December rebuffed a British appeal for

American participation in the Paris conference, insisting that under no circumstances could the United States enter into discussions about war debts.[80] The only positive contribution to come from the Harding administration was the offer, made publicly by Hughes in a speech at New Haven on 29 December, of American collaboration in an examination of Germany's capacity to pay reparations by an international committee of experts.[81]

V

During the last week of December 1922, the finishing touches were applied to Bradbury's draft proposals, soon to become known as the Bonar Law Plan. Bradbury returned to London for final consultations with Bonar Law and other senior ministers, and on 29 December the scheme was (in the words of Tom Jones) 'approved but probably not understood' by the Cabinet.[82] There was little confidence that it would be accepted by France. This was reflected in the great attention paid to tailoring various aspects of the plan to suit French wishes. The chief negotiators at the forthcoming Paris conference, the Prime Minister and the President of the Board of Trade, Lloyd-Greame, were given considerable latitude in that respect. The Cabinet decided that, from the point of view of presentation of the plan to the French government, it might be useful to introduce a clause indicating that France would obtain from the proceeds of the loan to be raised during the moratorium some advantage to meet part of the expenditure incurred on reconstruction of her devastated areas – provided that this could be achieved without serious prejudice to British interests and without antagonising Belgium or Italy. The question of whether such a clause would help matters was left to the judgement of Bonar Law and Lloyd-Greame, in consultation with Bradbury and Niemeyer. Bonar Law alone was authorised, if he considered it advisable, to drop the requirement that France should transfer to Britain the first series German bonds to be received by her in respect of the Belgian war debt. The Cabinet also agreed that the plan should not be presented immediately to the French government, but that the two ministers involved in the negotiations should have full discretion as to timing. Finally, it was decided that, in the event of French insistence on *gages*, Bonar Law and Lloyd-Greame might accept proposals 'which were not seriously mischievous, even though they were not likely to prove productive'.[83]

As feared, when the British plan was unveiled at the Paris conference on 2 January 1923, it met with a barrage of criticism, and not only from the French.[84] The Belgians were understandably resentful at being asked to surrender their right to priority over reparations,[85] while the Italians (whose principal negotiator in the absence of Mussolini was the Marquis della Torretta) took strong exception to two of the proposals in particular: that Italy should transfer to Britain 1.5bn gold marks of first series German bonds and should (along with France) relinquish all claims on the gold deposited in London during the war.[86] This latter proposal also displeased the French. But their complaints about the plan went far beyond such points of detail. They were opposed to it root and branch.

It was decided to release details of the plan the day before the opening of the conference. With the benefit of hindsight, some British policymakers came to regard this as a tactical blunder which contributed greatly to the breakdown of the negotiations. Thus Curzon, who clearly held Bradbury responsible for the decision, told Bonar Law on 6 January that he doubted whether it had been 'altogether wise to publish our scheme in advance and expose it to the ruthless fangs of the Paris press'.[87] Certainly the outcry which arose from all sections of the French press did mean that Poincaré came under intense pressure to reject the British proposals even before the conference got under way. The French Cabinet's reaction to the proposals was equally hostile, and there were rumours that Poincaré would simply refuse to discuss them.[88]

Although these rumours proved baseless, the French Premier's critique of the Bonar Law Plan was so devastating that prospects of a settlement were left in tatters.[89] According to Poincaré, the plan involved both an unacceptable reduction in French reparation claims and serious violations of the Treaty of Versailles.[90] It was, moreover, excessively favourable to the Germans whose obligations – with maximum discounts – might be reduced to as low a figure as 20bn marks. Germany had no external debt. Much of her internal debt had been wiped out by depreciation of the mark. Her industry was intact and her population growing. Under these circumstances, Poincaré claimed, the British programme was 'tantamount to a restoration in a very short time of German hegemony in Europe and in the world'. Nor did it contain any provision for the productive pledges deemed esential by France, and Poincaré was convinced that at the end of the proposed four-year moratorium Britain would show even more patience and even less desire to put pressure on Germany than was currently the case. As a result, the Allies would not be able to obtain a sou.[91]

There were other objections. Britain's insistence on a free hand to determine the reparation liabilities of Austria, Bulgaria and Hungary was viewed as a surreptitious attempt to promote British financial interests in central Europe. More generally, it was felt that the sacrifices being asked of France were disproportionately heavy. Thus Poincaré produced figures purporting to show that the plan would leave her with a total net indebtedness of 73bn gold marks, comprising 14bn owed to the United States and 59bn (after allowing for reparation receipts of 11bn) for pensions and reconstruction. Britain, by comparison, would face a debt to the Americans of 15.5bn (after deducting the sums to be transferred to her by France and Italy), plus a pension bill of 30bn – a total of 45.5bn, or only 62 per cent of the burden France was expected to bear. From the French point of view, therefore, what was on offer repesented a bad bargain. In return for remission of the war debt owed to Britain and valued at 11bn marks, she was expected to renounce 38bn of existing C series bonds and transfer to

Britain 2.5bn of the new first series bonds relating to the Belgian war debt. In addition, she would have to give up the 1bn marks (£53.5m) of gold deposited in London as security for wartime loans.[92]

This last issue was a particularly emotive one. Poincaré insisted that France had a legal right to recover the gold under article 2 of the 1916 Treaty of Calais and categorically rejected the British government's contention that this provision had been superseded by subsequent agreements.[93] His strong stand was partly dictated by concern that the already vulnerable franc would be further weakened if it was definitely accepted that the gold should cease to be included in the official French reserves. But it was also necessary to take heed of popular feeling on the question, reflected in a series of newspaper articles expressing outrage at Britain's attempted 'theft' of French gold and at the revelation – for the first time, as far as the general public was concerned – that the gold was no longer in London but had in fact been shipped to the United States during the war.

Not surprisingly, the British viewed matters differently. They denied that article 2 of the Treaty of Calais remained in force. Nor did they think it unreasonable that France (like Italy) should surrender the gold as a set-off for cancellation of her debts. Returning the gold would create difficulties for Britain, and since the end of the war the Treasury had consistently maintained that it was unthinkable. As Bonar Law explained to Poincaré:

> That gold does not exist. It was sent years and years ago, before the end of the war, to America to pay our joint debts. We have always regarded it simply as a diminution to that extent of the French debt. There is no gold. If we have to give it back to the French, we must buy it.[94]

Bonar Law dealt with Poincaré's other objections to the British scheme in an equally forthright manner, in the process challenging the figures which had been put forward as to the comparative financial sacrifices involved for Britain and France. He also raised objections of his own to the rival plan circulated by the French during the first session.[95] This plan was prefaced by the usual insistence that France could only consider reduction of the German debt if certain of the Allies (i.e. Britain) were prepared to accept a smaller share of reparations than their entitlement under the Spa agreement and if priority was accorded to reconstruction of the devastated regions. Subject to these conditions, it proposed that French and other European war debts should be liquidated by the transfer and subsequent cancellation of an equivalent amount of German C series bonds. Germany was to be allowed a moratorium of only two years at most, and even during that period was to continue making deliveries in kind and to meet the costs of the allied occupation forces. German finances were to be reorganised under the strict control of the Guarantee Committee, resident in Berlin and given greatly enlarged powers over expenditure and taxation. Various pledges were to be taken in order to enforce payments, and in the event of non-co-operation by the German government there would be automatic sanctions: military occupation of Bochum, Essen and other parts of the Ruhr Basin designated by Marshal Foch, together with the establishment of a customs barrier on the eastern frontier of all the occupied territories.

In the opinion of Bonar Law, these proposals were a recipe for disaster. He was dismissive of the suggestion regarding cancellation of the C series bonds, having already rejected it when it was first put forward officially at the London conference of 9–10 December. His most serious reservations, however, concerned what he regarded as the inadequate relief to be granted to Germany. Substantial reparation receipts could only be obtained, he argued, through the restoration of German credit. But that would not be possible if the Allies imposed on Germany during an excessively short moratorium obligations which could only aggravate her existing problems of inflation and a budget deficit.[96]

From a comparison of the French and British plans, as well as from the reactions which they elicited, it was immediately obvious to all concerned that there was little if any chance of a compromise. Yet Bonar Law at least was loath to see the conference fail. He therefore sought to keep it alive by indicating that the British proposals were not unalterable and that he might be willing to modify some of those which the French found unpalatable – including the idea of an independent tribunal to adjudicate on Germany's capacity to pay. Poincaré, on the other hand, seems to have decided at an early stage that there was nothing to be gained by dragging the discussions out when the differences which separated the two sides were irreconcilable. The sticking point was the French insistence that there could be no moratorium without pledges. If the British found this principle unacceptable, Poincaré stated bluntly at the third session on 4 January, then it was futile to prolong proceedings for another day.[97] Bonar Law reluctantly agreed and, following a short adjournment, a final exchange of views took place from which there emerged a communiqué combining expressions of mutual good will with a frank admission of fundamental policy differences between the British and French governments.[98]

The collapse of the Paris conference, which was to have such dire consequences, has been variously explained. In recent times, there has undoubtedly been a shift in emphasis, with historians tending to attach rather less importance than before to Poincaré's alleged stubbornness and implacable determination to crush Germany.[99] Attention has been focused instead on a perceived failure of political imagination on the part of British policymakers. According to this interpretation of events, Bonar Law and his colleagues were unpardonably slow to realise that Poincaré meant what he said about going into the Ruhr and that domestic pressures made it impossible for him to draw back unless he could show that he had secured in return a generous financial deal from London. As a result, they were for a long time disinclined to make the kind of concessions on reparations and war debts which might conceivably have brought a change in French policy. Even when they did belatedly grasp that Poincaré was not simply engaged in a game of bluff, their response was unequal to the occasion. Not only was the Bonar Law Plan unduly complicated and ineptly presented. It suffered from the more basic defect of offering too little to achieve its purpose. Sally Marks has argued that the proposals were such as no continental politician could have accepted and remained in office.[100] Artaud is no less critical, describing them as 'parsimonious'.[101] Following the line taken by Poincaré, she seeks to demonstrate that they were unfair to France. Britain, she calculates, stood to receive between 70 per cent and 80 per cent of the sums needed to pay her debts to the United States, whereas France would have obtained little more than half of the amount already spent on her devastated regions (16.3bn marks against 30bn marks) and nothing at all for future expenditure. Given French claims over the past year, Artaud concludes, it was inconceivable that the British scheme would be accepted.[102]

Such criticisms of the Bonar Law Plan and of the general policy that lay behind it have some force. At the same time, they fail to take sufficient account of the real difficulties facing the British government or of the serious effort made by Bonar Law himself to bring about a comprehensive settlement. Bonar Law was not unsympathetic to the French case. There was, though, a limit to the concessions he could make, one which was set by his own sense of fairness and by political realism. In the weeks before the Paris conference, he had repeatedly made it clear that Britain was prepared to relax the Balfour Note principle in order to facilitate an agreement. But he was equally emphatic that there could be no question of renouncing all British claims so long as America insisted on repayment. That would be unjust, he told the House of Commons on 14 December, and for Britain to meet her obligations to the United States without receiving anything from her European debtors 'would reduce the standard of living in this country for a generation, and would be a burden upon us, which no one who talks of it now has any conception of'.[103] Throughout the Paris conference itself, this was the line he continued to take. As he informed Poincaré, while willing to consider some minor adjustments in the plan which he had submitted, he was convinced that its essential features represented the furthest that Britain could go in making concessions, having regard to her financial difficulties and the attitude of the Americans:

> The net result of our proposal is that in the most favourable returns we will get less from Germany and our Allies than the amount of our debt which we have to pay to the United States. Greater generosity than that I should not think was possible.[104]

But even if Bonar Law personally had favoured a more magnanimous approach, it is extremely doubtful whether he could have carried public opinion with him. In this respect, it was significant that the negotiations in Paris took place just as the Chancellor of the Exchequer, Baldwin, arrived in Washington to begin some very hard bargaining about a debt settlement. With the Harding administration giving no indication whatever of a softening in its stance, circumstances could scarcely have been less favourable to the idea of quixotic gestures to the French and other debtors.

Finally, and most important, it is by no means certain that the chief reason for the failure of the Paris conference was French dissatisfaction over the net receipts which they would notionally obtain under the Bonar Law Plan. Certainly there were complaints on that score. As far as Poincaré was concerned, however, the key consideration was not what France would be entitled to in theory but the assurance that Germany would pay. It was on this point above all others that the British and French were unable to compromise. Poincaré believed that productive pledges were an absolute necessity. Bonar Law was unalterably opposed to them. As Poincaré himself pointed out, the difference was one of principle. The only way in which a breakdown could have been averted, therefore, was if the British government had been prepared to acquiesce in a policy which it believed to be profoundly misguided.

5

From the Occupation of the Ruhr to the Advent of the Second Baldwin Government, January 1923–November 1924

I

At the Paris conference the Bonar Law Plan was rejected by the French government as outrageous and insulting. In the light of subsequent developments, however, it began to seem rather less objectionable – not least because the sobering experience of the Franco-Belgian occupation of the Ruhr left France with much lower expectations regarding reparations and war debts. Following the replacement of Poincaré by the Radical-Socialist leader Edouard Herriot at the head of the *Cartel des Gauches* in May 1924, there was a marked shift in the official line and from that time onwards the French made increasingly desperate efforts to secure an assurance that the concessions which the plan had made on inter-allied debts remained on offer. Unfortunately for them, there had been a simultaneous change in British policy. For some months after the breakdown of the Paris conference British policymakers were undecided about whether to adhere to the proposals set out there, especially since the situation had been completely transformed by events in the Ruhr. The position was clarified during August 1923. On the 11th of that month Curzon sent a note dealing with reparations and the Ruhr crisis to the French and Belgian governments. This contained a separate section on inter-allied debts in which the central features of the Bonar Law Plan were again put forward as the basis for a comprehensive settlement. As in the previous January, the response from Poincaré was completely negative. After this second rebuff, the British stance became unequivocal: the proposals originally advanced by Bonar Law had not been accepted and had therefore lapsed.

The adoption of this uncompromising posture was symptomatic of a more general hardening of official attitudes towards Britain's debtors, and towards the French in particular, during 1923 and the early part of 1924. This was a consequence of various factors. It was natural that there should be a hostile reaction to the outright rejection at the Paris conference of terms which the British regarded as generous in the extreme. There was mounting impatience at the failure of the French to tackle their chronic financial problems by increasing taxation towards the British level. The fact that France began to lend abroad while claiming to be unable to pay interest on her war debts was a source of considerable irritation. Many, including Bradbury, were also angered by what they saw as the French government's refusal to treat its obligations to Britain with a proper degree of seriousness. There were, however, two factors above all others which contributed to a stiffening in the British approach: negotiation of the Anglo-American debt settlement in early 1923, and the impact of French policy in the Ruhr.

II

On 4 January 1923, the day on which the Paris conference collapsed, a British debt funding mission arrived in the United States, headed by the Chancellor of the Exchequer, Baldwin: the other members of the team were Norman and Geddes.[1] As has been seen, the WDC had been authorised to fund only on the basis of an interest rate of at least 4.25 per cent and a maximum repayment period of 25 years – conditions which would mean annual payments equivalent to £61m. In the period before the British negotiators set off, however, the American ambassador in London, Harvey, had encouraged Bonar Law and others to believe that there was a real prospect of settling for as little as £25m per annum, with interest set at 2 per cent and sinking fund at 0.5 per cent. Baldwin's instructions, therefore, were to negotiate a settlement which was within these limits.[2]

It soon became apparent that the hints conveyed by Harvey had been thoroughly misleading. On 12 January the chairman of the WDC, Mellon, proposed an agreement based on 3.5 per cent interest plus 0.5 per cent sinking fund over a period of 61 years – a proposal entailing annual payments of some $187m (£39m). When informed by London that this was completely unacceptable, Balwin countered on 14 January with an undertaking to recommend to the Cabinet 3 per cent interest and 0.5 per cent sinking fund over 50 years, i.e. $140m (£30m) annually. The most that the Americans would concede, however, was 3 per cent instead of 3.5 per cent for the first ten years and a reduction in back interest from 5 per cent to 4.5 per cent. By this stage, Baldwin and his fellow delegates were convinced that it was vital to settle on the basis of this latest offer. An agreement, they believed, would pave the way for American participation in the economic restoration of Europe and perhaps, ultimately, in a conference on reparations and war debts. Not to reach agreement, on the other hand, would be damaging to British prestige. Nor did they think that there was any chance of obtaining better terms in the future: there seemed a real danger, indeed, that delay would only result in more onerous demands from the Americans, especially if the issue became entangled in party politics in the forthcoming presidential elections in November.[3]

Such arguments failed to move Bonar Law. He believed that the rate of interest being demanded was 'intolerably unjust' and his opinion was reinforced by talks with the former Chancellor of the Exchequer Reginald McKenna, who advised rejection of the American terms.[4] At a Cabinet meeting of 15 January, attended by only six ministers, Law's view was endorsed. Baldwin was accordingly instructed to return to London for consultation.[5]

When the matter was discussed by the full Cabinet on 31 January, Bonar Law spoke passionately against accepting what he termed an unjust bargain. Britain, he insisted, was no more obliged to pay the United States than France was to pay Britain. If nothing was obtained from the French and Germans, the effect of paying would be to impose a heavy burden on the British people for the next 63 years: there would be no possibilty of a cut in taxation and the cost of living would be 80 per cent above the prewar level. He obtained little support, with only Novar (the Secretary of State for Scotland) giving him strong backing. Most ministers shared his resentment at the Americans' commercial approach to the question. At the same time, the predominant feeling was that Baldwin was right when he argued that the economic and political case for acceptance was overwhelming: repudiation was not to be contemplated. After threatening resignation, Bonar Law finally bowed to the will of the majority and on the following day the Cabinet agreed that the Treasury should draft a note of acceptance.[6] There then followed several months of negotiation over the details of the settlement, with the result that it was not until 18 June 1923 that it was formally signed.[7]

Under the agreement, Britain was to pay $161m (around £33m) per annum for the first ten years and an average of $185m (£38m) per annum thereafter. According to Stephen Schuker, these were 'relatively generous terms'.[8] Since Britain could afford to pay her obligations in full, he suggests, America's willingness to accept lower interest rates and thereby renounce 30 per cent of the amount due represented a substantial concession. Such a judgement is at least open to question. It is obviously true that interest rates of 3 per cent and then 3.5 per cent were an improvement on the 5 per cent charged for the demand obligations and even on the 4.25 per cent fixed as the minimum by Congress – both of which reflected current market conditions in the United States. It might be argued, therefore, that Britain was being required to pay less than was warranted by strictly commercial considerations. But this is to beg the question of whether it was appropriate to apply such a narrow criterion to the treatment of wartime credit arrangements between allies. If one judges the Anglo-American debt settlement not by comparison with a standard commercial transaction of the time but with other inter-allied debt agreements, then its terms do not appear as generous as Schuker claims. The funding agreements which the United States subsequently negotiated with other debtors were far more lenient, with France being asked to repay 47 per cent of the nominal value of her debt and Italy only 26 per cent, compared to 82 per cent in the case of Britain.[9] So, too, were the terms offered by Britain to her own debtors: neither in the Bonar Law Plan nor in any of the various settlements which were actually concluded was the remission less than 60 per cent. Granted that the terms agreed with America were within the British capacity to pay, the financial sacrifices involved were nevertheless severe, with payments each year being the equivalent of 8d in the pound income tax. To give some idea of the size of the burden being assumed, Keynes – a fierce opponent of the settlement – calculated at the time that the sum to be paid each year was the equivalent to two-thirds of the annual cost of the British navy, nearly equal to state expenditure on education and greater than the total burden of the pre-war national debt. He further calculated that the amount to be transferred to the United States over the next 61 years would be sufficient over the same period to 'abolish slums and re-house in comfort the half of our population which is now inadequately sheltered'.[10]

There can be no doubting the intensity of Bonar Law's feelings on the question. He contemplated resignation. He took the unusual step of writing an article in *The Times* under the pseudonym of 'A Colonial 'to urge rejection of the terms;[11] and even though he reluctantly acquiesced, he remained (in the words of Tom Jones) 'very sore about it' for some time afterwards.[12] As Chancellor of the Exchequer during the war, Bonar Law had been directly concerned with British borrowing from America and had unsuccessfully put to the United States Treasury proposals designed to remove the need for any further credits. He therefore had particular reason to feel aggrieved about the matter. But there were many others who shared his basic conviction that the debt had been incurred in a common cause, that the Americans were driving a hard bargain and that the Britsh taxpayer was being saddled with an unfair burden. The majority of his Cabinet colleagues favoured acceptance of the terms recommended by Baldwin not because they regarded them as just and reasonable, but because the alternative courses of action seemed even more unpalatable.[13]

One result of the American debt settlement was that it now became possible to put a figure – an estimated present value of 14.2bn gold marks (£710m) – on the sum that would have to be collected from Germany and allied debtors combined to cover Britain's payments to the United States. Another was that its perceived severity strengthened British determination to secure an equivalent amount from their own debtors. This attitude was further reinforced by exasperation at developments in the Ruhr.

In the months leading up to the Franco–Belgian occupation of the Ruhr in January 1923,[14] both the Lloyd George and Bonar Law governments had repeatedly made it clear that they were absolutely opposed to the adoption of such a coercive measure, and had warned Poincaré that it could not succeed in its declared aim and was bound to have damaging effects not only on Germany but on the economy of Europe as a whole. In British eyes at least, their warnings had been amply vindicated by subsequent events. The operation failed to yield reparation receipts on the scale Poincaré had predicted: on the contrary, as he himself was eventually obliged to admit in public, the amount obtained by force in 1923 was actually smaller than in the previous year. At the same time, it had disastrous consequences. The Cuno government's response to the entry of French and Belgian troops was to initiate a policy of passive resistance. Poincaré retaliated by stepping up efforts to directly exploit the Ruhr's resources, and the upshot was massive dislocation of Germany's most productive industrial region, headlong depreciation of the mark and an escalating political crisis which threatened to plunge the whole country into chaos. Nor were British interests unaffected. During its early stages, the occupation, by disrupting German production, provided a stimulus to some sectors of British industry, including coal and steel. The longer term effects, however, were mostly adverse.[15]

In London, the major responsibilty for all these disturbing developments was laid squarely at the door of the French. When the occupation began, the British government, while dissociating itself from what it considered to be a breach of the Treaty of Versailles, sought to remain on the friendliest possible terms with France – not least because of the continuing need for her co-operation over Turkey. As the situation in the Ruhr deteriorated, however, so too did the state of Anglo-French relations. Although it was felt that Berlin was not blameless for the stalemate that had developed, Poincaré's obduracy was seen as the main obstacle to a sensible compromise. Throughout the crisis he insisted that, whatever else happened, France must obtain from Germany, net of her debt repayments, 26bn gold marks – the sum which was said to be necessary for restoration of the devastated regions and which also happened to correspond to the French 52 per cent share of the 1921 Schedule A and B series bonds. Such a demand made it impossible to devise a reparation settlement which took into account both the interests of other allied creditors and of Germany's capacity to pay. Poincaré was also thought to be unhelpful in other ways. He consistently refused to begin talks with the German government until it had unconditionally abandoned its policy of passive resistance. He twice dismissed German proposals on reparations without consulting Britain, without giving them the mature consideration which the British felt that they merited and without inviting a further offer. In addition, he delayed and obstructed British efforts to have the question of how much Germany could pay referred to an independent body.

III

It was against this background of turmoil in the Ruhr and strong disapproval of French policy there that British policymakers pondered the issue of inter-allied debts. The most basic question requiring a decision was whether the time had come to ask the debtor countries to open negotiations on funding arrangements or at the very least start paying interest in cash on the amounts owed by them. The matter was taken up by the Treasury in the spring of 1923, partly because of the attention it was receiving in the House of Commons and partly because of a feeling – as Niemeyer expressed it – that France and the others were 'laughing at us'.[16] An added sense of urgency was given to the debate by the imminent prospect of having to pay the United States the equivalent of some £33m a year.

To request payment of interest in cash was the simplest and in some respects most appealing option. Since the end of the war interest on the original loans had been steadily accumulating, with the cost of servicing the debts being borne in the meantime by the British taxpayer. By January 1923 France alone owed £88m in back interest, and by March the figure had risen to £145m. At that time the net amount due to Britain from all the Allies (excluding Russia) was £1,123m. The annual yield from that, at 3 per cent, would be just over £33m – enough to offset British payments to the United States.[17] But would the allied debtors be willing or able to pay?

So far as France was concerned, Treasury officials were in little doubt that she possessed the means to meet her interest charges of some £16m a year, despite protestations to the contrary by the French government. Certainly indications were not lacking that money was readily available for other purposes. In January 1923 the French Finance Minister, de Lasteyrie, stated in the Chamber that France had repaid foreign creditors 10bn francs, the equivalent of £114m, over the past four years.[18] This claim provoked an indignant reaction at the Treasury, where it was felt to be 'adding insult to injury to boast of payments on this scale while refusing to make a beginning with paying any interest on France's debt to us'.[19] Reports of projected French government loans to Poland and various other countries produced similar complaints. As one Treasury oficial wrote in March 1923: 'Thus France owes us £541m. and is paying not a penny interest; yet she can lend Poland £5,500,000. Moreover, she can incur heavy military expenditure which in turn drives us into increased expenditure.'[20]

But the capacity of France and the other debtors was not the only factor needing to be taken into account. Also to be considered were the political implications of asking for interest to be paid in cash. This aspect of the matter had weighed heavily when the possibility of making such a demand first received serious attention in early 1922; and though the governments concerned had been formally notified that Britain reserved the right to request cash payments for interest falling due on or after 1 October of that year, this notification had not been followed up by any practical steps to obtain the money – largely for political reasons. When the question was further examined by the Treasury in early 1923, political considerations again figured prominently in their deliberations.[21]

In a paper prepared in March 1923, Frederick Phillips, while pointing out the obvious desirability of receiving payments, also warned of some likely difficulties in trying to secure them. In the first place, it would cause friction. France

and Belgium were currently engaged in a desperate struggle to extract reparations from Germany and would therefore regard it as a most unfair time to
approach them for cash. Secondly, there was the risk of losing a valuable means
of persuading France to moderate her policy on reparations and the Ruhr occupation. The mere threat of asking for debt interest to be paid provided the British
government with a powerful weapon for exerting pressure. But once the French
had flatly refused a direct request, as Phillips was certain they would, that weapon
would be rendered useless. For these reasons, Phillips was opposed to a policy of
demanding immediate cash payments. It would be better, he argued, to invite
Britain's debtors to make proposals for funding arrangements.[22]

Niemeyer indicated broad agreement with this conclusion in a note of 13
March for the Chancellor of the Exchequer.[23] It is clear, though, that he found
the arguments finely balanced. He could see that there was a strong case for not
taking any action yet over the debts. Having been bitterly critical of American
debt policy, he was anxious that Britain should not appear in the garb of a
Shylock. Nor was he convinced that there was anything to be gained by 'adding
to the impossible demands now lying so thick on the international carpet'. Like
Phillips, he was also concerned that France and Italy wuld simply refuse a request
to pay and thereby destroy the value of the debts as a lever. A few months ago,
Niemeyer told Baldwin, he would have found these arguments overwhelming.
Now he was less sure. The lever was becoming so rusty from lack of use that it
would 'soon cease to move anyone', and the debtors openly regarded their obligations as written off. Even if a funding agreement were concluded with them,
there would still be the bait of cancellation as a means of exercising influence.
Finally, there was the worry that if the British government held back the
Americans would get in first and that any forbearance by Britain would merely
facilitate payments to the United States. On the whole, Niemeyer thought that
there was a great deal to be said for informing the European debtors that the time
had come to place their debts on a permanent footing. 'Whatever is done about
cash (and I think they ought to pay something), there ought surely to be a scheme
of future payments instead of a mere hand to mouth renewal as at present.'[24]

While there was growing support for the adoption of such a policy, however,
it was recognised that the war debts owed to Britain could not be dealt with in
isolation from the overall problem of inter-allied indebtednes and reparations. It
was further recognised that it would be extremely difficult to come up with
proposals for a general settlement of these questions which would be acceptable
to all the interested parties. The task had proved beyond those at the Paris conference and had become more formidable still because of the occupation of the Ruhr.
As a result of the financial and economic damage which this had inflicted on
Germany, the Cuno government was unwilling to accept a total reparation
liability of more than 30bn gold marks. Although this was well below the figure
of 50bn posited in the Bonar Law Plan, the British government nevertheless
regarded it as excessive, given the disastrous deterioration that had taken place

in Germany's fortunes in the interim. Yet France demanded almost the whole of this amount (26bn) as her own share, Belgium sought a minimum of 5bn, plus an additional priority beyond the one already accorded to her and Britain insisted that she was not prepared to accept less from Germany and allied debtors combined than the 14.2 billions needed to pay America. To reconcile such competing claims, within the constraints of Germany's capacity to pay, was simply not possible.

Bradbury acknowledged as much when he set about drafting yet another plan in the spring of 1923. The key factor, in his opinion, was the attitude of the French. At this stage, they had not yet woken up to the folly of the Ruhr adventure and would only do so when they began to understand its financial and economic consequences for themselves. The futility of the operation was likely to become apparent before Christmas. The effect of this would be to undermine French credit and precipitate a rapid fall in the franc. Until that happened, however, the outlook for a settlement would remain unpromising. What was needed was a 'complete change in French temper', but Bradbury doubted whether that could be hoped for until there had been 'a general debacle in Germany and a financial crash in France'.[25]

Despite holding these views, Bradbury still believed that efforts should be made to negotiate an agreement and in late April 1923 he submitted to the Chancellor some new proposals to that end.[26] These conformed closely to the Bonar Law Plan, with a number of modifications being introduced to take account of the reduction in Germany's capacity to pay reparations as a result of events in the Ruhr. As in the original scheme, Germany's maximum obligation was set at 50bn gold marks, about one-fifth of which would be allocated to meeting the costs of the Rhineland occupation and other expenses arising from implementation of the Versailles Treaty. The main difference was that a bigger proportion of the total figure was to be made up of contingent payments. Since the Spa percentages were to remain in force, Britain would obtain about 9bn marks: 5bn from unconditional obligations and a further 4bn from the others. This would not suffice to cover repayments to America, however, and Bradbury suggested that the shortfall should be made good by the transfer to Britain of 3bn and and 1.5bn of first series German bonds from France and Italy respectively. The remainder of the French and Italian debts – by now standing at £595m and £522m – were to be cancelled. According to Bradbury, the effect of these arrangements would be to reduce French indebtedness to Britain by around 80 per cent and Italian indebtedness by more than 86 per cent. At the same time, Britain would be left with a margin of nearly 2bn marks over the 14.2bn present value needed for payment to America – providing no part of the German conditional obligations were cancelled by the proposed Arbitration Tribunal.[27]

From the British standpoint, such an outcome would be reasonably satisfactory. As Bradbury himself realised, however, it would not suit France. This, in fact, was the most serious weakness in his scheme. Allowing for the 3bn German bonds to be surrendered to Britain, the French would receive at most 19.5bn marks – well below the 26bn repeatedly stated to be the irreducible minimum they were prepared to accept.[28] Admittedly, the new proposals did include a concession over the allied gold deposited in London during the war, a concession made possible by the boost to sterling provided by the funding of the British debt to America. At the Paris conference, the British had insisted that there could be no question of the gold ever being handed back. Bradbury now proposed that it should initially be retained by Britain as security for the ceded German bonds and then returned *pro rata* as these were redeemed.[29] This apart, though, there was little in the new scheme to appeal to France.

This was one of the main complaints about Bradbury's draft when it was circulated for comment. The other, predictably enough, was that it suffered from being far too complicated. After trying to make sense of it, Lampson minuted on 1 May:

> Sir J. Bradbury's schemes have the reputation of being entirely unintelligible to nine-tenths of mankind. The present 'modifications' to his original scheme are no exception to this rule. And I fancy that our representatives (with the possible exception of Lord d'Abernon) will be rather flabbergated when they find themselves invited to criticise so technical and intricate a plan.[30]

Lampson's forecast was accurate. Certainly the Marquess of Crewe, who had recently succeeded Hardinge as ambassador to France, was out of his depth. It seemed to Crewe that the hardest part of negotiating an agreement would be to obtain the acquiescence of the French government. Given its current mood and the great discrepancy between French demands on Germany and the reparation figures which all competent authorities considered feasible, he was doubtful whether any scheme which could be suggested would secure assent from France. Another French rejection of British proposals would threaten the Entente. If some were to be put forward, therefore, great care must be taken over their presentation. The Bonar Law Plan had been sprung upon the other delegations without adequate consultation: any future scheme should be discussed beforehand with French experts. The Bonar Law Plan had also failed to get the serious consideration which it deserved because it had been conceived and drafted in purely financial terms, and without regard for French *amour propre*. According to Crewe, French susceptibilities were at present so tender that no proposal which did not 'go far to satisfy their declared requirements, or at least to avoid humiliating them over withdrawal from recent pretensions', stood any chance of being accepted by them. Quite apart from this psychological aspect of the matter, it was also impossible to ignore the French government's desperate need for money: the gap between revenue and expenditure for the current year was 30bn francs.[31]

By implication at least, much of this analysis was highly critical of Bradbury's scheme. So too were the main conclusions that Crewe drew from it. It was essential, the ambassador argued, that any proposals which were advanced should be drawn up in a manner that made them easy to grasp and publicise. An offer must be made which would immediately appeal to French official and public opinion. One possibility was an assurance that France would obtain early substantial cash payments or large-scale deliveries in kind, especially of coke – even if conditions in Germany meant that this could only be done through raising loans in London or New York. Another was a more generous concession on the French gold than that envisaged by Bradbury. The issue had given rise to 'serious trouble' at the Paris conference and Crewe's own feeling was that it would be better to return the gold at once rather than hold on to it for a time.[32]

Foreign Office and Treasury reaction to these observations was scornful. Crowe minuted that he found it difficult to extract from them 'any practical suggestion or line of argument free from contradiction'. It was urged that France must be provided with large and immediate payments. Yet such payments were considered impossible by financial experts. Talk of floating reparation loans on the British and American markets seemed to show an equal lack of realism.[33] At the Treasury, officials were particularly scathing about Crewe's recommendation for dealing with the French gold. On 7 June, Niemeyer wrote to Lampson:

> The notion that in any circ[umstance]s we can return £53 millions in gold to France is wholly absurd and it is most undesirable that any such idea should be dallied with for a single moment either by the Paris embassy or those with whom they may be in touch. The proposal is absolutely impossible. Where do they imagine we are to get the £53 millions from?[34]

In the meantime, while these deliberations were taking place, Bradbury produced yet another paper, dated 1 June, on reparations and war debts.[35] On 20 May Bonar Law had been obliged to resign on grounds of ill health and the avowed purpose of Bradbury's latest offering was to brief the new Prime Minister, Baldwin, on the modifications needing to be made in British policy in the light of developments since the Paris conference. At that conference, Bonar Law had declared his willingnes to accept a general settlement which gave Britain a reasonable prospect of recovering from her debtors and Germany together enough to service the American debt. He had also indicated that the Allies might discharge their obligations by transferring an agreed proportion of reparation receipts. According to Bradbury, this particular offer could no longer be countenanced. It had been made on condition that Germany's total liability was set at a figure consistent with the restoration of her credit and that there must be no military intervention in her affairs. The latter, however, was 'now past praying for'. The Franco–Belgian occupation of the Ruhr had depreciated the value of the reparation asset and it was therefore no longer possible to justify taking German bonds in satisfaction of allied debts. Under existing circumstances, indeed, it seemed to Bradbury that the best course would be to deal with reparations completely separately from the question of inter-allied debts.

Bradbury remained convinced that a present value of 50bn gold marks was the maximum liability Germany should be asked to assume. With about 42bn of this being available for reparation proper, Britain's 22 per cent share would yield 9.25bn. That would leave some 5bn to be obtained from the alllied debtors in order to fulfil the Balfour Note principle. It was important to ensure, however, that this total was apportioned according to capacity to pay. Here Bradbury urged caution. The British government had criticised France for basing her claims on Germany on her own supposed financial needs. By fixing the som which it aimed to collect from Britain's debtors at the 14.2bn to be paid to the United States, it ran the danger of being exposed to precisely the same criticism. To avoid that, it must be made clear that British indebtednes to America could 'only be made the measure of the amounts we should exact in respect of inter-allied debts to the limits of what our debtors can pay'.

Bradbury's assessment of the capacity to pay of each of the individual debtors had ominous implications for the French. They alone were judged to have the resources to make substantial payments, especially if they managed to secure an appreciable amount from Germany: 'So long as France has a favourable trade balance as at present, and is in a position to make foreign loans to countries like Poland and Roumania for political purposes, any plea of incapacity is heavily discounted beforehand.' Bradbury believed that even if the French received no reparations at all, in the longer term at least they should still be able to pay 'a substantial part if not the whole' of their debt to Britain – provided they did not ruin themselves by excessive military expenditure or foreign adventures. Immediate payments, on the other hand, might present problems. Until her current budgetary imbalance was rectified, it would be difficult for France to make any large payments in sterling without disturbing the exchanges. Whether the budget was balanced by allowing the franc to depreciate or by 'a real fiscal effort comparable to that made by Great Britain' was for the French people themselves to decide. Bradbury was disposed to give them five years to sort out their difficulties, during which time, as an interim arrangement, interest would be paid in francs at the rate of 25.22 to the pound: the balance of interest due would be written off. In order to protect the franc exchange, each interest payment received might be reinvested in France unless and until it could be remitted without depressing the franc below its current level. In effect, this would be to place the debt on the same footing as France's internal war debt, and so long as the French government paid interest on that it could not 'with any pretence of decency claim to treat less favourably the debt which the British Government incurred to [sic] its nationals on behalf of France'. At the end of the five-year period, a funding scheme should be negotiated which took into account both the amount to be paid by Britain to the United States and the French capacity to pay.[36]

Bradbury was not in favour of putting these ideas to the French. The first step, he urged, was to invite them to make proposals of their own, while pointing out that the debt was currently in the form of three-month Treasury bills, payable in cash at maturity. The opportunity could also be taken to scotch suggestions being made in various quarters in France that inter-allied debts should be settled by the surrender of C series bonds. Such bonds were 'entirely worthless' and the French government should be informed that any proposal along those lines would be completely unacceptable to Britain.[37]

IV

Bradbury's schemes were ingenious but premature. Until the crisis in the Ruhr had been resolved, there could be no progress towards a general agreement on reparations and war debts. The British government's first priority, therefore, was to break the deadlock between France and Germany. During the first few months of the occupation, it had pursued a policy of holding aloof from the struggle taking place, unwilling to give backing either to French action that it considered illegal or to German passive resistance. The longer the occupation continued, however, the harder it became to sustain such a position. There was mounting pressure from the Labour and Liberal Oppositon as well as some sections of the Conservative party for the adoption of a more active policy. Moreover, the government itself became increasingly alarmed at the deteriorating situation in Germany, as the depreciation of the mark began to accelerate from June and separatist agitation flared up in the Rhineland. At the beginning of August Lord d'Abernon, the British ambassador to Berlin, warned: 'If things are allowed to drift, they can only drift into anarchy, Communism and disruption.'[38]

Left to themselves, it seemed, the French and Germans would never find a basis for compromise. Poincaré refused to negotiate with the German government until it had abandoned its policy of passive resistance, while the Germans, for their part, were equally insistent that such a move could not be considered without some counter-concessions over evacuation of the Ruhr. Speaking in the House of Lords on 20 April 1923, Curzon sought to provide a way out of this impasse by advising Berlin to make an offer on reparations.[39] In the course of his speech, he referred to the possibility of an examination of Germany's capacity to pay by an independent body – an idea mooted by the American Secretary of State, Hughes, in his New Haven address of the previous December, and one which had great appeal for the British government as the approach most likely to a produce a sensible figure.

The Germans responded to this prompting with a note of 2 May proposing total payments of 30bn gold marks.[40] In order to meet objections from several members of the Cuno cabinet, this offer was hedged with restrictions which rendered it less attractive to the creditor powers. There were no specific guarantees of payment, merely a statement that these could be determined by discussion with the Reparation Commission. It was emphasised that passive resistance would continue until the Ruhr and other newly occupied areas had been evacuated and restored to normal conditions. In addition, the whole proposal was made conditional upon stabilisation of the mark and German equality in international commerce.

The reply from France was swift and predictable: in a joint French and Belgian note of 6 May the proposals were scornfully rejected. To the British government and to Curzon personally, this came as a severe disappointment.[41] The British, like the rest of the Allies, regarded the German offer as inadequate.[42] According to the Treasury, indeed, the only part of it which was of any value at all was the indication that Germany was prepared to submit the whole reparation problem to an international tribunal. Despite its undoubted shortcomings, however, the German note was seen as a positive reaction to Curzon's appeal of 20 April and as such deserving of more serious consideration than the French and Belgians had given it. By acting without even consulting their Allies, Curzon complained to Crewe, the French had 'taken it upon themselves to slam the door which I had tried to open'.[43]

In an effort to ensure that the door did not remain shut, the British joined with the Italians – with whom they were co-operating closely at this stage – in asking the Cuno government to reconsider and expand its proposals.[44] The upshot was another German note, transmitted on 7 June. While omitting any figure for reparations, this set out specific guarantees of payment and placed greater emphasis upon the idea of an independent assessment of Germany's reparation liability.[45] The French government was no more enamoured of these new proposals than it had been of the earlier ones. Poincaré expressed dissatisfaction with their failure to promise cessation of passive resistance or to fix a definite sum for reparations. He also objected to the idea of referring Germany's capacity to pay to an international commission, arguing that the only body legally competent to give a verdict on the matter was the Reparation Commission.[46] In London, the German proposals created a more favourable impression. The official view there was that they marked 'a serious advance' and ought to be followed up.[47] This basic difference of opinion led to weeks of wrangling, culminating in a public exchange of strongly worded notes in August 1923.

V

The period following receipt of the second German note saw a marked hardening of French attitudes. This was partly a consequence of hostility to the note itself. But it also derived from a growing assurance on the part of Poincaré that his policy in the Ruhr was at last beginning to achieve results. In late May he was able to announce to the Chamber that recent deliveries of coke and coal had been running at a satisfactory level, and the Chamber responded with a resounding vote of confidence.[48] With Poincaré's position thus strengthened, the British government's chances of persuading France to join the rest of the Allies in sending a moderate and encouraging reply to the German proposals were considerably diminshed.

The French government saw no need for any reply to be sent. As was made clear in an aide-memoire which Saint-Aulaire left at the Foreign Office on 11 June, it continued to rule out any discussions with Germany until passive resistance had been abandoned. Once that had been done, negotiations might begin. But the sort of settlement that the French envisaged was not one that was likely to secure British approval. Under no circumstances, it was insisted, would France sacrifice any portion of her 52 per cent share of the A and B series bonds: 26bn gold marks, plus whatever was needed to repay the United States and Great Britain, remained an irreducible minimum. Reviving the proposal put forward by Poincaré at the Paris conference, it was further stated that the French and other allied debts might be repaid by surrendering C series bonds.[49] Curzon held out no hope whatever of an agreement being reached on such a basis. If France's share of the A and B series bonds was not to be reduced, he told Saint-Aulaire, it followed that any revision of Germany's liability would be at the expense of the other creditors and of Britain in particular. As for the suggestion that France should liquidate her obligations with C series bonds, that had already been emphatically rejected by the British government.[50]

After further equally fruitless exchanges of a similar character, on 6 July Curzon informed the French ambassador that the British government was unwilling to tolerate 'an indefinite prolongation of the present situation, which was driving towards a disaster that would overwhelm us all'.[51] It was therefore going to prepare a draft answer to the German note of 7 June. This would be circulated to the Allies in the hope that it might be adopted as a collective response. If it failed to obtain their agreement, however, the British government would probably send it on its own behalf. The draft of a reply was accordingly despatched to the Allies on 20 July, together with a covering note stressing the necessity of prompt action in view of deteriorating conditions in Germany. It recommended abandonment of passive resistance, progressive evacuation of the Ruhr, the appointment of a body of impartial experts to advise both on Germany's capacity to pay and on guarantees of payment and the commencement of inter-allied discussions 'for the purpose of elaborating a comprehensive plan of a general and final financial settlement'.[52] The absence of any specific mention of war debts aroused French and Italian suspicions. The omission was partly because of an assumption on the British side that reference to a general financial settlement would be understood by all to include that subject as well as reparations. But there was an additional explanation. Curzon was hopeful of persuading the Americans to participate in the proposed independent investigation of Germany's capacity to pay and anxious that their co-operation should not be jeopardised by drawing attention to an issue on which they were notoriously sensitive.[53]

The French and Belgian replies, both of which were presented at the Foreign Office on 30 July, dashed any lingering hopes that it might be possible to adopt a common allied position towards Germany. Curzon described the French response as a rebuff.[54] But the one from Belgium was regarded as scarcely less disappointing. The Belgians offered no comments at all on the draft submitted to them. All they said on the matter was that an agreement might be reached on the text of a common reply to Germany – but only if the proposals and conditions set out in their note were favourably received. If there was any reduction in Germany's total liability, it was stated, Belgium and France were to be given priority because of their devastated regions. In addition, the Spa percentages must be altered in their favour. The French reply was more discouraging still, repeating the familiar refrain that there could be no talks with Germany until passive resistance had ceased, that France was not prepared to relinquish any part of her entitlement to A and B series bonds and that there could be no question of evacuation of the Ruhr until Germany had discharged in full all her obligations.[55]

In view of the uncompromising nature of these replies, the Cabinet now abandoned the idea of sending an answer to Germany, and on 2 August it was announced in Parliament that the government intended to publish the correspondence on reparations that had recently taken place between the Allies, together with a final British note designed to make known to the world the extent of the problem and the need for urgent action to deal with it.[56] A draft of this note, prepared by Curzon and Crowe, was submitted to the Cabinet on 9 August and received general approval. Some ministers were worried that it was too abrasive, however, and as a sop to them Baldwin agreed to examine it with Curzon and soften those parts of it which might give offence to the French.[57]

The note that was finally addressed by Curzon to France and Belgium on 11 August was said to be offered in a 'friendly spirit', but there was in fact little evidence of such cordiality in either its content or its tone.[58] The Foreign Secretary was clearly angered not only by the way in which the two countries had stultified his efforts to expedite talks with Germany, but also by what he saw as their greed and selfishness. These feelings were now given free rein. Having expressed acute disappointment at the French and Belgian governments' replies to his note of 20 July, Curzon then proceeded to a devastating critique of their position on reparations. The occupation of the Ruhr was castigated as both illegal and disastrous in its consequences, the Reparation Commission as 'an instrument of Franco-Belgian policy alone'. Even if France and Belgium succeeded in their stated aim of breaking German resistance, it was argued, Germany's ability to pay would remain paralysed by the continued occupation of her most productive industrial region. French and Belgian claims were dismissed as unrealistic and unfair to Britain. Modification of the Spa percentages, as they proposed, would mean further sacrifices for the British taxpayer, already more heavily burdened than his French and Belgian counterparts. Priority for the devastated areas was equally unaceptable, resting as it did on an artificial distinction between different types of enemy damage: lost ships and cargoes were just as much material damage as the ruined villages of France and Belgium. Moreover, Britain had suffered in other ways, having been obliged to liquidate foreign securities worth £700–£800m, in the allied cause, during the war. Belgium's position was privileged enough. Her war debts (£300m) had been written off and she had already received a disproportionate share of reparation receipts – 1.5bn gold marks (£75m). Yet she now demanded, in addition, the full 5.2bn marks to which she was entitled by her 8 per cent share of the 1921 Schedule. France, for her part, was seeking to obtain a net amount greater than she would get if the London Schedule and inter-allied debt agreements were to remain in force. According to the *rapporteur* of the French budget, Bokanowski, the capital value of the Schedule was 65bn gold marks. On that basis, France's share would be 34 bn. Since she owed Britain and the United States the equivalent of 12bn and 15bn gold marks respectively, that would leave her with only 7bn – less than a third of her current demand of 26bn.

In a separate section on inter-allied debts, the note expressed the view that it was hopeless to try to deal with them until a better estimate could be made of the sums likely to be obtained from Germany. The first step, therefore, must be to determine the most she could reasonably be expected to pay by means of an impartial enquiry. When that had been done, the British government would be prepared to write down the allied debts owing to it to a sum representing the difference between Britain's share of Germany's revised obligation and the 14.2bn gold marks to be paid to the United States: the liability of each of the debtors would be determined in accordance with its capacity to pay.

Another important feature of the note was that it repeated the offer contained in the Bonar Law Plan to consider accepting payment of allied debts by means of German reparation bonds. This was the last time such an offer was made, and even on this occasion it was pointed out that the idea was not as attractive as it had originally been since the deterioration in Germany's financial prospects – resulting from the 'unwise' policies pursued by France and Belgium – had made reparation receipts a less secure asset. Finally, it was stressed that Britain's willingness to cancel a portion of outstanding debts did not signify any waiving of her rights as a creditor – rights which were governed by the terms of the various wartime loan agreements. It could not be admitted that repayment should be dependent on recoveries from Germany, or that French Treasury bills given to the British government were somehow less binding than those given to a private investor. The bills were accepted subject to renewal for a limited period only, on the clear understanding that as soon as French credit was sufficiently reestablished they would be redeemed by loans raised on the London market. By renewing the bills beyond the agreed deadline, the British government had tacitly recognised that the time had not yet come to put this intention into effect. But the recent practice of simply adding interest to capital could not continue indefinitely and payment of at least part of the interest must be made as soon as the sterling-franc exchanges became reasonably stable.[59]

The note showed Curzon at his worst: pompous, sanctimonious and insensitive. Poncaré's reply was equally characteristic in its asperity and bluntness. The British embassy in Paris provided advance warning that it was likely to be acrimonious. On 13 August 1923 Phipps reported that the Quai d'Orsay had issued a briefing note for the French press – probably inspired by Poincaré himself – which contained a stinging attack on British reparation and war debt policy. The Balfour Note principle was singled out for special criticism, the familiar argument being advanced that it was fundamentally unfair that the less France received in reparations the more she would have to pay Britain.[60] Phipps' report produced an angry reaction in London, particularly from the Treasury which dismissed the French asertion as a perversion of the facts. What rankled most was that a voluntary British concession was being treated as a ground for complaint by the French. Under the London Schedule, Britain was entitled to £1.55bn from Germany. In addition, she was owed £1.2bn by her allied debtors (excluding Russia). By limiting her total claim to £710m (14.2bn gold marks), therefore, she had cancelled some £500m of the allied debts. These debts had then been further written down by the full amount of Britain's share of the reparations actually paid by Germany. 'It is this last concession', the Treasury argued, 'which Great Britain was never under any obligation to make, and which operates solely to the advantage of her Allies, which is now actually represented as a grievance to France'.[61]

Poincaré's official reply of 20 August, followed a week later by one from Belgium, only added to the irritation felt by British policymakers. It vigorously defended the occupation of the Ruhr and denied that there was any need or justification for an impartial investigation of Germany's capacity to pay. It also insisted that war debts could only be paid after Germany had fully discharged her obligations and that France would not accept less than 26bn gold marks over and above what was required for payments to Britain and the United States. In a similar vein, the Belgian note refused to recede from earlier demands for modification of the Spa percentages plus an assured minimum of 5bn gold marks for Belgium on top of the reparations she had already received.[62]

VI

By this stage, the Baldwin government's efforts to bring the Ruhr crisis to an end had manifestly failed. Its attempt to organise a joint allied response to the German note of 7 June had foundered on the rock of French and Belgian resistance, and there was little more that could be done so long as France and

Germany continued to cling to their irreconcilable stances on passive resistance. Powerless to break the deadlock and thus pave the way to a general financial settlement, the British began to devote more attention to the protection of their own interests. There were already clear indications of this trend in the Curzon Note of 11 August, with its strong emphasis on Britain's rights as a creditor. In the following months, it became more pronounced. One historian has written of the Treasury at this time 'moving swiftly towards the view that France should pay the war debt to the uttermost farthing'.[63] This is an exaggeration, since nobody in official circles, whether at the Treasury or elsewhere, imagined that the French ever would or could pay more than a portion of what they owed. Even so, there was undoubtedly a harder edge to British policy. This was not without an element of calculation – the constant reminder that Britain was entitled to demand repayment in full serving as a none-too-subtle threat of what might lie in store for the French if they continued to hinder progress towards a comprehensive agreement.

Bradbury, for one, felt that it was important to make clear to the French government that Britain's rights as a creditor remained intact. This was one of the main messages that he sought to hammer home in a paper which he wrote for the Prime Minister in early Sepember 1923.[64] At that time Baldwin was on one of his customary summer breaks in Aix-les-Bains. Arrangements were currently being made for him to meet Poincaré in Paris on his return journey, and Bradbury wanted him to use the opportunity to clarify current British policy on reparations and inter-allied debts. Bradbury himself was firmly convinced that there was no possibility of reaching any agreement with the Poincaré government which would not be 'disastrous both to British interests and the peace of Europe'. Certainly there could be no agreement along the lines suggested in the French and Belgian notes of 20 and 27 August, both of which envisaged the imposition on Germany of a minimum liability of 50bn gold marks – apart from other peace treaty charges – plus provision for further contingent payments. Such figures were excessive and unless Poincaré was prepared to modify them, or at least agree to an impartial examination of Germany's capacity, he should be told that the British government 'must reluctantly take such steps as we may find necessary to protect our own interests'. This would mean insisting both on Britain's agreed share of reparations and on repayment by allied debtors to the full extent of their capacity. Any discussion of debts must be preceded by a frank recognition by the debtors of existing contracts – contracts which could only be altered with the consent of the creditor. Nor would it be possible to adhere to the proposals set out in the Bonar Law Plan. Those had been based on a total German obligation of at least 31.5bn gold marks. Because of the deterioration in Germany's position since January 1923, however, Bradbury did not think it was now safe to rely on an irreducible minimum of even 30bn marks; and it followed that Britain's 22 per cent share of reparations could not be regarded as worth more than 6.6bn gold marks at most for the purpose of calculating what offer might be made on allied debts. Bradbury acknowledged that the current instability of the franc exchange, together with uncertainty over the value of reparations, made it difficult for the time being to come to a comprehensive agreement. He saw no reason, however, why France should not begin to pay some interest on her debts as soon as the franc became reasonably stable – especially since the French balance of payments position was 'eminently favourable'.[65]

What Bradbury's arguments amounted to was the suggestion that Poincaré should be presented with an ultimatum. His advice went unheeded. The possibility that the course which he advocated might have a damaging effect on Anglo-French relations was not something that caused Bradbury much concern. Baldwin, on the other hand, was determined to do everything within his power to preserve the Entente. He felt considerable sympathy for France and since becoming Prime Minister had gone out of his way – notably in his important policy statement to the Commons on 12 July – to gain French trust.[66] As far as he was concerned, this was to be the main purpose of his talk with Poincaré On 14 September he wrote to Curzon explaining the approach he intended to adopt:

My chief desire in seeing this singularly difficult President of Council is to get into his head that our Government speaks the truth and can be trusted, and that the P.M. and the F.O. speak with one voice. I am convinced that profound distrust of Lloyd George was the primary cause of the lessened confidence between Paris and London . . . If I can make him believe the truth I propose to tell him of the various currents of feeling in England. An attempt to settle properly with Germany and to provide other sanctions in the military occupation will infallibly alienate English sentiment and this sentiment, once alienated, will be difficult to recapture . . . In short, my object is to work for the Entente and for a prompt settlement by every means that may occur to me.[67]

In the event, Balwin's conversation with Poincaré, held at the British embassy on 19 September, went as he intended. It was conducted in very general terms, with Baldwin making no attempt to follow the line advised by Bradbury. His comments were chiefly designed to dispel mistrust and explain the mood in Britain: to tell Poincaré of the widespread feeling there that France appeared to take little account of British willingness to make substantial concessions over allied debts, and to convince him of the depth of disapproval within the Labour and Liberal parties, and to some extent within the Conservative party, of French policy in the Ruhr.[68] The nature of the discussion was reflected in the vague and anodyne communiqué issued at its conclusion which declared that 'on no question was there any difference of purpose or divergence of principle which could impair the co-operation of Britain and France'.[69]

The Baldwin-Poincaré meeting had no immediate practical effect, except the unfortunate one of arousing German fears that Britain had surrendered her opposition to the occupation of the Ruhr in order to save the Entente. Whether it had any longer-term influence in opening the road to a settlement is hard to assess. Other developments were taking place, however, which did offer some hope. One of the most significant of these was Germany's capitulation over passive resistance. After the fall of the Cuno government on 13 August, the new Chancellor, Gustav Stresemann, the leader of the German People's Party, had lost little time in seeking to reach an informal understanding with the French on its cessation. His initial overtures were rebuffed. He remained reluctant to surrender without obtaining a *quid pro quo*, but was left with no alternative: Poincaré refused to negotiate, and the financial situation in Germany was deteriorating to the point where Hilferding, the Minister of Finance, advised that resistance could no longer be sustained. On 26 September, therefore, Stresemann officially announced its abandonment.[70]

The British government's satisfaction at this step – which it had been urging on the Germans for several months – proved short-lived. Poincaré now insisted that it was not enough for Berlin to withdraw the ordinances which had been issued ordering resistance. Talks could not begin until reparation deliveries were resumed. To Baldwin, this escalation of French demands came as a bitter disappointment. He felt, indeed, that Poincaré had deliberately misled him during their recent talks in Paris. 'Poincaré has lied', he told Tom Jones on 22 October. 'I was led to believe that when passive resistance ceased he'd negotiate with the Germans.'[71] Curzon, too, was angry, and this was reflected in the extraordinary attack which he launched on alleged French disloyalty over the past few years in a speech to the Imperial Conference on 5 October.[72] As advised by Crowe, Curzon used his speech to try to force Poincaré into the open about his intentions by stating that Britain was awaiting proposals from the French government.[73] This was badly received in France where it was seen as an imperious summons to produce a plan.[74]

While the Imperial Conference was still taking place, the prospects of a settlement of the reparation problem were greatly improved as a result of intervention by the Americans. On 9 October 1923 Calvin Coolidge, who had become President in early August following the death of Harding, announced publicly that he was 'in accord with the proposal advanced by Secretary Hughes' for an investigation by experts of Germany's capacity to pay.[75] The British government, which had for some time been considering ways of getting the United States involved, grasped eagerly at the opportunity thus presented. On 12 October Curzon sent a despatch to Washington saying that it was intended to seek the co-operation of Britain's European Allies in inviting the American government to assist in the proposed enquiry in whatever way it thought appropriate. After receiving an encouraging response, he then approached the French, Belgian and Italian governments on 19 October.[76]

As anticipated, it was the French who created the most serious difficulties. On 26 October Poincaré indicated that France was willing to participate in a study of Germany capacity. The method of proceeding for which he expressed a preference, however, was not the one favoured by either the British or the Americans. In replying to Curzon's despatch of 12 October, Hughes had set out two ways of approaching the problem. One was to call an economic conference, in which the United States and the recipients of reparations would participate, for the purpose of considering Germany's capacity to pay and drawing up a plan to secure payment. The other was for the Reparation Commission to appoint an advisory body to make recommendations, with a competent American citizen taking part in an unofficial capacity. The British government left the French in no doubt that it had a strong preference for the first alternative, since it would involve the direct participation of the American government and would there-fore probably be more fruitful. Yet despite this, Poincaré successfully insisted on the other option, arguing that to take the matter out of the hands of the Reparation Commission would constitute an infringement of the Treaty of Versailles.[77] From the British standpoint, this setback was irritating enough. Far more more serious, however, was the disagreement which subsequently arose over the terms of reference of the proposed expert enquiry. Poincaré claimed that no committee appointed by the Reparation Commission could have the power to recommend a reduction in Germany's liability. When the Americans dismissed this contention as absurd, he then sought to limit the investigation to Germany's *present*, as opposed to her long-term, capacity to pay – a stipulation which would have rendered the exercise pointless, given the current state of German finances. He also insisted that the question of the occupation of the Ruhr must be excluded from the committee's remit. In view of these conditions and of continuing disagreement amongst the European Allies about the scope of the expert enquiry, on 9 November 1923 Hughes issued a statement indicating that the United States government did not believe it would be worthwhile initiating such an enquiry under current circumstances.[78]

VII

While the French were causing a delay over the appointment of an expert committee, and largely because of that, the Foreign Office raised with the Treasury the possibility of exerting some form of financial pressure on France in order to induce her 'to adopt an attitude more in harmony with the interests and sentiments of Great Britain'.[79] This was not the first time that the use of such a tactic to influence French reparation policy had been considered. A few months earlier, in May 1923, there had been some discussion about trying to overcome French resistance to an impartial investigation of Germany's capacity to pay by restricting their borrowing on the London money market. When Norman was consulted, however, he had advised that such a scheme was unlilkely to be effec-tive since France gave no indication of needing to borrow abroad. The idea was therefore abandoned.[80] In November, conditions were more favourable for the successful application of financial pressure because of the sharp fall taking place in the international value of the franc as a result of the continuing crisis in the Ruhr.

On 14 November 1923 the Foreign Office sent a note to the Treasury seeking information on the kinds of pressure that might be applied to France. The Treasury were asked about the advantages and disadvantages of using war debts as a lever, with particular reference being made to non-renewal of French Treasury bills as they matured. They were also asked about the possible withholding of the credits or other forms of financial assistance on which French companies or public bodies were able to rely in the London market.[81]

As might be expected, Bradbury's opinion was canvassed. He had already been turning the question over in his mind for some time and he now came up with a number of options, of varying degrees of severity. One of these was that the £53.5m of French gold deposited in London during the war should be used to pay the interest on maturing French Treasury bills, with the process continuing until the gold was completely exhausted. Another suggestion was that legislation might be passed prohibiting the raising of loans in Britain by the French and other debtor governments – except with the express approval of the Treasury and on condition that part of the proceeds must be applied to the payment of outstanding debts. A third possibility was the enactment of a law empowering the Treasury to impose a levy on imports from all debtor countries, along the lines of the 1921 Reparation Recovery Act. Any of these methods, Bradbury believed, could serve as a practicable way of putting pressure on France. What he did not like, however, was the idea of placing British holdings of French Treasury bills on the market. Such an operation, he argued, would have to begin on a small scale and with the bills being sold at ludicrously low prices. It would 'have the appearance of a mere pin-pricking transaction, without serious financial utility'. In addition, there was the risk that France would be provoked into a flat repudiation of her debts.[82]

Bradbury felt that, if it were decided to exert financial pressure on France, it would be worthwhile holding informal talks with the Americans about a possible co-operative effort. The Treasury agreed. Some of his other suggestions, however, were received with a certain amount of scepticism. It was objected that passing a law to prevent loans to France without Treasury sanction would place on the department an onus that 'we would sooner be without'.[83] There would be a clamour in the City. Nor was it certain that the necessary parliamentary assent could be obtained. This last problem applied equally to the proposed 'Reparations Recovery Act' against France which, in any case, might have adverse effects on Britain herself.[84]

Despite such reservations, the Treasury were reasonably confident, as they told the Foreign Office, that effective pressure could be brought to bear on France.[85] According to the Treasury, the only thing likely to cause the French to adopt a more reasonable policy – apart from a growing feeling of isolation and concern at the disapproval of world opinion – was 'a fall in the franc sufficiently serious to shake the confidence of the French peasant in his national securities'. Fear of that happening would make the French government 'very susceptible to pressure', and the Treasury were convinced that Britain was in a position to produce such fear. A number of sanctions were available. The French gold held in London could be used to meet interest payments on the unfunded debt. It had already been made clear that this gold would not be returned 'until all French debts are paid (ie never)'. But its public application to pay off interest would oblige France to take £53.5m out of her official reserves – a move that would damage her credit. The sale in the market of some of the British holdings of French Treasury bills – inevitably at a very low price – would have a similar effect on the standing of French credit in most parts of the world. Most humiliating of all, French bills held by the Treasury might be exchanged for German bonds, with the result that Germany could then meet her reparation obligations by tendering those bills. (Here the Treasury were echoing a proposal first made by Norman in late 1921). In the opinion of the Treasury, it might not be necessary to actually implement all or any of these measures to produce the desired result: the threat alone would probably suffice. The Treasury's general conclusion was that the existence of short-term French debts could be made a 'very potent lever' for persuading France to agree to a reasonable reparation settlement, provided the government were prepared to act resolutely: 'It would be esential that the French Government should believe that Great Britain really meant business.'[86]

It was not until 4 January 1924 that the Treasury communicated these views to the Foreign Office – almost two months after receiving the latter's original enquiry. There can be no doubt that this delay was intentional. As requested, Treasury officials quickly prepared a memorandum with the relevant information. They refused to be rushed into sending it, however, despite constant Foreign Office pressure for a prompt reply. On 3 December Niemeyer fobbed Crowe off by telling him that he did not think he should let the paper be transmitted as an official Treasury document until it had been seen by the Chancellor of the Exchequer, whom he was supposedly unable to get hold of at that time.[87] The excuse was a thin one and certainly not sufficient justification for a further four-week delay.

Some historians have found the Treasury's procrastination inexplicable. Thus Schuker writes: 'They [Treasury officials] rather relished the idea of using the available financial levers to break French recalcitrance. Unaccountably, however, they did not present a concrete set of recommendations for seven weeks, by which time it was too late for the lame-duck Conservative government to take action.'[88] Yet the reason why the Treasury acted in a dilatory manner is not far to seek. When Baldwin came out in favour of protective tariffs in a speech at Plymouth on 25 October, he triggered off feverish speculation about an imminent general election. This lasted until Parliament was dissolved on 16 November. Even after polling had taken place on 6 December, the situation remained unclear. Although the Conservatives had suffered a setback, they were still the largest single party in the Commons, and it was not until 22 January that James Ramsay MacDonald took office as head of the first Labour government. Throughout November and December, therefore, the period when the Treasury were considering how financial pressure might be exercised on France, the domestic political climate was one of great confusion. In theory, permanent officials at the Treasury should not have been influenced by this uncertainty. But there is evidence that they – or at least some of them – were. Thus Phillips minuted on 23 November: 'It is to be hoped that no decision will be reached until the whole thing has been maturely considered, which could scarcely be till after the election.'[89]

Whatever the Treasury's motives, their tardiness in supplying the information requested of them meant that by the time this came to be discussed at the Foreign Office in January the question of whether financial pressure should be exerted on the French had lost much of its urgency. Initial Foreign Office interest in the matter in mid-November had been prompted mainly by a desire to find some way of breaking French resistance to an impartial examination of Germany's capacity to pay. By January 1924 that was no longer a problem: a committee of experts, under the chairmanship of an American, Charles Dawes, had already been appointed and was about to begin its work in Paris. Even so, the debate which took place within the Foreign Office after receipt of the Treasury's memorandum was not merely academic. Financial pressure, it was felt, might still come in useful if France proved obstructive over implementaton of the experts' recommendations. It was also seen – as it had been from the outset – as a means of obtaining some relief for the British taxpayer by compelling the French to fund their debts or at least pay some interest on them.

Foreign Office reactions to the Treasury's conclusions were varied. Lampson (now the Head of the Central Department), was almost exultant at the revelation that Britain apparently possessed 'a weapon of overwhelming power'.[90] Nor could he see any reason why it should not be used. It was outrageous, he minuted on 8 January 1924, that the British taxpayer should be paying £30m a year (the equivalent of 6d in the £ income tax) to service French war debts, 'whilst meanwhile the French Government proceed gaily on their way giving credits to their friends of the Little Entente for the purpose of strengthening her [sic] military dominance of Europe'.[91] Writing on the same day, Curzon, who was similarly angered by reports of French lending abroad, expressed regret that it was now too late for him to put the suggested financial sanctions into effect – a state of affairs for which he laid the blame squarely on the Treasury:

> It seems to me a great pity that the Treasury have taken nearly two months to reply to our enquiry and have thereby prevented the present Government from taking any action in the sense indicated . . . Had we received it before I should have brought the matter before the Cabinet and invited them to consider measures for

our relief from an altogether intolerable situation, brought about by the purely selfish and exclusive policy of France. I hope that the position may be considered at an early date by our successors.[92]

Crowe struck a more cautious note, saying that he could see 'no practicable object' in giving the Treasury memorandum any wider circulation or in bringing it to the attention of the incoming government.[93]

Within days of taking office on 22 January, MacDonald, who had assumed the post of Foreign Secretary as well as that of Prime Minister, sought the advice of Foreign Office officials on a number of issues arising out of the memorandum. He wanted to know, in particular, whether it would be wise to approach the Americans about possible co-operation, whether financial pressure would stir up hostile feeling in France and strengthen support for Poincaré's current policy, and whether it would be more likely to help or hinder acceptance of the expert committee's recommendations.[94] By this time, Lampson's earlier enthusiasm for adopting the measures suggested by the Treasury had cooled. He now urged that nothing should be done until after the experts had reported. Reminding France of her debt would not only lessen the chances of her accepting their findings, but would also give a boost to Poincaré's waning popularity. 'Rather let him have more rope; and his obstinacy, left alone, will do the rest.'[95] Crowe reached a similar conclusion, and MacDonald found his and Lampson's arguments convincing. It was therefore decided that the matter should be allowed to lie dormant until after the Dawes committee had completed its work.[96]

IX

The appointment of the Dawes committee followed intensive negotiations between Bradbury and other members of the Reparation Commission, including the unofficial American observer, James A. Logan, during the second half of November 1923. It will be recalled that the idea of an independent examination of Germany's capacity to pay had suffered a serious setback when the Coolidge government announced on 9 November that it saw no point in participating in such an inquiry because of differences amongst the Allies about its scope. After several weeks of discussions, however, the Reparation Commission came up with a proposal which resolved those differences. Whereas the French wanted an investigation which concentrated on the export of German capital abroad, the British took the view that such a limited exercise would be futile. What was needed, they insisted, was to look at the whole question of how German credit might be reestablished. Bradbury sought to bridge the gap between these conflicting viewpoints by suggesting the estabishment of two committees, one to carry out a study into Germany's foreign assets and the other having much broader terms of reference. As far as Bradbury was concerned, the former was mere 'eye-wash': it would serve no useful purpose except to help in securing French approval. In the event, Bradbury's stratagem worked. Poincaré acquiesced and on 30 November the Reparation Commission unanimously resolved to appoint two committees of experts. The last remaining hurdle was cleared on 11 December when the United States government declared that it viewed 'with favour' the participation of American private citizens in its deliberations.[97]

As Bradbury anticipated, it was the committee with the wider terms of reference, the one chaired by Dawes, which produced the most important practical results. Its task was to consider the necessary measures to balance the German budget and stabilise the mark – a formula which was sufficiently elastic to permit a thoroughgoing examination of all aspects of the reparation problem. The committee began its labours in the middle of January 1924 and on 9 April produced a report that was to form the basis of a settlement which lasted for five years.[98] The plan which was included in this report – the Dawes Plan – called for an initial payment of 1bn gold marks for the year 1924–5. Annual payments were then to increase gradually until they reached a standard figure of 2.5bn in 1928–9. Thereafter, they might be revised upwards again according to a complicated index of prosperity.[99] The British members of the committee, Sir Robert Kindersley and Sir Josiah Stamp, had pressed for a standard annuity of no more than 2bn, but their views had not prevailed. A novel feature of the Dawes Plan was that it aimed to relieve Germany of responsibility for making payments across the exchanges. The German government was to pay the requisite sums in gold marks into a newly created Bank of Issue. Having done that, it would have fully discharged its obligations. The conversion of the marks into appropriate foreign currencies would then be carried out by a Transfer Committee, presided over by a new official, the Agent-General for Reparation Payments. This committee would also determine how much Germany could prudently transfer to the Allies without risking exchange difficulties. In order to get the plan off to a good start, it was proposed that Germany should be aided by an international loan of 800m gold marks.

During the early phases of the Dawes committee's deliberations, Poincaré was unusually accommodating. This was the more surprising in view of the deep hostility he had initially shown towards the very idea of such an expert inquiry. His relatively co-operative attitude during this period was the result in part of French financial weakness. After a steady decline during 1923, the franc began a disastrous slump in January 1924, adversely affected by continuing uncertainty over the occupation of the Ruhr and by the government's mounting difficulties – exemplified by the failure of the Eighth *Crédit National* bond issue – in raising short-term loans to cover its budget deficit. The special financial programme that was introduced in panicky response to this crisis provided only a short respite, and in March there was a further alarming fall in the franc's value. A $100m credit organised by J. P. Morgan early in that month exercised a stabilising influence on France's financial position, but it remained precarious.[100] No political strings, such as a prior commitment to accept the experts' recommendatons, were attached to the credit. In a real sense, however, the French were on probation, since the credit was subject to renewal after three months and was unlikely to be extended unless they adopted a reparation policy which American and British bankers considered sound.[101] Poincaré himself was doubtless aware of this. Certainly influential senior officials like Jacques Seydoux and Emmanuel Peretti de la Rocca, the Political Director at the Quai d'Orsay, were at this time urging the importance of reaching an understanding with Britain because of French dependence on Anglo-American financial assistance.[102]

There were other factors at work. Even Poincaré was not wholly impervious to the chorus of international criticism directed at French policy in the Ruhr. By the beginning of 1924, moreover, there were unmistakable signs that that policy was not achieving either its financial or political objectives. The Rhineland separatist movement (which the French had encouraged) had completely collapsed, and Poincaré was obliged to admit in March 1924 that reparation receipts since the start of the occupation had been disappointingly low.[103] It is true that the so-called MICUM agreements, the first of which had been concluded on 23 November 1923, appeared to represent a considerable success for the French government.[104] It has been plausibly suggested, however, that the effect of this, paradoxically, was to induce in Poincaré a more relaxed attitude on the question of reparations.[105] Finally, there were indications that the French Left was intending to fight the next elections on a platform of blaming the recent fall of the franc on the failure of Poincaré's Rhineland policy.[106]

Whatever the reasons, Poincaré initially showed little inclination to hamper the Dawes committee's progress. From mid-March, however, London was given clear warning of some of the controversial issues that he was likely to raise over implementation of the experts' report. A speech which he made to the Senate on 13 March contained strong hints that military evacuation of the Ruhr would be a protracted business and that direct Franco-Belgian exploitation of its resources would only cease if the British government promised to assist in applying sanctions in the event of a German default – a condition which Crowe described as 'impossible'.[107] These indications of his intentions were amply confirmed by the contents of a message delivered to the Foreign Office by Saint-Aulaire on 24 March.[108]

Faced with the likelihood of a serious disagreement over such matters, the British were understandably anxious to retain the option of using French indebtedness as a lever in future negotiations. As Niemeyer pointed out, shortly after the Dawes committee had released its report, the debts were Britain's 'only weapon if the Allies seek to disturb the settlement unduly'.[109] For that reason alone (but also for others which will be discussed later), the British government was determined not to get drawn into talks about inter-allied debts until after the Dawes Plan had been put into effect. This was in direct opposition to the approach favoured by the French, who were equally determined that the two questions should be dealt with together. In this way, it was calculated, France would be in the strongest possible position to insist on a reduction in her obligations in return for accepting the experts' recommendations. Poincaré would need to obtain some such concession in order to save face over abandonment of his Ruhr policy, and it was no less important to his sucessor, Herriot, to be able to demonstrate that he had not agreed to an abatement of French reparation claims without gaining substantial compensation in other areas.

Since Poincaré – in common with other French leaders – had consistently asserted that there must be a linkage between the amount France received from Germany and that which she paid to her creditors, it is scarcely surprising that he should have pressed for negotiations over the Dawes Plan and those over war debts to take place simultaneously. Rather more surprising perhaps is that he also wanted to bring in the question of security. This was contrary to the line that he had taken the previous summer. When presenting his government's note of 7 June 1923 setting out its proposals for a reparation settlement, the German ambassador to London, Friedrich Sthamer, had informed Curzon that Germany was in addition prepared to 'offer any guarantees for the security of France and Belgium that might fairly be sought, consistently with their being reciprocal in character and not infringing the sovereignty of the Reich'.[110] Although doubtful about the advisability or usefulness of raising such a matter in connection with reparations, Curzon had sounded Poincaré out about the German offer – only to be told in a 'curt manner, amounting almost to a snub' that

> the French Government did not regard the question of the Ruhr as in any way bound up with that of security. They had not raised, and they did not now desire to raise that question. Their occupation of the Ruhr was designed for economic purposes solely, and had no relation to the question of security for France, which was dealt with and defined by the clauses of the [Versailles] treaty relating to that problem.[111]

By the spring of 1924, however, Poincaré's attitude had changed and in March Saint-Aulaire was instructed to tell MacDonald that, in the French view, reparations and security were interrelated.[112] As for Poincaré's successor, Herriot, he was insistent almost to the point of desperation on the need for France to obtain some concession over security before a settlement was reached on reparations.

X

From the British standpoint, the French government's wish to have security and inter-allied debts discussed at the same time as implementation of the Dawes Plan was thoroughly unwelcome, since it opened up the prospect of protracted bargaining. Despite Foreign Office and Treasury reservations about various aspects of the experts' scheme, on 10 April the Cabinet decided to accept it in its entirety, providing other interested parties did likewise,[113] and from that time onwards London aimed at putting it into practice as soon as possible. The inclusion of other important matters in the negotiations, however, would inevitably increase the risk of delay. As an example of the sort of complications that might arise, it was felt that if Britain agreed to discuss debts with France then it would be impossible to refuse to engage in similar talks with Italy. The Italians had been pressing for an Anglo-Italian debt agreement for more than a year. In May 1923, following conversations between Treasury officials and an Italian financial expert, Alberto Pirelli, an informal understanding had been reached on the possible terms of such an agreement.[114] Subsequent Italian requests that this should be formalised had been turned down. The Italian government remained eager to conclude a definitive settlement, however, and on a number of occasions during May and June 1924 indicated that it was prepared to align its reparation policy with Britain's in return for generous treatment over debts. MacDonald, who had no wish to get involved in what he termed 'pettyfogging bargains', sought the Treasury's views on the matter in mid-July and was duly informed that they had strong objections to any discussion of debts at that stage, even if it was confined to experts.[115]

Throughout the period between publication of the Dawes Plan and the summoning of the London conference on reparations in July 1924, the Treasury consistently argued that it would be a great mistake to take up the question of inter-allied debts until the Dawes committee's recommendations had been put into force and were seen to be working smoothly. Apart from a desire not to get bogged down in unnecessary complications, Treasury thinking on this point was strongly influenced by concern about the suspicion and hostility that any talk concerning debt negotiations was bound to arouse in the United States.[116] The fact that a substantial portion of the projected international loan for Germany would need to be raised in New York was viewed as reason enough to avoid antagonising American opinion. Moreover, the Treasury had not yet completely given up hope of some future revision of the onerous Anglo-American debt settlement. This might come about, it was thought, through a general conference on war debts involving the Americans. In the opinion of the Treasury, however, the time was not ripe for such a conference. In the meantime, the American presidential elections were due to be held in the coming November and it was therefore important to refrain from any public comment on the United States' attitude to inter-allied indebtedness until those were safely out of the way. As a further argument for postponing negotiations with Britain's debtors, the Treasury maintained that the debts – in their current unfunded state – were 'a by no means negligible weapon' to ensure that the Dawes Plan was 'given a fair chance in the opening months' and that its control mechanisms were being exercised in a satisfactory spirit. On balance, therefore, the Treasury felt that it would be better not to discuss debts before December 1924 at the earliest. In order to make this more palatable to the debtors, it was suggested that they should be told that Britain would not demand any cash payments on account of interest until a settlement was concluded or until April 1925 – whichever came sooner.[117]

Like the Treasury – and for similar reasons – MacDonald also wanted war debts to be dealt with later than, and separately from, reparations. Yet that was not the impression that he initially conveyed to the French. Whilst in Opposition, the Labour leader had been bitterly and openly crtical of French reparation policy. On more than one occasion, moreover, he had characterised France as a militaristic and imperialist power which was seeking to establish a neo-Napoleonic hegemony in Europe. Not surprisingly, therefore, by the time he took office in January 1924 he had acquired a reputation for being Francophobe. Realising the crucial importance of securing French co-operation, he immediately set out to win Poincaré's trust. On 26 January he sent him a cordial personal letter in which he declared that he wanted the Entente to be 'much more than a nominal thing'. In a second letter, dated 21 February, he expressed his willingness to examine reparations and debts together.[118] Poincaré took this to mean that the two matters would be settled at the same time.[119] It soon emerged, however, that this was not MacDonald's intention and that he was determined to see the Dawes Plan in operation before starting talks about debts. Having made this clear in the House of Commons on 14 May,[120] he refused to change his position throughout subsequent negotiations with Herriot.

Saint-Aulaire was from the outset deeply sceptical about MacDonald's protestations of goodwill towards France and soon concluded that his vague offer of co-operation over both inter-allied debts and security was nothing more than a drug to soothe French public opinion.[121] The ambassador's suspicions were not without justification. The tone of the early letters to Poincaré was more important than their substance and MacDonald was careful to avoid any firm commitments. Even in those letters, moreover, serious criticisms were levelled at various aspects of French policy and there was a direct complaint about France's failure to pay interest on her debts. Claiming to be merely describing 'popular sentiments' in Britain, but in reality voicing his own views, in his second letter Macdonald referred to widespread anxiety about France's apparent determination to ruin Germany and dominate the Continent without any consideration for reasonable British interests; about the large ground and air forces that were stationed in western as well as eastern France (hence posing a threat to British security); and about French involvement in the military organisation of Poland and the states of the Little Entente. Not only were many British people uneasy about such matters, MacDonald said, they also questioned

> why all these activities should be financed by the French Government, in disregard of the fact that the British taxpayer has to find upwards of 30,000,000 a year interest upon loans raised in America, and that our taxpayers have also to find large sums to pay interest on the debt of France to us, to which France herself has as yet

neither made nor propounded, so far as they can see, any sacrifices equivalent to their own.[122]

There were other early indications that, despite his wish to create a favourable impression on French opinion, MacDonald's line on the war debts owed by France would be at least as firm as that of his predecessors. Shortly after he took office, he was reported in the *Matin* as stating that he would insist on their repayment. This prompted the prominent Belgian socialist Vandervelde to comment that, if correctly reported, MacDonald's remarks were completely contrary to what he had said at international socialist conferences. MacDonald in turn responded with a statement issued through Reuters in which he made it clear that; in the absence of a general settlement, 'we could not go on paying our American debt and allow France, which was in better industrial condition than we were, to disregard its obligations to us . . . We have never agreed and we never will agree, to anything which victimises Great Britain in the interests of any other state.'[123] In a similarly forceful vein, MacDonald told the Belgian ambasador in April 1924 that France and Belgium seemed to have 'a mythical idea of England's capacity to pay other people's debts and . . . I thought it was about time for the Allies to feel a little more than they apparently did their financial obligatons to us'. Certainly there could be no question of the debts being written off.[124]

Although MacDonald also assured the Belgian ambassador that he would not be a 'hard-fisted businessman', in the event he was to show little inclination to make concessions over war debts. In particular, he proved immovable in his refusal to even discuss them until after a settlement had been reached on reparations. It is hard to imagine that he would have enjoyed the overwhelming success that he did in withstanding French pressure on this point if he had had to continue dealing with Poincaré. As it happened, his task was facilitated by the latter's fall from power. On 11 May 1924 the *Bloc National* was defeated in the French elections. Poincaré resigned two days later and was succeeded by Herriot at the head of a left-wing coalition government.

Over the next few months the new Prime Minister was to display a lamentable lack of negotiating skill. In his defence, it must be conceded that he was hampered by France's continuing financial dificulties which rendered him vulnerable to foreign pressure.[125] Almost immediately after the elections, the franc was hit by a heavy bout of speculation. Although it eventually rallied with the help of support operations by the Bank of France, its underlying weakness remained. With the Morgan credit due for a further renewal in mid-September, Herriot was well aware of the need to retain American and British confidence. This in itself limited his room for manoeuvre.[126] The problem was compounded, however, by his own shortcomings. It was not simply that he lacked experience of conducting negotiations: he also had little taste or aptitude for it, as became obvious from his encounters with MacDonald both at the meeting which they held at Chequers in late June and during the ensuing London conference on reparations.[127] Herriot did not possess the mental toughness and obstinacy which made Poincaré such a formidable negotiator. Nor did he ensure that he was adequately briefed.[128] Most British ministers and senior officials with whom he came into contact found him unimpressive – Hankey describing him as 'a poor creature . . . very deficient in political courage'[129] – and the verdict of historians has also been highly critical: the general view amongst them is that he was basically incompetent. Certainly he was no match for MacDonald, who proved to be extremely effective in achieving his objectives.

XI

The first discussions between MacDonald and Herriot took place at Chequers on 21–22 June 1924. The original invitation (of 9 May) had been to Poincaré. Following his electoral defeat, however, Herriot was invited instead. Herriot initially envisaged the meeting as an informal exchange of views between himself and MacDonald, without any experts taking part.[130] This was reflected in his inadequate preparation. Consultation with relevant senior officials was perfunctory and Herriot arrived for the talks – accompanied by his *chef de cabinet*, Gaston Bergery, and Peretti de la Rocca – with only a vague idea of his minimum requirements on the issues that he wished to be discussed. The contrast with his British counterpart could scarcely have been greater. MacDonald was fully briefed and throughout the discussions he and Crowe operated (in the words of one historian) as a 'brilliant team'.[131] As a result, the outcome was very much what the British wanted.

While the main topic on the agenda at Chequers was implementation of the Dawes Plan, Herriot was anxious that inter-allied debts and security should be explored as well, if only to be able to counter the damaging charge of right-wing opponents that he was failing to obtain any compensation for concessions made over reparations and evacuation of the Ruhr. Herriot was highly sensitive to such criticism and to the political danger of appearing weak in comparison with Poincaré. The hardening of French attitudes which resulted from dramatic gains for the German Nationalists in the Reichstag elections of early May only added to the pressure he was under not to return to Paris empty-handed.

In the event, Herriot's attempts to widen the scope of the Chequers conversations proved to be pathetically ineffectual, with MacDonald and Crowe having little difficulty in brushing them aside. The first session, on 21 June, was devoted entirely to consideration of the Dawes report and in particular to the possibility of sanctions in the event of a German default.[132] Towards the end of the second meeting on the following day, however, Herriot tentatively raised the question of war debts. When he returned to Paris, he said, Parliament would be sure to ask him what he had done on the matter. He therefore wanted to know the British government's intentions: whether it had made any fresh proposals since the

Curzon Note of 11 August 1923 and whether it was prepared to discuss inter-allied debts at the forthcoming reparations conference. It was vital, Herriot stressed, that parliamentary critics should not be able to reproach him with having done nothing on the subject of French debts. Could not MacDonald 'give a general indication in such a way that we could see eye to eye?'[133] In response to this plea, MacDonald indicated a strong preference for dealing with reparations and war debts separately:

> My own view has always been not to mix up the question of inter-Allied debts with that of the experts' report: as soon as these last questions [sic] have been settled, we can negotiate on the subject of debts. A new element has entered into the situation, that of our payments to the U.S., and we should very much like to arrive at a general settlement of the question of inter-Allied debts. What would you say to this proposal: the question of inter-Allied debts will not be discussed at the next conference; but it is only adjourned, and will be broached on the first occasion after the experts' report has been put into operation.[134]

The main drawback to this suggestion, Herriot claimed, was that it would leave him badly placed in relation to previous French governments, since they had received offers in principle whereas he had not. When MacDonald correctly pointed out that these past offers had been rejected as unfavourable to France, Peretti de la Rocca intervened to produce a copy of that section of the Curzon Note of 11 August which related to debts. MacDonald's rather lame reaction was to say that he had forgotten about it. Crowe was more decisive, however, stating that in the opinion of the Treasury all that was 'dead'. Still dissatisfied, Herriot then sought further clarification of the official British position and help in dealing with his domestic critics:

> I should like to know where we actually are. My predecessors are going to say that in their time the question of [reparation] credits and debts were treated together. A democratic government comes into power, and I shall be the first without any general idea on the question of debts. I do not ask for engagements, but to know what to think.

At this point Peretti de la Rocca reverted to the Curzon Note, claiming that the French government had hitherto believed it still held good. Even if it did, he said, France could not dream of making any payments until she had obtained from Germany a full standard annuity, and that would not be for at least five years. If, on the other hand, that particular offer was no longer available, the French government would need to reconsider its position and would like to receive some new proposals in writing. Bringing the discussion on debts to a close, MacDonald bemoaned the financial difficulties in which Britain found herself, having to pay more than £30m per annum to the United States while at the same time paying the interest due from her debtors. He also insisted that he had not known that the debts question was going to be raised. Because of that, he could not enter into any binding commitments for the time being but would have to consult the Treasury first to find out if they were ready to begin talks on the subject. The only concrete concession he was willing to make was that British and French financial experts might hold a preliminary meeting.[135]

Herriot did not press any further. Instead, he turned to the question of security, only to be thwarted once again. The particular security matter engaging Herriot's attention at this time was the fate of the Draft Treaty of Mutual Assistance – a measure which the Assembly of the League of Nations had approved in 1923.[136] Since the Draft Treaty was designed to outlaw 'aggressive war' and strengthen the League's sanctions machinery, it was naturally welcomed by the French. It had little appeal, however, for the British. The armed forces, the Committee of Imperial Defence and the Foreign Office all raised fundamental objections to what was seen as a massive extension of British military obligations, and the Dominion governments were no less hostile.[137] At Chequers, MacDonald warned Herriot frankly that there was little likelihood of the Draft Treaty being accepted by Britain. Nor did he hold out any hope – given the public mood – of a British guarantee of France against German aggression. While professing sympathy for French apprehensions and indicating his willingness to discuss security at some later date, he stressed once again that his immediate priority was implementation of the Dawes Plan, to the exclusion of other issues:

> This is what I think: we are going today to settle the Dawes Report; but in doing so we are only taking the first step in the conclusion of a long series of agreements. When we have got the Dawes Report out of the way, I am ready to go to Paris to pay you a visit and spend a couple of days talking to you on the question of debts and security and so on . . . Let us therefore settle first the question of the Dawes Report; then we will go on to that of Inter-Allied debts, then to the problem of security and we will try to remove from Europe the risks of war which threaten it . . . [138]

Although Herriot thanked MacDonald warmly for what he had said, the latter had in fact offered little of substance. Indeed, Herriot unwittingly acknowledged as much when he asserted that the most important result of the meeting was 'a sort of moral pact of continuous co-operation between us for the good of our two nations and in the general interests of the whole world'.[139] The French insistence that reparations, debts and security must be dealt with simultaneously had been tacitly abandoned. Moreover, Herriot had failed to obtain an assurance that the proposals set out in both the Bonar Law Plan and the Curzon Note of 11 August 1923 still held good. Having previously rejected those proposals out of hand, the French were by now beginning to show a definite interest in them. What they did not realise before the Chequers meeting was that the British, too, had shifted their ground, largely as a consequence of the occupation of the Ruhr and of the Dawes Plan. As early as 28 April 1924, in response to a Foreign Office request for clarification on the point, the Treasury had argued strongly that there was no longer any justification for the offer contained in the Bonar Law Plan and repeated in the Curzon Note that allied debtors might be allowed to discharge their obligations by surrendering to Britain a percentage of their claims on Germany. The advice from the Treasury was that it should be made clear to the French government at least, and possibly to the other governments concerned as well, that the proposal had lapsed and could not be revived. At the time, however, the government had not wanted to inform France of its change of policy, partly because there was no 'convenient peg to hang it on' and partly because it was reluctant to take the initiative in raising the debts question before the Dawes Plan had been put into effect.[140] As a result, it was not until several weeks later, when they themselves brought the matter up at Chequers, that the French were told officially that Britain was no longer prepared to accept German bonds in part payment of allied debts.

While the Chequers talks were taking place, a curious incident occurred in this connection. Although Crowe stated categorically that the debt offer contained in the Curzon Note was 'dead', for a time there was a certain amount of confusion about the matter even on the British side. When Herriot and Peretti de la Rocca asked if the offer still stood, the Treasury were consulted by telephone and the message which came back was that it did. It later transpired that whoever had taken the call at the Treasury – his identity was not known – had provided misleading information.[141] Not surprisingly, therefore, those officials who were actually dealing with the subject were anxious to set the record straight, and at the beginning of July a paper was sent to the Foreign Office explaining the Treasury's position in full.

As this indicated, the department continued to take the view that there were important elements in the Bonar Law Plan and the Curzon Note to which the British government was no longer committed. The principle that Britain would limit her claims on allied debtors and Germany combined to the amount required to repay the United States still remained in force. As far as the Treasury were concerned, however, that was not the case with the proposal that allied debts might be settled by means of reparation bonds. It was unreasonable, the Treasury argued, for the French and other debtors to expect to avail themselves of such an offer, since current circumstances were totally different from those which had obtained when it was first made in January 1923. The original purpose of the offer then had been to induce France not to occupy the Ruhr. It had failed. The ocupation had taken place and, as a result of the economic dislocation that it had caused, reparations were now worth less than they would otherwise have been. If the Bonar Law Plan had been adopted, the Treasury believed, there would have been a fair chance of restoring German credit, and because of that it had been possible at the time it was put forward to treat the proposed claims on Germany as an asset having some real and calculable value. In the opinion of the Treasury, the Dawes Plan offered no such prospect, for it indulged in 'higher hopes which must mean lower expectations'. The initial annuities that the experts recommended were too heavy and would imperil the financial recovery of Germany on which future payments depended. There appeared to be a real danger that the suggested index of prosperity, while yielding insignificant amounts, would engender prolonged bickering. In the absence of any precise limit to her obligations or any discounts for redemption, Germany would have little incentive to make capital payments. A further problem was that the projected transfer mechanism – a necessary safeguard – would impose restrictions on how much she actually paid. The Treasury worked on the assumption that it might prove impossible to obtain more than 1bn gold marks (£50m) per annum. That would mean a capital value for the whole liability of only 16bn gold marks (£800m), of which at least 6bn (£300m) would be spent on peace treaty charges. Britain's share of the balance would be 2.2bn gold marks (£110m) – an amount falling well below the capital value of the British debt settlement with the United States of 14.2bn (£710m). In the light of these calculations, the Treasury concluded, and if Britain was to avoid becoming the only country making a serious effort to pay her foreign debts, she could not afford to 'let the Allied debt go merely in exchange for German obligations under the Dawes Plan'.[142]

In essence, therefore, what the Treasury favoured was a return to the policy of the Balfour Note of 1922 and a retraction of the additional concessions offered to Britain's debtors in the Bonar Law Plan and Curzon Note. The Chancellor of the Exchequer, Philip Snowden, a harsh critic of French reparation policy and probably the most Francophobe of the senior figures within the Labour government, wanted to go further still. Snowden had serious doubts about the wisdom of voluntarily restricting Britain's total claims to the amount repayable to the United States. As a result, he was not prepared to commit himself to such a line until it had received further consideration.[143]

In the meantime, while the Treasury were busy clearing up any lingering ambiguity about their attitude towards the Bonar Law Plan and the Curzon Note, preparations were going ahead for the inter-allied conference on reparations which had been agreed upon at Chequers. The conference was to be held in London and the Foreign Office issued invitations for 16 July.[144] The contents of the invitation sent to France caused considerable embarrassment to Herriot. This was especially true of the section expounding the British view that the authority to decide whether Germany was in default should be vested in a body other than the Reparation Commission. There were strong protests in the French Chamber and widespread accusations, both from nationalist critics like Pertinax of the *Echo de Paris* and from members of Herriot's own party, that there had been an abject surrender to British dictation. Herriot's unconvincing attempts to defend himself in Parliament on 26–27 June failed to silence the clamour.[145] Nor did MacDonald help matters by twice going out of his way, on 23 and 26 June, to emphasise to the Commons that the topics of war debts and security were to be specifically excluded from the agenda of the forthcoming conference.[146]

Disturbed by Herriot's predicament, Phipps urged upon London the importance of 'some spectacular action' to strengthen his hand and convince French public opinion that he had succeeded where his 'sinister predecessor' had failed.[147] At the same time, Herriot himself addressed a personal appeal for assistance to MacDonald.[148] The upshot was that the latter set off for Paris, accompanied by Crowe, on 8 July. In the ensuing conversations, which took place on the 8 and 9 July, MacDonald stoutly resisted all Herriot's desperate efforts to engage him in detailed discussions on inter-allied debts and security.[149] Nevertheless, he was sufficiently concerned by the apparent precariousness of Herriot's hold on power to be willing to make some minor concessions in order to help him. Thus the joint Franco-British memorandum which emerged from the talks – laying down the agenda for the London conference and suggesting the main guidelines for an agreement – contained a number of items which were primarily designed to appease French opinion. It was declared, for example, that the Reparation Commission must not be weakened. There was also a paragraph on war debts stating:

> The two Governments have had a preliminary exchange of views on the question of inter-Allied debts. The British Government declare they will, in consultation with the Governments concerned, seek an equitable solution of this problem, due regard being had to all the factors involved. This question is therefore referred for preliminary examination to the experts of the Treasuries.[150]

To MacDonald, this statement was first and foremost a device for saving Herriot's face. It amounted to nothing more than a vague undertaking that the question of debts would be dealt with at some unspecified date. Certainly it involved no retreat from the position he had taken at Chequers, where he had insisted that the subject could not be considered until after the Dawes Plan had been implemented and was seen to be working satisfactorily. Herriot, for his part, attached much more importance to the formula and saw it as providing an opportunity to discuss debts in the immediate future. These conflicting perceptions of what had been agreed were a contributory factor in some of the differences which later arose at the London conference.

XII

The London conference began on 16 July and lasted until 16 August, with the Germans taking part in the proceedings from 5 August.[151] In his opening speech,

MacDonald urged fellow delegates to refrain from the 'fatal habit of connecting one question with another' and to proceed 'step by step, isolating each question as far as possible and solving it before moving on to the next'.[152] The message was clear enough: the sole business of the conference was to be implementation of the Dawes Plan, and decisions on all other matters must wait until that had been accomplished. Despite this warning shot across the bows, Herriot was not deterred from trying to raise the questions of war debts and security, regarding it as essential to his political survival to obtain some *quid pro quo* in these areas for the major concessions he was being called upon to make over reparations. Diplomatically isolated because of the Belgians' overriding desire for a quick settlement and subjected to intense pressure both from the British delegation and from British and American bankers, he was eventually obliged to consent to complete miltary evacuation of the Ruhr one year after signature of the London Agreement, instead of the two years that he had earlier said was the absolute minimum he could contemplate. In addition, he had to agree to a compromise over the Reparation Commission's power to declare a German default, reluctantly acquiescing in a formula – providing for reference to arbitration – which effectively precluded any future independent action by the French government. These concessions were deeply unpopular in France and, given the basic weakness of Herriot's political position, it is hardly surprising that he should have wanted to render them more palatable to domestic opinion by demonstrating that they had only been made in return for counter-concessions wrested from Britain.

Throughout the London conference, Herriot's evident political vulnerability was the subject of much anxious speculation by Phipps, who reported from Paris – almost on a daily basis – on the mounting problems facing him and the unfortunate consequences which were likely to follow if he were to be forced out of office. During the last week of July and the first week of August, Phipps provided a graphic account of unfavourable French reactions to developments in London. There was, he told the Foreign Office, universal indignation at the pretensions of American financiers and, in particular, at their insistence on firm guarantees against unilateral action by France. This was accompanied by anger at what the *Matin* denounced as 'intolerable English threats' and bitter disappointment at the British government's recent announcement that it would not be signing the Draft Treaty of Mutual Assistance. In the Senate, the *Union Républicaine* group was demanding that inter-allied debts and security must be dealt with in conjunction with reparations, and if Herriot failed to ensure that this happened he would run into heavy criticism when he returned to Paris. Under these circumstances, Phipps warned, it would be a great mistake not to make 'a supreme effort' to save Herriot or 'rather to save his face'. The real danger was not that the British government should get too little out of him, but rather too much, thereby precipitating his fall and 'some unreasonable action on the part of France brought about by what might well develop into a new wave of Anglophobia'. According to Phipps, if Herriot did indeed fall, the likelihood was that he would be succeeded by Briand, who would be much more of a 'prisoner' of the Right-Centre. Briand himself would probably not last very long and would soon be followed by others such as Barthou, Loucheur or Klotz. The disastrous final outcome of this steady drift to the right might be the return of Poincaré. It was possible, Phipps feared, that 'Poincaréism' was only 'in a state of suspended animation'.[153]

At the Foreign Ofice, there was some feeling that such dire predictions and warnings were overstated, even alarmist. Indeed, it was suspected by at least one official, John Sterndale Bennett (of the Central Department) that Phipps was inadvertently playing the French game by exaggerating the danger of Herriot's downfall. It was in the French interest, Sterndale Bennett minuted on 28 July, to use the possibility of that happening as a lever, and they would exploit it to the full. Sterndale Bennett took the view that the demise of the Herriot government was actually far less likely than Phipps appeared to believe. It would almost certainly entail the collapse of the Dawes Plan and a sharp fall in the value of the franc. Herriot's opponents would therefore think more than twice before throwing him out.[154]

MacDonald was likewise not wholly convinced that the situation in which Herriot was placed was quite so critical as British representatives in Paris or the French Premier himself were prone to suggest. By the time of the London conference, moreover, whatever sympathy he might have originally felt for Herriot's political difficulties had all but disappeared. Indeed, he was rapidly losing patience with having to hear about them: after all, as the head of a minority government heavily dependent on Liberal support, he was not without such problems of his own. 'I am tired of M. Herriot's parliamentary position', he minuted on 13 August.[155] In any case, if (as Phipps advised) the only way to assist Herriot in withstanding his critics was to allow him to return home with concessions on debts and security, then for MacDonald, for one, that was too high a price to pay.

At no stage during the London conference, therefore, was MacDonald willing to countenance discussions on either of these topics, and all French eforts to persuade him to change his mind met with a rebuff. On 28 July, when agreeing in principle to evacuate the Ruhr within two years, Herriot (together with Theunis) cautiously sought to link up military evacuation with a European debt settlement. As MacDonald reported to the Cabinet shortly afterwards, he immediately ruled this out, making it clear that he was not prepared to 'mix up these questions'.[156] A week later Etienne Clémentel, the French Minister of Finance, made a rather more determined attempt to broach the question of debts, although with no greater success. On 4 August he submitted a note setting out the French view that reparations and inter-allied debts were closely related and ought to be dealt with together: MacDonald himself had confirmed as much, it was stated, in his letter of 21 February 1924 to Poincaré. The Clémentel note claimed that the Allies had from the outset implicitly acknowledged that payment of reparations must take precedence over settlement of debts. It further claimed that the

reduction of Germany's liabilities under the Dawes Plan would be disproportionately disadvantageous to France: she would obtain only a part of the sum
spent on damage to her devastated areas and nothing at all for military pensions,
whereas Britain would be able to recover at least some of her expenditure on the
latter item. Because of that, it was implied, there would need to be an alteration
in the Spa percentages. The main purpose of the note was to secure a British
commitment to speedy action on war debts. As it pointed out, paragraph 7 of the
joint Franco-British memorandum of 9 July had referred the question to experts
for preliminary examination. What Clémentel now wanted was for the British
and French governments to provide those experts with the necessary political
guidelines. A satisfactory basis for these, it was suggested, might be found in a
twofold declaration stating first, that the experts should seek 'an equitable and
simultaneous settlement' of all debts between the European Allies, with due
regard being paid to their relationship to reparations and other factors involved;
and secondly, that the British government understood by an equitable settlement
one based on previous British proposals, 'adapted to the Dawes Plan', and recognised that payment of war debts must be preceded by Germany's full
reimbursement of 'material reparations'.[157]

It would be no exaggeration to speak of the British delegation being incensed
by Clémentel's aide memoire.[158] This reaction was partly because the arguments
and proposals which it contained were regarded as wholly unacceptable. But the
indignation felt by MacDonald and Crowe in particular also owed much to the
belief that the French were reneging on the understanding reached in Paris on 9
July. Both men were convinced that Herriot had been given no reason to think
that war debts would be on the agenda at the London conference. On the
contrary, it had been expressly agreed that they should not, and the only undertaking on the British side had been that there might be an informal exchange of
views between Treasury officials at some future date. Yet the French government was now asking for the question to be settled in connection with the
conference and seeking a general agreement on it before the experts had even
begun to talk. This, Crowe minuted on 8 August, was 'running directly and
designedly counter to what was in fact agreed upon in Paris'. MacDonald heartily
concurred: 'I stick to what I said in Paris. The debts can be disscused as soon as
the French care between experts.'[159] Beyond that he was not prepared to go.
Clémentel and Herriot never received the written reply to the note of 4 August
that they had originally expected. Nor, for that matter, was the note given any
serious consideration.

MacDonald's point-blank refusal to discuss debts at this stage was in keeping
with the stance that he had adopted since well before the conference had been
called.[160] One of the various factors that influenced his attitude was the hope that
he might eventually persuade the United States to participate in negotiations for
a comprehensive reparation and war debts settlement, thereby making it possible
to reopen the Anglo-American funding agreement. At the time of the London

conference he was fairly – if mistakenly – optimistic on this score and determined not to prejudice his chances of success by getting embroiled in premature talks with Britain's European debtors.[161]

This consideration also entered into the calculations of the Treasury, which continued to favour postponement of any debt discussions until after the American presidential elections were out of the way. Clémentel's note took no account of the United States, calling for the summoning of an inter-allied conference confined to the Europeans. That in itself made it suspect in the eyes of the Treasury, since they attached little value to a conference which did not include the Americans. But it was by no means the only reason why they found it unsatisfactory. Niemeyer expressed the department's basic dislike of the note when he told Crowe on 14 August that the principles which it laid down as the basis of a settlement were 'absolutely impossible' and 'quite irreconcilable with the views consistently held by British Governments'.[162] The Treasury refused to concede, as they had always done, that French war debt obligations were contingent on prior reparation payments by Germany. Nor did they accept the distinction which the French were again attempting to draw between reparation for physical damage and that for pensions. Any change in the Spa percentages, the Treasury insisted, was out of the question – as was a revival of the offer made initially in the Bonar Law Plan to take reparation bonds in payment of French war debts to Britain. Finally, the Treasury were fundamentally opposed to war debts being discussed at the London conference. More than that, they doubted very much whether a general inter-allied meeting would provide the most suitable method for tackling the problem – at any rate for some time to come. The best way to proceed, the Treasury now argued, would be for Britain to deal with her debtors separately, in each case taking into account individual capacity to pay.[163]

This represented a considerable change in Treasury thinking and the situation was not without irony. Having spent the past five years or more striving for a comprehensive reparation and war debt settlement and criticising the United States for blocking such a settlement by its insistence on bilateral negotiations with its debtors, the Treasury themselves were now moving towards the approach favoured by the Americans.

With the British responding in such a negative manner to the ideas contained in the French note of 4 August, Herriot faced the embarrassing prospect of having nothing to show as compensation for the concessions on reparations and evacuation of the Ruhr to which he was being inexorably driven. True to form, he remained preoccupied with the weakness of his parliamentary position and the need to mollify his critics. In Parliament, he was coming under fire for his performance in London not only from supporters of Poincaré – that was predictable enough – but also from the Socialists, who were pressing hard for either a revision of the Spa percentages or an agreement along the lines of the Bonar Law Plan. Herriot knew that neither of these objectives was remotely attainable. The most he could hope to achieve was to throw up a smokescreen which would temporarily disguise from public opinion how little he was likely to obtain in the way of counter-concessions from the British government. On 9 August he and Clémentel returned to Paris for consultation with ministerial colleagues. A crucial Cabinet meeting took place the same day, following which the French press carried officially-inspired reports of progress to date on the key issues under consideration at the London conference. These reports conveyed the highly misleading impression that some sort of satisfactory understanding on reparations and war debts had already been reached. Clémentel was said to have told the Cabinet that the existence of a connecton between reparations and war debts had now been 'completely established' and that there was 'absolute' agreement on this point with MacDonald. He allegedly added that an inter-allied conference on debts would certainly take place once the American presidential elections were over.[164]

Although the intention of this deception was to afford Herriot a respite from his critics, its actual effect was to add to the pressure that he was already under by raising unrealistic expectations of British leniency. If Herriot himself still retained any illusions on that point, he was to be immediately disabused upon his return to London on 11 August to find that there had been no softening in MacDonald's attitude on the question of debts.

MacDonald's temper had not been improved during Herriot's brief absence by a clumsy, ill-judged attempt at intervention by a leading figure in the French Socialist party, Léon Blum. On 10 August Blum went to see Phipps at the British embassy in Paris, the purpose of his visit being to appeal for greater generosity on the question of French indebtedness.[165] France, Blum said, was now pursuing a new and more enlightened policy on reparations and the Ruhr, and it was to be hoped that this might find an echo in Germany over disarmament and in Britain over war debts, 'thus lifting the whole issue out of the morass of legal technicalities into a higher realm of international goodwill'. According to Blum, it was essential that Herriot should be given something to show in return for the great concessions that he had made: otherwise, he would be overthrown. Blum conceded that there could be no serious discussion on debts until after the American presidential elections. All that was needed was that the French delegation at the London conference should be given an assurance, even one couched in vague terms, that the British government was 'prepared to examine in a friendly spirit the question of inter-allied war debts'. Loucheur, who had just set off for England, had already said that he and about 50 other Radicals would vote against Herriot unless he brought back some such assurance. When pressed to explain what he understood by examination in a 'friendly spirit', Blum indicated that the outcome he envisaged was a solution whereby France would be relieved of all debt repayment for a period of four years, the time needed to recover from Germany the 5bn gold marks still due for the expense of restoring her devastated regions. There should be a revision of the Spa percentages. In addition, payments to Britain must be made contingent upon and proportionate to French reparation receipts.[166]

Phipps did not disguise his reservations about these particular proposals. He nevertheless believed that there was a good case for giving a general assurance of the sort suggested by Blum and strongly advised that that should be done in order to help Herriot to remain in power. Any change of government, he argued, could only be for the worse from the British standpoint and would also mean further delay in implementation of the Dawes Plan. This was a familiar refrain and it fell on deaf ears in London. Certainly there was no disposition to follow up Blum's ideas. Niemeyer dismissed them as 'quite absurd'[167] and the reaction from the Foreign Offices was almost as scathing. Lampson saw no objection to giving the French 'a little pat on the head' – in the form of a vague assurance that Britain remained prepared to examine debts in a friendly spirit – provided the French delegation continued to 'play up for the rest of the conference'. Sterndale Bennett pointed out that an assurance about inter-allied debts had already been given in the Franco-British memorandum of 9 July and that it was undesirable to offer any more definite commitment at a time when the government was trying to exclude detailed discussion of debts from the London conference.[168] It was not until 20 August, when the conference was over, that Phipps was eventually informed that MacDonald and Crowe felt it was best not to enter into controversy with Blum on such matters as allied debts.[169]

Blum's intervention followed hard on the heels of a similar – and equally fruitless – efort to influence MacDonald by another prominent French Socialist, Vincent Auriol, who was the chairman of the Finance Commission of the Chamber. On 6 August, as he was about to set off for London, Auriol had written to MacDonald on the subject of debts and reparations. He did not spare the flattery, addressing him as the 'beloved head' of the Labour party and a 'comrade so deservedly esteemed by the whole International'. He also made an emotional appeal to the solidarity of the Left. There were, he wrote, hopeful signs of an end to policies based on force: French Socialists had successfully fought against the 'mad' Ruhr adventure, and the electoral success of the Labour party in Britain and the *Cartel des Gauches* in France opened up the prospect of harmonious cooperation between the two countries. But the interests of European peace demanded a reparation settlement based on equity. To maintain the Spa percentages would represent 'a crying injustice' and they must be revised in such a way that German payments were earmarked solely for the work of making good war damage and not for pensions. This would be in keeping with the line taken by the Second International, which had consistently favoured both cancellation of inter-allied debts and limitation of reparations to the amount needed to restore devastated areas. What Auriol was concerned about was that the Labour government might follow a different course and adopt instead 'a solution contrary to the wishes of the international proletariat'. If that were to happen, it would be said that a French government of the Left had obtained from its Labour friends not only less than Bonar Law had offered but also less than MacDonald had led the French people to hope for in his letter of 21 February to Poincaré. This would provide Herriot's critics with a powerful weapon and deal a 'terrible blow . . . at the policy of peace and also at the prestige of one of the greatest forces of peace – our International'. Auriol was convinced, he said, that MacDonald would join the other allied heads of government in signing, at the same time as they signed protocols for implementation of the Dawes Plan, a provisional settlement on war debts. The letter finished with a grand rhetorical flourish: 'Wash out all the past. Make a settlement of justice. The world will bless you!'[170]

Auriol's dramatic appeal, like that from Blum, was wasted on MacDonald, who lacked his fellow-Socialists' capacity to identify the interests of European peace and the international proletariat with those of France. The idea of a revision of the Spa percentages was a non-starter. Nor was there the slightest possiblity of an agreement on inter-allied debts being completed at the London conference. Even the kind of general assurance suggested by Blum was not something that MacDonald was prepared to concede.[171]

As the conference drew to a close in the second week of August, Herriot would have gladly settled for such a concession. By that stage, he had abandoned hope of talks being held on the basis of Clémentel's memorandum of 4 August, or even of receiving a reply to that communication, and was desperately casting around for a fig leaf of however modest a proportion to hide the paucity of what he had achieved. Ideally, he would have liked a public declaration that the British government remained committed to the Bonar Law Plan; but on the few occasions that he and Clémentel hinted at this possibility, they were virtually ignored. During the last days of the conference, therefore, French endeavours were concentrated on inducing MacDonald to make some reference in his closing speech to his readiness to have the debt question gone into sympathetically at an early conference. Herriot informed Crowe on 13 August that MacDonald had promised him that he would do that. But MacDonald's own version of what he had agreed to – as told to Niemeyer on the same day – was rather different. According to this, Herriot had said that he only wanted a reiteration of the statement contained in the joint memorandum of 9 July, that British and French experts might exchange views in due course. MacDonald was 'quite definite' that he would not agree to anything beyond that, minuting: 'we stand by what has been said and do not budge'.[172]

Even such a limited concession was only consented to grudgingly and in response to frantic last-minute appeals from the French delegation. After the final meeting of the committee of Heads of Delegation on 16 August, Herriot, dismayed by the fact that there had been no mention of inter-allied debts, went to see MacDonald, accompanied by Clémentel and General Nollet, the Minister of War: at MacDonald's request, Hankey stayed for the ensuing talks.

Clémentel began proceedings by saying that the French government had originally hoped that the question of debts might be 'joined up' with the conference.

He then got down to the real business of the meeting, which was to ask MacDonald to include in his final speech to the plenary session the actual words used in the Paris memorandum about seeking an 'equitable solution' to the debt problem, with 'due regard being had to all the factors involved'. The public repetition of this formula, Clémentel claimed, would be invaluable in helping Herriot to deal with parliamentary critics, especially in the Senate, and would head off any reference in the French parliament to revision of the Spa percentages. At first MacDonald expressed reluctance to give an undertaking, indicating that he did not want to say too much 'owing to the bad atmosphere here in London. It might cause serious difficulties if he said too much'. In any case, MacDonald added, the matter was primarily one for the Chancellor of the Exchequer and he had been complaining earlier in the day that he was obliged to raise 8d. in the pound income tax to pay interest on the French debt. Since Snowden had spent the whole of the conference attacking French policy and insulting French delegates, the implied invitation to take the question up with him was not likely to be accepted.[173] Herriot voiced concern that failure to repeat the formula of 9 July would give rise to allegations in Paris that the British government was going back on it; and Clémentel warned that it might lead to the collapse of the conference. MacDonald then relented a little, promising that he would look into the matter and see what he could do. He also authorised Herriot to say in Paris that the formula would be carried out to the letter.[174] In the event, MacDonald's speech at the close of the conference did make an explicit reference to what had been agreed upon in Paris – though without complying with the French wish that the actual words should be used. The statement read: 'There is the question of inter-allied debts, which I propose shall be dealt with in accordance with the declaration made in Paris.'[175]

XIII

The outcome of the London conference was exactly what MacDonald had wanted. Satisfactory arrangements had been reached on implementation of the Dawes Plan, and the British government had managed to avoid any precise and binding engagements on either security or war debts. Nevertheless, by encouraging the French to believe that consideration of the other issues would be taken in hand as soon as reparations were settled, MacDonald had incurred a moral obligation to act without undue delay. At his Chequers meeting with Herriot, he had only ensured that London conference would be confined to the subject of reparations by promising that debts and security – in that order – would be the next items on the agenda. As it turned out, this promise was only partly fulfilled. In September 1924 MacDonald attended the autumn session of the League of Nations and, in collaboration with Herriot, set in motion the process which was to lead to the drafting of the Protocol for the Pacific Settlement of International

Disputes (otherwise known as the Geneva Protocol).[176] There was to be no comparable progress over inter-allied debts, however, mainly because of shortage of time. Soon after MacDonald's triumph at Geneva, the Labour government ran into serious difficulties arising from the prosecution of the editor of the *Workers' Weekly*, the official organ of the British Communist Party. On 8 October it suffered a defeat on what was in effect a vote of confidence and MacDonald then went to the country.[177] In the ensuing general election – held on 29 October and to the accompaniment of a 'red scare' over the Zinoviev letter – the Conservatives made sweeping gains.[178] As a result, Baldwin formed his second administration, appointing Austen Chamberlain as Foreign Secretary and Churchill as Chancellor of the Exchequer. It was during this government's term of office that negotiations for an Anglo-French debt agreement were to be brought to a successful conclusion, though not without many hitches and much delay.

6

Negotiations for the Churchill–Caillaux Provisional Debt Agreement of August 1925

I

By the time the second Baldwin government took office in November 1924 considerable resentment had built up in British official circles at the French delay in negotiating a war debt settlement. Earlier sympathy for their financial difficulties – always tempered in any case by a feeling that they were largely self-inflicted and the result of a chronic unwillingness to increase taxation – had by this stage all but disappeared. Instead, there was intense irritation, especially at the Treasury, fuelled by a growing suspicion that France was not making any effort to reach a funding agreement and had no real intention of ever doing so.[1] Indeed, the British ambassador to Paris, Crewe, identified this widespread belief as a major cause of the deterioration in Anglo-French relations which he noticed at that time.[2]

Relations between the two countries were further strained by a new-found determination on the part of the British government to set negotiations in motion. Earlier in the year (as we have seen) MacDonald had shown little interest in pressing the French to begin official talks on war debts. On the contrary, he had positively discouraged Herriot from raising the matter both at their Chequers meeting of June 1924 and at the London conference on reparations shortly afterwards. From late 1924 onwards, however, the British position started to change and the French government was thereafter subjected to growing pressure to negotiate an early settlement. There were a number of reasons for this. It was partly because, for the time being at least, the reparation problem had ceased to be as troublesome or as urgent as it had been for the previous three or four years. The successful operation of the Dawes Plan from September 1924 enabled the British government to switch its attention to the related question of allied debts. It also made possible a more informed assessment of likely receipts from Germany and hence of the French capacity to repay their debts and of the sums Britain would need to obtain from debtors other than Germany in order to cover the cost of her annual payments to the United States.

Another important factor was the advent to power of the Baldwin government and, more specifically, the appointment of Churchill as Chancellor of the Exchequer. Churchill had been out of office since the collapse of the Lloyd George coalition in October 1922 and was delighted, as well as surprised, by his unexpected return to such an important post. In some respects, the position of Chancellor was not one that was well suited to his particular talents, since he was notoriously uninformed about financial matters, but he threw himself into his new task with the formidable energy and determination that characterised all his activities.[3] One of Churchill's first priorities was a reduction in the current level of taxation which he, along with most of his colleagues, saw as a major cause of Britain's economic difficulties; and over the next few years this objective was to become something of an obsession. He aimed to achieve it mainly by cuts in government expenditure. But he hoped, too, that an early debt settlement with France and the other allied debtors would also help to ease the burden of the domestic taxpayer who was by now meeting interest payments of more than £30m each year on the French debt alone.[4]

Quite apart from this consideration, Churchill was keenly aware of the criticism that he was likely to face in Parliament – and not only from the Opposition benches – unless he took prompt action to get negotiations under way. The warning signs were clear: as early as 10 December 1924 the new Chancellor found himself obliged to explain and defend the government's intended policy on inter-allied debts during a debate on the subject initiated by the Liberals.[5] According to Baldwin, Churchill's statement in the Commons met with approval from all sides.[6] The likelihood was, however, that the respite he had gained would only be brief.

Within days of taking office, therefore, Churchill began making plans to approach the debtor governments. Fortunately for him, his determination to press ahead with negotiations was matched by a greater responsiveness on the part of the French than had previously been the case to the idea of a bilateral (as opposed to all-round) settlement.[7] This change of attitude was a consequence of the deteriorating state of public finances in France. By late 1924 Herriot and his Finance Minister, Clémentel, had come to accept the necessity of securing foreign loans in order to cope with the problem of a massive floating debt. They realised that there was no prospect of obtaining such loans until France had concluded a funding agreement with her creditors, and they were therefore more receptive to initiatives from Churchill than they would otherwise have been. As against that, their room for manoeuvre was severely constrained by public opinion which at this time was even more sensitive than usual about war debts, stirred up as it was by the start of informal talks on a funding agreement with the Americans and lengthy parliamentary debates on the subject during December

1924 and January 1925. The highlight of these debates was an emotive speech on 21 January from an influential figure in the *Bloc National*, Louis Marin. Speaking with great feeling of the 1,600,000 French war dead, Marin declared that it would be a monstrous denial of justice to expect France to repay the borrowed sums spent by her in the common allied cause. His speech was applauded by the entire Chamber and the press was unanimous in endorsing the sentiments he had expressed.[8] Reporting from Paris, Phipps provided Crowe with an eye-witness account of the dramatic impact of Marin's intervention, adding that 'at least ninety-nine Frenchmen out of a hundred share his views on the question'.[9] The ambassador, Crewe, agreed with this assessment and reported that the effect of Marin's speech would 'undoubtedly be to render it more difficult for M. Herriot to meet the point of view of His Majesty's Government during the discussion of the subject of inter-allied debts'.[10]

II

Despite such problems, Churchill approached the negotiations ahead in a highly optimistic frame of mind and convinced that there were real prospects of securing substantial payments in the near future. Certainly he believed the position to be a great deal more promising than at any time since the end of the war. In a note of 25 November 1924 for Niemeyer, Churchill contrasted the current situation with that obtaining in 1921 when the Treasury and the then Chancellor of the Exchequer, Austen Chamberlain, had urged the Cabinet to cancel all the war debts owing to Britain 'as a friendly gesture' while at the same time repaying British debts to the United States. At the time, Churchill had strenuously opposed the proposal as excessively generous and he was now extremely relieved that the Cabinet had decided to reject it.[11]

According to Churchill, what had recently transformed the whole situation to the great advantage of Britain was a combination of two factors: the Dawes Plan and an incipient recovery in the world economy. Under the Dawes Plan, Britain was scheduled to receive £10m per annum initially, rising to £25m after four or five years. On top of that, Churchill confidently expected to obtain large payments from France and Italy at an early date. The French and Italian economies were beginning to revive after several years of peace, and Churchill argued that as this process continued both countries would 'need and seek financial respectability' – something which could only be acquired if they agreed to fund their debts. Under the circumstances, therefore, Churchill considered it highly probable that Britain would be able to do a great deal better than merely recover her annual payments of some £33m to the United States, as envisaged in the Balfour Note. The sort of figure that he had in mind was a total annual receipt of £50m – about half of it coming from Germany and the other half from allied debtors.[12]

This raises the question of Churchill's attitude to the Balfour Note, a matter that was to assume considerable importance in his subsequent discussions with the French. In 1922 he had been one of its leading supporters. As he later admitted to Niemeyer, at that time he would have 'closed gladly on a European offer of 32 millions p.a. reparations and [debt] payments, thus leaving us neither gainers nor losers on the balance'.[13] Looking back from the vantage point of 1924, however, Churchill was glad that the Note had not been favourably received by other governments. The Americans and the French in particular had both rejected it decisively. It could therefore be argued that the proposals which it contained were no longer on offer and that the British government was free to insist upon its full legal rights, without being constrained by any self-imposed restrictions. Churchill similarly took the view that other British offers – notably the Bonar Law Plan and Curzon's scheme of 11 August 1923 – had also lapsed, since they had not been accepted when they were put forward. In other words, the line which Churchill proposed to take in dealing with the French and other debtors was that the British government did not feel bound by any previous proposals. It would continue to regard the position set out in the Balfour Note as a useful 'guide' to British policy but by no means as a binding commitment: 'Balfour, Bonar Law, Curzon – all have been swept away. They were not accepted, the conditions have changed and they no longer exist. The field is perfectly clear.'[14] As will be seen, this reading of the situation was markedly different from that of the French.

From the outset, Churchill's sanguine assumptions and expectations were not shared by his official advisers. They were much more sceptical in their estimates both of the likely scale of reparation receipts and of the French capacity to pay in the near future. A Treasury memorandum of 2 January 1925, while conceding that the French burden of taxation was lighter than the British, nevertheless laid great stress on the severe financial difficulties that France was currently experiencing. The franc was vulnerable to dangerous bouts of speculation and there was an enormous floating debt which had reached a figure of 90bn francs, equivalent to more than £1bn, in the previous summer. Until these major problems were successfully tackled, it seemed out of the question for the French to 'raise anything worth mentioning for the repayment of inter-Ally debts'. They must therefore be given a moratorium of something like three years.[15] A similar conclusion was reached by Bradbury, who continued to draft elaborate plans for a comprehensive reparation and war debt settlement. Writing to Churchill in mid-December 1924 about the terms which might reasonably be accorded to France, Bradbury commented:

> There is very little probability of getting substantial payments from France in the near future over the exchange. We must therefore resign ourselves to something like a complete moratorium for several years, or devise some scheme which will encourage France to borrow on the English market to meet her liabilities to us.

Nor did Bradbury believe – as Churchill appeared to do – that Britain could count on receiving the Dawes annuities in full. Because of transfer problems and political risks, he argued, 50 per cent of the nominal value was the most which could be prudently included in any balance sheet.[16]

The cautious note sounded by his advisers did little to diminish Churchill's enthusiasm or optimism. There was, however, one difficulty which he himself frankly acknowledged, namely the strain which would probably be placed on relations with France (and other debtors) when the delicate question of repayment was broached. Thus on 1 December 1924 Churchill wrote to the Foreign Secretary, Austen Chamberlain, informing him of his intention within the next few months to make a definite move to assert British claims against France and Italy, seeking Foreign Office co-operation in the matter and apologising in advance for the difficulties which were bound to ensue:

> I expect to be rather a heavy burden to you in your diplomacy. It will be my duty to claim on behalf of the British taxpayer substantial repayments of debt from France, from Italy and from other Powers; and to resist the repeated attempts which they and the United States will make to gain advantages at our expense. This will cause a certain amount of friction, and every kind of pressure from threats to wheedling and from abuse to flattery will be employed by them . . . They will be furious, and if they think they can avoid their legal obligations by bluster there is no resource they will not try.[17]

It would be perfectly possible, Churchill admitted, to avoid all this trouble by taking no action and 'putting up with being fleeced'. This would doubtless earn Britain lots of compliments for being generous and agreeable. Such praise, however, would be a 'pretty thin diet' to offer the hard-pressed British taxpayer, and Churchill concluded his letter by begging the Foreign Secretary to 'take this debt reclamation policy upon your shoulders as one of the leading objectives of British foreign policy and only abandon it if some even greater interest is in danger'.[18]

At the Foreign Office, Churchill's communication was received with a mixture of annoyance and unease. Lampson detected in it a thinly veiled reproach against the department for not having shown sufficient vigour in defending British financial interests. Tyrrell thought that it was a 'perfectly legitimate note of warning' – provided that it was not intended to negotiate a settlement on a 'purely financial basis'. This caveat was endorsed by Crowe, who emphasised the importance of 'not dealing with this question in isolation, but of making it a pawn in a general understanding with France regarding foreign policy in general'.[19]

Here, as these comments suggest, was the potential for a serious disagreement over policy between the Foreign Office and the Treasury. This was in fact a constant danger throughout the 1920s. Nor is it really surprising that the two departments should have approached the question of recovering war debts from France and other countries from different angles and with different priorities in mind. At the risk of simplification, it could be said that, whereas the Treasury tended to treat the issue as an important one in its own right, the Foreign Office often seemed to view it chiefly in terms of the diplomatic leverage that it provided. Once the Treasury had reluctantly accepted that all-round cancellation of war debts was not feasible, their efforts were redirected towards getting the best possible deal for the British taxpayer. In pursuing this aim, they paid little or no regard to broader political considerations, and the questions that occupied their attention were usually ones of a technical nature concerning the capacity of France and the other debtor countries to pay or the likely impact of payments on Britain's trading performance. Such a narrow focus, however, was not appropriate for the Foreign Office, where there was necessarily greater concern for the political complexities involved.

The Foreign Office was not unmindful of the financial benefits to be derived from reaching an agreement on war debts with France and the other debtor countries. But it was also anxious about possible political costs, especially in the case of France. Great importance was attached to remaining on friendly terms with the French, whose co-operation was needed in many fields throughout the world. Not unnaturally, therefore, the Foreign Office was extremely reluctant to risk the loss of such co-operation by taking a strong line on debt payment. Conversely, it regarded French indebtedness as a useful bargaining counter which might be employed to obtain concessions to the British viewpoint over a whole range of other issues, including disarmament, reparations and evacuation of the Rhineland. Such an approach, as Crowe perceived, might well run counter to the Treasury's purely financial concerns. Treasury officials themselves were constantly worried that debt negotiations might be hampered by a desire to avoid friction; and it was their concern on this score which was to prompt the suggestion from Niemeyer and his deputy, Frederick Leith-Ross,[20] in the summer of 1925 that negotiations with the major debtors, France and Italy, should be conducted by some sort of independent body analogous to the WDC set up by the United States in 1922.[21]

In the event, Churchill's warnings to Chamberlain of the strain that would be imposed on relations with France by his attempts to negotiate a debt settlement were largely unfulfilled. The main reason for this lay in the Chancellor's own conduct. While negotiations with the lesser debtors were handled by senior Treasury officials, those with France (and Italy) were carried on by Churchill personally, and throughout the discussions leading up to the Franco-British agreement of July 1926 he showed a willingness to accommodate French interests which, as we shall see, dismayed his advisers.

On the face of it, Churchill's performance represented a complete *volte face* from his earlier tough stance. Yet this judgement must be qualified. It is true that in the various briefing papers that he prepared for Treasury officials and Cabinet colleagues in November and December 1924 Churchill cast himself in the role of unyielding debt collector. Nor can there be much doubt – judging from his reference to 'being fleeced' – that he was at that time genuinely determined to fight tooth and nail for the interests of the British taxpayer who, in his opinion, had suffered equally badly at the hands of a harsh creditor, the United States, and irresponsible debtors. On the other hand, it is possible to detect even at this stage an ambivalence in his attitude, an ambivalence which was to become increasingly pronounced as the negotiations proceeded. In a draft memorandum for the Cabinet, dated 1 December 1924, remarks about the need for firmness and resolution in dealing with the French are coupled with the revealing observation that in any agreement which was reached the government would be bound to take into account something which the Americans never had, namely the enormous contribution France had made to the allied war effort.[22] Equally significant is a warning contained in a note for Niemeyer about the importance of not being 'too sentimental'.[23] Since this was the very thing that Churchill was later to be criticised for in his handling of the debt negotiations with France, it is hard to avoid the conclusion that here is a classic case of a man protesting too much.

III

In January 1925, Churchill took the first tentative steps towards negotiating a war debt agreement with France when he held talks in Paris with Clémentel. The talks took place during a conference of finance ministers being held to settle the apportionment of the Dawes annuities. Churchill saw the conference as an ideal opportunity for broaching the question of French and Italian war debts. He was not sure at this stage, however, that the time was right for raising the matter formally. His reluctance to do so stemmed from two considerations. First, there was his belief that the French and Italians should be allowed a certain amount of time – 'though not too much' – to enable their economies to recover still further. They would then be 'more anxious to acquire a certificate of financial solvency than they are at present'.[24] Secondly, the question of timing was also affected to some extent by current British difficulties in Egypt, where a political crisis had erupted following the assassination of the Governor General of the Sudan, Sir Lee Stack, in November 1924. To Churchill it seemed a bad time to make demands on the two major Mediterranean powers, France and Italy, when their goodwill might well prove to be useful over the 'Egyptian imbroglio'. He decided, therefore, not to take up the debt question formally at the conference, but to dicuss it instead in private conversations with the finance ministers involved. As he informed his Cabinet colleagues, he intended to make it clear to the French and Italians that the British government expected them to put forward proposals for repayment in the near future and that 'failing such proposals we should not indefinitely remain inactive'.[25]

Shortly before the Paris conference was scheduled to meet, Churchill became involved with two matters which had a bearing on the question of French war debt payments. While visiting Paris in early December, Austen Chamberlain had a brief and informal conversation with Clémentel. One of the subjects that the latter was anxious to talk about was the possibility of raising a loan in the City in order to repay French obligations falling due there the following year. A letter containing a request along these lines was handed to Chamberlain for the attention of the Chancellor of the Exchequer.[26] This development was not unexpected, for it followed a series of indirect approaches through various channels. In late October, the Governor of the Bank of France, Robineau, had (on Clémentel's behalf) sounded out Norman as to whether the Bank of England was prepared to assist in the issue of a loan for the French government.[27] Several weeks later, on 17 November, Norman had received a similar request in a letter from a financial agent called Ernest Rechnitzer, who claimed to be speaking for 'some friends in Paris, who act as advisers to the French Minister of Finance'.[28] Finally, on 1 December the Governor had had a meeting with a representative of Bernard Scholle and Co., a banking organisation with extensive experience in procuring international short-term credits for the French government. According to this man, Clémentel had told him that French obligations in London totalling between £13m and £15m were due to mature in the course of the following year and he therefore wished to obtain sterling loans for at least that amount. Bernard Scholle had sought a letter of authority to negotiate along these lines. Clémentel had declined on the grounds that he could not risk a refusal, but had nevertheless asked them to make enquiries and report back.[29] As in earlier cases, Norman ruled out the possibility of a loan. This was partly for straightforward financial reasons: he felt that the City had been over-lending abroad to an extent which might weaken sterling and had for some time been using his influence to discourage foreign loans except in very special cases. There was also a political element involved, however, in that the current ban was being enforced with particular rigour against France and other debtor countries as a means of bringing pressure to bear on them to fund their war debts.[30]

Clémentel's own efforts to obtain a loan were equally unsuccessful. In his letter to Churchill, he sought to make the idea of a French loan more acceptable to the Treasury and the Bank of England by emphasising that it was not intended that any of the money raised from a flotation would actually leave London.[31] But Churchill was not persuaded. As he informed Chamberlain, his refusal to accede to Clémentel's wishes was based on three main arguments. First, it would set an undesirable precedent for other debtors who might also seek to get round the City's embargo by suggesting that a loan need not involve 'any transfer of funds'. Secondly, it was important to keep up the pressure on France: 'If we are ever going to get the French to pay interest on their debts we must not let them think this can be done by borrowing from us'. Finally, foreign loans were a matter on which the City itself must decide.[32] This last point was disingenuous in the extreme. The embargo was being implemented in accordance with Treasury wishes. Yet the fiction was maintained that the government had nothing to do with it, and on 16 December Chamberlain was asked to tell Clémentel that it was the established practice of the Treasury to leave market loans to the judgement of the City.[33]

The other matter that occupied Churchill's attention on the eve of the Paris conference was the question of France's debt to the United States. In late 1924 the WDC decided that future debt agreements should be negotiated on the basis of capacity to pay, with interest rates being adjusted to take account of the special circumstances of each of the debtor nations. Compared with the earlier rigid formula, as applied in the case of Britain, the new one undoubtedly represented a softening of attitude. On 1 December the French ambassador to Washington, Jules Jusserand, was informed of the change of policy by the Treasury Secretary, Mellon, and shortly afterwards Herriot and Clémentel began unofficial talks on repayment of the French war debt with the United States ambassador in Paris, Myron T. Herrick.[34] The talks made no progress because of the gulf still separating the two sides. Nevertheless, the alarm bells sounded in London, where the Treasury were concerned that British interests were being overlooked and that the French might give America preferential treatment over debts. Churchill was determined that this should not happen. Speaking in the Commons on 10 December, he stated in the strongest terms that any payment by European debtors to the United States must be accompanied simultaneously and *pari passu* by proportionate payments to Britain.[35] It was his intention to reinforce this message when he attended the forthcoming conference of finance ministers. 'It will be necessary', he wrote on 4 January, 'to point out quite clearly to M. Clémentel that we will be bound to ask from France the same terms as America may concede to her. We preserve absolute independence in the matter, and the question of terms on which we settle with France will not be governed by decisions reached between France and the United States'.[36]

IV

At the Paris conference Churchill found it unnecessary to take the initiative in raising the question of French war debts, since the French themselves proved eager to do so. He was not displeased by this. In addition, he was pleasantly surprised by the attitude displayed by Clémentel and the other French politicians he met while in Paris: the Premier, Herriot, the President, Gaston Doumergue, and Loucheur, who was not a member of the current government but clearly acting in a semi-official capacity. Churchill was gratified to find that there appeared to exist little or no resentment towards Britain: for the time being at least that seemed to have been transferred to the other main debt collector, the United States – doubtless because of the unofficial Franco-American talks on a funding agreement that had been taking place recently. He was also strongly sympathetic to the difficulties French political leaders were facing. This emerges clearly from his subsequent reports on the Paris meeting. An interview with Herriot, who was unwell at the time, prompts the comment: 'Poor man – he seemed very seedy and worn with worry and phlebitis. We got on very well.' French politicians in general are described as 'depressed . . . tame and sad'.[37] Nor does Churchill find their mood hard to understand, observing: 'The position of France, ground between the upper and nether mills of American avarice and German revenge, affords full justification for her present sober mood.'[38]

Throughout the unoffical talks that took place in Paris, the main concern of the French was to establish a firm link between their debt payments and their receipts from Germany. For his part, Churchill made it clear that he had no authority from the Cabinet to engage in detailed discussions about either the terms or methods of repayment. At the same time, he told Clémentel that he was willing to consider any proposals that the French government might care to advance. On 11 January Loucheur called on Churchill, after attending a meeting of ministers and some ex-ministers, the purpose of his visit being to put forward a plan and sound him out about it. The suggestions offered by Loucheur were extremely vague. The sort of proposal he would favour, he said, was that France should discharge at least part of her debt by ceding to Britain a proportion of the Dawes receipts to which she was entitled: instead of 50 per cent of the total, she might be prepared to accept 48 per cent. Even if the Dawes payments ceased completely, Loucheur added, France would do her best to pay something. In the course of a later conversation with Leith-Ross, Clémentel put forward much the same ideas.[39]

On each of these occasions it was stressed that the whole proposal was conditional on Britain's willingness to stand by the Balfour and Curzon Notes, the latter of which envisaged payment of part of the French debt with German bonds. Having initially been hostile to both these statements of policy, the French had for some time now regarded them as useful tools for curbing British demands. Not surprisingly, therefore, Clémentel made repeated attempts to find out whether the British government still adhered to them. This was despite the fact that he had already been told at the Chequers meeting of the previous June that the Curzon Note had definitely lapsed.[40] Churchill refused to be drawn. Instead, he invited Clémentel to put the question in writing, which he duly did in a letter of 10 January.[41] Clémentel pressed for a definite answer before the conference ended, but Churchill remained non-committal. His own view, as we have seen, was that the Balfour and Curzon Notes no longer held good. It is possible, however, that he did not wish to discourage the French by saying so outright. Besides, he was understandably reluctant to commit himself until the matter had been fully discussed by the Cabinet. After consulting Baldwin and Chamberlain, therefore, he wrote to Clémentel on 13 January informing him that the question was too complicated to permit a considered answer as yet but would be given 'prompt and earnest consideration' when he returned to London. 'Meanwhile', he continued, 'I can only repeat that the Balfour note remains for us a dominating guide of principle set up freely by our own hands.' Churchill's letter concluded with an assurance that discussions on the French debt settlement would be approached 'in the same spirit of loyal comradeship which led us safely through the agonies and perils of the war, and will alone enable us to surmount the vexations and difficulties which remain after the military victory has been won'.[42]

V

Churchill returned from Paris delighted with the French government's apparent willingness to begin serious discussions about a debt settlement and impatient to capitalise on it by responding as soon as possible to Clémentel's initiative.[43] Others were more circumspect. There was in fact considerable disquiet about Churchill's handling of the matter amongst both Foreign Office and Treasury officials. At the Foreign Office, the particular concern of Eyre Crowe was that an early settlement of the debts question would deprive the government of a valuable bargaining counter in negotiations currently taking place on other important issues. The Baldwin government was at this time engaged in difficult discussions with the French about a possible security pact, following its decision to reject the Geneva Protocol. It was also trying to persuade France to agree to evacuation of the Cologne zone by allied occupation forces – something which was supposed to take place in January 1925, but which Paris was delaying because of German infringements of the Versailles Treaty.[44] In a note for the Foreign Secretary, dated 3 February 1925, Crowe argued that Britain's position as a creditor of France could be used to facilitate a satisfactory solution to both these questions. So long as the debts remained unfunded, a certain amount of pressure could be exerted on France. Once a debt settlement had been reached, on the other hand, Britain would no longer have a 'lever of any kind by which to put pressure on France – pressure which it may possibly be most useful to exercise at any given moment'.[45] It was for this reason that Crowe had serious reservations about Churchill's enthusiasm for pressing on with the debt talks. His own preference was for spinning them out until the other issues had been settled.[46]

Anxiety about Churchill's eagerness to reach an early settlement was felt even more keenly by officials at the Treasury, albeit for somewhat different reasons. The prevailing view amongst his departmental advisers was that the task of negotiating a debt settlement was one for which Churchill was not well suited. It was not so much his undoubted lack of technical expertise, but rather his temperament, which gave rise to concern. As Leith-Ross was later to write in his memoirs, it was felt that 'Winston had too generous a heart to be a hard debt collector'.[47] Officials feared that he was too prone to making impulsive and romantic gestures. There were also doubts about his ability to bargain in matters of finance, the feeling being that lacked patience and might be tempted to go for a quick settlement if the French showed sufficient determination.[48] Early in February 1925, Niemeyer confided to Crowe that everybody in the department had misgivings about the way the Chancellor intended to proceed.[49] Their unease stemmed from a fear that Churchill, through a combination of rashness and excessive generosity, was in danger of letting the French off too lightly. Certainly he appeared to be retreating at a rapid rate from the repayment figures he had been putting forward only a few weeks previously – before his talks with Clémentel – when he had spoken confidently of securing a total of £25m per annum from Britain's debtors. Niemeyer expressed his own worries on this score in a note of 31 January for Leith-Ross. 'Winston', he wrote, 'now talks of letting the French off with £7 million a year. He then indulges in mathematical pyrotechnics to demonstrate that this is consistent with the Balfour Note'.[50]

Like Crowe, Niemeyer thought there was a strong case for putting the brake on debt talks with the French. His own view was that there should be no settlement for at least two years. He believed there was a good chance that in a year or two's time French finances and the French economy would have recovered sufficiently to enable France to negotiate a debt agreement yielding substantially bigger payments to Britain than those currently under consideration. In any case, it seemed to Niemeyer that time was needed to see how the Dawes Plan worked out. Only when it became clear how much Britain actually received from Germany would it be possible to make an accurate calculation of what France and other debtors would need to pay in order to meet the principle contained in the Balfour Note that Britain must receive enough from reparations and debt payments combined to cover her own obligations to the United States. For the moment Britain and France were unable to agree on what sums the Dawes Plan was likely to produce in practice, and the best way to settle their disagreement was to wait and see what happened over the next year or two.[51]

It was because he wished the pace of negotiation to be slowed down that Niemeyer approved of the rather stiff reply that was sent to Clémentel's letter of 10 January. Commenting on a draft prepared by Churchill on 31 January, he expressed the view that the French would regard it as 'one in the eye', adding: 'I rather like it for that reason as I am convinced in my own mind that the proper policy is to make no debt settlement or at any rate not for the next two years until we see what happens to the Dawes Plan.'[52]

The preparation of the reply was mainly the work of Churchill himself, based on Treasury briefs and subject to approval by the Cabinet. The role of the Foreign Office was minimal. A preliminary Treasury memorandum set out the main guidelines. Addressing the central point raised by Clémentel, this stated that the British government still adhered to the principles of the Balfour Note but that certain sections of the Curzon Note – those referring to the Bonar Law Plan – were no longer applicable. The British government, the memorandum continued, was prepared to consider proposals for a reduction of the French debt, provided France undertook to make definite payments from her own national resources and without reference to reparations. Such payments would be fixed with due regard to her wealth and tax-paying capacity. They would be supplemented, moreover, by an additional annuity consisting of a percentage of French Dawes receipts. Attention was drawn to the fact that Britain was committed to paying the United States £33m annually until 1932 and approximately £38m annually for more than 50 years afterwards. Payments already made to the Americans exceeded by over £70m the amount Britain had received from Germany, and this deficit would have to be made good – though the British government might possibly be prepared to envisage a small gap between receipts and payments. In view of the fact that Britain had already made considerable financial sacrifices, it was stated, and in view of the further fact [sic] that the British debt to the United States would not have been incurred but for the loans which Briain had made to her Allies, the very least France should do was to make strenuous efforts to provide some relief for the British taxpayer. Nor would this involve sacrifices as great as Britain had already acccepted. Taking all these factors into account, the British government was prepared to discuss proposals from the French government, and would deal with such proposals 'with every consideration for the special circumstances of the critical years'.[53]

On 27 January 1925 the Treasury's memorandum was sent to the Foreign Office. The reaction there was mixed. Sterndale Bennett did not take issue with its substance, acknowledging that it was for the Treasury to decide what concessions might be made and what constituted acceptable terms. His reservations concerned presentation, an area where he felt that the Foreign Office did have a legitimate role to play. In the past the French had always objected to the underlying assumption in the Balfour Note and related offers that a reparation default by Germany must mean a proportionate increase in allied debt payments to Britain, in order to preserve the principle that British obligations to the United States should be fully covered by reparations and debt repayments combined. In the opinion of Sterndale Bennett, the draft prepared by the Treasury completely failed to get round this objection.[54] Lampson was less critical, taking the view that the Treasury were on the right lines. If anything, he argued, their proposals erred on the side of generosity to France, since they represented an advance even on the Balfour Note principle. To implement that principle would in itself involve cancelling £500m of the debt owed to Britain, a charge which would have to be borne by the British taxpayer and which would be the equivalent of 5d in the pound on income tax. A further concession was now being contemplated, and Lampson suspected that when the draft reply came to be discussed by the Cabinet certain ministers would feel that the 'hard-pressed British taxpayer' was not being treated fairly. 'Generosity is all very well', minuted Lampson, 'but there are limits'.[55]

On 3 and 4 February 1925 the Cabinet met to decide the final wording of the reply to be sent to Clémentel. The main document that they had before them was a paper from Churchill consisting of the draft letter written by him on 31 January and a covering note in which he set out his general views and some rough figures. As Churchill pointed out, one of the key issues to be settled was the extent to which French repayment should be dependent on reparation receipts. It was essential, he told his colleagues, to have a clear idea of what would happen in the event of a total or partial failure of the Dawes annuities. If Germany met her obligations in full, then Britain would probably be able to secure from Europe a 'complete equivalent' of her payments to the United States. On the other hand, 'as reasonable men' ministers must face the fact that a total breakdown in the Dawes Plan would leave Britain with a heavy deficit. Even a partial one might mean a retreat from the Balfour Note principle. The draft reply to Clémentel contained the statement that Britain expected her American payments to be covered even if only half the Dawes annuities were received. But Churchill made it clear that he regarded this as a prudent preliminary negotiating position rather than a fixed principle. His main aim was to get talks going, and what he wanted to avoid was sending a note which would 'chill and check any further proposal by France'. He wished to 'encourage her to make a proposal, and so take a step towards a practical result rather than to give satisfaction to our natural inclination to exact our strict legal or at least our full moral rights'.[56]

Having secured Cabinet approval for his draft, subject to certain amendments, Churchill wrote to Clémentel on 6 February.[57] Besides setting out in some detail the financial sacrifices Britain had already made during and since the war, his letter also provided answers to the specific questions about the Balfour and Curzon Notes which Clémentel had put to Churchill in Paris. It pointed out that Curzon's Note of 11 August 1923 incorporated parts of the Bonar Law Plan and that the latter had now become inoperable since it was posited on a total reparation figure lower (and more realistic) than the one subsequently adopted in the Dawes Plan. It followed that Curzon's statement could no longer serve as a basis for British policy. The Balfour Note was a different matter: the British government continued to adhere to the principles contained in that. What the government could not accept, however, was a position in which the Balfour formula could only be fulfilled by assuming a full yield from the Dawes annuities or by taking at their face value debts which could not be treated as good assets. On this understanding, the French were invited to put forward proposals for a settlement.[58]

Churchill's letter was taken to the French Finance Ministry on 8 February by Crewe. A slight complication then arose when it was learned that Herriot intended to leave Paris for the weekend late that afternoon and might therefore get his first glimpse of Churchill's letter from press reports. Since this was thought highly undesirable, Crewe and Clémentel went to see him immediately, and both he and Clémentel were given an oral translation of the letter. The initial reaction from Clémentel was that he had hoped for something more favourable but that everything depended upon the actual figures that were eventually agreed. Clémentel also stated that France was not in a position to make any cash payments for the time being and would therefore need a moratorium. The impression formed by Crewe was that Churchill was likely to face a lot of pressure on this last point.[59]

On 9 February Aimé de Fleuriau, Saint-Aulaire's successor as French ambassador in London, brought up the question of war debts during a meeting at the Foreign Office with Crowe. After reading out a telegram from Clémentel expressing 'warm gratification' at the friendly tone of Churchill's letter, the ambassador raised the possibilty of early negotiations. He understood that Herriot and Clémentel hoped to come to London for talks in the near future, but only if a successful outcome were guaranteed beforehand. What he suggested, therefore, was a preliminary meeting of Treasury experts to sort out any difficulties in advance. Jean Boyer, the head of the 'Allied Accounts' section of the French Treasury, would be arriving in London shortly and, if the British government wished, could place himself at the disposal of the Treasury for that purpose.[60]

This suggestion had little appeal to the British Treasury, as they made clear when the Foreign Office sought their opinion on it.[61] There was some doubt whether Boyer was a sufficiently senior figure to handle such important negotiations: Niemeyer described him dismissively as 'a very pleasant young Inspecteur des Finances but not of any great standing'.[62] Concern was also expressed about the risk of embarrassing leaks, especially from the French side.[63] The most serious objection, however, was that the experts' talks would almost certainly resolve themselves into 'fishing enquiries by the French to see how far we are prepared to go'.[64]

The Treasury view, then, was that it would be a tactical mistake to agree to a preparatory meeting between officials and that the next step must be a definite offer by the French government on the basis of the principles laid down in Churchill's letter of 6 February. Such an offer should be transmitted through normal diplomatic channels and, until that had been done, the Treasury could see little point in a meeting of experts taking place.[65] De Fleuriau was informed of their feelings on the matter on 19 February, but he repeated his suggestion – though putting it in a slightly different way – a few days later.[66] During a conversation with Crowe on 24 February, he again indicated that Clémentel wanted to come to London at an early date in order to put his views on a settlement to the Chancellor. It appeared, though, that there were certain points in Churchill's letter which left Clémentel unsure about the British government's intentions. Talks between British and French experts, the ambassador suggested, might be the best way to clarify matters. When asked for their reaction, the Treasury reiterated their view that a meeting of experts would serve no useful purpose until a definite offer had been received from the French government. They agreed, however, that if the French required elucidation of certain points orally, they would be prepared to oblige them.[67] In the meantime, Churchill was informed by Clémentel that the French government intended to set in train a thorough study of his letter to provide a basis for future discussions.[68]

VI

When, as the French had requested, British and French officials held informal talks at the Treasury in the first week of April 1925, detailed accounts appeared in the press, both in Paris and London, with particular coverage being given to the French viewpoint.[69] The reports, which were substantially accurate, were clearly the result of inspired leaks and on 3 April Niemeyer, the main British representative at the talks, wrote to one of the French representatives, de Rinquensen, the financial counsellor at the London embassy, to complain. Niemeyer pointed out that such publicity could only hinder progress. Drawing attention to the French position would probably attract parliamentary questions and, in that event, the government would have no alternative but to state that the terms suggested by the French were quite inconsistent with the Churchill letter of 6 February.[70]

During the discussions between the experts, it soon became apparent that there was a wide gulf separating British and French interpretations of this letter. This arose from a fundamental disagreement about how the Balfour Note principle should be put into practice, with the two sides basing their calculations on completely different assumptions. The French understanding of what it meant rested on two main suppositions, both of which tended to minimise the amount they would need to repay: first, that Britain would set off against her debt payments to the United States the full nominal value of her share of the Dawes annuities; and secondly, that the balance needed to cover the American debt payments would be allocated between Britain's debtors – including Russia – in proportion to the capital value of their respective debts. The French attached great importance to this latter point, fearing that they might be saddled with an unfair and disproportionate share of the collective burden if the British government were to exclude the Russian debt from their calculations, as well as making special allowances for the financial weakness of Italy and the smaller debtors.

In accordance with these general views, the French experts put forward some specific proposals as a basis for negotiation. France would transfer to Britain 4.5 per cent of her Dawes annuities so as to increase the British share of total receipts from 22 per cent to 26.5 per cent. In addition, the French government would also pay out of its own resources a limited annual sum – described as an 'insurance premium': £500,000 for the years 1925–6 and 1926–7; £750,000 for 1927–8 and 1928–9; £1m for 1929–30 and 1930–31; £1.5m for 1931–2 and 1932–3; and £2m for 1933 and for each remaining year of the Dawes Plan. These figures, along with the arguments on which they were based, were set out in an informal aide-memoire.[71] From the British standpoint, as Niemeyer immediately indicated, such figures were wholly inadequate, fell well short of meeting the Balfour Note principle and could only be justified by accepting the French case in its entirety. Reporting to Churchill, Niemeyer commented that the French aide-memoire revealed a complete misconception of the British position.[72] He believed that this was deliberate and that the record should be set straight as soon as possible. A note was accordingly sent on 4 April explaining what was intended by the Balfour Note and Churchill's letter. It was emphasised that Britain expected to receive from the European Allies payments which covered the difference between the *actual* amounts obtained from Germany and the *actual* amounts to be paid to the United States. Britain could not accept a situation in which the Balfour Note principle could only be fulfilled upon the basis of a maximum annual yield from reparations or by taking at their face value allied debts which could not be regarded as good assets. It followed that the British government was not prepared to write down the French and other allied debts on the assumption that the Dawes annuities would be received in full. Nor could it accept the contention that the liability which remained to be met by the European debtors should be allocated between them in strict proportion to the nominal value of their respective debts. Instead, the different annuities would be fixed with regard to capacity to pay. As a concession, the note included a statement that in any year where Britain's total receipts from reparations and debt payments exceeded the sum to be paid to the United States, the surplus would be applied to reducing the following year's payments by the allied debtors.

If, as the French claimed, the purpose of the experts' exchange of views had been to clear up certain ambiguities in Churchill's letter, then it had certainly achieved that. In doing so, however, it had merely served to underline how far apart were the British and French negotiating positions. Yet the talks had not ended in complete deadlock; and when the French experts left to spend Easter in France on 7 April, they stressed that they did not wish their departure to be seen as a sign that negotiations had been broken off.[73] As for the British side, although Niemeyer had totally rejected the arguments put forward by the French, he had no complaint about their attitude, telling Churchill that their bearing throughout the discussions was very friendly, if 'somewhat melancholy'.[74]

Nor was Churchill himself too disappointed by the way the conversations had gone. Thus he reported to the Cabinet on 8 April that the proposals outlined in the French aide-memoire, whilst unacceptable, nevertheless 'constituted a considerable advance on the position taken up by the French Government a year or two ago'.[75] Churchill's own view by this stage was that it was unrealistic to expect France to pay more than £15m per annum, having regard to the obligations which she also had to the United States, and that it might well be necessary to accept less:

Sooner or later [he told Niemeyer] we shall have to make up our minds upon a figure, a real figure. At present we are opening our mouths for 20, and they are screwing up their courage to offer 4. Shall I try to settle on 12? Or shall we treat their offer as ludicrous and wait for them to come up to scratch later; or query: not come up to scratch at all?[76]

VII

In the period immediately following suspension of the experts' discussions, Niemeyer was in no great hurry to move towards a settlement. As he explained to Lampson on 14 April, he favoured 'spinning out' the talks in the belief that it would be possible to get much better terms out of the French in a year's time than at present.[77] Churchill took a completely different line. He was eager to follow up the preliminary conversations at the earliest opportunity. He was frustrated, however, by the onset of a political crisis in France, the background to which was a severe deterioration in the country's financial situation. The crisis had begun while the talks in London were still taking place, and one of its first casualties was the Finance Minister, Clémentel, who resigned on 3 April, to be replaced by Anatole de Monzie.[78]

The financial difficulties now facing the Herriot government had three main elements: a chronic deficit in the budget; a huge floating debt, which had by this stage reached an alarming total of 80bn francs; and a shortage of liquidity.[79] It was the government's attempt to deal with this last problem that precipitated its fall. Rumours that the note circulation was to be increased above the current maximum legal level of 41bn prompted fears of inflation and led to a drop in the value of the franc on 1 April. When these rumours were confirmed the following day by an announcement from Herriot that the government did indeed plan to authorise an extraordinary issue of extra notes to the value of 6bn, the franc fell further still. Herriot made an ineffectual attempt to restore confidence, hampered as he was by the conflicting views of his Radical and Socialist supporters, before resigning on 10 April following the passage in the Senate of a vote of no-confidence. After an abortive attempt by Briand, Paul Painlevé managed to form a new government on 16 April, with Briand as Foreign Minister and Joseph Caillaux at the Ministry of Finance.[80]

During this period of political instability, there was obviously no chance of further progress with the debt negotiations. Moreover, even after the formation of the Painlevé government there was a further delay. The new Finance Minister, Caillaux, a leading figure in the Radical party who had staged a remarkable political recovery since his wartime disgrace and subsequent trial on charges of high treason, was initially preoccupied with the financial problems inherited from the previous administration.[81] In any case, he needed time to consider the position that the debt talks had reached so far, as the French ambassador reported to

Austen Chamberlain on 25 April, following a visit to Paris for consultations with new ministers. According to de Fleuriau, both Caillaux and Painlevé were determined to proceed to a settlement. The former, however, did not wholly accept the line taken by Clémentel and wished to examine the matter further.[82]

Caillaux was in a dilemma. He aimed to deal with the French financial crisis by balancing the budget, converting the floating debt into longer-term obligations and stabilising the franc. As he appreciated, however, his entire programme was dependent on the availibility of foreign credits, and the prospects for obtaining these would remain bleak until France took steps to settle her debts.[83] For several months past, as we have already seen, the London market had been operating an unofficial loans embargo against France and other recalcitrant debtor countries. In April 1925 the United States authorities instituted a similar policy and this effectively compelled the Painlevé government to begin serious negotiations over war debts.[84] At the same time, Caillaux and his colleagues were naturally reluctant to incur the deep unpopularity such a course would provoke.

Caillaux's response to these conflicting pressures was to put forward proposals indirectly and on an unofficial basis. This was a tactic which had a number of advantages, not the least of which was that it enabled him to probe for possible British concessions without disturbing domestic opinion and while keeping open the option of disavowal. As a bonus, it offered scope for playing off the British and Americans against each other.

On 19 May an 'inspired' statement appeared in *Le Temps* to the effect that the French government would shortly be making proposals on war debts to Britain and the United States.[85] The same day saw the first of three extraordinary unofficial approaches from Caillaux, each made through Phipps. While attending a dinner given by Prince Arthur of Connaught at a British exhibition in Paris, Phipps was asked by a friend of the Finance Minister whether he would be prepared to meet a man described as 'one of Caillaux's most faithful henchmen' in order to discuss possible terms for a debt settlement. When Phipps replied that he was not a financial expert and that the best course would be for Caillaux to send one of his officials to have talks with the Treasury, he was told that this was imposible since Caillaux wanted to keep any negotiations entirely secret for the time being.

The supposed reason for this was fear of arousing the suspicions of Briand, the Foreign Minister, with whom Cailaux was said to be 'on exceedingly bad terms' and who would 'immediately imagine that Caillaux was trespassing on his preserves and initiating political discussions with Great Britain'.[86] As the conversation continued, it emerged that Caillaux's 'delightfully simple' solution to the debts question was to make over to Britain and the United States, on a *pro rata* basis, France's share of the Dawes receipts. This, it was said, was the maximum offer that Caillaux could contemplate, and it was doubtful whether he would be able to persuade Parliament to accept even that. Phipps informed London that he proposed to make no reply to this 'strange and highly unsatisfactory proposal made in such a tortuous manner'. He concluded his report on the meeting with the observation: 'Caillaux is incorrigible and is at his old subterranean tricks again.'[87]

These sentiments were echoed at the Foreign Office and Treasury alike, with officials from both departments expressing full approval of the cool and discouraging attitude displayed by Phipps. At the Foreign Office, Lampson argued forcefully that the government must have nothing to do with such underhand dealings. Tyrrell commented: 'It is typical of Caillaux, but I never thought he would show his hand so soon.' As for the Foreign Secretary, Chamberlain was deeply sceptical about the allegation that Briand would be suspicious and hostile if Caillaux negotiated openly.[88] When consulted, the Treasury, too, dismissed out of hand the idea of responding to Caillaux's unorthodox approach. Niemeyer took the view that negotiations could only be held with official representatives of the French government and suggested that the Foreign Office should be left to draft a tactful note declining to become involved in Caillaux's 'backstairs' methods. 'It would clearly be worthless', he told Churchill, 'to deal on a basis which could be discredited at any time'.[89]

Despite Phipps' unresponsive attitude, Caillaux was undeterred and quickly followed up his initial approach with another one. This time he used as his intermediary a *Daily Herald* journalist called Slocombe, through whom he sent Phipps an urgent message on 22 May. According to Slocombe, Caillaux had heard from Painlevé that some time the following week Briand intended to propose to the Cabinet that a debt agreement should be negotiated with the United States behind the back of the British government. This scheme allegedly had the backing of Philippe Berthelot, the influential Secretary at the Quai d'Orsay. Caillaux himself was said to be strongly opposed to it, taking the view that unless an arrangement were reached with Britain the franc would slump – a development that would be disastrous not only for France but for Britain as well, since it would lead to the dumping of French goods on the British market. In order to strengthen his hand at the forthcoming Cabinet discussions, however, he needed to be able to tell his colleagues that he could guarantee a reasonable settlement with Britain at an early date.[90]

As reported by Slocombe, the sort of settlement that Caillaux had in mind would involve dividing the payments into two parts: one part made up of a proportion of French reparation receipts; the other completely independent of reparations. It would also include a safeguard – similar to that enjoyed by Germany under the Dawes Plan – to ensure that payment would only be made when it did not have an adverse effect on the French exchanges. With a view to exploring the possibility of an agreement along such lines, Caillaux hoped that Phipps would agree to see him or 'an intimate friend' of his. Alternatively, this friend could travel to London or Caillaux himself would be willing to meet any representative that the British government cared to send to Paris.[91]

Whether Briand really did intend to propose a prior settlement with the

United States, or whether the story was fabricated by Caillaux as a means of putting pressure on the British government, is difficult to say. Phipps himself was highly sceptical about Caillaux's claim. Churchill was not so sure, however, and was determined to nip in the bud any attempt to give the Americans preferential treatment. His suspicions were aroused by a conversation he had with the prominent American banker Otto Kahn (of Kuhn, Loeb & Co.), during a luncheon which took place shortly after the meeting between Phipps and Slocombe. Kahn, it appeared, had recently spoken to Briand, who had asked him whether he thought the British government would object if France gave better terms to the United States than to Britain. The obvious implication was that this was being contemplated. Briand's argument was that Britain was precluded by the Balfour Note from taking more from Europe than she needed to pay the United States. It followed that if she received the full amount to which she was entitled under the Dawes Plan, nearly £25m annually, her European debtors – including Russia – would only have to pay her a total of £10m between them. Such an arrangement would mean a relatively light burden for France, and Briand indicated that he was prepared to offer the United States much more favourable terms. Churchill's reaction to this account of Briand's alleged intentions was one of intense anger, combined with a firm insistence that the French must treat Britain as well as they treated the United States. As he told Kahn:

> In no circumstances would we tolerate any payments by France to America which exceeded or antedated similar proportionate payments to us. Such an act of scandalous injustice would be resisted by us by every means short of physical force.[92]

The luncheon with Kahn prompted Churchill to write to Austen Chamberlain on 27 May to express his disquiet at the direction French policy seemed to be taking, as well as to make it clear that he rejected completely Briand's notion of the Balfour Note principle as a binding constraint on the British government. By this stage, Churchill was becoming impatient with the lack of any real progress towards a settlement, and he reminded Chamberlain that no reply had yet been received to his letter of 6 February to Clémentel. In view of this, and of the fact that the Americans were already pressing France for payment, Churchill suggested that Britain, too, should soon make a formal request for proposals from the French government. If Chamberlain agreed, he wished to raise the matter in Cabinet. For Chamberlain's information, Churchill added that the President of the Board of Trade, Philip Cunliffe-Lister (earlier called Lloyd-Greame when holding the same post in the first Baldwin government),[93] who had also been present at the lunch with Kahn, fully endorsed his views.[94]

Chamberlain agreed that it might, indeed, be time to consider drafting a despatch to Paris. He also agreed that there could be no question of Britain's being treated less favourably than the United States.[95] Having himself already conveyed the strength of British feeling on this last point to Clémentel and Herriot, Chamberlain repeated the message to Briand when they met in Geneva in early June, while attending one of the regular sessions of the League of Nations. If Britain agreed to remit part of the French debt, he told Briand, it would be to help France and 'not to enable her to pay the United States more'. Apart from this insistence on equal treatment with the Americans, the other stipulation Chamberlain laid down was that French payments should be at least partly independent of reparation receipts. He also suggested to Briand that future negotiations on the subject of war debts should be left to the Chancellor of the Exchequer and the French Finance Minister.[96]

This last point casts an interesting light on Chamberlain's whole attitude to securing payments from the French. All the available evidence indicates that the role of debt collector was not one that he relished, especially when the debtor was France, a country he once claimed to love 'as one loves a woman . . . for her defects as well as her qualities'.[97] As an ardent Francophile and a friend of Briand, Chamberlain clearly found it uncongenial to press his French colleague on the matter. But his evident reluctance to exert pressure was not simply a question of personal sentiment. There was also a political element involved. When, as Chancellor of the Exchequer in the Lloyd George government, he had advocated a unilateral cancellation of the debts owed by Britain's European Allies, one of his main reasons for urging this policy was the desire to remove a source of potential friction. This was a consideration which weighed even more heavily with him now that he was Foreign Secretary. Chamberlain regarded close co-operation with the French as a key element in his overall strategy for European 'appeasement' and was averse to doing anything which might jeopardise it.[98] It is scarcely surprising, therefore, that he should wish to distance himself as far as possible from the unpleasant task of trying to obtain payments from an unwilling France and be content instead to leave the negotiations to a forceful colleague whose eagerness to reach a settlement showed no sign of flagging.

Meanwhile, as instructed, Phipps had told Slocombe that the proposals transmitted by him on behalf of Caillaux were not acceptable.[99] Yet despite this further rebuff, the French Finance Minister persisted with his tactic of unofficial soundings. On 10 June Phipps received a visit from Robert Pelletier, an aide of Caillaux who occupied the position of *chargé de mission au Cabinet du Ministre des Finances*. The message that Pelletier brought was a familiar one. Caillaux was anxious for a quick debt settlement with Britain. Indeed, it was his aim to reach an agreement with the British government before proceeding to one with the Americans. Before travelling to London for negotiations, however, he wanted to clear the ground first, and Pelletier's task was to expound his views to Phipps. By now Phipps had gained considerable experience in coping with this sort of approach and his immediate response was to suggest that Caillaux's views should be put in writing. He added that he presumed Briand was aware of Caillaux's intentions – to which Pelletier replied in the affirmative. Later the same day, Pelletier handed over a letter from himself and a memorandum which he claimed faithfully set out Caillaux's views.[100]

The memorandum began with a statement that France could not accept the assumption that Russia would pay nothing, before going on to offer some guidelines for a settlement. It was envisaged that annuities should consist of two elements: a proportion of France's Dawes receipts, and payments to be made from her own resources. But nothing could be paid immediately. Given France's current financial position, there would need to be a moratorium for a number of years. From 1930 onwards she would be able to pay between £4m and £5m annually – though even then there must be adequate safeguards to protect her exchanges, similar to those offered to Germany under the Dawes Plan. Finally, it was suggested that there might be provision for a periodic review of the French financial position, with a view to modifying the terms of the debt settlement should it prove necessary.[101]

These proposals were given an extremely hostile reception by the Treasury, being dismissed as 'a try on' which came nowhere near meeting the British government's requirements.[102] They strengthened Leith-Ross' existing suspicions that the French were engaged in a devious game of playing off the British and Americans against each other, and what he feared was that France would settle with the United States first, obtain credits there and then simply not bother to negotiate a settlement with Britain.[103]

The possibility of a prior Franco–American deal detrimental to British interests was a major worry for Leith-Ross at this time. Indeed, in a note of 6 June 1925 he told Churchill he had reliable information that Briand had already discussed the matter with American bankers. In the note, Leith-Ross pointed out that on several occasions French political leaders, and Poincaré in particular, had tried to establish a distinction between France's debts to Britain and those to the United States on the grounds that involvement in the war had been less of a necessity for the Americans and that the loans from them were in any case of a more commercial nature. Given this attitude and France's desperate need for foreign credits, a French settlement with Washington could not be ruled out – especially since the latter now seemed prepared to offer more favourable terms than Britain had obtained in 1923. Under these circumstances, Leith-Ross recommended that an official note should be sent to France (and Italy) seeking formal assurances of *pari passu* treatment and reserving the right to abandon the Balfour Note principle if such assurances were not given and fulfilled.[104]

According to Leith-Ross, the main purpose of this note would be to forestall any attempt by the French (and Italians) at a separate settlement with the United States. At this stage he saw little point in pressing for definite proposals, since there was no likelihood of a worthwhile offer being made until the French Treasury had sorted out some of their current difficulties. On the other hand, six months had now elapsed since Churchill had first raised the debt question with Clémentel, and it was essential to make some sort of progress. Leith-Ross' own preferred solution to the present deadlock was to press for a temporary settlement. One of the main advantages of this, he maintained, was that it would satisfy the House of Commons where there was growing discontent at the absence of any productive negotiations. Since Churchill was extremely sensitive about parliamentary criticism of his policy on war debts, this was an argument which was likely to impress him.

Leith-Ross expected that the sending of a note to France and Italy would initially cause some resentment in the United States but might then lead on to a more co-operative attitude on the part of the Americans. It seemed to him that such a development would be highly desirable, and that there was a great deal to be said for Britain and the United States conducting joint negotiations with their common debtors. It was futile to hope that Britain could extract better terms than America, while there appeared to exist a real danger that the Americans would obtain something and the British nothing or that the debtors would continue to play them off against each other and so avoid paying anything to either. At the very least, the adoption of a joint negotiating position by the two main creditors would put an end to such delaying tactics. During a recent visit to London, the United States Under-Secretary of the Treasury, Garrard Winston, had raised the possibility of presenting a common front to the debtor countries. Leith-Ross suggested that the government should give an encouraging response if the Americans were to make a proposal along such lines.[105]

Another suggestion that Leith-Ross put to Churchill in his note of 6 June 1925 was that negotiations with the French and other major debtors should be dealt with not by the Chancellor of the Exchequer or the Foreign Secretary, as had so far been the case, but by a parliamentary commission. The analogy he had in mind was the United States' WDC.[106] This idea was supported by Niemeyer who, in a note of 15 June, put forward a number of names as possible members of the commission: Churchill, Lord Bradbury, the prominent Liberal politician Sir Donald McLean, and two senior Treasury officials – Leith-Ross and Niemeyer himself.[107] The reason given for this proposal was that such a commission, unlike the government (and the Foreign Office in particular), would not be hampered in conducting negotiations by a concern to maintain harmonious relations with France and other ex-allied debtors. There seems no reason to doubt that Niemeyer and Leith-Ross were, indeed, primarily motivated by this particular consideration. It is not improbable, however, that they also had another objective in mind – one that they would certainly not wish to divulge to Churchill. As we have seen, they and the rest of their colleagues at the Treasury were thoroughly dissatisfied with the line that the Chancellor was taking, their chief concern being that he would demand too little from France. One obvious way to prevent this from happening and to curb Churchill's generous impulses was to ensure that negotiations were carried on not by him personally, but by a commission on which Treasury officialdom was strongly represented.

Besides sharing Leith-Ross' enthusiasm for negotiation by a non-governmental commission, Niemeyer also shared his dislike of the proposals conveyed by Pelletier. He believed that these were open to a number of serious objections. To begin with, he took exception to the way the capital value of France's debt to Britain had been written down substantially by a series of what he regarded as dubious calculations. The first step in this process was to take the present value of the *full* Dawes annuity, that is £1.8bn, despite the fact that this was completely contrary to the statement in Churchill's letter to Clémentel of 6 February that the British government could not accept a position in which the Balfour Note principle could only be achieved on the basis of a full normal yield from reparations. It had been made clear that a present value of £900m was the maximum that Britain was prepared to take as a practicable transferable sum. By calculating the British share (*including that of the Dominions*) of the full £1.8bn and by also excluding from their calculations the value of the payments Britain had already made to the United States since 1923, the French had arrived at a capital sum of £310m as the difference between British reparation receipts and the annuities to be paid to the Americans. They had then fixed their own share of this figure at £155m – well below the actual debt of £620m.

Nor was this Niemeyer's only complaint about the proposals. He was highly critical of other features, including the failure to specify what proportion of the French Dawes receipts would be transferred to Britain, the low figure of £4–5m set as that part of the annuities which was to be independent of reparations and the suggestion that there should be no payments at all until 1930. His reaction to the request for some protection against disturbance to the exchanges was particularly scathing. According to Niemeyer, talk of transfer guarantees like those afforded to Germany under the Dawes Plan was 'mere eyewash' unless a committee comprising representatives of France's foreign creditors were established and given the powers to enforce a sound monetary and exchange policy on the Bank of France. Without this element of foreign supervision, the analogy with the arrangements for Germany was meaningless: France would be able to evade paying her annuities by letting the exchange rate depreciate, either as a deliberate act of bad faith or by a 'mere continuance of her traditional foolish money policy'. Given the record of the Bank of France, Niemeyer argued, it was impossible to 'attach any value to a proposal which left any payment entirely dependent on that Bank's courage and wisdom'.[108]

The conclusion Niemeyer drew from his analysis of the Pelletier proposals was consistent with the line that the Treasury had been urging for the past six months, namely that it was too soon yet to obtain a satisfactory permanent settlement. The French and British governments were basing their negotiating positions on completely different estimates of what the Dawes Plan was going to yield in practice, and it seemed to Niemeyer that the only sensible course was to wait and see whose forecast was correct. Like Leith-Ross, therefore, what he favoured was an interim arrangement. A permanent funding agreement should be postponed until 1928, the year in which Germany was scheduled to pay the

first full Dawes annuity; and in the meantime France should pay unconditionally, as an earnest of her good faith, £5m annually – a sum which Niemeyer
believed to be well within her capacity to pay, even if the same amount also had
to be found for the United States. In the opinion of Niemeyer, immediate cash
payments were important not only for Britain, but also for the sake of French
credit, since France had created widespread doubts about whether she ever
intended to pay anything: 'She has got to stabilise her currency and balance her
budget with some foreign debt payment met at once.'[109]

When Niemeyer showed the Pelletier memorandum to Churchill, the latter
expressed great disappointment both with its contents and with the fact that it
had been transmitted by someone who was not in a position to speak for the
French government. Phipps was accordingly instructed to tell Pelletier that the
British government would only consider official proposals. He was to add that
the latest offer was inadequate and did not conform to the terms of Churchill's
letter to Clémentel.[110]

VIII

The Pelletier affair, following as it did upon the two earlier unofficial approaches,
convinced Churchill and his advisers that the time had come to send a formal
note about payment of war debts not only to France, but also to Britain's five
other main debtors. The Foreign Office had misgivings, however, as became
evident when the Treasury sent a draft despatch for its comments on 20 June.
Opinion at the Foreign Office was divided, though there was general agreement
that the timing presented difficulties. Lampson pointed out that negotiations
were currently taking place with France, Germany and other countries over a
multilateral security pact (to lead ultimately to the Treaty of Locarno), and
argued that these might well be hindered if the French were presented with an
offficial demand to pay their debts. On the other hand, he could also see good
reasons for doing what the Treasury suggested. Britain was still making
payments to the United States, as she had done for the past two years, whilst
receiving nothing from her own debtors. Moreover, the Americans themselves
were now taking more active steps to obtain funding agreements from France and
other debtor countries, and it was important that Britain should not be 'left in
the lurch'. On balance, therefore, Lampson felt that the Treasury's suggestion
ought to be adopted. Tyrrell, who had recently succeeded Crowe as Permanent
Under-Secretary, strongly disagreed. He did not dispute that every effort should
be made to get the debts paid, but felt that it would be a tactical mistake to exert
pressure on France at that particular time. There would be a better chance of
getting a debt settlement, Tyrrell argued, once the security talks were out of the
way. In addition, the economic condition of France herself would compel her to
seek a debt agreement in the near future. For both these reasons he was opposed

to the course of action favoured by the Treasury.[111]

Although conceding that there was a great deal to be said for Tyrrell's views, the Foreign Secretary nevertheless came down in favour of sending a note to the French government – if only to bring Caillaux into the open – and one was duly despatched on 26 June.[112] The note drew attention to the fact that Britain had already paid £85m to the United States, while receiving only £25m in reparations and nothing at all from debtors. This meant that she was £60m down on the Balfour Note formula. While acknowledging France's financial difficulties, therefore, and while wishing to act in a generous spirit, the British government felt bound to press for definite proposals for cash payments in the near future. Reference was made to the French government's failure to respond to Churchill's letter to Clémentel of 6 February. The note also insisted that Britain must be treated on an equal footing with the United States.[113]

It was these last two points in particular which triggered off an unpleasant wrangle with the French government. In their reply of 2 July, the French claimed that they had in fact responded to Churchill's letter in the sense that in late March they had sent a group of experts to discuss what certain aspects of the letter meant with British Treasury officials.[114] This claim provoked an indignant reaction in London where it was regarded as a piece of sophistry. The Treasury pointed out that no formal written reply had been received and suggested that the matter should be raised again. The Foreign Office was equally dismissive of the French claim but, unlike the Treasury, took the view that it would be pointless to get embroiled in a semantic debate about whether or not there had been a proper reply to Churchill's letter.[115]

The issue of being treated *pari passu* with the Americans was a different matter altogether. On this particular question, the Foreign Office was no less determined than the Treasury that the British government's position must be accepted. It was noted with concern that the French reply of 2 July made no mention of equal treatment for Britain.[116] This was interpreted as a deliberate omission and served to strengthen long-standing fears that France intended to offer preferential terms to the United States. On 3 July Briand assured the British ambassador, Crewe, that the provisions of any settlement that France might conclude with America would 'in no way operate to the prejudice of Great Britain'.[117] This assurance was not regarded as adequate, however, especially when it was learned that on the same day as it was given the French government had informed the Americans that they proposed to send a delegation to Washington to discuss a debt settlement. Since no such statement of intent had been received by Britain, the inevitable result of this revelation was to heighten existing suspicions that the French meant to settle with the United States first. During an interview with de Fleuriau on 7 July, Chamberlain sought assurances that this was not the case and that Britain would be treated on an equal footing. The ambassador's reply was that he had been instructed by Briand to say that in forthcoming negotiations with America the French government would 'carefully abstain from any settlement that would place the United States of America in a position of advantage over His Majesty's Government'.[118]

Before his meeting with the French ambassador, Chamberlain had a talk with Churchill to ascertain his views, and the latter made it clear that he would take strong exception to any suggestion on the French side that the debts owed by France to Britain and the United States did not rest 'on an identic basis'. Churchill also outlined his thoughts on what he expected the French government to do next. What he wanted was an official proposal in writing setting out the amounts that France was prepared to pay. The annuities should consist of two elements: substantial payments which were completely independent of reparations, and additional sums which were contingent on French receipts under the Dawes Plan. Churchill could see no reason why the latter category of payments should not begin immediately, though he was prepared to concede that in the first few years the burden might be eased by permitting smaller annuities to be paid.[119] These suggestions were later conveyed to de Fleuriau by Chamberlain during their conversation on 7 July.

Churchill had indicated to Chamberlain that he himself was prepared to see de Fleuriau, and as a result talks took place between the Chancellor and the ambassador on 9 and 17 July. On both occasions Churchill took an extremely firm stand against any priority being accorded to the United States. If it were, he said at the first meeting, the British government would have no hesitation in abandoning the Balfour Note principle and insisting that France should meet her obligations in full. Furthermore, Churchill continued, when an Anglo-French debt agreement was negotiated it would need to contain a provision for renegotiation if France were to give the Americans better terms at a later date. De Fleuriau was upset at this statement and retorted that it might be better for France to settle with the United States first. Churchill dissented, however, saying that he thought a French delegation should be sent to London as soon as possible.[120]

The second conversation covered much the same ground. It began with de Fleuriau asking Churchill how he could reconcile the Balfour Note principle with his insistence on being treated *pari passu* with the United States. Churchill did not give a direct answer. Rather, he repeated his earlier threat that Britain would withdraw the concessions contained in the Balfour Note if she were treated unfairly. He then proceeded to explain why he believed it to be in French interests to reach an agreement with Britain first rather than with America, arguing that the latter had so far shown scant sympathy for Europe's difficulties and would in all probability impose a severe settlement, the terms of which would be bound to influence Britain's own demands. According to the British record of the discussion, de Fleuriau expressed cordial agreement with this analysis of the situation.[121]

The question addressed to Churchill at this second meeting foreshadowed a nasty and confusing squabble over two related issues:[122] whether the British demand for equal treatment with the United States was consistent with the Balfour Note principle; and whether Briand's assurance – as transmitted by de Fleuriau to Chamberlain on 7 July – that the French government would 'abstain from any settlement that would place the United States of America in a position of advantage over Britain' was equivalent to acceptance of London's claim to equal treatment. At the heart of the disagreement was an unspoken assumption on the part of the French that there was a chance of obtaining more generous terms from the British than from the Americans.

IX

In the meantime, while de Fleuriau was engaged in a hair-splitting debate with the Foreign Office,[123] Caillaux was preparing the ground for talks with Churchill. On 16 July Pelletier called at the British embassy in Paris to tell Phipps unofficially that the French Finance Minister proposed to visit London, accompanied by Briand, in the near future. He would only do so, however, if a settlement was really in sight since it would be 'disastrous for his position to return to Paris having failed to reach agreement'. What was envisaged, therefore, was a preliminary discussion between officials.[124] Confirmation of French intentions came on 22 July when de Fleuriau informed Chamberlain and Churchill that Caillaux wished to send a team of experts on 26 July before coming to London himself.[125]

Churchill welcomed this news and authorised his officials to hold talks.[126] These began in London on 27 July. The British representatives were Niemeyer, Leith-Ross, Thomas Bewley, and David Waley, while the French team consisted of two senior Treasury officials – Moreau-Néret (*Sous-Directeur du Mouvement Général des Fonds*) and Barnaud (*Inspecteur des Finances*), who had been one of the experts sent to London by Clémentel some months earlier – plus Thion de la Chaume, a director of the Banque de L'Indo-Chine, and Henri Pouyanne, the financial attaché at the London embassy.[127]

In all there were three meetings. The first was taken up almost entirely by a statement from Moreau-Néret setting out the French proposals. For the purpose of these proposals, it was assumed that British payments to the United States averaged £35m per annum. It was further assumed that the probable value of Britain's 22 per cent share of the Dawes receipts was £22–23m. As a concession, however, the French were prepared to accept two-thirds of this figure – £15m – as a basis for calculation. In return, they wanted an arrangement to compensate them if, as they expected, this estimate turned out to be too low. If by September 1929 Britain had obtained from reparations more than four times the annual amount of £15m allowed for, then half the surplus should be allotted to France. Thereafter, any necessary adjustments were to be made each year.

By deducting £15m from the annuity of £35m which Britain paid to the United States, the French arrived at a sum of £20m to be provided annually by

Britain's debtors. So far they had always insisted that the collective burden must be apportioned between the various debtors, including Russia, in accordance with the level of their indebtedness – an arrangement which would mean France paying 30 per cent of the total. Now they offered to assume responsibility for 50 per cent of it, i.e. £10m, to be made up of £4m independent of reparations and nine points from the French share of the Dawes receipts, valued at £6m. They also offered to pay off part of the difference between British receipts and British payments to the United States to date by allowing £37m of the gold deposited in London during the war to remain there without interest for the next 60 years. The remaining £16.5m of the gold, however, would be returned to France at a rate of £275,000 per annum.

It was proposed that the debt payments should be spread over 60 years so that they would cease at the same time as British payments to America. Moreau-Néret made it clear, however, that France would have the utmost difficulty in paying anything before 1930. One of the main problems, he explained, was that she was already committed to transferring substantial amounts of sterling over the exchanges in repayment of the wartime loans contracted by the Bank of France from the Bank of England. In accordance with the agreement negotiated by Norman and Robineau in 1923, the Bank of France was due to pay back £6m in 1925, £7m in 1926, £8m in 1927, £9m in 1928, £15m in 1929 and £5m in 1930, and it was felt that any additional transfers of sterling would cause a further fall in the international value of an already weak franc. A solution might be found, Moreau-Néret suggested, if the British government asked the Bank of England to reschedule the existing loan repayments in a way that would lessen the burden in the period before 1930. France would then be in a better position to put into operation at once the proposals now being set out.[128] Given the fierce hostility felt by Norman towards any political interference in the affairs of the Bank of England, such a suggestion was unlikely to find favour in one quarter at least.

Following Moreau-Néret's statement, de la Chaume emphasised Caillaux's desire for an early settlement in order to facilitate a stabilisation of the franc and suggested that a stable French currency would be worth far more to Britain than an additional £1m or £2m each year in debt payments. Niemeyer followed up with a number of questions, and the meeting was then adjourned until the following day to give the British experts an opportunity to examine the proposals.[129]

The initial British reaction to the proposals was generally favourable, though the Treasury did have strong reservations about a number of points. It was, after all, the first time a definite offer had been made; and it had been put forward by official representatives of the French government rather than the dubious inter-mediaries Caillaux had previously used. What was more, the actual terms of the offer, while not entirely to British liking, were at least felt to be worthy of serious scrutiny – unlike the 'try on' attempted by Pelletier.

As might be epected, staff at the British embassy in Paris urged that the

French proposals should be given sympathetic consideration. In a memorandum of 28 July, Ralph Wigram, the First Secretary there, warned of the danger of failing to respond positively. Phipps took a similar line. According to Wigram, Caillaux needed some sort of settlement to clear up France's financial difficulties and, if the British government refused to negotiate one based on capacity to pay, there was a 'grave risk' of jeopardising his current financial programme and forcing him to adopt an alternative policy of inflation. Such an outcome was unlikely to serve British interests: 'We can of course argue that we shall wait and see what we shall get when the inflation period is over. That may however well be a very problematical course.'[130]

The Foreign Office, too, felt that the French proposals presented a real opportunity for a settlement which ought to be seized. After receiving details of them from the Treasury, Lampson commented that they seemed 'like real business', adding: 'On the face of it, it sounds not at all a bad offer – and far better than we had hitherto looked for. If this goes through it should exercise an extremely good effect on public opinion here.'[131] In a minute of 29 July, Austen Chamberlain agreed that the prospects looked promising, though he could not refrain from a jaundiced observation about Churchill's role in the negotiations so far: 'It is hopeful. If we reach agreement we shall owe much to C/E – and he will owe even more to us! But he will never know.'[132]

The Treasury were less impressed by the French offer. They were unsympathetic to the request for a moratorium until 1930 and regarded the proposed figure of £10m per annum as both well below the French capacity to pay and insufficient to fulfil the Balfour Note principle. Their attitude was reflected in an indignant note of 28 July by the Permanent Secretary of the Treasury, Sir Warren Fisher. Writing to Baldwin in Aix, Fisher summarised the main points of the French proposals and made clear his own view that they were wholly inadequate. 'Nothing short of £20m from France', he told Baldwin, 'will make us reasonably safe in the matter of our American Debt (Balfour Note terms)'. For the government to accept anything less would be excessively generous and he was sure that the taxpayer would feel the same way.[133]

When the financial experts met again on 28 July, Niemeyer set out the Treasury's position on the French proposals, after reminding those present that the debt stood at roughly £626m and was costing the British taxpayer £32m per annum to service. Niemeyer acknowledged that the general principles underlying the proposals represented a 'great advance' towards the British point of view, but he felt that there still remained a considerable gap between what Britain required and what had been offered. He challenged the French calculations on a several grounds. In the first place, he argued, Britain's average annual payment to the United States was £37m and not £35m as the French claimed. Secondly, he was not prepared to accept the estimate of £15m for Britain's yearly receipts under the Dawes Plan: the figure ought to be £10m at most. Thirdly, he disagreed with the French valuation of the nine points of their share of the Dawes

receipts which they proposed to transfer to Britain. Whereas the French estimated their worth at £6m, Niemeyer thought that £4m was a more realistic
figure. For all these reasons, the French offer of £4 million per annum from their
own resources would need to be 'considerably increased' in order to satisfy the
Balfour Note principle.[134]

There were other points on which Niemeyer demurred. He rejected, for
example, the suggestion that France should be paid interest on the gold deposited
in London under the Calais agreement of 1916. Indeed, the Treasury view was
that Britain should be allowed to keep the gold for herself in recognition of the
fact that the French war debt was to be written down to one-third of its nominal
value. If the French wished to recover the gold, then they ought to make an additional payment. Niemeyer also made it clear that the Treasury saw no
justification for a moratorium on payments across the exchanges for the first few
years since France was 'essentially a rich country with a favourable trade balance
and would be receiving large sums in respect of reparations'. In response to the
French request for help in the early period, however, he offered to put their
proposal for a rescheduling of existing commmercial debts to the Bank of
England, though warning that a favourable response could not be guaranteed. As
an alternative, he suggested that France might borrow on the London market.
This suggestion had a sting in the tail, however, for Niemeyer indicated that one
of the factors that would have to be taken into account when a loan was being
considered was the strength of public feeling about the losses suffered by British
holders of French war bonds as a result of depreciation of the franc.[135] Clearly
this was an attempt to secure some measure of compensation.

When, after listening to this catalogue of reservations, de la Chaume asked
whether the Treasury at least accepted the principle that France should pay 50
per cent of the sum due from Britain's European debtors, Leith-Ross indicated
that the figure he and his colleagues had in mind was higher. It would need to be
75 per cent, since the advances to Russia must be regarded as a bad debt and the
minor Allies could not be expected to pay very much. The discussions then broke
up. It was agreed that there should be further talks the next day and that in the
meantime the Treasury would try to send the French experts a set of counter-
proposals.[136]

The third meeting between the experts, which took place on the afternoon of
29 July, was preceded by a Cabinet discussion earlier in the day. Reporting on
the French offer, Churchill stated that it was not entirely satisfactory but was 'at
any rate serious' and a 'great advance' on what had so far been thought possible.
He then proposed that the French should be asked to pay £15m annually during
the period of Britain's payments to the United States: £10m from the resources
of France herself and £5m from her Dawes receipts. The Cabinet's response was
to set up a small committee, composed of Baldwin, Austen and Neville
Chamberlain (Minister of Health), and the Secretary of State for War,
Worthington-Evans, with the task of formulating a detailed scheme along the

lines suggested by Churchill.[137] By the time the Treasury representatives met their French counterparts in the afternoon, therefore, they must have been aware that the Chancellor of the Exchequer, with whom Niemeyer had consulted, was moving towards a figure of £15m. Yet their opening proposal was £20m – doubtless nothing more than a bargaining position. Moreau-Néret replied that such an amount was out of the question. If France was obliged to pay Britain £20m, she would have to pay the United States £30m; and if these sums were added to the commercial debts to be paid after 1929 (averaging £10m per annum) it would mean a total of £56–£60m – the equivalent of one-fifth of the whole French budget – needing to be transferred abroad each year. Moreau-Néret argued that it would be impossible to transfer so much across the exchanges and, to support his argument, pointed out that in the past British experts had insisted that £40m was the most that Germany could manage. He also contrasted the heavy burden France would have to bear with the relatively light one Italy was likely to have. The probability was that the Italians would only be expected to pay Britain £5m per annum, even though their debt was almost the same as that of the French, their population was similar in size and they had suffered comparatively little devastation during the war.[138]

Niemeyer was not convinced by this or the other arguments. France, he said, was to receive a large share of the Dawes payments – much more than Italy. Moreover, she was currently enjoying a healthy surplus on her balance of trade. These two factors combined meant that the transfer problem should be considerably eased. To this de la Chaume retorted that the trade balance was only temporary: it resulted from a weak currency and would quickly disappear once the franc had been stabilised. De la Chaume then stressed that Caillaux could not make any substantial increase on the offer already made, since any bigger sum would be beyond the French capacity to pay and would in any case be rejected by Parliament. If, therefore, the existing proposal was considered unacceptable, he could see no point in continuing the discussions.

The prospect of a breakdown in the talks prompted Niemeyer to try a different tack. Interest on the French debt was costing the British taxpayer around £30m per annum, and what he suggested was a settlement based on payments of £15–16m so as to reduce the burden by half. This approach was immediately ruled out by de la Chaume who claimed that if Caillaux were to accept such a figure he would be 'thrown overboard'. The meeting then ended with a brief summary by Leith-Ross of some of the main points on which the two sides agreed and differed. There was agreement, he said, that France could start making payments out of the Dawes receipts at once. However, the British government was not prepared to go along with the French contention that payments out of France's own resources could not begin until 1930.[139]

There were no further meetimgs between the experts. On 30 July, however, somewhat later than originally intended, the French representatives were sent a memorandum containing British counter-proposals which had been approved by the small Cabinet sub-commitee set up the previous day. In the memorandum, it was proposed that France should pay 62 annual payments of £16m. Of this sum, £10m was to be independent of reparations. This part was to be paid in equal instalments twice-yearly (on 1 January and 1 July), with payments beginning in January 1926. The rest was to be made up of 12 per cent of the total Dawes receipts, estimated to be worth £6m, and payment of this contingent annuity was to start almost immediately, on 1 September 1925. No concession was to be made, then, to the French request for a moratorium. Nor was one envisaged over the matter of the £53.5m of gold. This was to be kept by Britain as compensation for reduction of the debt. Alternatively, if the French preferred, it might be kept on deposit in London, without interest, for the duration of the repayment period, and then returned against extra cash payments. The memorandum sought to bind France to an undertaking that she would automatically extend to Britain any terms she negotiated with the Americans which, *in the opinion of the British government* [my italics], were more favourable than those granted to Britain. Finally, an attempt was made to safeguard the interests of British nationals whose property in France had suffered war damage – the so-called *sinistrés* – by getting an extension to them of the compensation granted to French nationals under a law passed on 17 April 1919.[140]

The French experts returned to Paris with these proposals. Caillaux found them disappointing and was at first reluctant to agree that he and Briand should proceed to London for talks with Churchill. He later relented, however, and it was arranged that dicussions should begin on 24 August 1925.[141]

X

In the weeks preceding Caillaux's visit, the constant message from the British embassy in Paris, and from Phipps especially, was that it would be a mistake to press him too hard. It seemed to Phipps that the omens for a reasonable settlement were good, since Caillaux was engaged in a political duel with Briand and could not afford to return from London empty-handed. On the other hand, there appeared to be a real risk that stiff terms would mean a hefty increase in French taxes and resultant difficulties for the French government.[142]

Such warnings left the Treasury completely unmoved.[143] They could see no reason whatever why France should pay less than £16m per annum. A memorandum prepared by Leith-Ross examined the French capacity to effect payments abroad, and – on the basis of figures from the Board of Trade about France's industrial production, balance of payments surplus and reparation receipts – concluded that France was in a position to transfer substantially more than was being asked of her.[144] Nor were the Treasury disturbed by the argument that French taxation would have to be increased. On the contrary, they positively welcomed the prospect of that happening on the grounds that it would benefit

British trade. According to Niemeyer, the expansion of French exports in recent years had been assisted by the low level of taxation French industrialists had to bear in comparison with their British counterparts. A debt settlement on the basis of the latest proposals by Britain might thus help to equalise the burden. In a note of 7 August for Austen Chamberlain, Niemeyer argued strongly that there was no case whatever for further concessions to France:

> I believe that France is economically and industrially in a very strong position; that she can quite well afford to pay anything up to £40 million overseas; and that if she does not make these payments for her legal debts she will have that money to invest it abroad to the growing detriment of our own trade.[145]

The Treasury continued to take a strong line throughout the negotiations between Churchill and Caillaux, which lasted from 24 to 26 August. According to one critic of their policy, they were 'very sticky, preferring to break and wait 2,3,5 years rather than take less than they thought France might some day be able to pay'.[146] The Governor of the Bank of England adopted a similar stance, believing that 'by holding on we shall get better terms later from a resuscitated France'.[147] Norman was insistent that the French should be made to pay at least the £16m per annum that was being asked of them.[148] This was also the view of the President of the Board of Trade, Cunliffe-Lister, who (like Niemeyer) was concerned about the competitive advantage given to French industry by the relatively light taxation that it enjoyed. In other quarters, however, there was a growing recognition that Caillaux would never agree to such a figure and that there were only two possible outcomes to the discussions taking place: either a complete breakdown or an agreement based on significantly lower payments than the British government had so far been willing to consider. Both Chamberlain and Churchill wished to avoid the former. The Foreign Secretary was anxious to settle the debts question as speedily and as amicably as possible so that it would not get in the way of the negotiations for a multilateral security pact in which he was currently engaged with the French and Germans. For his part, Churchill seems to have quickly convinced himself that Caillaux was making a genuine effort to reach a settlement and that there was a better chance of doing a deal with him than with any other French finance minister. As he wrote to Baldwin while the negotiations were taking place: 'He [Caillaux] is taking his life in his hands and if he collapses under the strain we may look long for another French statesman with either his courage or his command of the situation.'[149]

Churchill was not alone in being favourably impressed by Caillaux who, unlike most of his predecessors (and, indeed, Churchill himself), had a strong grasp of financial matters, having become Minister of Finance for the first time as long ago as 1899 and having before that worked as an official in the *Inspection des Finances* – an experience which gave him a thorough knowledge of the French taxation system. Caillaux's recent efforts to resolve the French financial crisis had gained him the respect of many British observers. Thus a leading article in *The Times* of 25 August expressed a widespread view when it praised him as a 'man of courage and understanding' who had already brought about an improvement in his country's financial position.[150] His reputation was further enhanced by his behaviour during the London talks. He was extremely charming, spoke in English, convinced those he met that he meant business and – in what was seen as a refreshing change – dispensed with the usual attempt to play for sympathy. Reporting on the discussions to Baldwin, who was at this time taking his customary summer break in Aix-les-Bains, Hankey wrote: 'Caillaux seems to have made a very favourable impression as a man of business. No speeches or gas. Not even the inevitable "Nous avons beaucoup souffert." Down to hard tacks.'[151] Although Chamberlain neither liked nor trusted him, he found him easy to deal with.[152] So did Churchill, who struck up a good personal relationship with him.[153]

XI

The London discussions opened on 24 August with a French proposal of £10m annually for 62 years, half of it to be made up of four percentage points from France's share of the Dawes receipts.[154] Several conditions were attached. The fate of the £53.5m of gold was to be decided by a later agreement. Each year an account would be drawn up showing total British payments to the United States since 1922 and the total amount received by Britain from Germany and allied debtors combined; and if there was a surplus it was to be credited to the debtors in proportion to the sums each had paid up to that time. Immediate implementation of the settlement was to be subject to modification of the existing debt repayment arrangements between the central banks of the two countries, as well as to the grant of a partial moratorium for the first four years. In any case, the combined sums to be paid annually during this early period to the Bank of England and the British Treasury must not exceed by more than £2m the amount that the French Treasury were presently obliged to transfer to the Bank of England. Finally, the British government was to do all in its power to facilitate French loans on the London market in order to meet particularly heavy obligations in the first four years.[155]

When this initial offer was unequivocally rejected, Caillaux submitted a revised version on 25 August. The principal feature of this was that the suggested annuities of £10m would be based entirely on France's own credit. In addition to the conditions accompanying the earlier proposal, two others were put forward. If it appeared to the French government that payments would seriously affect the exchanges, it might request their postponement. As a further safeguard, the French government was to have the right to ask for revision of the debt agreement in the event that Germany failed to fulfil her obligations under the Dawes Plan either wholly or in part.[156]

While the new proposal represented, in Churchill's words, 'a great advance on any previous offer made by any French Government',[157] it still fell well short of British requirements. There remained a wide gap between Caillaux's apparent upper limit of £10m annually and the figure of £16m which was the minimum that the Cabinet had so far been prepared to contemplate. Churchill informed Caillaux that he had no authority to go below £16m. Nevertheless, in an effort to bridge the gap and prevent the talks from breaking down, he undertook to recommend to the Cabinet that it should consider an agreement based on annuities of £12.5m, with smaller payments in the early years, on condition that Britain received a guarantee of equal treatment with the United States.[158]

On 25 August a set of British counter-proposals, along the lines indicated by Churchill, was sent to Caillaux. Although the latter expressed disappointment at their content, as a matter a fact they contained a number of concessions to the French viewpoint. In the first place, there was provision for payments substantially below the standard £12.5m during the period up to 1930. If, as the French had requested, the Bank of England agreed to a rescheduling of payments due from the Bank of France, then the French government was to pay £2m in 1925, £4m in 1926, £6m in 1927, £8m in 1928 and £9m in 1929. Otherwise, the payments were to be reduced still further. Secondly, a measure of protection was to be afforded against the risk of difficulties for the French exchanges or a failure by Germany to meet her commitments under the Dawes Plan. If at any time before 1935 transfers to Britain were to seriously affect the stability of the franc, the French government would have the right – subject to 90 days' notice – to postpone payment of half of an annuity for a period of up to twelve months. In the event of a complete German default on reparations, the British and French governments were to 'consider together, in the spirit of friends and allies, what modification, if any, in the present [debt] agreement is justified'.[159]

As he had promised, Churchill put these proposals to the Cabinet on 26 August.[160] He argued strongly in favour of their acceptance, although Chamberlain, sending an account of the meeting to Baldwin, described his performance as vacillating: 'I was profoundly relieved to find Winston sensitive to all the larger issues involved and moderate, tho' he seemed to me to vacillate a good deal'.[161] Chamberlain likened his colleague's shifting views on what Caillaux could do and what the French government would accept to those of 'the speculator who when his £100 shares went to £10 was ready to give them away, when they rose again to £15 said I will sell at £20, when they touched £19 wrote to his broker to say they are evidently going higher. I will wait for £30 and so on and so on'.[162] What this implied criticism ignored was the dificulty of the task facing Churchill. To persuade the Cabinet to approve the terms outlined in the British counter-proposals was no easy matter in itself. It was made harder still by the reaction to those terms from Caillaux. Dismayed by what had been proposed, on the afternoon of 26 August he sent a written statement to the Treasury setting out his main reservations. In this he declared that France could pay nothing for the calendar year 1925: for that to be done, the Chamber would be required to vote an extraordinary credit. He also suggested that it should be left to an arbitration board to determine how far the state of the French exchanges would permit a transfer of debt payments. From the British viewpoint, however, what caused most concern was his assertion, not made before, that France should be entitled to claim a revision of the debt agreement if her reparation receipts were not sufficient to cover all payments to her allied creditors.[163]

It was this last point that dominated Cabinet discussion of the subject. As ministers immediately realised, acceptance of Caillaux's stipulation would have the effect of making French debt payments dependent not on French credit, but on the successful operation of the Dawes Plan.[164] The Cabinet, in the absence of Baldwin chaired by Austen Chamberlain, found itself sharply divided. According to the official record, there was general agreement that the negotiations should not be allowed to break down, 'but the majority of the Cabinet were strongly in favour of adhering to their previous decision that at least a substantial part of the French payments should be based on French credit, irrespective of the Dawes payments and without any provision for reconsideration of the agreement in the event of a German default'.[165] The minutes provide little information about the views expressed by individuals. However, reports of the proceedings sent to the Prime Minister by Hankey and Chamberlain are more helpful in this respect, and from them it is possible to gain some idea of the position taken by different ministers – even though in the case of one, the Secretary of State for India, Birkenhead, the evidence is contradictory.

The question which divided the Cabinet was whether the debt settlement should include – as the British counter-proposals envisaged – a formula for joint reconsideration of its terms, as friends and allies, in the event of a default by Germany. Those who supported such a formula certainly included Churchill and Austen Chamberlain, as well as Robert Cecil, the Chancellor of the Duchy of Lancaster, who argued that it was best to accept the fact that France would never pay except out of her share of the Dawes receipts.[166] The attitude of Birkenhead is more problematical. In his account of the deliberations, Chamberlain wrote: 'F.E. [Birkenhead] a protagonist of moderation, Bob [Cecil] and I in support.'[167] Yet this is completely at variance with the version provided by Hankey, in which Birkenhead is presented as a staunch opponent of the formula.[168] Whatever the truth on that particular matter, what is not in doubt is that the chief spokesman for the 'hardliners' in the Cabinet was the President of the Board of Trade, Cunliffe-Lister, who was doubtless influenced by the many complaints he had received from businessmen and employers' organisations like the FBI about the advantage French industry was deriving from low taxation at a time when France claimed she was unable to pay her debts. British industrialists, Cunliffe-Lister said, were 'sick of seeing French manufactures pour into this country in an ever growing stream, while the French Government refuse to pay their debts'. Britain had agreed to repay the United States from her own resources and regardless of what she received from her debtors. Why should France receive better treatment? [169] According to Hankey, Birkenhead 'was most insistent on this side' and argued strongly against any part of the French payments being dependent on reparations. What he feared was that at some future date a French government might think it worthwhile to connive at a German default. [170]

In the end, the issue was decided by a vote – always a sure sign of fundamental differences – and the result was a majority of eight to four against any provision for reconsideration. [171] As recorded in the minutes, the Cabinet 'refused categorically to entertain any clause modifying the responsibilities of France in the event of a German default'. [172] It was agreed that 62 annuities of £12.5m on the sole credit of France 'might be accepted in principle as governing the debt settlement'. As an alternative, the Cabinet was willing to consider £10m on French credit and £2.5m from the Dawes receipts. Having taken these decisions, the Cabinet then adjourned so that Churchill could resume talks with Caillaux, whom he had arranged to meet at 5pm: the Cabinet was to reconvene at 6 p.m. At his meeting with Caillaux, Churchill made it clear that the Cabinet's proposals represented its last word on the matter, and the other undertook to lay them before his government. Churchill reported back to his colleagues and later that evening, after a telegram had been received from Baldwin indicating his general support for the terms approved by the Cabinet, a press statement was issued to the effect that the Chancellor of the Exchequer had been authorised to propose a settlement based on the principle of 62 annuities of £12.5m on the sole responsibility of France. [173] The statement emphasised that the offer was subject to agreement on a number of outstanding matters of detail and to the condition that Britain was treated no less favourably than France's other creditors: 'It would be no service to Europe, already so grievously stricken, if the sacrifices of one creditor of France merely conduced to the advantage of another.' A communiqué by Caillaux, released at the same time by the French embassy, said that he reserved his position on the British proposals but intended to put them to the French government. [174]

Caillaux's communiqué referred to the need for a 'partial moratorium' until 1930. It also contained a reserve that in no circumstances should France have to pay her creditors collectively more than she herself received from Germany. In the period immediately following 26 August, it appeared that these stipulations might prove troublesome. Reports from the Paris embassy suggested that Caillaux was perhaps misleading his colleagues about what had been agreed, and there was particular concern lest he should encourage them to hope for a settlement in which payments were dependent on reparation receipts. [175] There was some relief, therefore, when on 5 September Churchill received a letter from Caillaux informing him that 'the figures fixed by the British Government do not give rise to any objection of principle on the part of the French Government' and that he did not doubt that agreement would be reached on the other questions involved. In his reply, Churchill tried to dispel any misunderstandings and to obtain a formal acknowledgement that payments must be made irrespective of what France received under the Dawes Plan. After expressing pleasure that agreement in principle had been reached, he added: 'I presume that you have made clear to your colleagues that the figure of £12½ millions was only acceptable to His Majesty's Government on the express condition that the French Government undertook to make any payments on this scale as an absolute liability.' Caillaux refused to take the bait, however, and his reply of 15 September was non-committal.[176] What his carefully-worded letter revealed was that he remained unwilling to concede unequivocally that there should be no connection between French debt payments and the amount they obtained in reparations. As he told Phipps on the same day he wrote to Churchill, 'he would be stoned in France if he agreed to pay England and America regardless of whether or not France received payments from Germany'.[177]

XII

On 16 September 1925 Churchill publicly announced the French government's acceptance in principle of the British offer. Speaking at Birmingham, he reminded his audience that the provisional agreement had to be viewed in a broader political context:

> We have not sought . . . to extract the utmost farthing. We think it our duty to consider not only the capacity of our debtors to pay, but the circumstances in which the debts were incurred. We believe it to be in the interests of Britain to promote a general appeasement and revival on the Continent of Europe. It is in our moral interests, it is in our national interests.[178]

The tone of the Birmingham speech was essentially defensive. This doubtless reflected Churchill's discomfort at the generally hostile reaction the agreement had provoked. It is true that there was a certain amount of support from some sections of the press, with *The Times*, *The Morning Post*, *The Observer*, *The Daily Mail* and *The Daily News* arguing that the terms were the best that could be secured and that the bargaining and haggling with Britain's closest friend and ally had already gone on far too long.[179] But even these newspapers showed little enthusiasm, conceding that the agreement would involve substantial financial sacrifices for Britain and could only be justifed on political grounds. Others, such as *The Daily Express*, *The Evening Standard*, *The Daily Chronicle*, *The New Statesman* and *The Manchester Guardian* were unreservedly critical, with the last-named accusing the French of repudiating their debts.[180] The consensus in these newspapers was that France was a prosperous country which could afford to pay a great deal more and that Churchill had negotiated an indefensible arrangement which would benefit French taxpayers and manufacturers at the expense of their hard-pressed British counterparts. *The Daily Express* – expounding the views of its proprietor, Beaverbrook – was particularly scathing, claiming that £20m per annum was the very least that France should pay.[181] Although a close friend and political associate of Churchill, Beaverbrook was by no means uncritical of the policies he had pursued as Chancellor. His newspapers had previously conducted a fierce campaign against the decision to restore the pound to its pre-war parity in April 1925.[182] Now they turned their fire on the agreement reached with Caillaux.[183] An editorial in *The Daily Express*, entitled 'A Very Bad Bargain', declared that Britain was no longer in a position 'to play the role of the world's rich uncle' and concluded with an attack on the Chancellor of the Exchequer personally: 'We could almost wish that Mr Churchill were head of the French Treasury and M. Caillaux the guardian of our own financial affairs. M. Caillaux would assuredly have done a better day's business for Britain'.[184]

From the outset, then, the provisional agreement of August 1925 was widely unpopular. During the months that followed, as Churchill experienced repeated setbacks in his efforts to turn it into a definitive settlement, its unpopularity was to grow.

7

Towards a Final Settlement

I

The provisional agreement of August 1925 established the framework for a settlement based on 62 standard annuities of £12.5m, but it left a number of outstanding questions to be dealt with in future negotiations. No definite arrangement had been reached over the gold deposited in London during the war. It remained to be seen whether the Bank of England would consent to a rescheduling of the payments due from the Bank of France in the years up to 1930. Nor had a decision been taken on whether there should be bigger annuities in the later years to compensate for the alleviation accorded during the early period of repayment. Another item requiring further consideration was a proposal by the British to include as part of the eventual debt settlement a provision guaranteeing British nationals whose property in France had suffered war damage the same level of compensation as French nationals – something Caillaux had promised to examine. Troublesome as all these matters were, however, they were of minor importance in comparison with two other contentious issues that still had to be resolved: the claim by the French to be allowed to suspend transfers in the event of difficulties on the exchanges, and their insistence that in no circumstances should French payments to Britain and the United States combined exceed their receipts from Germany.

With characteristic optimism, Churchill hoped and expected that it would be possible to dispose of these difficulties without too much delay. Not for the first time his optimism proved to be misplaced. For almost a year after the conclusion of the provisional agreement he was engaged in fruitless attempts to negotiate a definitive settlement, and it was not until July 1926 that he at last achieved his objective. This disappointingly slow progress was partly a result of the gap that separated the two sides on the questions listed above. But there were other factors at work, not least the complication introduced by French debt negotiations with the Americans. As Churchill had emphasised in his press statement of 26 August, the British government was adamant on the principle of *pari passu* treatment and therefore regarded the terms of the provisional agreement as subject to the outcome of impending discussions between France and the United States. For reasons of their own the French, too, were not unwilling to postpone a final settlement with Britain until after they had concluded one with America, their calculation being that a generous offer from the latter would strengthen their bargaining position when talks were resumed with the former.[1] Initially, this fitted in with Churchill's own plans, since he believed that the Americans would be 'extremely stiff' on the very points that the provisional agreement had left outstanding.[2] The failure of a mission to Washington by Caillaux in late September 1925, however, ushered in a protracted period of uncertainty which was to last until France and the United States reached an accord, the Mellon-Bérenger agreement, on 29 April 1926.[3]

Matters were further complicated by the Anglo–Italian war debt settlement negotiated by Churchill and the Italian Finance Minister, Count Giuseppe Volpi, on 27 January 1926.[4] This was extremely lenient, involving a remission of more than 80 per cent of the amount owed.[5] The French rightly took the view that they themselves had been treated less favourably and began to press for a revision of the terms offered to them the previous August.[6] But what most hampered Churchill in his efforts to consolidate the provisional agreement was the financial and political instability which afflicted France at this time.[7] A succession of governments headed by Painlevé (two administrations), Briand (three administrations) and Herriot made half-hearted and ineffective efforts to deal with the financial chaos facing them, and their preoccupation with the domestic crisis inevitably meant that the question of a debt settlement with Britain was given a lower priority. At a more basic level still, Churchill found it almost impossible to get negotiations started for the simple reason that none of his French colleagues remained in office long enough. On 15 October 1925, Churchill wrote to Caillaux expressing the hope that talks might be resumed now that he had returned from his visit to Washington.[8] It was a forlorn hope. Within a fortnight Caillaux was out of office. His successor, Painlevé, who combined his new post with that of Prime Minister in a reconstructed government, lasted barely a month as Finance Minister and was followed in rapid order by Louis Loucheur, Paul Doumer and Raoul Péret.[9] It was this phenomenon of kaleidoscopic changes at the rue de Rivoli which prompted Lloyd George to observe sarcastically that the French had 'discovered a most ingenious method of avoiding paying their debts, by changing their cashiers whenever the bill is presented to them'.[10] For Churchill the experience was a profoundly frustrating one, and his increasingly desperate correspondence with successive ministers presents to the reader a spectacle which is both touching and faintly comic. The pattern was repeated with monotonous regularity. Scarcely had the Chancellor written to a new finance minister to congratulate him on his appointment and invite him to begin discussions than he found it necessary to send another letter offering commiserations upon his resignation.[11]

Failure to make any progress was a source of acute embarrasment to Churchill, provoking as it did mounting criticism of his policy in Parliament and the press. This criticism, in turn, fuelled his impatience at the delay. It also provided him with a useful argument in his dealings with the French government. Writing to Painlevé on 2 November 1925, Churchill pointed out to the new Finance Minister that Parliament was due to reconvene after its summer recess in a fortnight's time and when it did awkward questions were bound to be asked about the latest position on French war debts. What he suggested was that if Painlevé came to London with Briand for the formal signature of the Locarno Treaties at the end of the month, then the opportunity could be used to negotiate a final debt settlement. One advantage of doing this, Churchill explained, was that it would enable him to make a statement to the Commons announcing that negotiations had been arranged and excusing himself from giving any details.[12] Unfortunately for this stratagem, Churchill's suggestion met with objections from the Foreign Office, with Austen Chamberlain declaring himself 'horrified' by the idea that Painlevé should accompany Briand to London when the Locarno pact was signed.[13]

Chamberlain's strong reaction has to be seen in the context of his attitude towards Briand and of his general policy for promoting a Franco–German reconciliation. During the months leading up to the Locarno settlement, Chamberlain had been deeply impressed by the French Foreign Minister, believing that his statesmanlike qualities and willingness to make concessions had played a major part in the success of the negotiations.[14] He now saw Briand as the leading French exponent of a policy of moderation towards Germany – in sharp contrast to the chauvinistic and Germanophobe tendencies represented by Poincaré[15] – and therefore wished to do everything possible to bolster his political position. For that reason he was concerned that the presence of Painlevé might distract attention from Briand who 'must be the hero of the French delegation', and he begged Churchill to discourage Painlevé from coming to London for talks at that particular time.[16] Churchill agreed, though with obvious reluctance, telling Chamberlain that he would be 'forced to make a statement to Parliament pretty soon as people will not put up with this matter dragging on indefinitely'.[17] When Painlevé was subsequently asked whether he might be able to begin negotiations in London at an earlier date, he demurred on the grounds that he would be involved in vital financial discussions in the Chamber until at least the end of November.

On the whole, Chamberlain was prepared to leave the conduct of the war debt negotiations to Churchill, and his intervention in this instance exemplified Foreign Office anxiety over the Chancellor's impatience for quick results. There was a real danger, it was felt, of forcing the pace too much, especially when the French were trying to cope with daunting financial problems. In a letter of 11 November 1925 to P. J. Grigg, Churchill's Principal Prvate Secretary, Lampson put the case for a more patient approach:

Frankly, it seems to me that you are expecting just a little too much of the French Government at the present moment. Is it really likely that they will be prepared to settle the debt whilst the present financial chaos in France continues to exist? I speak as a layman, but if I were on the verge of bankruptcy, the last thing I would do would be to pledge myself to pay a large sum of money to a creditor.[18]

Churchill, who saw the letter, was furious with it, minuting that he 'did not wish to see such cheeky letters . . . '.[19] Grigg himself, however, could see the force of this argument and on occasion sought to exercise a restraining influence on the Chancellor, although not with any great success.

An example of this occurred in late January 1926 when Churchill had just negotiated the Anglo-Italian debt settlement on extremely generous terms. Churchill's intention was to follow this up immediately with a note to Paris demanding an early start to negotiations. In view of French sensitivity over the favourable treatment received by Italy, however, Grigg had serious doubts about the advisability of such a move, as he indicated to Churchill in a note of 29 January. Grigg thought it was important to avoid being exposed to complaints from Briand that 'while you are treating Italy with great generosity you are chivying France at a time when they are in great distress', and he asked Churchill: 'Is it quite certain that a little forbearance now will not make it easier to preserve the £12½ million basis?'[20] His advice went unheeded. On 1 February, after telling Grigg that he had weighed his arguments carefully, Churchill sent a stiff letter to the current French Finance Minister, Doumer, pressing him to set a date in early February for talks in London to reach a final settlement.[21]

The sharp tone of Churchill's letter reflected his irritation at the latest in a whole series of hitches. In response to earlier prodding, Doumer had assured Churchill on 5 January that in a fortnight's time, once he had completed plans for the 1926 budget with the Finance Commission of the Chamber, he would be able to give a date for coming to London.[22] This was followed by a message sent a week later stating that it was not yet possible to fix a date but he was thinking of some time in early February.[23] On 9 February Doumer wrote to tell Churchill that he had not forgotten his earlier promise. He thought that the financial debates in the Chamber should be completed by the end of the following week and he would then be in a position to make definite arrangements.[24] A further letter of 18 February, which was not actually transmitted by the French ambassador until a week later, informed Churchill that the votes on the financial proposals were unlikely to be completed as early as expected, but that Doumer should be free to come to London at the end of the first week in March. When Churchill suggested a meeting during the second week of the month, Doumer agreed.[25] The meeting never took place, however, for on 6 March Briand's government resigned over the defeat of its financial proposals and when he formed another administration several days later Doumer was replaced by Péret.[26]

This tortuous episode epitomised the difficulties Churchill had to contend with for almost a year. Events followed a consistent sequence. Each newly-appointed Minister of Finance invariably asked for a period of grace while he settled in and prepared his financial programme; he then pleaded the impossibility of leaving Paris until after he had secured the passage of that programme through the Chamber; and finally, he was out of office before Churchill had succeeded in getting discussions under way.

II

In the absence of any progress whatever towards a final settlement, Churchill's policy inevitably came under renewed attack in the spring of 1926. This development was accompanied by a rising tide of popular indignation against the French which was evident in Parliament, the press,[27] and amongst industrialists. The President of the FBI, Colonel Willey, voiced the feelings of the last-named when he told a meeting in early February:

> British manufacturers suffering competition from French industrialists – at present being subsidised by British taxpayers to the extent of some 20 millions sterling a year – are getting impatient. They are awaiting some pronouncement from our government of an actual payment which can be quickly put to the relief of the British taxpayer.[28]

Such criticism of French procrastination was widespread, and the opinion was frequently expressed that the interests of the British taxpayer were being completely disregarded in Paris. Nor was there much sympathy for the financial chaos in which France found herself. The view of most British observers was that it was largely of her own making – the consequence of gross mismanagement by a succession of irresponsible governments and of the failure of French political leaders to tell the electorate frankly that the only way to balance the budget was by reducing expenditure and increasing taxes. It was generally believed that Britain had acted responsibly in paying her creditors and restoring the pound to its pre-war parity, despite the heavy sacrifices involved for industry and individual taxpayers alike. France, by contrast, was felt to be avoiding her obligations, and reaping the benefit of doing so in terms of low taxation and a depreciated currency, both of which were helpful to French manufacturers at the expense of British competitors.[29] At a time when Britain's major export industries – coal, textiles, shipbuilding, and iron and steel – were in dire straits, while France was showing signs of economic recovery, with a lower level of unemployment than the figure of more than one million in Britain, many regarded it as intolerable that a substantial portion of the French debt was to be written off and that it was taking so long to reach a final settlement. A typical expression of this viewpoint was to be found in a letter to *The Times* of 19 March 1926 from a correspondent signing himself 'Nottingham Merchant'. After quoting anecdotal evidence from a French friend who told him of 'the insolent luxury in Paris, Trouville and elsewhere', the writer added that this information tallied with his own impression of the healthy state of the French economy.

> From personal knowledge I should say internal conditions are extremely prosperous. Agriculture, industry and trading have enormously increased, and externally French manufacturers have a booming trade. Compare conditions with Great Britain in the past five years after intensive taxation, deflation of all our business assets, acute trade depression and stagnation. There is no doubt that our interests are not being properly considered. France can well afford to pay her debts.[30]

There was one development in particular which served to intensify resentment of this kind about the French government's conduct. That was the negotiation of the Anglo–Italian war debt agreement in January 1926. There were two main reasons why this had such an effect. In the first place, it made French delay appear in an even worse light than before: if Italy found it possible to fund her debts, was the common reaction, then why not France? Secondly, the aggrieved manner in which the French responded to the agreement was a futher goad to British opinion. News of the terms caused an explosion of anger in Paris. All sections of the French press united in claiming that Italy had been treated far more leniently than France and began to agitate for renegotiation of the Churchill–Caillaux agreement.[31] In official circles, too, there was a clear feeling – as Caillaux informed Phipps – that the Italian settlement must lead to a scaling down of French annuities below the agreed figure of £12.5m.[32]

The French press campaign for a revision of the provisional agreement provoked something of a counter-campaign in Britain where the prevailing view was that the terms already ofered to France were generous enough.[33] The issue was highlighted by reports of a meeting held under the auspices of the *Comité National des Etudes Sociales et Politiques* on 1 February 1926, at which the former finance minister, Klotz, and the current *rapporteur* of the Chamber's finance committee, Lamoureux, made speeches suggesting that the French debt to Britain was much smaller than was generally supposed.[34] According to some reports, indeed, Klotz went further still and produced figures purporting to show that, if anything, Britain owed France some £40m.[35] These claims were greeted with a mixture of astonishment and derision by the bulk of the British press, with *The Times*, *The Manchester Guardian*, *The Daily Express* and other newspapers pouring scorn on what *The Financial Times* called 'the fantastical exercise in figures which has just been put forward at Paris'.[36]

In an article headed 'France and Its Debts: A Statistical Extravaganza', *The Financial Times* declared that the whole business was prompted by petty jealousy over the Italian settlement and dismissed out of hand the case for any further remission of the French debt. France's capacity to pay, the article argued, was unquestionably several times greater than that of Italy, since she was entitled to a much bigger share of reparation receipts and had acquired as a result of the war important new territories and productive resources. The terms accorded to France in the provisional agreement were 'open to the serious objection that they were totally inadequate to safeguard the position of the home taxpayer', and it was 'sincerely to be hoped that in her own interests France will not attempt to play the part of a shifty debtor by seeking complete absolution following upon the marked indulgence already extended to her'.[37] A later article in the same newspaper, occasioned by speculation that the French Finance Minister, Doumer, intended to use the Italian settlement to reopen the agreement of August 1925, was equally unyielding. The agreement could not be reopened, it stated, because it was a binding one. Nor should it be, given the continuing irresponsibility of French financial policy, as reflected in the Chamber's recent pruning of Doumer's measures for balancing the budget.[38]

Such manifestations of public sentiment were observed with a certain amount of satisfaction at the Treasury, where they were regarded as a useful card to be played against the French government. Hence Leith-Ross' comment on this particular article in *The Financial Times*: 'Alas poor Doumer. But this is healthy stuff.'[39] Less welcome, however, was mounting evidence of a lack of confidence in Churchill's handling of the whole matter. Individual manufacturers and representatives of the FBI – annoyed not only by what they saw as the continuing subsidisation of French industry by the British taxpayer, but also by recent increases in French tariffs – urged the Chancellor of the Exchequer to take a tougher line with the French government;[40] and similar views were expressed in the Commons where a Conservative backbencher, Terence O'Connor, speaking on 21 February 1926, voiced the fear of many MPs that there were going to be further concessions to Paris, in spite of a widespread feeling 'that the terms offered to France by this country were too generous'.[41] On 11 March, Churchill sought to allay such concern by stating in Parliament that the agreement he had reached with Caillaux was a binding one.[42] Despite this assurance, however, attacks on his policy continued unabated, coming to a head during a Commons debate of 24 March.

In this debate Labour Opposition members had a field day, relishing the opportunity it presented to vent the anti-French sentiments which many of them held, while at the same time deriving considerable party advantage by posing as defenders of the hard-pressed British taxpayer whose interests were allegedly being sacrificed by Churchill and his colleagues. It is true that a few speakers, including Frederick Pethick-Lawrence and Sir Frank Wise, sounded a note of caution against pressing the French too hard, warning that there might be an increase in British unemployment if the debt were repaid in goods and services[43] – something that was not actually being contemplated. The majority, however, were highly critical both of the French, for failing to pay their debts, and of the Baldwin government, for not ensuring that they did so. A typical contribution came from Joseph Kenworthy, an inveterate critic of a wide range of French policies. He accused the government of being excessively lenient towards France and argued that it might have at least insisted on some *quid pro quo* for its financial concessions – perhaps by demanding French support for British views on disarmament.[44] But it was the speech made by Snowden, the former Chancellor of the Exchequer and Labour's chief spokesman on financial affairs, which dominated the proceedings. Snowden was a master of invective. He was also intensely Francophobe, and his speech – full of hyperbole – consisted for the most part of a fierce diatribe against the French. Their procrastination since the previous August, Snowden said, was absolutely inexcusable in view of the healthy state of French industry and trade. Throughout the postwar period, indeed, their financial record had been 'one of the most discreditable . . . in the history of international finance'. In recent years, in particular, they had presented 'a contemptible spectacle to the whole world', and their failure to tax themselves was 'bringing France to the verge of national bankruptcy'.[45]

III

Complaints about the delay in obtaining a final agreement, together with allegations that France was about to be offered further concessions, were not taken lightly by Churchill. Indeed, one of the reasons why he was so sensitive to the criticism levelled against him personally was that he shared to the full the exasperation and impatience of his critics. Like them, he felt that Britain was being treated unfairly and that the French were not doing all they might to get early discussions going. His attitude was well expressed in a letter written in March 1926 to a Conservative backbencher who had lobbied him about the French war debt on behalf of an old business friend from the North of England.[46] 'I am well aware', he wrote, 'of the importance to British trade of securing payment from France in respect of her war debts, and I intend to take every possible step to that end'.[47] This was not mere verbiage, designed to appease one of the party faithful. Rather it reflected his genuine determination to achieve a settlement as soon as possible. *Pace* Churchill's critics, the failure to register any progress in the months after August 1925 was not due to any lack of effort on his part. On the contrary, he pressed the French government repeatedly for a resumption of negotiations, losing no opportunity to point out the strength of public opinion on the matter and the way in which interest charges were all the time piling up at the rate of some £30m per annum. As has been shown, indeed, there was a feeling in some quarters, especially at the Foreign Office, that his pursuit of an agreement was relentless to the point of being counter-productive.

Nor was there any substance in speculation that Churchill intended to revise the terms already agreed with France in the light of the favourable treatment subsequently received by Italy. As a matter of fact, his main reaction to the Italian settlement of January 1926 was that it made an agreement with the French more urgent than ever. As he explained to Doumer: 'It will make, I fear, a disagreeable impression on Parliament if contemporaneously with the settlement of the Italian debt, I have to admit that the final steps to complete the settlement with France are not yet concluded, or at least on the way to a definite conclusion.'[48]

In refusing to consider modification of the August agreement, Churchill was no doubt influenced to some extent by the views of his permanent advisers who declined to accept that the terms offered to Italy had any bearing on the arrangements already reached with France. On the basis of press reports, Treasury officials were convinced that the French would take a different view of the matter, and they were worried that various aspects of the Italian settlement might provide them with ammunition.[49] There was concern, for example, over how the French government might react to the clause in the settlement relating to gold lodged with the Bank of England during the war. In August 1925 Caillaux had agreed that the £53.5m of French gold should remain in London, without interest, until 1987. It might then be recovered by means of an additional payment. The Italians had managed to secure a more satisfactory arrangement whereby their gold was to be returned gradually at the rate of about £300,000 annually between 1928 and 1987. To extend a similar provision to France would involve, on a proportionate basis, handing over £1m of gold each year. This was an eventuality which the Treasury were not prepared to countenance. In any case, it seemed to the Treasury that the French were in a different position from the Italians – not least because their need for gold was less, since the Bank of France already had as much gold as the Bank of England.[50]

Nor were the Treasury prepared to concede that the Italian settlement provided any justification for a reduction in the standard French annuity of £12.5m. As Leith-Ross tersely put it: 'We should not accept such a demand.'[51] Both Leith-Ross and Niemeyer felt strongly on this point. Indeed, the latter wanted a statement to be issued making it plain that this was the view taken by the British government. Such a statement, Niemeyer felt, would be doubly useful. It would help to forestall unrealistic expectations on the part of the French. It would also 'serve as a pointer to the Americans', who might otherwise misinterpret British intentions, with unfortunate consequences.[52] 'One of the dangers of our position', he warned Churchill in a note of 2 February 1926, 'is that the Americans, concluding from the Italian agreement that we mean to be more liberal with the French, might themselves make a more liberal arrangement with the French, which in turn would make it more difficult for us to maintain the £12½ millions'.[53]

In another note of the same date, Niemeyer set out in full the arguments Churchill might deploy for countering French attempts to use the Italian settlement as an argument for reducing the standard annuity below £12.5m.[54] First, in September 1925 Caillaux had informed Churchill that his government accepted in principle the figure of £12.5m per annum. He had made this commitment, moreover, after consulting his Cabinet colleagues, including the present Prime Minister, Briand. 'The French Government having admitted £12½ millions in September last as within France's capacity to pay, cannot now argue that it exceeds that capacity.'[55] Secondly, although the French might appear to be on strong ground when contending that France should only pay as much as Italy since the amounts the two countries owed to Britain were approximately the same, in fact such a line of reasoning did not stand up to closer examination. It was true that the sums outstanding were similar: on 1 January 1926 the Italian debt stood at £560m, the French at £570 million. But these figures were beside the point. What really counted was capacity to pay – the criterion which had explicitly governed the Italian settlement – and nobody seriously doubted that the French capacity to pay was 'immeasurably greater than the Italian'. At a conservative estimate, it was thought to be three times greater. France's national income (about £1.9bn) was admittedly only double that of Italy, but was 'much more firmly based'. Thirdly, the Treasury took the view that an even more important factor than internal wealth was the power to transfer payments abroad, and in this respect too France was seen to be 'immeasurably superior' to Italy. She was a lot better endowed with natural resources such as coal, iron ore and agricultural produce, and was therefore far less dependent on imports. Her earnings from tourism were three or four times greater. She also – unlike Italy – derived substantial income from overseas investment. All these factors meant that the French enjoyed a considerably bigger balance of payments surplus than the Italians and, as a result, were more favourably placed to effect transfers. Their position would be further eased, moreover, by the fact that they were entitled to 52 per cent of the Dawes receipts, compared to only 10 per cent in the case of Italy. (This argument should be used carefully, Niemeyer warned, since it might invite a French retort that their payments ought to be dependent on France's reparation receipts.) Fourthly, it had to be remembered that France was to be allowed to make lower payments until 1930, whereas Italy was to pay the full annuity (£4m) from the beginning. Finally, there was the broader question of the likely reaction from Berlin to claims by the French that payments of £12.5m a year were beyond their capacity. Under the Dawes Plan, Germany would eventually pay the equivalent of £125m annually. If it were conceded that France was unable to pay total annuities of some £30m (£12.5m to Britain and £18m to the United States), it would then 'be impossible to keep Germany – a poorer country than France – to £50 millions, let alone £125 millions'. For all these reasons, Niemeyer concluded, the Treasury could see no reason why France should expect any further alleviations. 'To sum up: we regard the £12½ millions standard figure as accepted by the French as not open to question. We do not regard the Italian settlement as affecting this point.'[56]

IV

As Niemeyer's memorandum plainly indicates, Treasury officials were not disposed to make any concessions to France, the more so since they detected clear signs that the French economy was beginning to prosper. They were set to drive as hard a bargain as possible, and every argument that the French advanced in favour of greater leniency was vigorously rebutted. The negotiation of the Mellon–Bérenger agreement in late April 1926 gave rise to considerable speculation that the French government intended to use it to bargain for changes in the terms agreed by Churchill and Caillaux.[57] The Treasury, however, flatly rejected the idea that changes were justified, claiming that the American and British settlements with France were 'substantially equivalent'.[58] Similarly, a report in February 1926 of warnings from Caillaux that it was not in the interests of British industry to press the French government too hard over war debts met with a firm rejoinder from Niemeyer. 'On the contrary', he minuted, 'it is in the interests of British industry to do so'[59] – his argument being that the commencement of debt payments by France to Britain would help to redress the long-standing imbalance in taxation between the two countries.

The Treasury's determination not to give ground was also reflected in papers prepared by officials to brief Churchill for expected talks with Péret at the beginning of April 1926. The most important of these – a memorandum by Leith-Ross – consisted of a detailed analysis of the points left outstanding by the agreement of the previous August and of the likely position the French government would adopt on them.[60] There was scarcely a hint of concession. For example, while not opposed to the principle of smaller annuities in the early years, Leith-Ross was thoroughly dissatisfied with the 'over-generous' figures that had been put to Caillaux. He felt that the French should be pressed to pay more. They should also be left in no doubt that there must be payments above the standard £12.5m at a later stage, as compensation for the initial lightening of their burden. As far as the question of transfer was concerned, Leith-Ross anticipated that the French would ask for the right to postpone payments if it was thought the stability of the franc was being endangered. His own view, however, was that this request should be treated with the utmost caution and only agreed to 'if we were given control of the French financial and currency policy as a whole'. Since this was not a practicable proposition, all that could be done was to allow France a limited power of postponement for a maximum of two years, along the lines of article 4 of the Italian settlement. With regard to French claims about dependence of payments on reparation receipts, Leith-Ross was equally unaccommodating, pointing out that the French were apt to overlook the fact that a breakdown of the Dawes Plan would involve losses not only for France, but also for Britain, which was counting on at least £10m per annum from Germany in order to fulfil the Balfour Note principle. At the time of Caillaux's discussions with Churchill in August 1925, the latter had favoured a formula providing for joint consultation about possible modifications to the agreement in the event of a total failure. But this had been immediately rejected by the Cabinet and was therefore no longer on offer. The issue was certain to be raised again, and Leith-Ross had no objection if the French Finance Minister wished to make a settlement more palatable to domestic opinion by stating that £12.5m to Britain and a proportionate amount to the United States did not exceed a prudent estimate of France's receipts under the Dawes Plan. It seemed probable, however, that the French would seek more. They would want a definite stipulation that their payments to Britain and America must be covered by reparation receipts, and such a proposal – which would be totally unacceptable to either American or British public opinion – ought to be strenuously resisted: 'The simple and straightforward course is to maintain no dependence on Dawes; and it ought to be possible to hold to this.'[61]

At the root of the unyielding attitude of Leith-Ross and other Treasury officials lay their conviction that France had already been treated with excessive generosity. Certainly there was little sympathy for French complaints about the supposedly crushing burden of debt repayment. Hence Leith-Ross' coolly ironic reaction to a report in the *Temps* of 25 April 1926 of a speech by Poincaré stating that the French taxpayer was in danger of being overwhelmed by demands from foreign creditors: 'The French taxpayer will survive', he minuted.[62] Throughout the discussions leading up to the accord of August 1925, both Leith-Ross and Niemeyer had consistently maintained that the French could afford to pay at least £15–16m a year, and they regarded the agreed figure of £12.5m as too low. Their disappointment on this account was compounded in the months that followed by the French government's evident reluctance to begin making payments. Nor were their feelings softened by the financial difficulties facing France in the spring of 1926. On the contrary, they became increasingly contemptuous as they observed the fruitless attempts of successive French governments and finance ministers to halt the continuing depreciation of the franc. The Treasury were anxious to see the franc stabilised, believing that the uncertainty currently surrounding it was having a damaging effect on European trade in general and on the British export trade in particular. They saw no evidence, however, that the policies being pursued by the French authorities were likely to succeed. In the judgement of leading Treasury officials, France's financial malaise could only be cured by balancing the budget – through increased taxation and reduced expenditure – and by stabilising the franc. But the latter required a restoration of confidence in French credit and that, in turn, was dependent on the negotiation of funding agreements between France and her creditors. From the British standpoint, the logical conclusion of this analysis was extremely convenient: far from being a major impediment to a definitive debt settlement with Britain, the French financial crisis made such a settlement an essential first step towards national solvency.

V

Given the Treasury's uncompromising stance, as well as the French preoccupation with their domestic financial and political crisis, it is scarcely surprising that progress towards a final debt agreement was practically non-existent in the opening months of 1926. Despite all Churchill's endeavours, the French government remained reluctant to begin talks. Undeterred by his lack of success, in March and April Churchill redoubled his efforts. This was partly because of his concern over the growing volume of parliamentary criticism to which he was being subjected, criticism which came to a climax during the Commons debate of 24 March referred to earlier. No doubt it also reflected his determination to capitalise on the minor breakthrough he had achieved with Doumer in actually fixing a definite date for dicussions to be held in London during the second week in March. Although the talks failed to take place because of Doumer's departure from office on 9 March, Churchill was eager to sustain the momentum by arranging a meeting with the new Finance Minister, Péret, at the earliest opportunity. There was, however, another consideration behind the Chancellor's greater sense of urgency. He was desperate to be able to include a figure for French debt repayment in his Budget proposals for the financial year 1926–7, if only to silence his critics. As a result, 26 April 1926 – the date on which he was scheduled to make his Budget statement – became the deadline for a settlement.

As soon as Péret was installed in office, Churchill wrote to him expressing the hope that he would be able to come to London in the near future in order to settle the points left outstanding in the agreement of the previous August. In his letter, Churchill reiterated the well-worn arguments he had addressed, without any tangible results, to Péret's predecessors: a settlement was as much in the interests of France as of Britain, since it was a necessary precondition for balancing the French budget and stabilising the franc; over £15m of interest had been added to the debt in the last six months; and the state of parliamentary opinion in Britain made it 'impossible to allow the matter to drift further'.[63] Peret's response was to send Barnaud, a senior Treasury official (*Directeur Adjoint du Mouvement des Fonds*) who had taken part in the experts' discussions leading up to the Churchill–Caillaux accord, to explain to British officials the new Finance Minister's views on the questions still to be settled. While he was in London, Barnaud was asked to transmit to Péret the suggestion that talks might be started during the week following 6 April.[64] Churchill then confirmed this date in a letter of 1 April in which he stressed to Péret the importance of reaching agreement before he made his Budget speech on 26 April.[65]

This initial exchange was now followed by the familiar ritual of trying to find a mutually convenient time for meeting. The main consideration for Churchill was the need to bring negotiations to a successful conclusion before the date of his Budget speech. He therefore wanted to proceed with the minimum of delay.

Péret had different priorities. Being immersed in the task of piloting his financial programme through the Chamber and Senate, he felt unable to come to
London until the end of April – far too late for Churchill's purpose. Matters were
made more complicated still by the imminence of a debt settlement between
France and the United States.

On 5 April 1926 Roger Cambon, a member of the French embassy staff in
London, called at the Foreign Office to say that he had received an urgent
message from Paris concerning Péret's proposed visit. He had been informed that
it would be almost impossible for Péret to make it before the end of the month
because he was obliged to appear before the Senate Finance Commission on 8
April and then before the Senate as a whole in order to secure the passage of his
budget. What Cambon wanted to know, therefore, was whether Churchill was
prepared to modify his original plan to meet before 16 April. According to
Cambon, if Péret came to London in the middle of the French budget discussions, not only would he be unable to negotiate a final settlement, but he would
also suffer political damage. The outcome, he implied, might well be a grave
political crisis in France.[66] In response to this plea, Churchill suggested that talks
should be held between 16 and 18 April.[67] When Phipps conveyed this suggestion to Péret on 8 April, he was told that the Finance Minister had that very
morning written to Churchill assuring him that he would be in London before
26 April, the date of his Budget statement. While this was welcome news, it was
immediately offset by an announcement from Péret that he thought it desirable
to wait until France's current negotiations with the United States had been
completed before beginning discussions with Britain. He was hopeful that an
agreement would be reached in Washington within the next few days. That
would enable him to be in London on 16 April. Phipps was dismayed by this
unexpected complication, and urged upon Péret the importance of his going to
London even if the negotiations with the Americans took longer than anticipated.
Péret accordingly promised that, unless something completely unforeseen
happened, he would be in London on 16 April, with a view to reaching agreement by the 18th.[68]

Despite this promise, the French Finance Minister failed to meet Churchill
before the latter made his Budget statement. This was partly because of developments in Washington, and partly because of Péret's continuing involvement
with parliamentary discussion of his financial proposals which, in the event, did
not receive final approval until 29 April. The first real hint of difficulties over
meeting the agreed deadline came when Phipps had an interview with Philippe
Berthelot, the Secretary at the Quai d'Orsay, on 17 April. Berthelot told him that
Henry Bérenger, the recently-appointed ambassador to Washington and the
principal French representative in the debt negotiations taking place there, had
telegraphed saying that it was highly desirable that Péret should not go to London
until the American settlement had been concluded. When Phipps expressed
astonishment at this news and asked why Bérenger took such a position, he was

told that the Franco-American talks had reached a critical stage and that a draft agreement was about to be submitted to the WDC. Phipps replied that this was most unfortunate. He was sure that Churchill would want to see Péret before Budget day, and he urged that everything possible should be done to meet his wishes.[69]

Although it proved impossible for Péret to be in London before 26 April, he did devise a face-saving arrangement for Churchill. On 22 April he wrote to inform the Chancellor that he would not be available to see him before the 26th because he needed to stay in Paris to attend to the budget discussions taking place in the Chamber and Senate. What he proposed, therefore, was to enable Churchill to include a figure for debt payment in his Budget by giving an undertaking that France would pay £4m during the financial year 1926–7, with half the sum being paid between 1 January and 31 March 1927.[70] While this was not entirely satisfactory from Churchill's viewpoint, the fact that he could refer to Péret's undertaking during his Budget speech at least offered him some measure of protection against his critics.[71] His real objective remained a definite agreement, however, and on 4 May 1926 he suggested to Péret that talks should begin in London as soon as possible.[72] On the following day Leith-Ross received a message from Pouyanne, the financial attaché at the French embassy, indicating that his government wished to send Barnaud and some other experts from the Ministry of Finance for preliminary discussions starting on 13 May: Péret would join them a few days later. The Treasury saw no objection to this suggestion, although Niemeyer was somewhat concerned that the General Strike, which had just begun, and in combatting which Churchill was already heavily engaged, might prove a distraction.[73]

In the event, this particular difficulty did not arise, since the strike was over before Péret arrived on 16 May. That his visit failed to produce any substantial results was the result of other factors. At this stage the French were still content to play for time. They were, moreover, in the throes of a serious financial crisis, and dealing with that occupied a much higher place on their list of immediate priorities than reaching a final debt settlement with Britain. The Mellon–Bérenger agreement had been accepted grudgingly in the expectation that it would improve French credit and help to steady the franc. But that had not happened: on 29 April 1926, the day on which the agreement was concluded, the franc stood at 148 against the pound; by 14 May it had fallen to 161; and on 19 May it plunged to a low of 178.[74] Having failed in a series of desperate attempts to obtain credits from American bankers, Péret made no secret of his hope that he would have more luck in London.[75] On the eve of his departure, it was suggested semi-officially at the Ministry of Finance that Péret counted on securing fresh credits from the City and that his visit would not be considered a success unless he did so. This announcement produced an enthusiastic chorus of approval from the French press which, by contrast, showed little interest in what was supposed to be the main purpose of the forthcoming discussions – the negotiation of a definite debt settlement.[76] There was in fact considerable justification for the verdict delivered by the Paris correspondent of *The Times* that, as far as the French were concerned, the object of the talks appeared to be 'less to arrange how France may pay off her debt than how she may borrow more'.[77] Certainly Norman was later to tell Benjamin Strong that the only thing Péret wanted to talk about during his visit to London was a credit.[78]

While there was undoubtedly much more interest in clinching an agreement on the British side, it was not matched by any great willingness to accommodate French wishes. Certainly the Treasury continued to take an uncompromising line. This was partly because they now knew precisely how much France would have to pay the United States – a relatively small starting figure of £6m in 1926, rising to £7m by 1930 – and were more convinced than ever that what France received from Germany would easily suffice to cover both these annuities and the sums suggested by Britain. It was felt, indeed, that France would have 'a *very ample* Dawes margin above her USA payments *plus* our proposed scale'.[79] The fact that the Americans had refused to include in the Mellon–Bérenger agreement a 'safeguard clause', by which the amount payable by France would be directly related to her receipts from Germany, further hardened the Treasury's attitude. In addition, there was a strong belief amongst Treasury officials that the French were in an extremely weak bargaining position because of the recent intensification of their financial crisis. This was accompanied by an equally strong disposition to take advantage of the fact. Contrary to French hopes, the American debt settlement had failed to arrest the depreciation of the franc. Nor was there any realistic prospect that France would be able to secure in the United States the credits needed to stabilise it until the settlement had been ratified – a move that was likely to be postponed for some considerable time, given the French public's hostile reaction to it.[80] Not surprisingly, therefore, the Treasury were confident that the British government was in a position virtually to dictate terms to France. As Niemeyer triumphantly told Churchill on 15 May, after recounting the manifold difficulties facing the French: 'In these circumstances they cannot afford to break with us, because even if a debt settlement does not immediately put up the franc, a *failure* to settle will immediately precipitate the franc (and with it the French Government). They are really at our mercy.'[81]

Looking ahead to the discussions shortly to take place, Niemeyer and Leith-Ross envisaged the possibility of a few minor concessions. They were not opposed, for example, to granting France a limited right to suspend transfer of payments for a period of up to two or three years, along the lines of the provisions contained in the Anglo-Italian and Franco-American agreements. On what they identified as the key points, however, they favoured a much stronger line. Now that the United States had definitely refused to concede a safeguard clause over reparation receipts, they regarded that particular issue as 'dead'. Nor, they argued, should there be any question of revising the arrangements already reached in the provisional agreement of the previous August over the £53.5m of

French gold. Caillaux had accepted the British proposal that it should be left in London, without interest, until the whole debt had been paid off, and then redeemed by additional payments. Any attempt to reopen the matter because of the more favourable treatment received by Italy in the interim should be strenuously resisted. It was urged that the principle of a standard annuity of £12.5m – to be reached by 1930 – must be presented as not open to discussion, although some difficulty was anticipated over the level of payments to be made during the early years. The figures Niemeyer had in mind were £6m for 1926, £8m for 1927, £10m for both 1928 and 1929 and £12.5m for 1930, but he thought that the French would press for much smaller sums because of the unexpectedly low annuities fixed for the corresponding period in the Mellon–Bérenger agreement. Finally, both Niemeyer and Leith-Ross wanted pressure to be exerted to secure justice for British nationals whose property in France had been damaged during the war, and also for British holders of French war bonds who had suffered heavy financial losses as a result of the depreciating franc. While it was acknowledged that the bondholders had no legal claim against the French government, the latter was considered to have a moral obligation in the matter, and it was felt that Péret ought to be told – as Caillaux had been – that 'he would probably have to make some arrangement satisfactory to these holders of French loans before any other French loan in London could be successfully floated'.[82]

VI

On 16 May 1926 Péret at last arrived in London. He was accompanied by Barnaud and other experts from the Ministry of Finance. The negotiating team also included three senior Bank of France officials, one of them the *Secrétaire Général*, Albert Aupetit. According to press reports, Aupetit and his colleagues had come to talk to Norman about a possible revision of the 1923 agreement on repayment of the Bank of France's wartime debts to the Bank of England.[83] Yet they themselves seemed at a loss as to the purpose of their visit.[84] Indeed, Aupetit told Norman that he had nothing to propose or discuss, having come to London at the request of the Minister of Finance 'with no instructions or expectations'.[85] Norman was equally baffled. Nor was he sure what Péret – whom he described as 'a poor "critter"' – hoped to achieve.[86] On 19 May he wrote to his friend Benjamin Strong:

> I cannot imagine why he came. If it was to seek credits on the same line as Parmentier, it was the journey of a madman: if it was to make changes in the principles of Caillaux's settlement with this country, he must be more of an optimist than a realist: if it was to settle details, he had better have left the work to experts, for as it is he has failed to agree on 3 or 4 points of so-called detail and has gone away – nominally to come back and complete the task.[87]

Talks between Péret and Churchill began on 17 May, while a parallel meeting of British and French Treasury experts took place simultaneously. In neither set of discussions were any definite decisions reached, mainly because the whole proceedings were brought to an abrupt and premature end by Péret's enforced return to Paris.

Exchanges between Churchill and Péret were dominated by the latter's insistence on some formal recognition of a direct relationship between French debt payments and reparation receipts. Churchill pointed out that the Cabinet had already rejected any such link at the time of his earlier talks with Caillaux and made it clear that he had no authority to modify the position adopted then. He was reluctant to see negotiations collapse on this one point, however, and thus reacted positively to a suggestion from Péret of a possible solution to the deadlock by means of an exchange of letters setting out the two ministers' respective views on the situation that would arise in the event of a collapse of the Dawes Plan. It was agreed that Péret should draft a letter and, if it was acceptable, Churchill would submit it to the Cabinet – providing all other outstanding issues had been satisfactorily resolved.[88]

In the course of informal talks about the wording of this letter, a draft prepared by the French provoked a number of objections. At Péret's request, Churchill then undertook to put some ideas of his own in writing.[89] Before he could do so, however, it was suddenly announced that the Finance Minister would have to return to Paris immediately because of an alarming deterioration in the French financial position. On 18 May, while negotiations were taking place in London, there was a slump in the international value of the franc which fell from 162 to 168.65 to the pound.[90] An emergency meeting of ministers, bankers and senior officials of the Bank of France was arranged for the following day, and Péret was summoned to attend it.[91] This necessarily put an end to the search for an agreed form of wording. In any case, Churchill had learned in the meantime that there were a number of other points on which the experts had not yet reached agreement and that there was even some disposition on the part of the French to question the central principle of 62 annuities of £12.5m on the sole credit of France. He therefore told Péret that it would be better to defer until he returned to London any futher discussion of an exchange of letters 'even in the most tentative and non-committal form on either side'.[92]

Before Péret departed for Paris, Churchill set out the British position in writing. In a letter of 18 May he stated that the government stood on the agreement reached with Caillaux in August 1925.[93] At that time it had been stipulated that if France later made a more favourable settlement with the United States, Britain should be entitled to press for bigger payments. Since the terms of the Franco–American agreement of January 1926 and of the Churchill–Caillaux accord were held to be substantially equivalent, this particular point did not arise. That left three other issues still to be settled. First, there was the question of smaller annuities in the period up to 1930, and here Churchill emphasised that any reductions in the early years must be made good later. On the second question – the provision of a right to postpone transfers in certain exceptional circumstances – Churchill anticipated little difficulty in finding a solution. It was the French demand for a safeguard clause which threatened to be the sticking point. The debt payments had been fixed at a low level, Churchill reminded Péret, on the express condition that they were not dependent on reparation receipts. The British government had always taken the view that payments must be on the sole credit of France and had been confirmed in its opinion by the recent refusal of the United States to concede a safeguard clause. A possible substitute for such a clause might be found, however, in an exchange of letters for the contingency of a serious or complete failure of the Dawes Plan. If Péret cared to draft a letter, in suitable terms, Churchill would not refuse to submit it to the Cabinet.[94]

VII

When Péret left London late on 18 May, it was generally expected that he would soon be back to resume negotiations, once measures had been taken to halt the fall of the franc. But this was to underestimate the gravity of the financial crisis facing him. A series of desperate technical operations by the Bank of France and the French Treasury produced a sharp recovery in the value of the currency during the last week of May.[95] This improvement was only temporary, however, and by early June the franc was experiencing renewed pressure. Under these circumstances, as Pouyanne informed Leith-Ross on 4 June, Péret felt unable to return to London for the time being.[96] It was considered highly unlikely, indeed, that he would be able to make it until after the proposed state visit of President Doumergue which had been arranged to take place between 22 and 25 June. Quite apart from any other considerations, the French government had just appointed a special committee, headed by Charles Sergent, to make recommendations for dealing with the country's underlying financial problems. The probability was that it would take some three weeks to produce a report. The government would then try to get the Chamber to accept the committee's recommendations *en bloc*, and Péret thought it prudent to stay in Paris until that had been done. This meant that the week beginning 28 June was the earliest he could be available for talks with Churchill.[97]

While conveying this information to Leith-Ross, Pouyanne took the opportunity to sound him out about whether the British government would object if France ratified the Mellon–Bérenger agreement at once, before concluding a settlement with Britain. After consulting Churchill by telephone, Leith-Ross indicated that such a development would be regarded as 'most unfortunate', reminding Pouyanne that the accord reached between Churchill and Caillaux predated the American agreement by some six months. The Chancellor felt most strongly, he said, that the first step must be a definite settlement with Britain.[98] Given London's long-standing suspicions about the possibility of preferential treatment for the United States, such a hostile reaction cannot have come as a surprise to the French. Yet they continued to toy with the idea of ratifying the Mellon–Bérenger agreement before completing one with Britain, whilst not ruling out the reverse order of proceeding. Indeed, throughout June British representatives in Paris were sending contradictory messages about the French government's intentions. On 4 June the ambassador, Crewe, reported that on the previous day Péret had told the Finance Commission of the Chamber that he would not try to get the Washington agreement ratified during the current parliamentary session.[99] A few weeks later, however, Phipps was relaying information from Berthelot that Briand favoured immediate ratification and that the newly-appointed Finance Minister, Caillaux, was moving towards the same view.[100]

It seems a fair assumption that there was an element of tactical calculation behind the French equivocation: it was a useful way of keeping London and Washington guessing. But it also seems the case that – as so often in the past – French policymakers were genuinely undecided about whether to deal first with the British or the Americans. Whichever course they chose would have both advantages and disadvantages. Immediate ratification of the American settlement would greatly improve French chances of securing credits in New York. The franc would thereby be strengthened. A debt settlement with Britain would then become less urgent and could be negotiated from a stronger bargaining position. There was, however, a serious drawback: ratification would be deeply unpopular with a French public which had shown great antagonism towards the Mellon–Bérenger agreement. The main disadvantage of the other option was that, without prior ratification of the American settlement, and without the resultant access to credits, further negotiations with Britain would have to be conducted from a position of relative weakness. As against that, at least with the British government there was always the chance of obtaining some form of safeguard clause which might then be used to reopen the issue with the United States. According to Leith-Ross, it was precisely this that the French were aiming at. Their object, he told Churchill on 7 June, was 'to try to get some sort of safeguard clause here, and then play us off against the United States of America by refusing ratification of either settlement till they get the United States of America to accept a similar clause'.[101] Leith-Ross believed that such a policy was foolish, since there was not the remotest prospect of the Americans changing their mind on the matter.

Meanwhile, as the French government hesitated over which course to adopt, discussions had been taking place between British and French officials. After Péret's return to Paris on 18 May, some of the French experts had remained in London. Barnaud stayed until the 20th. Thereafter, it was left to the financial attaché, Pouyanne, to keep in touch with the Treasury and act as an intermediary between Churchill and Péret. It was understood that important issues of principle, and in particular the problem of finding some alternative to a safeguard clause, were to be settled by the two ministers concerned. The role of the experts was to examine the other outstanding points and work out the details of a draft agreement.

As the talks got under way, the mood at the Treasury was one of supreme confidence. This was based partly on the fact that Péret had already given an undertaking that £4m would be paid during 1926–7. As Niemeyer put it: 'We can I think await further events with equanimity as we have secured our payments for this year . . . '.[102] But the growing financial and political turmoil in France was the main reason why Treasury officials felt confident. Given current French difficulties, they believed that it was neither necessary nor desirable to compromise. 'The more I think about it', Niemeyer told Churchill in a note of 20 May, 'the less inclined am I to volunteer any further concessions beyond the very large ones we have already made. At any rate, it is no good giving concessions to an unstable Government whose power of delivering the goods is somewhat dubious'.[103]

At an early stage in the experts' discussions, Niemeyer proposed payments of £6m, £8m, £10m and £12.5m for the years 1926–30 inclusive, these to be followed by £13.5m annually between 1931 and 1987. The figures for the period up to 1930 were significantly higher than those suggested by the French or even by the British during the Churchill–Caillaux talks of the previous August. In order to make them more palatable, therefore, the French were informed that the payments would be made to correspond with the British financial year instead of the calendar year, the effect of which would be to give a three months' postponement. This represented a minor concession of sorts. In all other respects, however, both Niemeyer and Leith-Ross were unyielding. They indignantly rejected a claim from the French side that the present value of payments under the Mellon–Bérenger agreement amounted to only 42 per cent of the debt, compared to the 48.7 per cent being demanded by Britain. Nor were they apologetic when attention was drawn to the fact that the rates of interest so far charged by Britain exceeded those charged by the United States. While acknowledging that this was indeed the case, they argued that the disparity simply reflected the different market rates obtaining in the two countries. There was no hint of concession over the £53.5m of gold. Indeed, the French representatives were reported to be 'rather shaken by the actual wording of the texts now governing this gold'. A strong plea was made on behalf of British nationals whose property in France had been damaged during the war. As a result, it was agreed in principle that compensation should be paid at the same level as for French nationals. The French experts indicated that, because of a possible adverse reaction from domestic opinion, their government might wish this matter to be dealt with in a separate document and not publicised. Niemeyer said that he was prepared to consider the idea of a separate document. He could not undertake to keep the arrangement secret, however, and the British government must be free to disclose its existence. Finally, pressure was exerted on behalf of British holders of French war bonds who had seen the real value of their holdings diminished by some five-sixths because of the progressive depreciation of the franc.[104]

Reporting to Churchill after preliminary discussions, Niemeyer was unmistakably satisfied about the way they had gone. He recorded his 'very strong impression' that the French would eventually give way on all points at issue, including those to be dealt with at ministerial level. The safeguard clause was seen as a possible exception, though even here Niemeyer was 'by no means certain that they won't give way on that in the end'.[105] This particular issue was one on which both Niemeyer and Leith-Ross had pronounced views. They were adamantly opposed to conceding any such clause, especially since the United States had already refused to do so. In a note of 21 May 1926, Niemeyer warned Churchill of the various problems involved in allowing debt payments to be linked to reparation receipts. What particularly concerned him was the growing interest being shown in French and German political circles in the idea of a package deal including a commutation of France's share of the Dawes annuities for a lump sum payment by Germany. Such a 'private bargain' might well leave Britain 'out in the cold', and the damage to British interests would be compounded in the event of France having been allowed a safeguard clause:

> Thus the danger we have to avoid is that France, having (a) got something from us in the direction of dependence on Dawes of her payments to us, next (b) makes a bargain with Germany to commute on very favourable terms France's Dawes payments, and then (c) comes to us and says 'our Dawes payments have now been reduced: you must therefore reduce our debt payments to Great Britain'.[106]

Niemeyer foresaw another difficulty. However much care was taken over the wording of a safeguard clause, the French were bound to read into it more than was intended. 'No one can ever admit that a pledge is meaningless: therefore it must mean something: therefore, to French logic it means what the French say it means.' Because of this risk, any form of safeguard clause must be treated with 'great suspicion'. The best course was to have none whatsoever.[107]

As Niemeyer was well aware, the Chancellor's attitude on the question of a safeguard clause was not identical to his own. That probably helps to explain the strength of his warnings. On more than one occasion, Churchill had shown that he was prepared – albeit reluctantly – to consider some kind of formula covering the eventuality of a cessation of reparation payments. In August 1925 he had reached a tentative agreement with Caillaux on a suitable form of wording about consultation, only for the Cabinet to reject it, and during his recent talks with Péret the matter had been explored again. The fact that the Cabinet remained hostile obviously made Churchill's task harder. But it did not stop him from continuing to search for the elusive phraseology which would somehow satisfy the French without promising anything of substance. Unlike his officials, who saw no reason for haste now that there was a guaranteed payment of £4m for 1926–7, Churchill was desperate to reach a definite settlement as soon as possible, and all the indications were that one could only be had if France obtained a safeguard clause. On 4 June 1926, Crewe reported from Paris that, in view of the intense hostility aroused there by the Mellon–Bérenger agreement, he could 'scarcely believe that M. Péret would now venture to sign an agreement in London which does not in some form or other introduce the "safeguard" principle'.[108] This message was reinforced by a communication from Péret himself. In a letter of 12 June, which was intended as a belated reply to Churchill's own letter of 18 May, Peret said that he was more than ever convinced that a safeguard provision was essential – both to help French financial stability and because of the strength of French parliamentary and public opinion on the matter. During his recent visit to London he had sought to get round British objections to having a safeguard clause incorporated in the agreement by suggesting instead a ministerial exchange of letters. He now invited Churchill to send a draft of such letters.[109]

Before Churchill could respond, Péret was out of office. On 15 June he resigned, to be replaced by Caillaux. The Briand government fell on the same day and there then followed a period of confusion during which there was a sharp drop in the value of the franc. After a failed attempt by Herriot, Briand succeeded in forming a Cabinet on the 23 June. Once again Caillaux was appointed Minister of Finance.[110]

In the meantime, the experts' discussions had not proceeded as smoothly as British Treasury officials had complacently anticipated. Far from capitulating on all the points at issue, as Niemeyer had predicted, the French showed a disturbing tendency to offer stout resistance and even to reopen matters that had apparently been settled to the Treasury's satisfaction. A case in point was the question of compensation for Britons whose property in France had suffered war damage. Having initially said that they saw no objection to compensation being paid on the same basis as for French nationals, French Treasury officials now claimed that for their government to make the payments would present political difficulties. The solution they put forward was that the British government should pay and then recover the necessary amount from the so-called French Suspense Account. As Leith-Ross pointed out to Churchill, such an arrangement would have serious drawbacks. It would mean the British government becoming directly involved in the business of compensation, which it wished to avoid. Besides, all the credits in the French Suspense Account would be needed for the debt settlement. Leith-Ross was disappointed at the way the French had changed their position. The claims for compensation were of limited financial importance, he told Churchill, but they had aroused a great deal of feeling amongst the British colony in France. Unless the French government treated British property owners in a manner that was seen to be fair, there would be an outcry which might well 'provoke criticism of our debt concessions.'[111]

VIII

With Caillaux's return to office in late June, there was a speedy resumption of talks at ministerial level and negotiations for a settlement entered their final phase. For his part, Churchill was gratified to be dealing once more with a colleague whom he respected as courageous and businesslike. On the French side, there was now a greater sense of urgency, the main reason being the financial predicament in which they found themselves. The position was aptly summed up by Sir Charles Mendl, the well-informed press attaché at the British embassy in Paris, who described the situation facing the Finance Minister as 'indeed terrible'.[112] On 4 July the Sergent committee, which had been set up by the previous Briand government to examine the causes of France's financial difficulties, produced its report. One of its main conclusions was that foreign assistance was essential to stabilise the franc and that this would only be forthcoming if France funded her debts.[113] Caillaux did not disagree with this analysis, the logic of which was there would need to be an early settlement with Britain. This did not mean, however, that he was prepared to settle without a great deal of hard bargaining.

Caillaux's opening move was to repeat the tactics he had used the previous year, when he had sought to conduct informal negotiations through an assortment of unofficial intermediaries. This time the agent chosen to convey his views to Churchill was James Dunn, a businessman and financier. In late June 1926, Dunn and Caillaux had a conversation in Paris in which the Finance Minister expounded at some length his thoughts on the debt question.[114] He began by comparing the terms of the Mellon–Bérenger agreement with those currently being offered by Britain, claiming that the former were far more lenient: the early annuities were very small; this alleviation was not to be compensated for by additional payments at a later stage; and there was provision for a suspension of payments for a period of three years. The American settlement was not without deficiencies, though, the most serious being the absence of a safeguard clause, which Caillaux considered absolutely essential. Next, he spoke of some broader considerations which the British government might care to bear in mind. In particular, he stressed how important it was for British trade, as well as for the health of the European economy in general, that France should have a strong government and that the franc should be stabilised. It was also important that France should not be asked to pay more than French public opinion was prepared to tolerate. Nor must anything be done which might impair the personal prestige of Caillaux himself, so that it would be necessary to sort out all outstanding differences and have an agreement ready for signature before he set off to meet Churchill in London. As far as the actual terms were concerned, he had no intention of departing from the central feature of the understanding reached the previous August, namely a standard annuity of £12.5m. As he had made clear at the time, however, acceptance of this figure must be subject to a number of conditions. First, payments would have to start at a low level and not reach £12.5m until the fifth year. Nor should there be any compensation for this shortfall in later years. Secondly, France must be given the right to postpone any one payment for a period of three years. Thirdly, and most important of all, there must be a safeguard clause to cover the contingency of a suspension or complete failure of reparation payments.[115]

These conditions cannot have been unexpected, since Caillaux was essentially reiterating the reservations he had formally expressed in August 1925. But he also raised another issue which did cause a certain amount of surprise in London – at least about his approach to it. According to Dunn, he frequently referred to the large sums to be repaid by the Bank of France to the Bank of England over the next few years. It could not be said that Caillaux's preoccupation with this particular matter was new. His remarks to Dunn, however, appeared to suggest that his views on it had undergone a change of emphasis since he was last in office. During his talks in London the previous year, he had tried to enlist Treasury help in persuading the Bank of England to agree to a rescheduling of payments. His argument then had been that a reduction in the Bank of France's transfer obligations in the years up to 1930 would enable the French government to pay bigger annuities to Britain during the corresponding period. Now he seemed to be going further by suggesting that the inter-bank debt should be treated as an integral part of French government obligations and that the latter should be reduced by the amount paid by the Bank of France.[116]

Concluding the interview, Caillaux emphasised the importance he attached to an early settlement. He asked Dunn to see that the 'proposals' which he had outlined were put to Churchill as soon as possible and to bring back information about his reaction to them.[117] In the event, Dunn made no attempt to contact the Chancellor directly. Instead, he wrote to Birkenhead, a Cabinet colleague and close personal friend of Churchill, setting out the views Cailllaux had expressed.[118] His letter was then sent on to the Treasury. Caillaux's approach was thus even more circuitous than usual.

At the Treasury, Caillaux's manoeuvring produced a strong feeling of *déja vu*. As on previous occasions, there was not the slightest intention of responding. Leith-Ross saw 'no reason, and much risk, in attempting to negotiate through unofficial intermediaries'.[119] The French were already perfectly aware of the British government's views – which had been set out in a draft agreement of 14 May 1926 and thoroughly discussed with the French experts. The next step must be official negotiations. Niemeyer fully agreed. Caillaux was 'famous for his love of subterranean intermediaries', he warned Churchill in a note of 30 June, and it would be 'utterly imprudent to deal with fundamental questions in this way. Mr James Dunn is also a most dangerous channel'. If Caillaux really wanted to know the Chancellor's views, then he 'must come and negotiate and not seek a steady trickle of concessions through irresponsible agents'.[120] Such warnings were superfluous. Churchill minuted on Niemeyer's note: 'I am well aware of all this and had in fact declined the adventure as soon as it was received.'[121]

The Treasury's distaste for Caillaux's unorthodox methods was matched by their irritation at what he had to say. His insistence that France should have the right to postpone a payment for three years was not regarded as a problem, since it had already been decided to grant a concession along those lines.[122] But the Treasury dismissed as 'completely unfounded' the argument that, because the Bank of France was repaying its loan from the Bank of England in full, payments by the French government to the British government should therefore be scaled down.[123] According to Leith-Ross, the two debts were entirely separate matters. It was true that the British government had guaranteed the Bank of England against loss in connection with its credit to the Bank of France. It had only done so under strong pressure from the French government, however, and the then Chancellor of the Exchequer, Austen Chamberlain, had made clear his dislike of the arrangement. In any case, the fact remained that the transaction between the central banks was a purely commercial one and had no connection with the debt owed by the French Treasury.[124]

There was short shrift also for the other arguments advanced by Caillaux. Despite what Caillaux had said, Leith-Ross thought it essential that reduced annuities in the early years should be made good by payments above the standard rate of £12.5m at a later stage. Without such a provision, France would be repaying only 44 per cent of her total debt compared to 50 per cent in the case of her debt to the United States. Waiving compensation for lower payments before 1930 could only be considered as a *quid pro quo* for French concessions over the gold question or the safeguard clause. On the latter, Leith-Ross was adamant: France must not be allowed the right to delay or suspend payment in proportion to any shortfall in reparations. Even if Germany paid only half of the Dawes annuities over the next fifteen years, France would still receive in excess of £35m per annum – more than enough to meet her obligations to both Britain and the United States. Caillaux appeared to think that there was some chance of persuading the Americans to change their mind and agree to a safeguard clause. But Leith-Ross believed that there was no prospect whatever of that happening.[125]

IX

While the information provided by Dunn was thus being subjected to critical examination at the Treasury, Caillaux was making his negotiating position known through more conventional diplomatic channels. Indeed, so short was the time lag between Caillaux's unofficial approach and his official one that it is difficult to see precisely what purpose the former was intended to serve. On 30 June Churchill received a visit from de Fleuriau, who brought with him two documents setting out the Finance Minister's views on points still to be settled. Caillaux was anxious to come to London as son as possible, the ambassador said, but could not do so until he saw some real prospect of reaching agreement on those points.[126]

The arguments put forward in the documents handed over by de Fleuriau were essentially the same as those already outlined by Dunn. Churchill replied immediately in a letter to Caillaux.[127] This was accompanied by a draft agreement reflecting the position reached so far in the discussions between the experts. In his letter, Churchill began by expressing disappointment at the lack of any progress in recent months. Since negotiation of the provisional agreement in August 1925 the interest on the French debt had grown by nearly £30m. Over the same period, moreover, Britain had suffered the 'double disadvantage' of being obliged to pay the United States £30m, while receiving nothing from France – despite the fact that the latter had obtained substantial reparation payments. This situation was admittedly no fault of Caillaux, who had not been in office. But Churchill begged him to 'realise the painful impression which these developments have made upon British public opinion'. There were a number of matters which Churchill regarded as settled and not open to discussion. These included the principle of 62 standard annuities of £12.5m, the actual level of payments for each year and the need to compensate for the initial reduced annuities. The French request for the right to postpone transfers was not seen as a difficulty, since this was already provided for in the enclosed draft agreement. The only question of substance remaining to be dealt with, therefore, was that of a safeguard clause. On this, Churchill's position remained as set out in his letter to Péret of 18 May. The Cabinet had consistently taken the view that payments must be on the sole credit of France, without reference to reparations – the annuities having been scaled down on that understanding – and its opposition to a safeguard clause had been strengthened by the refusal of the Americans to concede one in the Mellon–Bérenger agreement. Despite this, Churchill was prepared to try to accommodate Caillaux's wishes by means of a ministerial exchange of letters, along the lines originally suggested by Péret. Although unable to accept the wording proposed by Péret during his London visit, he was nevertheless ready to consider some amended version which was suitable for putting to the Cabinet. In that way he hoped 'to meet to some extent the views you have already expressed without vitiating the principle of sixty-two £12½ million annuities on the sole credit of France'.[128]

In the ensuing negotiations, it was the issue of a safeguard formula which dominated and which for a time threatened to be a sticking point. Churchill's position was a difficult one. On the one hand, he was fully aware of the continuing hostility felt by Cabinet colleagues towards any arrangement linking repayments with French reparation receipts. On the other hand, he was equally aware that France would not agree to a debt settlement unless it included such an arrangement. The only way round this intractable problem was to find some form of wording which would satisfy the French that they had the protection they desired, while at the same time convincing the Cabinet that there had been no erosion of the principle that payments must be on the credit of France alone.

Most of the detailed discussion about phraseology was conducted by Pouyanne and Niemeyer, with Churchill and Caillaux putting the finishing touches. On 4 July 1926, Pouyanne, who had been in Paris for consultation with Caillaux, returned to London with fresh instructions. The same day he had talks with Niemeyer, as a result of which agreement was reached on a draft exchange of letters and a number of other items. Pouyanne then went on to see Churchill at his country home, Chartwell.[129] The Chancellor was somewhat uneasy about the draft, feeling that it represented a substantial concession by the British side and might expose him to 'accusations of having been worsted again by the Americans' who had refused to consider any kind of safeguarding provision. Nevertheless, despite these misgivings, he thought that he might be able to persuade the Cabinet to accept it – providing everything else was settled along the lines discussed by Niemeyer and Pouyanne.[130]

The meeting at Chartwell took place on a Sunday which meant that it was not possible to consult colleagues immediately. Churchill's intention, therefore, was to put the matter to the Cabinet on the following day, secure a favourable decision if possible, and inform Caillaux of the outcome at once. On 5 July, however, the French embassy reported that Caillaux wanted some slight changes in the draft letters, and this necessitated further discussions between Niemeyer and Pouyanne. On 10 July, it became known that the French Cabinet had suggested additional alterations, and these were studied by Leith-Ross, Pouyanne and Barnaud. Leith-Ross indicated that he was able to accept some of them, but others would need to be discussed by Churchill and Caillaux when the latter came to London.[131]

When Caillaux flew to London[132] on 12 July, therefore, there was still some negotiating to be done. But the remaining differences were not of major importance and were settled without any great difficulty during a meeting at the French embassy between Churchill and Caillaux. The last obstacle was removed when Churchill accepted four proposed alterations in Caillaux's safeguard letter, and the final texts of the agreement were signed at 6 p.m.[133]

8

The 1926 Settlement and
its Aftermath

I

The debt settlement concluded by Churchill and Caillaux in July 1926 provided for total payments of £801.5m spread over a period of 62 years.[1] According to *The Economist*, using an interest rate of 4.25 per cent as a basis for its calculations, this represented a present value of £264m – a reduction of 56 per cent on the debt as funded of £600m.[2] The Treasury, working on the assumption of a 5 per cent interest rate, arrived at corresponding figures of £227m and 62 per cent.[3] Whichever of these calculations one accepts, there was clearly a substantial writing down of the amount owed, although not as great as in the case of the Anglo-Italian settlement which involved a reduction of more than 80 per cent.

The central feature of the Churchill–Caillaux agreement was that France was to pay an average of £12.5m during each year between 1926 and 1988. Until 1930 payments would be on a rising scale or *échelle*: £4m in 1926–7, £6m in 1927–8, £8m in 1928–9 and £10m in 1929–30. Between 1930 and 1957 there would be a standard annuity of £12.5m. Thereafter, France would pay £14m annually in order to compensate for the low level of the early figures. Payments were to be made in two equal half-yearly instalments on 15 March and 15 September of each financial year. In accordance with the Balfour Note principle, article 5 of the agreement stated that if Britain's receipts from Germany and allied debtors combined exceeded her own annuities to the United States, France was to be credited with a proportionate share of the surplus. Another article (4) gave France the right to postpone payment of one half of her annual obligations for a period up to three years in the event of exchange difficulties. All these provisions were incorporated in the main body of the agreement. The latter was supplemented, however, by no fewer than six pairs of letters between Churchill and Caillaux. At the final negotiating session it had been agreed that only the exchange of letters relating to the safeguard question should be made public, with the result that the White Paper on the settlement contained no reference to the others. The letter from Caillaux which was published included the statement:

> If, therefore, for reasons outside the control of France, such [reparation] receipts should cease completely or to a greater extent than one half, in such an event a new situation would be created and the French Government is bound to reserve the right in such an event of asking the British Government to reconsider the question in the light of all the circumstances then prevailing.

In his reply, Churchill noted this reserve. He made no promises, however, maintaining the usual British line that payments must be 'on the sole credit of France' and insisting that, if there were to be any alterations, he would expect France's other creditors (i.e. the United States) to make similar ones in order to ensure equal treatment. While this exchange of statements was far from being the guarantee of an automatic adjustment which Caillaux and other French finance ministers had consistently sought, it was hoped that it would at least suffice to make the settlement somewhat more palatable to French public opinion.

The rest of the supplementary letters – those whose existence had not been disclosed – were of varying degrees of importance. In some cases, they were purely technical, specifying the form of bonds to be delivered by the French government and clarifying arrangements for closing the accounts. One pair of letters dealt with the claims of British nationals for war damage to their property in France. Another concerned the repayment by the Bank of France of its wartime loan from the Bank of England, with Churchill acknowledging that the level of payments to be made by the French government in the period up to 1930 was conditional upon modification – within one month of the signature of the intergovernmental war debt settlement – of the existing 1923 agreement between the two banks.[4]

This last matter was a particularly sensitive one since the necessary approval of the Governor of the Bank of England had not yet been obtained. At the time the Churchill–Caillaux agreement was signed Norman was on holiday in Antibes with his friend Benjamin Strong, and it was more than a week afterwards before he was officially approached about it. On 23 July, Niemeyer wrote to him explaining what had been agreed. He pointed out that when the Bank of France had borrowed from the Bank of England in 1916 it had been acting as an agent of the French government. As a result, the French Treasury was under an obligation to reimburse the Bank whenever the latter made repayments and therefore desired a reduction in the amounts to be paid in the years up to 1930. 'I greatly hope', Niemeyer concluded, 'that it will be possible for you to reach some accommodation with the Bank of France on this question in order that no alteration need be made in the scale fixed in the debt funding arrangements'.[5] In the event, Norman went along with the Treasury's wishes. But he was understandably angry.[6] Not only did he resent political interference of any kind in central bank affairs. He also felt, with some justification, that he had been presented with a *fait accompli* and placed in the invidious position of having to agree to something of which he heartily disapproved. It was true, as Niemeyer indicated in his letter, that the Treasury had always made it clear to the French that a final decision about altering the inter-bank agreement must be left to the Governor. In theory, therefore, Norman was free to reject the Treasury's request if he so wished. In practice, however, he was under irresistible pressure to acquiesce, since a refusal on his part would have necessitated fresh negotiations over the payments to be made in the period up to 1930. To compound Norman's irritation, he was also dissatisfied with the arrangements made for returning the French gold deposited in London during the war.

Nor were Treasury officials entirely satsfied with the terms of the final settlement. Throughout the negotiations leading up to it, Leith-Ross and Niemeyer had consistently taken a tougher line than Churchill, arguing that the British government was in a very strong bargaining position and should hold out for substantially bigger annuities than the French were offering. They had always been fearful that the Chancellor would be excesively generous. It now appeared that their fears had been warranted. Certainly the sums that Britain was to receive fell far short of the £16m per annum Treasury officials had considered reasonable, and also of the estimates – perhaps unrealistic – that Churchill himself had bandied about before embarking on negotiations. One aspect of the settlement which was a source of particular disappointment to Leith-Ross and his colleagues was the low level of payments fixed for the early years. Nor were they mollified by the fact that annuities of more than £12.5m were to be paid as compensation from 1957 onwards, regarding the prospect of big sums in the remote future as 'pure eyewash'.[7]

II

News of the settlement was announced to the House of Commons on 13 July 1926,[8] and on the following day Churchill defended it at length when speaking at the Mansion House. His main concern was to stress the political benefits of moderation. Anticipating criticism that the terms were too lenient, he told his audience:

> We could no doubt have won a great deal of praise from some quarters which pass for being instructed and are certainly articulate if we had used the same rigour to our debtors as has been meted out to us. But I am sure it would not have been a wise or far-sighted policy for a British government to win cheap cheers and a thin and ramshackle reputation for firmness by making demands which would never be carried out. The compact and solid substance is worth the pretentious and majestic shadow.[9]

Not everyone was persuaded by this line of argument. Indeed, the agreement was given a decidedly mixed reception both in the press and in Parliament. Some newspapers, such as *The Times*, expressed relief that a troublesome business had at last been brought to a moderately satisfactory conclusion.[10] But those which were less friendly to the government, including *The Manchester Guardian, The Nation and Athenaeum* and *The New Statesman*, were highly critical, claiming that France had got off lightly and that Caillaux had been far more successful in defending his country's interests than Churchill had. According to *The New Statesman*, indeed, the Chancellor had been 'completely bamboozled' by the Finance Minister of what was 'notoriously the most prosperous country in Europe today'.[11]

A similar division of opinion was evident when the matter was debated by the Commons on 19 July 1926. Speeches were predominantly hostile, although there was a limited amount of backing for the terms Churchill had negotiated. One Conservative backbencher, Major Albery, spoke in favour of a policy of generosity to 'that great country which, after all, was our very faithful and loyal Ally during the bitter years'.[12] Another, Sir Gerald Strickland, declared his support for complete cancellation of French war debts, provided France would consent to 'stop the undermining of the Empire and all intrigues which are contrary to our interests in the Mediterranean and the East'.[13] Almost without exception, however, even the staunchest government supporters found it difficult to summon up much enthusiasm for the settlement. The best they could say in its favour was that it would remove a persistent cause of friction between Britain and France and that remitting a portion of the debt would probably be good business in the long run.[14] Most speakers appeared to agree with the verdict of the Liberal MP Edward Hilton Young that it was 'not a brilliant settlement'.[15]

It was Hilton Young, a former Financial Secretary to the Treasury and an acknowledged expert on financial matters, who contributed what was perhaps the most balanced assessment of the funding agreement. He could see the merit of not overburdening France, since it was in Britain's own interest to promote the stability of the franc and thus encourage American funds to come to Europe. He very much doubted, however, whether the agreement that had just been reached would in fact assist towards that end. To stabilise their currency, the French would need foreign loans, which would only be available when there was confidence in French credit. It did not help to restore confidence, however, when France was repaying her debts on the basis of 6/8d in the pound and making repayment conditional upon receipt of reparations. According to Hilton Young, herein lay a crucial difference between British and French attitudes: 'We claim to receive from our debtors only so much as we pay to our creditors. The French agree to pay only so much as they receive, and in that way credit cannot be re-established.'[16]

The Liberal MP William Wedgwood Benn likewise expressed doubt as to whether French credit stood any higher as a result of the settlement. He was also sceptical about government claims that the settlement would help to create more stable political conditions in France, pointing to the fall of the Briand ministry on 17 July as evidence to the contrary. It seemed to Wedgwood Benn that the debt agreement was open to criticism on a least three counts. First, it betrayed the interests of the 'average taxpayer' in Britain who had looked for relief from his burdens in a 'proper settlement of the debt owing to us'. Secondly, the Baldwin government had failed to make use of its bargaining power as a creditor of France to insist upon certain concessions, such as a reduction of French tariffs or military expenditure. Finally, by consenting to a 'safeguarding arrangement', the government had put Britain in a position where she might find herself combining with France 'in bringing pressure to bear upon Germany to pay [reparation] annuities which may or may not be within her capacity to pay'.[17]

This feature of the settlement worried other critics, including the former Liberal minister Walter Runciman.[18] Nor were they reassured by Churchill's insistence that the exchange of letters between himself and Caillaux involved no binding obligations. It was obvious from press reports, Runciman said, that this opinion was not one shared by Caillaux.[19]

Lloyd George was amongst those disturbed by this particular point. He was, moreover, forcibly struck by the glaring incongruity which he saw between French claims of severe financial hardship when it came to repaying debts and the conspicuous prosperity that France appeared to be currently enjoying:

> There is no unemployment and on the whole there is a balance on French trade. All the old factories are going up and the account I get from all parts of France is one of new buildings, great prosperity, and at the same time this failure to pay debts.[20]

Other speeches against the settlement came from Labour backbenchers like Kenworthy, a persistent critic of France. Not unexpectedly, however, it was Snowden, Labour's chief spokesman on financial affairs and an ardent Francophobe, who launched the fiercest attack. His main complaint was that Churchill had given France far more generous terms than she had received from the Americans. According to Snowden, the United States would obtain from France a sum equivalent to more than twice the capital debt, whereas Britain would be getting only slightly more than the capital owing to her. He calculated that Churchill's misguided magnanimity – not only to France, but to Italy and the rest of Britain's foreign debtors – would cost the British taxpayer an extra £100m annually for the next 62 years.[21]

Behind all the specific criticisms from Snowden and other Labour speakers lay a general bitterness about the Baldwin government's alleged generosity to France. For the Opposition, the issue was quite simple: the more money Britain could squeeze from foreign debtors, the lighter her own intolerable burden of taxation would be. By cancelling a large part of the debts owed by France, the government was effectively easing the position of the French taxpayer at the expense of his British counterpart. In the aftermath of the General Strike, at a time when feelings about it were still raw, Labour claimed to see a revealing contrast between the consideration Churchill and his colleagues showed to foreigners and their apparent lack of sympathy for British workers. The MP for Merthyr Tydfil, Richard Wallhead, spoke for many in his party when he voiced a complaint on this score – a complaint which was to be heard frequently over the next few years, especially during debates on unemployment:

> We are demanding the full pound of flesh as far as our own working classes are concerned and they are worse hit than any other working class in Europe . . . France is a tremendously rich country. The working classes there are well off, while on the other hand our own working people are to be compelled to find an enormous sum of money to pay the debts of France and Italy and half the world besides.[22]

In one repect at least there was a curious *lacuna* in the reasoning of the Opposition, who dwelt enviously on France's commercial and industrial prosperity as if it were an offence. The French financial crisis was acknowledged, indeed relished. Yet it seemed not to be regarded as a mitigating factor in France's failure to pay her debts promptly and in full. Rather, it provided a convenient excuse to castigate the French people for irresponsibility and selfishness. There is a certain irony, too, in the fact that Wedgwood Benn, Kenworthy and others should have advocated the use of financial pressure to secure political concessions, since they were amongst the harshest critics of such tactics when used by the French.[23]

Labour's onslaught on the settlement was doubtless prompted to some extent by considerations of party advantage: it was not improbable, after all, that attacking the government for sacrificing the interests of the taxpayer would be popular with the electorate. The indignation was genuine enough, however, fuelled by moral outrage at the French failure to fulfil their obligations. Moreover, anger at the terms was all the stronger because there already existed widespread antipathy towards France within the Labour party. While this antipathy was the product of many factors, it was bound up above all with Labour's deep-seated hostlity towards the Treaty of Versailles. There was a tendency to blame France for the severity of the treaty, and French attempts to enforce its provisions by military means in 1920, and again in 1923, had helped to fix in Labour minds the image of France as a brutal oppressor of peaceful, democratic Germany. These episodes, together with the fact that France insisted on maintaining a high level of armaments throughout the 1920s, had also given her a reputation in British Labour circles as a militaristic and imperialistic power bent on establishing a neo-Napoleonic hegemony in Europe.

III

French war debts were far from being a dead issue after the settlement of July 1926. There were a number of reasons for this. Serious difficulties arose over a lengthy delay in ratification by the Poincaré government. Negotiations between the Bank of England and the Bank of France about modification of their 1923 loan agreement proved to be troublesome and acrimonious. Fruitless attempts to secure financial compensation for British holders of French war bonds caused ill-feeling on both sides.[24] Moreover, the fact that France enjoyed greater economic success than Britain in the period after the settlement served to fan the resentment many felt in any case over the apparent leniency of its terms.

In the years after 1926 the performance of the British economy was distinctly unimpressive, with Britain experiencing what one economic historian has termed 'a rather feeble boom' compared to most other advanced industrial countries.[25] The traditional exporting industries, such as coal and shipbuilding, continued to struggle, their difficulties now aggravated – after the return to the Gold Standard in 1925 – by an overvalued currency. Nor was there a great deal of growth in the service sector or in newer industries, such as motor manufacturing, chemicals and electrical engineering. Between 1926 and 1929 overall output increased at a slower rate than in the first half of the decade, with industrial production and investment actually falling between 1927 and 1928.[26] By comparison, the position in France was much healthier. There the *de facto* stabilisation of the franc (in December 1926) at around 122 to the pound, or less than one fifth of its pre-war international value, gave exports a strong competitive edge. At the same time, the formation of a Government of National Union, headed by Poincaré (who also assumed the post of Minister of Finance), helped to restore financial confidence. The net result was that from 1926 onwards France prospered. The franc became one of the strongest currencies in the world; industrial production forged ahead; unemployment remained low; there was a healthy surplus on the balance of payments; and the Bank of France acquired massive holdings of gold and foreign currency reserves.[27] The general state of the economy thus compared very favourably with that in Britain, where sluggish growth and an unemployment figure that remained stuck around the one million mark were the salient features of economic life in the second half of the 1920s.

Given this sharp contrast in the economic fortunes of the two countries, it is hardly surprising that the concessions which had been made to France over war debts continued to rankle in many quarters long after 1926. This feeling was reflected, for example, in a *Daily Herald* leading article of 18 April 1929 which made a swingeing attack on the various debt settlements negotiated by Churchill, singling out the one with France for special attention:

The French position is especially serious. France is enjoying . . . a large measure of prosperity; this country is steeped in unemployment. It is plain injustice that British taxpayers shall have to pay . . . £37 millions a year to America while they will be receiving (under the Churchill settlements) from France, Italy and other Continental countries, for debts far exceeding what Britain owes to America, only £20 millions a year.'

In Parliament, Churchill was subjected to constant criticism, especially from Snowden, on the grounds that he had been excessively generous. Churchill's private secretary at that time, P. J. Grigg, suggests in his memoirs that Snowden's attacks were not really serious and that he merely 'went through the motions' of belabouring the Chancellor.[28] Yet Churchill himself appears to have taken the attacks seriously enough. What is more, he increasingly came to feel that there was a substantial element of truth in the complaint voiced by Snowden and other critics that he had been too generous and that the French had badly misled him about their capacity to pay.[29] He came close to admitting as much when grumbling to Baldwin in September 1928 about the way Britain had been treated by foreign debtors and creditors alike: 'I was', he wrote, 'much criticised for the lenient treatment of France and Italy on the war debts, and it is clear that France is well able to pay us larger annuities than the Caillaux terms though I do not think she would ever have agreed to do so'.[30] Treasury officials similarly felt aggrieved on this score. Having consistently taken the view that the French could afford to pay more than they were offering, Leith-Ross and Niemeyer were naturally irritated to discover some time after terms had been settled that the French negotiators had been authorised to agree to bigger annuities.[31]

IV

In the period immediately following the signature of the Churchill–Caillaux settlement, the first priority was to revise the loan agreement which the Bank of England and the Bank of France had concluded in 1923. It will be recalled that, in one of the six pairs of ministerial letters exchanged as part of the settlement, it was agreed that the level of French government payments fixed for the years up to 1930 was conditional upon a reduction in the amounts due to be paid during the same period by the Bank of France to the Bank of England. These amounts had been determined by their 1923 agreement and were to be modified by means of direct negotiations between the two central banks. The sums of money involved were not very large and there seemed no reason to anticipate any serious difficulty in bringing the matter to a swift and successful conclusion. Yet the ensuing negotiations between the Governor of the Bank of England and his French counterpart, Emile Moreau, dragged on for almost a year – from July 1926 until April 1927. Moreover, they were conducted throughout in a spirit of intense rancour on both sides.

Both the sour atmosphere and the failure to make rapid progress can be explained to some extent by the circumstances in which the negotiations had originated, with one of the principal participants, Norman, feeling that the Treasury had failed to consult him properly before committing him to a course which he believed to be unwise. It is arguable, too, that they were a legacy in part of Norman's own somewhat tactless behaviour in 1923, when the then Governor of the Bank of France, Robineau, had asked for a rescheduling of payments to be made under the inter-bank loan agreement of 1916. Norman had made his consent to this request subject to certain stringent conditions. These included a stipulation that the extended credit must be available only to the Bank of France, not to the French Treasury, and that it must be secured on the whole of the £18m of gold deposited in London against the original loan.[32] At the Bank of France, this outcome left a lingering feeling of resentment against Norman. Moreau, who replaced Robineau as Governor in April 1926, regarded the 1923 agreement with deep hostility. It was, in his view, a humiliatng symbol of the weak and subservient policies of his predecessor, a blot on the national honour that he meant to expunge at the earliest opportunity.[33]

Such a background was scarcely conducive to a co-operative approach over modification of that agreement. Negotiations were rendered more difficult still by a serious clash of personalities between the two main negotiators, Norman and Moreau, and by the development of major policy differences in other areas.[34] It would be no exaggeration to speak of Norman and Moreau being engaged from the summer of 1926 onwards in a fierce power struggle. At the root of their rivalry was the growing relative strength of the Bank of France and the problems this posed for the Bank of England. During the early postwar years, the latter had played a predominant part in the financial reconstruction of Europe. From mid-1926, however, its influence and authority were increasingly challenged by the Bank of France. Moreover, in the ensuing contest between the two institutions it soon became clear that the French authorities' possession of substantial gold and foreign currency reserves placed them in a position, if they wished, to exert considerable pressure on sterling. Keynes expressed the realities of the situation with his customary pithiness when he wrote at the beginning of 1929: 'It is evident that we all survive, and the Bank of England in particular, by the favour of the Bank of France.'[35]

The revelation of this dependence naturally came as an unpalatable shock to Norman and his colleagues, and they experienced great difficulty in adjusting to the new balance of power.[36] The reversal of fortunes was swift and unexpected. In the summer of 1926 France was wracked by a financial crisis of the utmost gravity.[37] Yet within a year the franc had become the strongest European currency and the Bank of France had obtained what amounted to a stranglehold on the London money market. Norman discovered, to his consternation, that there existed a new spirit of confident self-assertiveness in Paris and that the Bank of France was no longer prepared to play second fiddle to the Bank of England.

One of the men responsible for this remarkable upsurge in French confidence was Moreau; and it is more than coincidence that his assumption of office as Governor of the Bank of France was followed by a sharp deterioration in its relations with the Bank of England. Moreau was a staunch nationalist, provincial to the core and deeply attached to his native Poitou. He had travelled little and spoke no foreign languages.[38] Almost by instinct he divided people into two categories: those whom he believed to be friends of France and the rest. After his first meeting with Norman, on 26 July 1926, he was under no illusion as to where the latter's sympathies lay, recording in his diary:

> Il n'aime pas les Français . . . par contre, il semble éprouver la plus vive sympathie pour les Allemands. Il est tres lié avec le docteur Schacht qu'il voit souvent et avec qui il dresse des plans secrets; ce penchant est d'ailleurs conforme au sentiment général de la Cité.[39]

Moreau nursed a grievance about the humiliations, real or imagined, that the Bank of France had suffered in the recent past.[40] He particularly resented the subordinate position it had been forced to occupy in its dealings with the Bank of England and was determined that the relationship in future should be one of absolute equality.

Norman, for his part, regarded the ascendancy of the Bank of England as part of the natural order of things and was not accustomed to contradiction either within the Bank or from foreign bankers. As Moreau correctly surmised, he had no great liking for the French.[41] Indeed, his secretary, E. D. H. Skinner, included them in a list of his 'fundamental dislikes', along with 'Roman Catholics, Jews, chartered accountants and in a more goodhumoured way the Scots.'[42] The distaste which Norman felt for the French was in some ways the obverse side of an affection for Germany, which dated from one of his rare periods of happiness as a student at Dresden.[43] He shared much of the City's traditional sympathy for Germany, a sentiment based on respect for German banking and on trading links which stretched back to the time of the Hanseatic League. In addition, he was a close friend of Hjalmar Schacht, the President of the Reichsbank.[44]

But Norman's attitude towards the French was not simply a matter of personal feelings. Like senior officials at the Treasury, he had grave doubts about the French authorities' expertise and was critical of many aspects of their policy. In the period after 1926, French financial policy flew in the face of all the orthodox advice offered by Norman and other British experts. The French were repeatedly warned that it would not be possible to stabilise the franc without first ratifying their war debt settlements.[45] Yet they proceeded to show that it could be done. The stabilisation took place, moreover, at a level which the British considered to be far too low. The successful stabilisation of the franc at less than one-fifth of its pre-war value against sterling was doubly vexatious to Norman. Not only did it add to his existing difficulties in defending an overvalued pound.

It also provided strong ammunition for those, like Keynes, who argued that the decision to restore sterling to its old parity was a major blunder. The French, it could be maintained, had learnt from Britain's error and had sensibly fixed their currency at a realistic rate.[46]

There was another feature of French policy which exasperated Norman. This was their growing involvement – or, as he saw it, unhelpful interference – in the work of restoring Europe's shattered finances.[47] A central element in the process of postwar recovery was the stabilisation of some of the weaker European currencies by means of international credit operations, and in the early 1920s such operations were invariably carried out under the auspices of the Financial Committee of the League of Nations – as in the case of Austria in 1922.[48] Norman thoroughly approved of this method of proceeding, considering the League to be the 'only safe and proper channel' where external financial control as well as assistance was involved.[49] He therefore became concerned when the French showed signs of wanting a change, following the dramatic improvement in their financial position and the appointment of Moreau as Governor of the Bank of France in 1926.

For various reasons Moreau wanted France to play a more prominent role in future currency stabilisation schemes. Unlike Norman, he did not view the Financial Committee of the League as an impartial and apolitical body. On the contrary, he regarded it as little more than a cloak for the promotion of British financial imperialism;[50] and when one considers its composition and the influence wielded over it by individuals like Sir Arthur Salter, Sir Henry Strakosch, Sir Otto Niemeyer and Norman himself, it is not hard to understand why he should have formed this impression.[51] Quite apart from this consideration, it seemed to Moreau that France would derive great political advantage from using her financial resources to buttress French influence and prestige in countries seeking credits. This would be particularly true, he felt, where the countries concerned already enjoyed close political and military links with France. Hence his determination to ensure that stabilisation projects currently being planned for Poland, Romania and Yugolavia should be organised on a different basis from earlier ones, with France rather than the League being given the leading part.[52]

Such ideas were anathema to Norman. He doubted the capacity of the French to provide, or even make a significant contribution towards, the capital which would be required – not least because of domestic restrictions on lending abroad. More worrying still, in Norman's judgement, was the fact that their motives seemed to be primarily political and that they were aiming to further their own national interests in a manner which would be disavantageous to both the League and the countries needing financial assistance.[53] It was because he took this view that Norman tried to frustrate a number of currency stabilsation schemes put forward by Moreau during 1927–28. The result was a bitter struggle.[54] Although this did not come to a head until the summer of 1928 – when Norman was finally obliged to concede defeat – serious friction had already arisen over the issue of credits for Poland in the opening months of the previous year. This was at the very time that discussions were being held about revision of the 1923 inter-bank loan agreement.

V

'Given the policy differences outlined above, as well as the personal animosity between Norman and Moreau, it is not surprising that these discussions did not go smoothly. In the opening stages, the advantage lay with Norman. It was the Bank of France, after all, which was seeking a change in the *status quo* and such change was dependent on approval from him. His basic tactic, therefore, was to make no constructive proposals himself, whilst pouring cold water on those put forward by Moreau. As the talks continued into 1927, however, the latter's bargaining position became progressively stronger – mainly because of a marked imnprovement in the state of French public finances – and Norman found it increasingly difficult to persist with a purely negative approach.

The discussions got off to an inauspicious start shortly after the Churchill–Caillaux settlement had been signed. Disregarding a request for their postponement, Norman announced by letter, on 28 July 1926, that he would be arriving in Paris on the following day.[55] When the talks began – on 29 July – he insisted on using an interpreter, though he spoke fluent French.[56] He made it plain that, while he might be prepared to ease the burden of repayment for the Bank of France, it was essential that the French Treasury should not benefit from this concession. His position was expressed in such a forthright manner that Moreau was rather taken aback, recording in his diary: 'Il me dit littéralement: "Je veux bien aider la Banque de France. Mais je hais votre Gouvernement et votre Trésorie. Pour eux je ne ferai rien."'[57] Further conversations were held the next day and were mainly taken up by a lecture from Norman on one of his pet themes: the need for the Bank of France to be completely free from government interference.[58] To guarantee this, he suggested, might require amendments to the Bank's statutes and even to its constitution. He also pressed for an early stabilisation of the franc.[59]

The question of the 1923 loan agreement was not taken up again until 17 February 1927 when Norman received a telegram from Paris asking him to set aside the 21st and 22nd of the month for talks in London with representatives of the Bank of France. This request was prompted by Poincaré who insisted on the matter being discussed before Moreau went off for a fortnight's leave on 3 March.[60] Norman replied at once that 21 and 22 February were not suitable because of prior engagements – including a visit to Schacht in Berlin – and proposed instead a date in March. At the same time one of his assistants, Harry Siepmann,[61] despatched a telegram to Pierre Quesnay,[62] a senior official at the Bank of France, inviting him to come to London. Moreau's suspicions were instantly aroused. He instructed Quesnay to say that he could not leave Paris because his wife was expecting a baby and telegraphed to Norman asking him to stop off in Paris on his way to or from Berlin.[63]

Norman, accompanied by Siepmann, duly arrived in Paris on 25 February and spent the next two days involved in negotiations with Moreau and Quesnay on revision of the 1923 loan agreement.[64] By this time, however, he was even less accommodating than he had been in July of the previous year, partly because he was still smarting from his discomfiture in the petty manoeuvring that had just taken place, but more especially because of recent differences with the Bank of France over providing credits for Poland and Yugoslavia. Thus, when Moreau submitted a scheme for modification of the 1923 repayment schedule, Norman reacted coolly and immediately countered by insisting that any such modification must be contingent not only upon French ratification of the Churchill–Caillaux debt settlement, but also upon stabilisation of the franc.[65] Although the franc had been stabilised *de facto* the previous December, the Poincaré government had as yet taken no steps to proceed to legal stabilisation. Norman felt that its failure to do so was hampering efforts to re-establish European finances on a sound basis and he told Moreau bluntly that the example set by France had led to the unfortunate result that an unstabilised currency was no longer regarded as discreditable.[66] Quite apart from this consideration, Norman was 'emphatic in saying that while he wished to do everything in his power to help the bank of France, he was absolutely opposed in principle to doing anything which would merely help the French Treasury'. To this Moreau answered that any concession was bound to help the Treasury either directly or indirectly.[67]

Norman found the changes to the 1923 agreement proposed by Moreau both surprising and unpalatable. Far from seeking an extension of the repayment period, as originally requested, Moreau was now asking for it to be shortened. In return, he expected a reduction in the annual interest charge from 6.38 per cent to 5 per cent and a concession over the £18m of gold still held by the Bank of England as security for the loan. Under the 1923 agreement, none of the gold was to be returned to France before the end of May 1928. What Moreau now suggested was an immediate release of £7m of it, followed by a further release in August 1927 so as to ensure that at no time should the value of the gold held be more than one-third of the outstanding debt.[68] It seemed to Norman that none of these proposals was warranted by undertakings given by the British Treasury during the negotiations leading up to the Churchill–Caillaux settlement. Leith-Ross, whom he consulted when he returned to London, was in complete agreement. As one of the main participants in those negotiations, Leith-Ross confirmed that at no stage had the Treasury promised to support the Bank of France in pressing for anticipated payments or for an early return of some of the £18m of its gold held in London. The Treaury's only commitment had been to use their good offices to secure a longer period of repayment in order to ease the overall burden of French payments before 1930.[69]

With Norman unwilling to give serious consideration to Moreau's proposals, the Paris talks of 21–22 February 1927 ended inconclusively.[70] Moreau, however, was rapidly losing patience with the delaying tactics that were being employed and decided to finish the business one way or another. The circumstances of the time placed him in a good position to do so. In July of the previous year, when negotiations were just starting and when French state finances were in chaos, he had justifiably lamented the fact that in his dealings with the Bank of England he was without any trump cards.[71] He could scarcely make the same complaint now. Since October 1926, the Bank of France had been purchasing sterling on a large scale as part of a campaign designed to prevent an unwanted appreciation in the value of the franc.[72] The possession of these holdings provided a powerful instrument for exerting pressure on a vulnerable pound, as well as the means to settle the Bank of France's debts under the 1923 credit agreement.

On 19 March Norman received a telegram from Moreau indicating that the latter was anxious to take up the negotiations where they had been left in Paris and requesting a meeting between Norman and Quesnay on the 23rd or 24th of the month. Norman replied that he already had engagements for those particular dates and suggested instead that Siepmann could make himself available for some useful exploratory talks. Moreau refused to be fobbed off, however, and sent a second telegram stating that he had something new and important to say and would like to see Norman personally on 24 March. Norman acquiesced and he and Siepmann had a meeting in London on that date with Moreau, Quesnay and Pouyanne.[73] To their obvious surprise, Moreau made no attempt to bargain over a rescheduling of payments. Instead, he simply offered to repay the whole of the outstanding amount of £33m during the first two weeks of April.[74] Moreau professed to believe that such an arrangement must be satisfactory to the Bank of England because 'it would dispose once and for all of a question which had an embittering effect on mutual relations'.[75] But the reality was that Norman had a number of reservations. He was worried that the 'immense operation' which would be required to complete repayment in full by mid–April would have an adverse effect on the exchange and money markets in London.[76] He therefore suggested payment by stages, only for Moreau to object that such a procedure would be too slow. Another area of concern was that the proposed scheme would not afford an opportunity to insist upon early legal stabilisation of the franc and ratification of the Churchill–Caillaux settlement as essential preconditions of its acceptance. Norman did ask whether an assurance could be given on these matters. Moreau's discouraging reply, however, was that – contrary to his advice – Poincaré had said that he would not be able to act before next year's elections. The meeting closed with arrangements being made for further talks in ten days' or a fortnight's time.[77]

What the London meeting had clearly shown was that Norman was now in an extremely weak bargaining position. This was reflected in the draft scheme which he sent to Moreau on 31 March, which was very much along the lines that the latter himself had just put forward. The outstanding debt was to be redeemed by a single payment of £33m on 22 April 1927. Part of the sum ($100m) was to be paid in US dollars and the balance of £12,415,619 in sterling. Gold to the value of £18,350,615 was to be made available to the Bank of France. Norman's only show of defiance was to try to insist, as he had done all along, that no benefit should accrue to the French Treasury.[78] This was a stipulation which Moreau had no intention of accepting.

An appropriately wretched climax to the whole episode was still to come. At the beginning of April 1927 representatives of the world's leading central banks gathered at Calais to discuss the topic of financial aid for Poland. Norman and Moreau took the opportunity to finalise arrangements on repayment of the inter-bank loan, and the result was an unedifying squabble, with threats and counter-threats, which ended in total capitulation by Norman.[79] At a meeting of 3 April Moreau indicated that, although he found the Bank of England's proposals of 31 March generally acceptable, he was not willing to agree to the condition that the French Treasury must not derive benefit from any relief granted to the Bank of France. Norman argued that Robineau had committed himself to that effect in 1923 and that his pledge was binding on his successor.[80] Moreau was adamant, however, and Norman was eventually obliged to give way: in a letter of 8 April he accepted unreservedly the other's position.[81] Even at this late stage further difficulties arose from a difference of opinion over whether the £33m repayment should be made partly in dollars. Unable to reach agreement on the rate at which the dollars should be valued for this particular transaction, the French decided to repay in sterling alone. This caused alarm at the Treasury where Niemeyer declared himself to be 'greatly perturbed' at the prospect. He had wanted to cover part of the Treasury's current dollar requirements from this source and on 12 April he wrote to Norman expressing the hope that it would be possible for the payment to be made partly in dollars. In reply, Norman made the obvious point that the Bank of England could not refuse to be paid in sterling.[82]

Despite this last-minute hiccup, the problem of modification of the 1923 agreement was finally resolved in April 1927. The negotiations had lasted far longer than expected and had been conducted throughout in an atmosphere of intrigue and deep mistrust on both sides. It is true that the matter had finally been disposed of – but only at great cost. The outcome was not a mutually accept-able compromise. Rather, it was an undisguised triumph for the French and a humiliation for the British.

VI

The acrimonious wrangle which took place over the 1923 loan agreement was by no means the only, or even the most serious, dispute to arise concerning implementation of the Churchill–Caillaux debt settlement. There were sharp differences also over the French delay in ratifying it. The disagreement in this case involved governments rather than central banks. It was more protracted – lasting until the summer of 1929 – and commanded a greater degree of public interest.

In the period immediately following the conclusion of the Churchill-Caillaux settlement, there was not the remotest prospect of its ratification since France was at that time in a state of financial and political turmoil. On 17 July the Briand government was brought down when its attempt to secure the necessary decree powers for putting into effect the recommendations of the committee of experts chaired by Sergent ran into fierce opposition from a combination of Radicals, Socialists, Communists and nationalists associated with Louis Marin. Under the short-lived Herriot government which followed, the franc plunged to a disastrous new low of 240 to the pound, and it was not until Poincaré formed a broadly-based Government of National Union to tackle the crisis on 23 July that a semblance of stability began to appear.[83]

Shortly before taking office, Poncaré told a leading French journalist: 'Je ne veux pas être le Ministre de la Ratification'.[84] Yet initial indications as to his new government's intentions on the matter were not unpromising. On 28 July the French financial attaché, Pouyanne, reported to Niemeyer that Poincaré saw no objection to the Anglo-French debt agreement, which he considered to be far more favourable than the French agreement with the United States. Poincaré's overriding priority was to get legislative approval for his proposed financial measures. That, he hoped, would be achieved by 8 August. The Chamber would then be adjourned until October, but when it reconvened ratification would be the first topic of discussion. Although gratified by this assurannce, Niemeyer regarded it as somewhat vague and was certain that Churchill would share his view. The Chancellor was scheduled to answer a parliamentary question on the subject and wanted to be able to state that Poincaré would seek ratification as soon as the Chamber reassembled in the autumn. Pouyanne anticipated no difficulty over this and promised to consult Poincaré about it. He also raised the possibility that France might be spared the expense involved in renewal of the bills held by the British Treasury against existing debt obligations. Under the Churchill–Caillaux agreement, new French bills were supposed to be delivered before 15 September 1926, the date of the first payment. In the absence of ratification by then, this would not happen. Instead, old bills would be renewed as they matured and stamp duty would be charged. Pouyanne asked whether renewal might be suspended. Although his request was refused, it was later agreed that payment of stamp duty would be waived for the time being.[85]

On 15 September 1926 London received the scheduled first instalment of £2m. Meanwhile, as promised, Pouyanne had obtained from Poincaré authorisation for Churchill to inform the Commons that ratification would take place in the near future, and on 3 August a reply in that sense was duly given to a parliamentary question from Wedgwood Benn.[86] This was to prove an embarrassment, for it soon became clear that Poincaré was not prepared to act for fear of jeopardising the passage of his financial programme. On 3 October Adrian Dariac, the chairman of a sub-commission of the Chamber Finance Committee appointed to examine the question of inter-allied debts, made a speech suggesting that the whole business should be referred to the League of Nations or to an international conference or tribunal. The British ambassador in Paris, Crewe, suspected that this might be in the nature of a *ballon d'essai* on behalf of the French government.[87] More disturbing still from the British viewpoint was the fact that Poincaré's draft budget for 1927 contained no provision for repayment of war debts. Leith-Ross' reaction to this was to suggest that it might be desirable to get the Foreign Office to make formal representations.[88] Niemeyer doubted whether that would do much good, however, and on 27 October had a meeting with Pouyanne in an attempt to clarify the situation. Pouyanne frankly admitted that there was no chance of the Churchill–Caillaux settlement being ratified before the end of the year because of the current strength of public feeling in France against the debt agreement concluded with Washington.[89] At the same time, he assured Niemeyer that the French Treasury's budget calculations made allowance for the second half-yearly instalment of £2m due on 15 March 1927 and that the money would definitely be paid.[90] Niemeyer asked whether this assurance could be put in writing in the form of a letter from Poincaré. After going to Paris for consultations, however, Pouyanne returned with the message that Poincaré felt that it would be improper and unconstitutional for him, in his position as Minister of Finance, to send any such communication to a member of a foreign government. Pouyanne had been charged to make a verbal declaration stating that the present parliamentary session would be devoted entirely to the budget and that ratification of the debt settlement would be considered in January 1927. At Niemeyer's request, he submitted a note summarising this declaration on 9 November. The note was less explicit than the oral statement, making no mention of a date when ratification would be discussed. Although disappointed, Niemeyer felt that there was no point in pressing for more at that stage since, in his view, the French would be compelled to ratify before long because of the dire state of their finances. 'I am inclined to think', he told Churchill, 'that time is on our side'.[91]

Churchill, stung by what he considered to be a clear breach of the undertakings given by Poincaré at the end of July, was less patient and instructed Niemeyer to consider the possibility of 'some alternative to inaction'.[92] Niemeyer accordingly prepared a stiff draft note for the French government. This detailed the history of French 'tergivisations' since the despatch of the Balfour Note in 1922. It warned that the Churchill–Caillaux agreement could not be regarded 'as an option which is indefinitely open to the French Government'. It also held out the threat of financial sanctions in the event of failure to ratify by 31 January 1927. The British government currently held overdue French Treasury bills to the value of more than £125m, and a further block of bills amounting to almost £40m were to fall due on 1 December. It had so far been agreed to extend the maturing of these bills until 31 December and to renew them without requiring payment of stamp duty. The draft note made it clear, however, that there could be no guarantee that this charge of some £100,000 per quarter would continue to be waived after 31 December or, indeed, that the British government would be prepared to accept the small annuities due under the Churchill–Caillaux settlement. On the contrary, the government reserved the right to make renewal of bills maturing on 1 February 1927 and after conditional upon payment in cash of full interest on the outstanding French debt: £3.8m on 1 February, £4.5m on 1 March and so on.[93]

The author of the draft note, Niemeyer, was opposed to it being sent off at that stage for two main reasons. First, he was by no means convinced that the threatened financial pressure would work. It looked fine on paper, he told Churchill, but what if the French simply refused to pay the sums demanded of them? 'Unless we are prepared, to the destruction of our general relations with France, to sell French paper in the street at knock down prices, our "sanction" is a bluff.' As such, it might be quite effective if applied when the franc was weak. Applied when the franc and Poincaré were in a strong position, however, the bluff 'could be called with impunity: and if it is, then it is no good as a bluff thereafter'. Secondly, Niemeyer believed that it would be a serious tactical error to give Poincaré the opportunity to pose as the defender of France against a grasping usurer and to risk turning the weight of French criticism on the war debts question from the United States to Britain. According to Niemeyer, Poincaré was not the type to be 'browbeaten by despatches'. Experience had shown, however, that he was 'frequently defeated by events' and Niemeyer was of the opinion that this would happen over ratification: 'I believe that events will drive France to ratify: and that she will pay the £6m in 1927. I would accept, with some ill-grace, the assurances we have received; and would keep more formal steps in reserve.'[94] In the event, Churchill reluctantly accepted Niemeyer's advice, minuting on 17 November: 'Let us keep the letter handy and see how things develop.'[95]

Although the draft despatch was not sent, its substance was conveyed to Pouyanne verbally during meetings with Leith-Ross on 10 and 11 December 1926. In an attempt to keep up pressure for ratification, Leith-Ross rejected the other's request for a deferment of renewal of existing French Treasury bills until 31 March 1927 as a means of avoiding payment of stamp duty.[96] Later in the month the attaché was apparently subjected to further pressure when he was summoned to the Treasury and, according to one French source, presented with what amounted to an ultimatum: if the debt settlement had not been ratified by 1 March, he was told, the British government would then feel free to rescind the various concessions made to Caillaux.[97]

December 1926 saw the *de facto* stabilisation of the franc. One of the consequences of this was to undermine completely Niemeyer's favoured tactic of simply waiting for the French to be driven to ratify by financial necessity. From the outset, Niemeyer had consistently maintained that the financial crisis which Poincaré had inherited could only be dealt with through stabilisation of the franc. That, in turn, would require foreign credits which would not be available until France had ratified both the British and American debt agreements. Poincaré, however, appeared not to appreciate these elementary truths and his financial measures were therefore bound to fail. 'I should expect the franc to fall steadily', Niemeyer had confidently told Churchill in July 1926, 'and this perhaps is the best and only method of teaching France the true facts'.[98] Unfortunately for this approach, Niemeyer's forecast had proved hopelessly wide of the mark. The franc had been successfully stabilised without recourse to foreign assistance, and after that there was less incentive than ever for Poincaré to pay any heed to repeated pleas and reproaches from London.

Attempts by the British government to hasten ratification by restricting French borrowing in the City proved equally ineffectual. From 1920 onwards the Bank of England and the Treasury orchestrated a general embargo on foreign loans as part of their preparations for the restoration of sterling to its pre-war parity against the dollar.[99] Although this was formally lifted in November 1925,[100] it continued to operate unofficially against those countries – including France – which had not yet negotiated a settlement of their war debts. In the case of France, the decision was taken that it should remain in force until the Churchill–Caillaux settlement had been ratified.[101] There is no evidence that this particular financial weapon had any great effect in the period before 1926, despite the fact that France was at that time desperate for credits. After 1926 it was rendered utterly useless by the dramatic improvement that occurred in French public finances. The embargo could only have been really effective if the French had found it impossible to raise loans in other countries besides Britain. But this was not the case. It is true that they were also denied access to the American capital markets, because of their failure to ratify the Mellon–Bérenger agreement.[102] On the other hand, they were not without alternative sources of finance. Indeed, once French credit had been re-established – as it was after the formation of Poincaré's Government of National Union and the *de facto* stabilisation of the franc – foreign loans were readily available. The Swiss, the Dutch and others showed themselves eager to fill the gap left by London.

For the Governor of the Bank of England in particular, the situation thus created was extremely disagreeable, not least because he had to deal on a regular basis with City bankers who were becoming increasingly dissatisfied with a policy which was depriving them of substantial profits. Lucrative commissions were being lost to foreign rivals, and what made the sacrifice seem even more intolerable was that many of the French loans which were officially being floated in Amsterdam and other financial centres were in fact financed in large measure through subscribers in London. As the person responsible for persuading the City to comply with what he termed the Treasury's 'unwritten law' against French borrowing, Norman found it increasingly difficult to fulfil his task.[103]

During the second half of 1926, it was relatively easy to do so. Thereafter, however, he faced growing pressure from leading figures in the City for the embargo to be terminated or at least relaxed. Nor could he himself see any real justification for its continuation. He was to be found expressing his doubts as early as February 1927, when he wrote to Niemeyer pointing out that France had recently contracted large loans in Holland and Switzerland and could do so again whenever she wished. Under these circumstances, Norman argued, when the French could clearly nullify the effect of the ban at will, there appeared to be little point in persisting with it.[104]

Two months later, in April 1927, he returned to the charge. He was prompted to raise the matter again by representations from two prominent merchant bankers, Emile d'Erlanger and Francis Tiarks, both of whom were annoyed at losing money as a result of following the unofficial guidelines laid down by Norman. Early in 1926 d'Erlanger's bank had negotiated an agreement by which it was to issue bonds on the London market on behalf of a French company, the *Compagnie Générale Transatlantique*. The bonds were to be guaranteed by the French government. At the request of the Treasury, the bank had withdrawn from the deal, only for d'Erlanger to learn at a later date that the same company had proceeded to raise the loan which it needed in Canada. Irritated by the loss of a large commission, d'Erlanger sent a note to Norman on 1 March 1927 suggesting that the time had come for a change of policy:

> Whilst it is quite natural that no loan should be raised directly for the French Government as long as the war debts are not settled and the United States follow the same policy, may I suggest that in other French business our policy is only depriving the City of legitimate and handsome profits without in any way benefitting us. The loans are officially issued in Amsterdam, Switzerland and New York. The commission is earned there whilst England always proves to be a heavy subscriber and subsequently large purchaser.[105]

Writing to Norman on 11 April 1927, Tiarks voiced a similar complaint about losing valuable business, this time in connection with a projected loan to an organisation called the Electric Company of Paris. Tiarks believed that the stance adopted by Norman was no longer tenable. Like d'Erlanger, he could understand the point of discouraging loans to the French government or to state institutions. It seemed to him utterly 'illogical', however, to prevent industrial loans of the sort that his bank was now having to turn down. Since the loan was now to be placed in Switzerland instead, the only result would be to benefit Swiss bankers and the Swiss electrical industry, while their British counterparts would be left out in the cold.[106]

Norman's response to these complaints was to pass them on to the Treasury, along with a reminder to Niemeyer of his own reservations on the matter.[107] Whatever his personal doubts about current policy, though, a strong sense of duty impelled him to carry it out to the best of his ability, as an expression of government wishes. Nor did he offer any encouragement to those seeking an easing of restrictions. Thus, while conceding to d'Erlanger that profits were being lost, he argued that such a change of policy would 'surely put us all into an undignified, if not ludicrous, position'.[108]

By the beginning of 1928, however, Norman was experiencing the utmost difficulty in holding to this line. What had transformed the situation and placed him in an almost impossible position was a change of policy by the United States. In a similar fashion to the British, the Americans had been operating since 1925 a ban on French borrowing because of their delay in ratifying the Mellon–Bérenger agreement. This policy encountered strong opposition from bankers, however, and in January 1928 Washington relaxed the ban so as to make it apply only to direct loans by the French government.[109] The effect of this change, as Norman clearly perceived, was to render existing British restrictions nugatory. On 4 February, he wrote to Sir Richard Hopkins,[110] who had recently succeeded Niemeyer as Controller of Finance at the Treasury, pointing out the implications of the recent American decision – which was bound to raise some awkward questions in the City – and calling for a fresh examination of the whole question:

> I wonder whether it is wise or necesssary or fair that London should be the one capital market in which certain French loans are not welcomed. Holland, Switzerland, Sweden, and now America are all open. I now find it difficult to justify this embargo whereas a year or two ago it was easy; and sundry methods of evasion have been adopted and others are being sought. So I feel like Cassabianca![111]

Several months after writing to Hopkins, Norman was again obliged to approach the Treasury seeking their views on three loans currently being considered in the City: one for the French colony of Indo-China; a second for Indo-China, this time guaranteed by the French government; and a third for the British Michelin Tyre Company, guaranteed by its French parent company.[112] As Norman had anticipated, the Treasury offered no objection to the Michelin loan. The other two were a different matter. Sir Warren Fisher, the Permanent Secretary, who replied to Norman's enquiry, offered two reasons why they should not be allowed to go ahead. First, he thought it 'absurd' that the French should seek funds in London when they had 'so much superfluous capital at home, tied up in their antediluvian fiscal system'. Here Fisher was voicing a recurring Treasury complaint about alleged inadequacies in the French banking and monetary systems and the failure of the French government to reform them. Secondly, there was the personal attitude of the Chancellor of the Exchequer, who was 'distinctly agrieved'[sic] at the French government's delay in ratifying the debt agreement and therefore wanted to see 'all possible difficulties placed in the way of any French official borrowing here'.[113]

Fisher's recommendation was that both of the Indo-China loans should be discouraged. It is interesting to note, however, that a considerable amount of discretion was left to Norman, who was told that he must be the sole judge of whether the embargo could be maintained without 'disproportionate trouble' in the shape of lost profits and possible reprisals.[114] In his reply of 2 October 1928, Norman indicated that on this occasion he was prepared to ask the bankers concerned not to raise loans for Indo-China, partly because he did not wish to go against the wishes of the Chancellor and partly because he believed that the whole question of the ban should be settled on general principles rather than on this specific issue. At the same time, he made no attempt to disguise his distaste for having to implement a policy which had become 'ridiculous', and begged the Treasury to advise him 'categorically' that the embargo on French borrowing was to end.[115]

What Norman wanted, therefore, was a clear directive from the Treasury which would release him from the quagmire in which he was trapped. This was something they had so far been unwilling to give, perhaps because of the Chancellor's strong feelings on the matter and a consequent nervousness about how he might react. Instead, they had left the initiative to Norman, placing upon him the onus of telling them unequivocally that the embargo should be called off because it was 'unenforcable or enforcable only at excessive cost'. Since this was something he was not prepared to do, if only because it would mean a loss of face, the result had been muddle and the continuation of a policy which had long since lost its *raison d'être*. By October 1928, however, Treasury officials themselves had come to share Norman's views about the futility of the embargo and were ready to see it stopped. Thus the only remaining obstacle to its termination, admittedly a formidable one, was the attitude of a thoroughly disgruntled Churchill, who had by now managed to convince himself – although on what grounds it is difficult to see – that he had only agreed to relatively small payments by France on the explicit understanding that there would be a speedy ratification of the 1926 settlement. Leith-Ross sought to overcome his resistance in a note of 6 October which endorsed Norman's judgement that the embargo was doing more damage to Britain than to France and that its continuation was 'endangering the prestige (as well as the profits) of the London market'.[116] This view was echoed by Hopkins. To carry on with the embargo, he minuted on 7 October, 'would only be to cut off our nose to spite our face'.[117]

With his official advisers and the Governor of the Bank of England now united in proposing a change of policy, Churchill was left with no realistic alternative but to acquiesce. Another consideration which must have had some influence on his capitulation was a warning from Norman that a group of bankers intended to send a deputation to the Treasury or to have the whole question raised in Parliament.[118] The government had always claimed in public that it had nothing to do with the embargo and that the markets were free to do as they pleased. Either of these eventualities would therefore have been acutely embarrassing. On

9 October 1928, Churchill approved the suggested change of policy. He did so with the greatest reluctance, however, as was reflected in his sour observation to Leith-Ross that the course which he was now being asked to sanction was 'exactly the opposite policy to which you invited my approval a week ago'.[119] The following day Norman was informed by the Treasury that it was no longer necessary for him to discourage French borrowing in London and the embargo was effectively brought to an end.[120]

Throughout its existence the ban on French loans was a dismal failure. It never came close to achieving its objective. Towards the end, indeed, it became completely counter-productive. As has been seen, other attempts to apply financial pressure over ratification of the Churchill–Caillaux settlement – whether by insisting on payment of stamp duty for renewal of French Treasury bills or, in the case of Norman, seeking to make ratification an essential precondition of his consent to a rescheduling of debt payments due from the Bank of France – were equally fruitless.

VII

In the absence of any effective financial leverage, the British government was obliged to rely exclusively on diplomatic pressure. This, too, yielded meagre results. During the latter half of 1926, as has been seen, Poincaré was able to ignore, or fend off with consummate ease, the various appeals that were addressed to him. This continued to be the pattern over the next two years. Indeed, far from making an effort to secure ratification, Poincaré offered instead written undertakings that the amounts due under the Churchill–Caillaux settlement would be paid on the allotted dates – £3m on the 15 September 1927 and 15 March 1928, and £4m on 15 September 1928 and 15 March 1929.[121]

In the meantime, Churchill came under mounting parliamentary pressure to take firmer action. His position was not made any easier by a statement from Poincaré to the Finance Commission of the Chamber on 25 January 1927 indicating that he was in no hurry to put the French debt settlements with Britain and the United States to a vote.[122] At the time of this statement Parliament was in recess. When it reconvened on 8 February, however, the matter was quickly taken up in the Commons. During one particularly difficult session, on 17 February, Churchill was faced with a whole series of questions from Snowden and other MPs about the French government's failure to ratify the debt settlement.[123] The hostile tone of some of these questions, which came from both sides of the House, can be gauged from one asked by the Labour backbencher John Beckett, who enquired whether it would be possible to 'make friendly representations to the French government suggesting that they should settle this debt with us before financing military dictatorship in Poland?'[124] On the same day, prompted by his ordeal in the Commons, Churchill sent off a personal letter to

Poincaré in which, while welcoming news that France intended to pay the sum of £6m due for 1927–8, he expressed the hope that in the interests of both countries the debt agreement would be ratified 'before long'.[125] He was expressing the same hope a year later, only to be informed that ratification would not be possible until after the French elections of April 1928 were out of the way.[126]

On the British side, it was regarded as understandable that Poincaré should wish to postpone such a controversial measure until after the elections. Expectations were nevertheless high – previous disappointments notwithstanding – that once these were over he would seek ratification without delay. Disillusionment was not long in coming; for even after the elections had taken place (on 22 and 29 April 1928) Poincaré continued to procrastinate, despite repeated promptings from London.[127]

Remarks which he made in the Chamber on 21 June were regarded as especially discouraging and unhelpful.[128] In the course of a speech about stabilisation of the franc, Poincaré made a number of references to war debts. In the first place, he stated that France's creditors had not exercised any pressure on her about ratification – a statement which was bound to add to the difficulties already facing Churchill, since it appeared to vindicate his critics' claim that he had not been doing enough to get the debt settlement ratified.[129] He also hinted that ratification might be rendered unnecessary if, as seemed possible, the existing French agreements with Britain and the United States were to be superseded soon by a general settlement of inter-allied debts and reparations.[130] Clearly what Poincaré had in mind here was the growing interest being shown at that time in replacement of the provisional Dawes Plan by a definitive arrangement for reparation payments.

Leith-Ross was extremely disappointed (though not surprised) by what he saw as the 'negative attitude' displayed in Poincaré's comments and suggested that the Foreign Secretary's attention should be drawn to the matter. As a result, on 12 July 1928 a note was sent to the British ambassador in Paris, Crewe, requesting him to speak to Poincaré about the importance of early ratification. The Treasury view, as expressed by Leith-Ross, was that there was not the slightest foundation for Poincaré's belief that ratification might be avoided by means of some general settlement on reparations and war debts. On the contrary, all the available information from the United States appeared to indicate that the Americans regarded ratification of the Mellon–Bérenger agreement as an essential precondition of their participation in any talks about a future general settlement. The Treasury were also concerned about the fragility of the coalition government over which Poincaré presided. It was by no means certain that it would last much longer, and it was therefore felt to be highly desirable that ratification should be carried out before there was any question of a ministerial crisis. Whilst appreciating that the move was certain to meet with considerable opposition, the Treasury believed that such opposition would only intensify the longer ratification was delayed. Nor was it doubted that Poincaré had sufficient prestige to push the measure through the Chamber if he chose to make it a matter of confidence.[131]

Crewe was instructed to put these points to Poincaré and tell him that the British government fully expected him to proceed to ratification as soon as possible after the Chamber's summer recess. The Foreign Secretary made it clear, however, in a way that reflected his overriding concern for the maintenance of good relations with France, that he did not wish the matter to be pressed 'in a disagreeable manner'.[132] Such a circumspect approach – however understandable in the context of Chamberlain's overall policy goals in Europe – was not likely to make much impression on a man whose sheer toughness and obduracy had on one famous occasion reduced Curzon to tears.[133] Nor did it. Poincaré paid as little heed to these particular representations as he had to earlier ones and his policy on ratification continued to be shaped not by half-hearted complaints from London, but by the dictates of French national interest.

In the second half of 1928 it seemed to Poincaré that French national interest would best be served by delaying ratification of both the American and British debt settlements until after agreement had been reached on a new and final schedule of reparation payments. The reason for this was quite straightforward. Like all other French political leaders, Poincaré always insisted that France's reparation receipts must be at least sufficient to cover the total cost of her war debt obligations. Since 1924 this requirement had been fulfilled by the Dawes Plan. The Dawes Plan was never intended as more than a stop-gap, however, and by the autumn of 1928 there was a general acceptance – largely as a result of intensive lobbying of the British, French and other interested governments by the Agent-General for Reparation Payments, S. Parker Gilbert – of the need for its early replacement by a permanent settlement.[134] On 16 September 1928, a significant step was taken in that direction when representatives of Germany and her five major creditors, meeting at Geneva, decided that a committee of experts should be set up to study the question.[135] It was expected that this committee would take several months to complete its work. In the meantime, until it had done so and until the governments concerned had negotiated an agreement on the basis of its conclusions, both the scale and allocation of future reparation payments must remain a matter of conjecture.

Given this considerable element of uncertainty, Poincaré's attitude was only to be expected. Only when he was sure that any new arrangements would provide France with enough to pay her creditors – with an additional amount to help towards the cost of restoring the devastated regions – would he be prepared to go ahead with ratifying the British and American debt settlements. It would be astonishing, too, if he did not appreciate that the promise of ratification might prove to be a useful bargaining counter in forthcoming negotiations about reparations.[136]

VIII

Poincaré's view that ratification must be preceded by a satisfactory agreement on reparations was made abundantly clear to Churchill when the two men held talks in Paris on 19 October 1928.[137] The main purpose of Churchill's visit to the French capital was to discuss reparations, but it also provided him with a convenient opportunity to raise other matters, including war debts. When he referred to the continuing delay in ratifying the 1926 settlement, Poincaré offered his opinion that no French Parliament would ever agree to it.

As a way out of the problem, however, he suggested a possible solution which had never been mentioned in any previous discussion of the question. The French constitution, he now claimed, only required the formal assent of Parliament in cases where an increased charge was imposed on France. Since the Churchill–Caillaux agreement involved a reduction rather than an increase in the the charges on France, it followed that the French government had the power to ratify it without parliamentary endorsement. But it would only exercise that power, Poincaré emphasised, when there was 'a real security' for the continuation of adequate reparation payments during the whole period of French debt repayment.[138]

This last assertion ran directly counter to the official British position that French annuities must be on the sole credit of France, without regard to reparation receipts. Yet Churchill did not take up the challenge. Instead, he turned to one of his recurrent concerns: the possibility that the United States might be given preferential treatment. He had heard rumours, he said, that the French government was thinking of ratifying the Mellon–Bérenger agreement first – something which 'would cause a most deplorable impression in England, and would upset us all very much indeed'. In reply, Poincaré assured him that such rumours were baseless and that it was his intention to treat the British and American settlements in exactly the same way.[139]

Churchill's overall impression of his meeting with Poincaré was that it had gone quite well, with the French Premier showing a more accommodating and constructive spirit than usual.[140] So far as ratification of the 1926 debt settlement was concerned, one of the most noteworthy features of the conversation had been Poincaré's disclosure that his government was constitutionally entitled to proceed without formal parliamentary approval. On the face of it, this was a helpful gesture which seemed to offer a way round one of the main stumbling blocks. But the development was in fact considerably less promising than it seemed. Whatever Poincaré might imply, even if he used the procedural device to which he had referred there was bound to be powerful opposition to ratification; and there is no evidence to suggest that he was any more willing to risk unpopularity over the issue than he had previously been. After October 1928 no more was heard about ratification without the consent of Parliament. Indeed, it is hard to resist the conclusion that Poincaré only mentioned it as a means of placating Churchill and buying more time. Of much greater importance, in any case, was his insistence that there could be no question of ratification until a final settlement had been reached on reparations. This stipulation in itself automatically precluded any early progress on the matter.

And so it proved to be. The deliberations of the committee of experts – chaired by the American representative, Owen D. Young – took longer than expected,[141] and it was not until August 1929 that an agreement embodying most of its recommendations was reached at the first Hague conference. In the meantime, while attention was focused on the proposed new reparation arrangements, the issue of ratification of the Churchill–Caillaux debt settlement inevitably tended to fade into the background. The Labour Opposition made intermittent attempts to breathe life into it, and their efforts were assisted by press speculation in the spring of 1929 that the Young committee intended to suggest a reduction in the share of reparation receipts allotted to Britain under the 1920 Spa agreement – the main effect of such rumours being to stir up indignation about the concessions that had been made to France over war debts.[142]

During the debate on the Budget in April 1929, Snowden led a Labour attack on the 1926 agreement and, along with Ramsay MacDonald and others, claimed that France's failure to ratify it provided an opportunity to renegotiate on more stringent terms.[143] This argument was immediately taken up by the Labour movement as a whole and featured -though not in a major way – in the general election campaign of May 1929.[144] Renegotiation was never a serious possiblity, however, and MacDonald was careful to deny that his party had any intention of repudiating the existing agreement if it came to power.[145] As for Churchill, by this stage he seems to have reconciled himself to the fact that ratification would take place when it suited Poincaré for it to do so. In the event, the agreement was not finally ratified by the French Chamber until 21 July 1929, by which time Churchill had been replaced by Snowden as Chancellor of the Exchequer, following the Conservatives' defeat in the general election of 30 May. The Mellon–Bérenger agreement was ratified at the same time.

One factor governing the timing of ratification was the desire to avoid incurring a substantial financial penalty. In the period following the November 1918 armistice France had received American credits of around $400m for the purchase of surplus war stocks, and the problem facing the French government in the summer of 1929 was that this debt would become payable in cash on 1 August unless the Mellon–Bérenger agreement had been ratified before then.[146] The timing was also influenced by the fact that Poincaré was now satisfied that French receipts under the Young Plan would more than suffice to cover France's debt payments to Britain and the United States.[147]

IX

The final chapter in the history of Anglo-French war debts was linked inextricably with the onset of the world economic and financial crisis and the consequent termination of reparations. On 15 March 1931 France paid the half-yearly instalment of £6.25m due under the Churchill–Caillaux settlement. Although it was not realised at the time, this was to be the last payment. Not long afterwards an initiative from the Amercan President, Herbert Hoover, resulted in a one-year moratorium on all inter-governmental debts. Before this expired, an agreement was reached at the Lausanne conference of June–July 1932 which effectively put an end to German reparations. During the conference Britain, France, Italy and Belgium also negotiated an accord between themselves by which ratification of this agreement was made conditional upon the prior conclusion of an acceptable settlement of inter-allied debts. As in the past, however, Washington refused to acknowledge any connection between reparations and war debts. Neither Hoover nor his Democratic successor, Franklin D. Roosevelt, was prepared to respond to the European Allies' decision on reparations by cancelling or significantly reducing war debts owing to the United States. Both presidents also rejected repeated British and French requests that payment of instalments stipulated by the existing funding agreements should be postponed. A stalemate thus developed, the eventual outcome of which was a default by France in December 1932 and by Britain eighteen months later. In the meantime, the French government was not required to meet its obligations to Britain.

The key event in all these interrelated developments, the Hoover moratorium, came in response to the deepening financial crisis in Europe in the summer of 1931 and to mounting evidence that the Young Plan, which had come into operation on 17 May 1930, was rapidly becoming unworkable in the current climate of international depression.[148] The collapse in May 1931 of the largest bank in Austria, the Creditanstalt, placed the country's entire banking system under severe strain. This, in turn, had serious implications for Germany because of her large-scale financial involvement in Austria. German finances were in any case already in a fragile condition because of the depressed state of the economy, an excessive reliance by government and banks alike on short-term foreign credits and shocks to confidence arising from the recently announced Austro-German customs union project and the National Socialists' spectacular breakthrough in the Reichstag elections of September 1930.[149] On 6 June 1931 the government of Heinrich Brüning, a leading figure in the Centre Party who had been Chancellor since March of the previous year, published a manifesto proclaiming that Germany must be relieved of her 'intolerable reparation obligations'.[150] This precipitated a massive outflow of gold and foreign exchange, and the Reichsbank suffered further heavy losses on 13 and 18 June.[151] Alarmed by the sharp deterioration in Germany's finances, disturbed by warnings from the American ambassador in Berlin, Frederic M. Sackett, about the Weimar republic's polit-

ical instability and concerned to safeguard American banks' substantial investments in Germany, President Hoover now reluctantly accepted the need for
decisive intervention on his part; and on 20 June he proposed a one-year moratorium on all intergovernmental debts, including reparations and war debts.[152]

Despite some delay in its implementation because of objections raised by the
government of Pierre Laval,[153] the Hoover moratorium provided a welcome
breathing-space. Throughout its duration, however, the central question preoc-
cupying all the governments concerned was what should be done when it expired
on 30 June 1932. Not surprisingly, the Germans insisted that a resumption of
reparation payments would be impossible. This was also the official view in
London, where MacDonald's National Government (formed after the demise of
the second Labour government on 24 August 1931) regarded the Hoover moratorium as an important step towards the complete cancellation of reparations and
war debts which had long been a cherished British objective.[154] Recognising that
this was not a realistic proposition for the time being – not least because of
approaching elections in France and Germany – London set its sights on an
extension of the moratorium, and from December 1931 the Foreign Office was
trying to interest the French in the early summoning of a conference at Lausanne
with a view to achieving that goal.[155] The French were unenthusiastic, however,
as Leith-Ross discovered from discussions in Paris with Finance Minister Pierre-
Etienne Flandin in December 1931 and January 1932.[156] The Laval government's
reluctance to participate in the projected conference was reinforced by the attitude of the Americans, which offered little prospect that any alleviation of
Germany's reparation burden which might be decided upon at Lausanne would
be matched by a lessening of European war debt payments to the United States.[157]
The wording of a communiqué issued after talks between Laval and Hoover in
Washington in late October 1931 had encouraged hopes of a possible softening
of the American line on war debts.[158] Such hopes, however, were illusory. When
first calling for a general moratorium, Hoover had emphasised that he 'did not
approve in any remote sense of the cancellation of the debts to us'. Although he
gradually became convinced that there was, indeed, a case for some revision of
the various settlements that had been negotiated so as to take account of much
altered circumstances, his room for manoeuvre was severely restricted by a deterioration in the domestic economy, a large budgetary deficit, opposition in
Congress and the imminence of presidential elections – due in November 1932.[159]

The Hoover administration's continuing inflexibility over war debts had a
vital bearing on the outcome of the Lausanne conference. In particular, it
increased the British government's difficulty in gaining approval from the
current French Prime Minister, Herriot, and his Finance Minister, Louis
Germain-Martin, for cancellation of reparations. Herriot, who had come to
power following gains for the Radicals and Socialists in the recent elections of 1
and 8 May, had already demonstrated during the 1924 London conference his
strong interest in close relations with Britain and a willingness to make substan-

tial concessions in order to maintain them. These tendencies were equally evident in the summer of 1932, as the growth of aggressive nationalist sentiment in Germany, combined with indications that France too was at last beginning to feel the impact of the world economic crisis, underlined the need for Anglo-French co-operation. In response to an invitation from Herriot, MacDonald and the Foreign Secretary, Sir John Simon, visited Paris on 11 June for preliminary talks on the Lausanne conference.[160] The desire of both sides to align their policies was reflected in the communiqué issued at the end of the talks which spoke of having arrived at 'a common point of view which makes it possible to foresee the adoption of fair and effective solutions' at the conference.[161] There was, however, a limit to how far Herriot was prepared or politically able to go in moving towards the British position on reparations, one which was determined in large measure by Washington's attitude to remission of war debts.

At the Lausanne conference, which began on 16 June, it soon became apparent that Herriot was no less insistent than his immediate predecessors Laval and Tardieu that he would only consent to a reduction in German reparation payments if there was a corresponding reduction in French war debt obligations.[162] Because of the stance adopted by the Hoover government, this posed a major threat to the success of the proceedings. What was needed to avert a breakdown was to find some means of reconciling the conflicting French and American viewpoints. The attempt to do this resulted in what came to be known as the 'Gentleman's Agreement' of 2 July.[163] As has been seen, this was signed by France and the three other major reparation creditors of Germany and sought to make implementation of any new reparation settlement subject to negotiation beforehand of a satisfactory readjustment of inter-allied indebtedness. It was only on the basis of this accord that it was possible to conclude an agreement on reparations on 6 July, the terms of which virtually guaranteed that Germany would never resume payment.[164]

The 'Gentleman's Agreement' was confidential and its existence was not officially acknowledged until after the Lausanne conference had ended. Its disclosure produced a furore in the United States, where it was justifiably seen as a device to pressurise the American government into renunciation of its debt claims.[165] Hoover was particularly angered by a parliamentary statement from the Chancellor of the Exchequer, Neville Chamberlain, implying that the United States had given some kind of undertaking to cancel the war debts owing to it if reparations were abolished at Lausanne.[166] His response was to send a public letter to Senator William E. Borah, the chairman of the Senate Committee on Foreign Relations, in which he denied having been consulted about the 'Gentleman's Agreement' and placed on record his opposition to debt cancellation.[167]

In the months leading up to the presidential elections, Hoover continued to take a tough line on foreign war debts for fear of giving the Democrats valuable political capital. The British government recognised that he was unable to act otherwise and, like the French government, refrained from raising the issue during the election campaign. Once this was over, however, it lost no time in doing so. On 10 November, only two days after Roosevelt's electoral victory, it sent a note to Washington requesting a general review of existing debt agreements and calling for payment of the next British instalment – due on 15 December – to be postponed while this process was taking place: the French immediately followed suit.[168] The despatch of these two notes marked the beginning of protracted and increasingly irritable diplomatic exchanges, throughout which there was regular consultation and collaboration between London and Paris.[169] Hoover was not entirely negative in his response. He personally – along with some of his most senior advisers, including Secretary of State Henry L. Stimson and Treasury Secretary Ogden Mills – favoured reconsideration of foreign debt settlements by a modified version of the WDC.[170] Regardless of Hoover's personal sentiments, however, his position as a lame-duck President facing a hostile Congress rendered him powerless to accede to British and French appeals over war debts.[171] This was especially the case after his efforts to secure the co-operation of Roosevelt in establishing an agreed policy on war debts were rebuffed by a suspicious President-elect.

On 23 November 1932, the day after a fruitless discussion between Hoover and Roosevelt at the White House, London was informed by the State Department that the President did not have the authority to postpone the instalment due in mid-December.[172] With time running out for further diplomatic activity, this raised the question of whether the British government should refuse to pay. Amongst policymakers there was only limited support for such a drastic step. Leith-Ross, who had been appointed Chief Economic Adviser to the Government in the previous March and who continued to deal with reparations and war debts, was strongly in favour, suggesting that the best course would be to act with the French and Italians in suspending payment. To pay, Leith-Ross argued, would only make it more difficult to obtain concessions from Roosevelt in the future, besides dealing a hefty blow at the Lausanne agreement.[173] Concern was felt in some quarters, however, about the possible damage that might be inflicted on British credit, and in the event the sum was duly paid. Three notes were nonetheless sent to Washington between 1 and 12 December in a desperate attempt to bring about a last-minute change of heart. In the first of these, attention was drawn to the scale of sacrifice involved in paying off the debt. It was pointed out that Britain had already paid $1.352bn out of a total of $4bn and that the depreciation of sterling since its departure from the Gold Standard in September 1931 meant an increase of some 50 per cent in the real burden of the forthcoming instalment. Currrent reserves of foreign exchange, it was claimed, were adequate for the support of sterling but not for making the December debt payment of $95.5m as well. The only means of meeting the obligation was with gold, therefore, and the problem here was said to be that available reserves were barely sufficient to enable London to fulfil its responsibilities as a financial centre.[174] When these arguments failed to make any impression on Washington, another note was despatched on 11 December indicating that the instalment would be paid on the appointed date. It was emphasised that this was not to be regarded as a resumption of the annual payments, but rather as a capital sum 'of which account should be taken in any final settlement'. Such a settlement, the note urged, should be concluded before 15 June 1933, the date of the next instalment.[175]

Meanwhile, the French government was working in tandem with the British and pursuing an identical strategy to theirs.[176] Following discussions with MacDonald and Neville Chamberlain in Paris on 8 December,[177] it was Herriot's intention that France would pay her instalment subject to the same reservation stipulated by Britain.[178] In a bid to win parliamentary approval for this policy, he made it a matter of confidence. The tactic backfired, however, and on 15 December Herriot was obliged to resign after being defeated on the issue in the Chamber.[179] On the same day France defaulted on her American debt. Thereafter negotiations continued intermittently between Washington and Paris, but without any agreement being reached.

Attempts by the Americans and British to resolve their differences over war debts similarly ended in failure. One of the main reasons for this was that Roosevelt felt unable to deliver significant concessions to Britain (or the other debtor countries) at a time when the American economy was entering upon a new downward spiral and when Congress was more hostile than ever to the idea of writing down inter-allied debts.[180] After several months of equivocation, the new President decided – like Hoover before him – that domestic recovery must take precedence over considerations of international co-operation, and he was unwilling to jeopardise the centrepiece of his economic programme, the National Industrial Recovery Act, by adopting a more generous policy on war debts.[181] For its part, the British government had only paid the the December 1932 instalment with extreme reluctance and was determined to avoid paying the next one on 15 June 1933.

Towards the end of April, MacDonald visited Roosevelt in Washington. After his departure on the 26th, Leith-Ross, who was one of the accompanying team, stayed on for talks on the subject of war debts with American experts. These might accurately be described as a dialogue of the deaf. An exasperated Leith-Ross complained that Britain was tired of paying out to the United States without recovering what was owed to her, and the discussions ended with an agreement to record the two sides' differences.[182] On 9 June the United States Treasury accordingly requested payment of the next instalment of $85m.[183] The British government, however, was only prepared to pay $10m. An even smaller amount – $7.5m – was paid on 15 December 1933.[184] This provoked an irate Congress to pass a resolution precluding the President from accepting any more 'token' payments and this, in turn, led on to a British default in June 1934, when a bill for $262m was sent to cover both the next instalment and the outstanding balance from previous ones.[185] As always, there was anxiety about the effect this might have on British credit. The decision to default was made somewhat easier, though, by the fact that a number of other debtor states, including France, had already set a precedent without appearing to suffer any adverse consequences.[186]

The ending of British debt payments to the United States brought with it the permanent cessation of French payments to Britain. On 8 July 1932, during the Lausanne conference, Neville Chamberlain had sent a letter to the French Finance Minister, Germain-Martin, indicating that suspension of these would continue until the Lausanne agreement on reparations came into force or until it had been decided not to ratify it. In the latter event, the legal position would revert to that obtaining under the Churchill–Caillaux settlement.[187] In theory, therefore, the British government reserved to itself the right to insist on repayment. This was a right which it had no intention of seeking to enforce, however, even supposing that there existed any real possibility of persuading the French to begin paying again in the absence of substantial receipts from Germany.

Conclusion

Throughout the 1920s the question of French war debts was a running sore in Anglo-French relations. It took several years of tortuous and sometimes acrimonious negotiations to produce a funding agreement in the summer of 1926, and even after that differences persisted because of a lengthy delay in ratification by the Poincaré government.

During the time that it was in operation between July 1926 and June 1931, the Churchill–Caillaux settlement yielded a total of less than £41m for the British Exchequer and, with the benefit of hindsight, it is tempting to question whether this modest financial gain was worth all the effort and friction involved. Some historians have cast a sceptical eye on allied attempts to extract reparations from Germany and concluded that the limited receipts were insufficient to justify the enormous political damage caused. Doubts have similarly been raised about the wisdom of seeking to secure payment of war debts by France at the expense of good Anglo-French relations. Artaud, Kent, Orde, Schuker, Silverman, Trachtenberg and others have tended to present British policy on the matter as short-sighted and lacking in statesmanship. Criticism has focused on the diplomacy of the Lloyd George and Bonar Law governments in the period leading up to the Franco-Belgian occupation of the Ruhr in January 1923, with particular stress being placed upon the supposed deficiencies of the Balfour Note and the Bonar Law Plan. This interpretation of events has been closely associated with a reassessment of Poincaré. Access to previously unavailable official French papers has led to modification of the traditional view – held in Britain at least – of Poincaré pursuing a misguided and totally inflexible strategy dictated by hatred of Germany. Such a corrective to the conventional wisdom was no doubt overdue. At the same time, the process of transferring responsibility for the Ruhr occupation to British shoulders has been carried too far. Thus it has been argued in this study that the alleged shortcomings of British political leaders have been exaggerated and that it is simplistic to assume, as has invariably been the case, that a little more generosity over French war debts in the months preceding the occcupation might have averted it. More specifically, it has been maintained that criticism of the Balfour Note has been much overstated.

A great deal of flak has been directed at the Balfour Note, the main features of which exercised a major influence on British war debt policy from August

1922. There was no shortage of contemporary critics of the Note and the verdict of historians has been overwhelmingly negative. The despatch of the Note is said to have ruined any prospect of dissuading Poincaré from seizing pledges in the Ruhr. It has also been claimed that the central principle set out in the Note – that Britain must obtain from Germany and allied debtors combined a sum sufficient to cover what she herself had to pay the United States – was fundamentally unjust in that it placed upon France the main responsibility for making good any short-fall in British reparation receipts in the event of a German default. For reasons that need not be repeated here these strictures have been challenged. Nor is it without significance in this respect that the French themselves, after initially castigating the Balfour Note, soon began to view it in a more favourable light and to press for it, along with the Bonar Law Plan, to remain the basis of British policy. Certainly the Note was not without flaws. At the very least, however, it represented a serious attempt to provide a coherent and equitable solution to a set of extraordinarily complex problems.

In formulating policy on French war debts British policymakers were obliged to take into account a plethora of financial, economic and political factors, many of which were outside their control. It was hard enough to devise a settlement which accommodated the interests of the two countries concerned. What made the task harder still was the impossibility of treating the question of French indebtedness to Britain in isolation from a whole range of matters affecting other parties. How much the French would be able or willing to pay and the British prepared to accept depended, for example, on the scale and distribution of German reparations and the amount that France and Britain received from their respective debtors. Another imponderable that entered into the equation was the likely effect upon British overseas trade of cancelling either wholly or substan-tially the French and other debts owed to Britain. No consensus emerged on this amongst ministers and officials. Some believed that such a move would increase purchasing power in the countries whose external debts were reduced in this way and thereby help to boost demand for British exports in France and elsewhere. Others took a contrary view, arguing that the best way to assist British exporters and industrialists in general was to make the French pay their debts. This, it was suggested, would put a stop to what was in effect subsidisation by British taxpayers of French producers and so reduce the latter's international competi-tiveness which was in any case aided by a depreciated franc. Although there was a great deal of speculation on this particular point, there appears to have been no serious attempt to get at the truth through systematic analysis by experts at the Board of Trade or the Treasury.

By far the most significant imponderable facing British policymakers was uncertainty as to the Americans' intentions regarding the wartime credits they had advanced to Britain – although it must be said that the consistently uncom-promising line taken by Washington offered no real grounds for optimism on that score. Whether or not, and to what extent, the United States insisted on repayment was without doubt the key determinant of British policy on French war debts. Any British government from 1918 onwards would have gladly agreed to waive its claims on France as part of a comprehensive package involving liquidation of all inter-allied indebtedness and a moderate reparation settlement. This particular option was not available, however, as became unmistakably clear with the conclusion of the Anglo-American debt agreement in 1923. It was the necessity of having to pay substantial annuities under this agreement which fuelled British determination to secure payments from France. Equally there was a great sense of relief in London when the decision to repudiate Britain's debt obligations to the United States in 1934 finally cleared the way for cancellation of the Churchill–Caillaux settlement, which had been suspended since July 1931 in accordance with the Hoover moratorium and the Lausanne Agreement.

It was thus the impact of the world economic crisis which eventually brought about – admittedly in a rather messy and unexpected way – what British policy-makers had striven for since the conclusion of the war: an end to inter-allied debts. Although this had always been regarded as the optimal solution, in practice it had often been necessary to follow a different course in response to the realities of the situation. So far as French war debts were concerned, British policy evolved through various phases. In the first of these, during the immediate postwar years, there was no question of exerting pressure on Paris to begin negotiations for a funding agreement. This was partly because it was recognised that such an exercise would have been pointless given the shattered state of French finances and the French economy at that time. Scarcely less important a consideration, however, was concern to avoid any bilateral settlement which might prejudice the chances of persuading the Americans to agree to all-round cancellation. It is therefore somewhat surprising, as well as unfair, that the French later came under a great deal of fire from the Treasury in particular for not having taken any steps in the early 1920s to begin paying off their debts. The British themselves took no initiative in the matter, and it was only after the advent to power of the second Balwin government in November 1924 and the appointment of Churchill as Chancellor of the Exchequer that serious discussions at last got under way.

One of the salient characteristics of this first phase of British policy, then, was restraint in pressing for repayment of French war debts. Another was the development in official circles of a certain amount of support for the idea of renouncing British war debt claims not only on France but also on all other allied debtors – even if Britain was required to meet her own obligations to the United States. This tendency was especially pronounced at the Treasury where Blackett put forward a proposal along those lines in 1920. Blackett and his colleagues identified the existence of war debts as a major obstacle to European recovery. They were also deeply sceptical about the possibilty of obtaining much if anything from impoverished debtors. Above all, however, their attitude was the product of frustration at their continuing inablity to persuade the Americans of the case for all–round cancellation of war debts. Blackett's proposal won strong backing not only from the then Chancellor, Austen Chamberlain, but also from the Foreign Office, where Curzon and his advisers felt that the suggested initiative would improve relations with the French and Italians and greatly enhance Britain's international prestige. It failed to secure the approval of the Cabinet, however, mainly because of opposition from Lloyd George and Churchill, and by the summer of 1921 had ceased to be a serious policy option.

The next phase of policy, from 1922 onwards, saw a gradual hardening of the official British stance. This was reflected most obviously in the despatch of the Balfour Note in August of that year requesting France and the rest of Britain's debtors to make arrangements for funding their debts. At this stage the Treasury continued to favour the line pushed by Blackett, and it is noticeable that the stoutest resistance to the Balfour Note came from ministers and officials associated with that department: Blackett himself, the Chancellor, Horne, and his predecessor, Austen Chamberlain. Soon afterwards, however, Treasury thinking began to change and a new mood gradually became evident amongst senior officials there. Less was heard from them of the case for unconditional financial sacrifices. Instead, emphasis was increasingly placed on protecting the interests of the British taxpayer, obtaining cash from foreign debtors to help in balancing the Budget and ensuring that France, in particular, made a fair contribution to the cost of liquidating inter-allied indebtedness.

This development was a consequence of various factors. Changes in personnel played a part. In late 1922 Blackett, the author of the proposal for unilateral debt cancellation, left the Treasury to take up a position on the Viceroy's Council in Delhi, and his succesor as Controller of Finance, Niemeyer, proved to be considerably less sympathetic to French pleas that they were unable to pay their debts. Leith-Ross, who became Niemeyer's deputy at the beginning of 1925 after a four-year spell assisting Bradbury on the Reparation Commission, was equally unaccommodating. The department as a whole reacted indignantly to the French rejection of the Bonar Law Plan – considered extraordinarily generous – in January 1923. There was also a growing feeling that Britain's restraint in pressing her legitimate claims as a creditor had been abused. In the immediate postwar years, the Treasury had been prepared to accept that France was in no fit state to begin repaying her debts. By 1923, however, they were less convinced. There was mounting irritation at French failure even to pay interest charges, the bill for which was thus being met by the British taxpayer. This was compounded by the conviction that Britain was not obtaining what was due to her largely because of appalling financial mismanagement by successive French governments, as well as a propensity for excessive military expenditure. All these factors contributed to the emergence of a tougher Treasury stance on French war debts. Most important of all, however, was the combined impact of the Anglo-American debt agreement and the occupation of the Ruhr. From June 1923, when payments to the United States actually began, it was no longer possible to indulge in wishful thinking about American generosity and all-round cancellation. Having seen the Americans adopting an essentially commercial approach, Treasury officials were inclined to do likewise and insist upon strict fulfilment of the Balfour Note principle. At the same time, they believed that recent events in the Ruhr had considerably reduced the real value of Britain's reparation receipts and that this necessitated an upward revision of the amount France would need to contribute towards the £33m–£38m required annually to cover British payments to Washington.

The third phase of British policy on French war debts was dominated by increasingly desperate attempts to negotiate an agreement. For a time, during the early part of 1924, the Treasury argued for a temporary arrangement on the grounds that it was not yet possible to make a sensible judgement about definitive terms because of the absence of reliable information on what Germany would be paying in the future. With the implementation of the Dawes Plan from September 1924, this element of uncertainty was removed and the quest for a French debt settlement began in earnest. Fear of being beaten to it by the Americans imparted an added sense of urgency to the proceedings.

Serious negotiations got under way in January 1925. Progress was hindered, however, by French financial and political instability. As a result, it was not until August 1925 that Churchill and Caillaux reached a provisional agreement and not until July of the following year that this was converted into a final one by the same two ministers. Throughout the negotiations it was the Treasury rather than the Foreign Office which played the leading role. While senior Treasury officials did much of the preparatory work in discussions with their French counterparts, there was also a great deal of input from the Chancellor of the Exchequer, and Churchill's close personal involvement in the bargaining process had two important consequences. First, it led to the French obtaining more lenient terms than they might otherwise have done. In spite of some early rhetorical flourishes about the necessity of standing firm against French special pleading, Churchill soon showed that he was not averse to making concessions. This was a cause of acute disappointment to his principal advisers, Leith-Ross and Niemeyer, both of whom wanted to hold out for bigger annuities than their political master considered feasible. Secondly, the relative generosity that Churchill displayed helped to minimise inter-departmental friction on the issue between the Treasury and the Foreign Office. Since the end of the war Austen Chamberlain had taken a thoroughly consistent line on French war debts. In his view, the prospect of recovering any worthwhile sum was a remote one and attempts to do so would only inflict unnecessary damage on Anglo-French relations. It was in accordance with this view that he had supported Blackett's proposal for unilateral debt cancellation and opposed the sending of the Balfour Note. As Foreign Secretary from November 1924, he saw no reason to revise his opinions, and both his personal affection for France and his desire for close collaboration with the French in consolidating the work of European 'appeasement' begun at Locarno made him apprehensive about the possible adverse political consequences of pressure being exerted for a debt funding agreement. Churchill himself warned that his determination to press on with negotiations was likely to create major difficulties for the Foreign Office. On the whole, however, this proved not to be the case, and the Chancellor's responsiveness to the arguments put forward by the French enabled Chamberlain to give broad, if unenthusiastic, support to his policy.

For some time after July 1926 the main objective of British policy on French war debts was to secure ratification of the Churchill–Caillaux settlement. This was not accomplished until the summer of 1929, and throughout this three-year period the debt issue thus continued to produce tensions in Anglo-French relations. What was more, the impressive economic and financial recovery which France enjoyed during this period, and which formed a marked contrast with the contemporary British experience, served to exacerbate the sense of grievance felt in London – especially by Churchill – over the delaying tactics of the Poincaré government. In the meantime, the sums laid down by the 1926 agreement were paid regularly and promptly on the scheduled dates of 15 March and 15 September of each year. With the onset of the Great Depression, however, the situation was transformed. At the end of June 1931 payments were suspended in conformity with the one-year general moratorium proposed by Hoover. They were never resumed.

From the end of the First World War successive British governments approached the task of collecting debts owed by the French with great reluctance. Yet a combination of financial and political factors stood in the way of outright cancellation. The most favourable time for the adoption of such a policy was in the immediate post-war years, when the general position regarding reparations and inter-allied debts was still in a fluid state and the Anglo-American war debt agreement had not yet been concluded. Even then, however, circumstances were by no means conducive to a generous gesture. During the early 1920s the British economy was sunk in a severe depression, with staple exporting industries being particularly badly affected. Unemployment was disturbingly high, rising to 2 millions at its peak. Public expenditure was subject to deep cuts in line with recommendations from various economy committees, and desperate efforts were being made to reduce taxation, the heavy weight of which was regarded as a prime cause of the country's current industrial and commercial difficulties. The domestic economic climate, in short, was not such as to encourage major concessions to foreign debtors. The Lloyd George and Bonar Law governments were no more able to disregard considerations of narrow national self-interest than those in France or the United States, and any official proposal that the British taxpayer should pick up the bill for the whole of the £450m or so that France had borrowed during the war would undoubtedly have led to a public outcry. This particular political constraint was to apply with even greater force after 1923 and the commencement of British debt payments to the United States.

There was another reason why no British government was at any time during the 1920s willing to surrender all war debt claims on the French. As long as at least some of these were retained, they were thought to provide a valuable bargaining counter. It was hoped that it would be possible to trade them off in negotiations either for an all-round agreement on reparations and inter-allied debts or for a reduction in Britain's own obligations to the United States. In addition, they were viewed – mistakenly as it turned out – as a useful means of exercising control over French policy towards Germany.

Although not prepared to cancel the whole of the French debt, all British governments between 1918 and 1926 nevertheless offered to write off a substantial proportion of it. This was a key feature of the Bonar Law Plan, for instance, as well as the scheme contained in Curzon's Note of August 1923 and the Churchill–Caillaux settlement itself. Instead of being received with gratitude, however, as expected in London, such concessions were dismissed as completely inadequate and provoked resentment. This reaction stemmed in part from a fundamental conviction in French official circles that it was unjust to expect France to repay debts which had been contracted under the very special circumstances of the First World War. But there was another explanation. For the French, the British debt was only one element in an overall balance sheet which also included their debt payments to the United States and reparation receipts from Germany, and what mattered most was not whether the sums requested by Britain were in themselves within their capacity to pay but whether France would find herself in a net creditor position when all other items were taken into account. What the French feared, and rejected as utterly unacceptable, was a scenario in which the amounts that they obtained from Germany would not suffice to cover their total payments to Britain and the United States, with something left over towards the cost of restoring the devastated regions. British policymakers, for their part, were equally determined that Britain, caught between a demanding creditor and unwilling debtors, should not make disproportionate financial sacrifices.

Notes

Introduction

1   J. Martet, *Le Tigre* (Paris, 1930), p. 59; David Robin Watson, *Georges Clemenceau: A Political Biography* (London, 1974), p. 388.

2   See, for example, Robert W. D. Boyce, *British Capitalism at the Crossroads: A study in politics, economics, and international relations* (Cambridge, 1987); Bruce Kent, *The Spoils of War: The Politics, Economics, and Diplomacy of Reparations* (Oxford, 1989); Anne Orde, *British policy and European reconstruction after the First World War* (Cambridge, 1990); Stephen A. Schuker, *The End of French Predominance in Europe: The Financial Crisis of 1924 and the Adoption of the Dawes Plan* (Chapel Hill, N.C., 1976); Dan P. Silverman, *Reconstructing Europe after the Great War* (Cambridge, Mass., 1982); Marc Trachtenberg, *Reparation in World Politics: France and European Economic Diplomacy 1916–1923* (New York, 1980).

3   Denise Artaud, *La Question des dettes interalliées et la reconstruction de l'Europe 1917–1929*, 2 vols (Lille and Paris, 1978). There are also, of course, much earlier studies of inter-allied debts, including Harold G. Moulton and Cleona Lewis, *The French Debt Problem* (New York, 1925); Harold G. Moulton and Leo Pasvolsky, *World War Debt Settlements* (New York, 1926); Harold G. Moulton and Leo Pasvolsky, *War Debts and World Prosperity* (Washington, 1932): Lucien Petit, *Histoires Des Finances Extérieures De La France Pendant La Guerre (1914–1919)* (Paris, 1929); Lucien Petit, *Histoires Des Finances Extérieures De La France: Le Règlement Des Dettes Interalliées (1919–1929)* (Paris, 1932).

4   *Parliamentary Debates, Official Report, House of Commons*, 5th Series [hereafter *HC*], Financial Statement by Chancellor of the Exchequer, vol. 153, col. 1021, 1 May 1922. It should be noted that all references to billions of pounds mean thousands of millions.

5   By January 1923 added interest had increased the original French government debt of £453m to £541m: T160/114/F4399/2, 'War Debts of Allies to Great Britain', note by Frederick Phillips, enclosure in Niemeyer to Chancellor of the Exchequer, 13 March 1923.

Chapter 1   *Origins of the War Debts*

1   Moulton and Pasvolsky, *War Debts and World Prosperity*, p. 48.

2   For a list of all the wartime loan agreements between the British and French governments see Niemeyer Papers, T176/1A; Petit, *Finances Extérieures De la France Pendant La Guerre*, pp. 758–77.

3   For information about how the war was financed see Derek H. Aldcroft, *The European Economy 1914–1980* (London, 1978), pp. 19–20; Derek H. Aldcroft, *From*

Versailles to Wall St, 1919–1929 (London, 1977), pp. 30–3; Kathleen Burk, *Britain, America and the Sinews of War 1914–1918* (London, 1985); J. A. Hemery, *The Emergence of Treasury Influence in British Foreign Policy, 1914–1921*, unpublished PhD thesis (Universaity of Cambridge, 1988); Gaston Jèze and Henri Truchy, *The War Finance of France: The War Expenditure of France* and *How France Met Her War Expenditure* (New Haven, 1927); Moulton and Pasvolsky, *War Debts and World Prosperity*, ch. 3; Petit, *Finances Extérieures De La France Pendant La Guerre*; Ellen Schrecker, *The Hired Money: The French Debt to the United States 1917–1929*, (New York, 1978), pp. 1–44; Silverman, *Reconstructing Europe*, pp. 14–17.

4   Silverman, *Reconstructing Europe*, p. 13. Another estimate puts the total direct cost of the war at \$260bn, with the Allies spending \$176bn: Aldcroft, *From Versailles to Wall St*, p. 30.

5   T160/646/F10685/1, 'Great Britain and War Debts', Treasury memorandum, December 1927.

6   According to the Treasury, between 1 April 1914 and 1 April 1917 73.7 per cent of British war expenditure was met from borrowing and 26.3 per cent from taxation: T160/646/F10685/1. 'Great Britain and War Debts', Treasury memorandum, December 1927. See also *HC*, vol. 105, col. 698, 22 April 1918.

7   Aldcroft, *From Versailles to Wall Street*, p. 31. Silverman puts the figure for France at 15 per cent: *Reconstructing Europe*, p. 133. For information on French deficit financing during the war see Harvey E. Fisk, *The Inter-Ally Debts: An Analysis of War and Post-War Public Finance 1914–23* (New York and Paris, 1924), pp. 48–9; Robert Murray Haig, *The Public Finances of Post-War France* (New York, 1929), ch. 3; Silverman, *Reconstructing Europe*, pp. 14–17; Martin Wolfe, *The French Franc Between the Wars 1919–1939* (AMS reprint of 1951 edition, N.Y., 1968), pp. 22–5.

8   Moulton and Pasvolsky, *World War Debt Settlements*, pp. 3–5, 24; Wolfe, *French Franc Between the Wars*, pp. 24–5; Philip F. Vineberg, *The French Franc and the Gold Standard 1926–1936* (Montreal, 1936), pp. 7–8.

9   For details of purchases by Britain and the other European Allies in the United States see Burk, *Britain, America and the Sinews of War*. *See also* W. B. Fowler, *British-American Relations 1917–1918: The Role of Sir William Wiseman* (Princeton, 1969), chs 2–3.

10   Burk, *Britain, America and the Sinews of War*, p. 62; Moulton and Pasvolsky, *World War Debt Settlements*, p. 4.

11   T160/F10685/1, 'Great Britain and War Debts', Treasury memorandum, December 1927; Burk, *Britain, America and the Sinews of War*, pp. 63–75.

12   Burk, *Britain, America and the Sinews of War*, p. 8; Moulton and Pasvolsky, *World War Debt Settlements*, pp. 4–5.

13   T160/F10685/1, 'Great Britain and War Debts', Treasury memorandum, December 1927; David Lloyd George, *The Truth About Reparations and War Debts* (London, 1932), p. 97. Lloyd George talks of advances of £1,950,000,000 excluding Russia and of a net difference of £460m between these advances and British borrowing from the United States.

14   Artaud, *La Question des dettes interalliées*, I, 3; Moulton and Pasvolsky, *War Debts and World Prosperity*, p. 27; J. M. Keynes, 'The Inter-Allied Debts', *The Nation and Athenaeum*, 10 January 1925. For details of French war purchases from abroad see Petit, *Finances Extérieures De La France Pendant La Guerre*, pp. 19–169.

15   Artaud, *La Question des dettes interalliées* I, 63, 111. Others put the French debt to Britain and the United States at \$7bn. See Aldcroft, *From Versailles to Wall St*, p. 93; Schuker, *The End of French Predominance in Europe*, p. 9; Silverman, *Reconstructing Europe*, p. 15.

16   Artaud, *La Question des dettes interalliées*, I, 63. Schuker gives a figure of $3.5bn: *The End of French Predominance*, p. 9.

17   Petit, *Finances Extérieures De La France Pendant La Guerre*, pp. 210–11.

18   T160/153/F5904, Note on French Credit Agreement, 13 September 1922.

19   For details of the 1916 agreement see Bank of England Papers [hereafter BE], Governors' File, G1/302/2582/3, Inter-Bank Loan, 25 April 1916; Petit, *Finances Extérieures De La France Pendant La Guerre*, pp. 211–16, 766–7.

20   For the text of the Calais agreement of 24 August 1916 see Petit, *Finances Extérieures De La France Pendant La Guerre*, pp. 767–8.

21   T160/153/F5904, Note on French Credit Agreement, 13 September 1922; T160/382/F8348/3, 'Comparison of Character of French War Debts to USA and G.B.', Treasury note, undated (1925); T172/1499A, note on Bank of France credit with Bank of England, enclosure in Niemeyer to Churchill, 2 April 1926.

22   T160/153/F5904, Norman to Niemeyer, 3 February 1923.

23   Otto Niemeyer served as Deputy Controller of Finance (under Sir Basil Blackett) from December 1920. He became Controller in early 1923 and held the position until late 1927 when he left the Treasury to join the Bank of England.

24   T160/153/F5904, Niemeyer to Governor of the Bank of England, 12 February 1923.

25   Ibid., Niemeyer to Governor of the Bank of England, 12 February 1923; Niemeyer to Chancellor of the Exchequer, 8 March 1923; Norman to Niemeyer, 8 March 1923.

26   BE, GI/302/2528/3, Norman to Robineau, 21 March 1923; Gold and Foreign Exchange Files, C44/268, note by Harvey, 19 May 1923.

27   BE, G1/302/2528/3, Norman to Robineau, 21 March 1923.

28   T160/227/F8514/1, note for Chancellor of the Exchequer by Niemeyer, 15 July 1926: T160/383/F8348/4, 'List of British Holdings of French Rentes Issues made in London during the War', Treasury note, undated, 1926.

29   T160/227/F8514/1, note for Leith-Ross by Waley, 17 March 1925.

30   For the history of British attempts to secure compensation from the French government for the bondholders' losses see Arthur Turner, 'British holdings of French war bonds: an aspect of Anglo–French relations during the 1920s', *Financial History Review*, 3.2, October 1996, 153–74.

31   *The Collected Writings of John Maynard Keynes* [hereafter *CW Keynes*], 29 vols (London, 1971–83), XIX, 266–7; Keynes, 'The Inter-Allied Debts', *The Nation and Athenaeum*, 10 January 1925; Hemery, *The Emergence of Treasury Influence*, p. 41 n. 4.

32   Petit, *Finances Extérieures De La France Pendant La Guerre*, pp.186–93. The terms of the agreement are to be found in ibid., pp. 760–1. See also Hemery, *The Emergence of Treasury Influence*, pp. 30–1; Moulton and Pasvolsky, *War Debts and World Prosperity*, pp. 28–9

33   For Keynes' appointment to the Treasury and his work there in managing inter-allied financial relations see R. F. Harrod, *The Life of John Maynard Keynes* (London, 1951), pp. 195–203; Hemery, *The Emergence of Treasury Influence*, pp. 7, 15; Robert Skidelsky, *John Maynard Keynes*, 2 vols (London, 1992–1994), I, 289–344.

34   For a complete list of all the wartime debt agreements between the British and French governments see Niemeyer Papers, T176/1A.

35   T160/185/F7029, 'French Debt to G.B.', note by Bradbury, 9 December 1922; Treasury memorandum, enclosure in Niemeyer to Under-Secretary of State, FO, 4 January 1924. See also T160/114/F4399/2, notes on bills falling due in February 1923, 10 January 1923.

36   T160/114/F4399/2, 'War Debts of Allies to Great Britain', note by Phillips, enclo-

sure in Niemeyer to Chancellor of the Exchequer, 13 March 1923; 'Great Britain and War Debts', Treasury memorandum, December 1927; *The Economist*, leading article, 'The Balfour Note Once More', 10 March 1923.

37 T160/646/F10685/1. 'Great Britain and War Debts', Treasury memorandum, December 1927.

38 FO 371/8295, Poincaré to Hardinge, 1 September 1922, enclosure in Hardinge to Curzon, 2 September 1922.

39 T160/115/F7029, Treasury memorandum, enclosure in Niemeyer to Under-Secretary of State, FO, 4 January 1924; T172/1499A, 'Comparison between French Debts to U.S.A and G.B.', Annex II to note for Chancellor of the Exchequer by Niemeyer, 20 May 1926.

40 T172/1499A, 'Comparison between French Debts to USA and G.B.', Annex II to note for Chancellor of the Exchequer by Niemeyer, 20 May 1926; Moulton and Pasvolsky, *War Debts and World Prosperity*, p. 31.

41 T160/149/F5742, McKenna to Ribot, 26 August 1916; Ribot to McKenna, 29 August 1916. See Petit, *Finances Extérieures De La France Pendant La Guerre*, pp. 320–1.

42 BE, Governors' Miscellaneous Correspondence, G30/2/4037/2, memorandum by Keynes, 10 March 1917.

43 Moulton and Pasvolsky, *War Debts and World Prosperity*, p. 31; T172/1025, Edwin Montagu to Austen Chamberlain, 28 March 1919.

44 T160/114/F4399/2, notes on bills falling due in February 1923, 10 January 1923; T160/185/F7029, Treasury memorandum, enclosure in Niemeyer to Under-Secretary of State, FO, 4 January 1924; T172/1025, Montagu to Chamberlain, 28 March 1919.

45 Sir Basil Blackett was Controller of Finance from September 1919 until late 1922 when he resigned from the Treasury to take up a position on the Viceroy's Councill in Delhi.

46 For the text of the Blackett–Avenol agreement see Niemeyer Papers, T176/1A.

47 *HC*, vol. 105, col. 692, 22 April 1918; T160/207/7768/2, Treasury Memorandum on the relation between the Anglo-American Debt and Allied Debts to Great Britain, 12 January 1925.

48 *HC*, vol. 105, cols. 692–3, 22 April 1918; vol. 147, col. 284, 20 October 1921; Cab 23/21, 30(20)163, Cabinet minutes of 21 May 1920, Appendix, Summary of a Statement by the Chancellor of the Exchequer on the Subject of Inter-Allied Indebtedness; T160/207/7768/2, Treasury Memorandum on the relation between the Anglo-American Debt and Allied Debts to Great Britain, 12 January 1925; Artaud, *La Question des dettes interalliées*, I, 23.

49 T160/207/7768/2, Treasury Memorandum on the relation between the Anglo-American Debt and Allied Debts to Great Britain, 12 January 1925; Artaud, *La Question des dettes interalliées*, I, 23. According to Austen Chamberlain, the Americans would have accepted the British proposal if Bonar Law had been willing to state that Britain was at the end of her resources: Cab 23/21, 30(20), 164, Cabinet minutes of 21 May 1920, Annex.

50 For a thorough analysis of Anglo-French discussions on the continuation of credits for France after the Armistice see Hemery, *The Emergence of Treasury Influence*, 1988), pp. 121–36. Also Orde, *British policy and European reconstruction*, pp. 35–51.

51 Trachtenberg, *Reparation in World Politics*, p. 13.

52 Ibid., p. 26; Keynes, *CW Keynes*, XVI, 411.

53 *CW Keynes*, XVI, 410; *The Times*, 27 February 1924, Keynes' review of Klotz's memoirs; Artaud, *La Question des dettes interalliées*, I, 95–6; Petit, *Finances Extérieures*

De La France Pendant La Guerre, p. 323.

54   See, for example, T1/12585, Rathbone to Reading, 4 March 1919; Reading to Chamberlain, 6 March 1919. For growing American reluctance to provide Britain with the credits requested see Artaud, *La Question des dettes interalliées*, I, 84–5; Burk, *Britain, America and the Sinews of War*, ch. 9; Hemery, *The Emergence of Treasury Influence*, pp. 125–6; Schrecker, *The Hired Money*, pp. 36–44.

55   Silverman, *Reconstructing Europe*, p. 63.

56   T160/646/F10685/1, 'Great Britain and War Debts', Treasury memorandum, December 1927; T172/774, 'The financial outlook', note by Sir M. Ramsay, 12 January 1919.

57   Artaud, *La Question des dettes interalliées*, I, 95; Orde, *British policy and European reconstruction*, pp. 36–8.

58   Petit, *Finances Extérieures De La France Pendant La Guerre*, pp. 322–5.

59   Artaud, *La Question des dettes interalliées*, I, 99–101; Orde, *British policy and European reconstruction*, p. 44. For Keynes' account see *CW Keynes*, XVI, 406–15.

60   According to Petit the British deliberately exaggerated the problems of securing financial aid from the United States in order to justify the termination of ending of credits to France: *Finances Extérieures De La France Pendant La Guerre*, p. 325.

61   Hemery, *The Emergence of Treasury Influence*, pp. 127–9.

62   T160/12256/49893/18, FO to Bailey, 23 December 1918; Bailey to FO, 4 January 1919; Artaud, *La Question des dettes interalliées*, I, 93; Orde, *British policy and European reconstruction*, pp. 38–9.

63   Cab23/115, WC536A, Cabinet minutes of 25 February 1919. An extract from the minutes is contained in *CW Keynes*, XVI, 406.

64   Petit, *Finances Extérieures De La France Pendant la Guerre*, p. 327.

65   Austen Chamberlain Papers, AC 35/7/5, Chamberlain to Keynes, 7 February 1924; Orde, *British policy and European reconstruction*, pp. 47–8; Hemery, *The Emergence of Treasury Influence*, pp. 127–9.

66   Hemery, *The Emergence of Treasury Influence*, p. 131.

67   Niemeyer Papers, T176/1A, Anglo-French Financial Agreement, 13 March 1919; FO 371/3754, Bradbury to Blackett, 19 March 1919; Artaud, *La Question des dettes interalliées*, I, 103; Hemery, *The Emergence of Treasury Influence*, p. 129; Orde, *British policy and European reconstruction*, pp. 50–1; Petit, *Finances Extérieures De La France Pendant La Guerre*, pp. 327–8.

68   T172/1025, Montagu to Chamberlain, 28 March 1919.

69   Idem.

70   See T1/12585, Chamberlain to Keynes, 2 March 1919.

71   T172/1025, Chamberlain to Montagu, 31 March.

72   Louis-Lucien Klotz, *De la guerre à la paix: Souvenirs et documents* (Paris, 1924), pp. 115–23.

73   *The Times*, 27 February 1924; *CW Keynes*, XVI, 407–13.

74   See *CW Keynes*, XVI, 406–14. For a discussion of the validity of Klotz' claims see Hemery, *The Emergence of Treasury Influence*, pp. 132–6.

75   See FO 371/3754, Bradbury to Foreign Office, 9 July 1919.

Chapter 2   *The Immediate Postwar Years, 1918–1922*

1   T160/185/F7029, 'French Debt to Great Britain', note by Bradbury, 9 December 1922; Treasury memorandum, enclosure in Niemeyer to Under-Secretary of State, FO, 4 January 1924.

2   T160/114/F4399/2, note by Phillips, enclosure in Niemeyer to Chancellor of the

Exchequer, 13 March 1922; T160/185/F7029, Treasury memorandum, enclosure in Niemeyer to Under-Secretary of State, FO, 4 January 1924.

3 T160/114/F4399/2, Niemeyer to Chancellor of the Exchequer, 13 March 1923.

4 Artaud, *La Question des dettes interalliées*, I, 241; Moulton and Pasvolsky, *War Debts and World Prosperity*, pp. 40–1.

5 T160/114/F4399/1, Blackett to Fass, 15 March 1922; P. J. Grigg, *Prejudice and Judgement*, (London, 1948) p. 79. The decision to resume interest payments to the United States was announced in the Budget statement of 1 May 1922: *HC*, vol. 153, col. 1029.

6 T160/114/F4399/1, Fass to Blackett, 22 March 1922; Niemeyer to Under-Secretary of State, FO, 24 March 1922; Foreign Office to Saint-Aulaire, 31 March 1922.

7 Ibid., note for the Chancellor of the Exchequer by Niemeyer, 14 September 1922; minute by Austen Chamberlain, 18 September 1922.

8 T160/114/F4399/2, 'War Debt of Allies to Great Britain', note by Phillips, enclosure in Niemeyer to Chancellor of the Exchequer, 13 March 1923.

9 Ibid., minute by Niemeyer, 18 September 1922: minute by J. R. Chambers, 27 March 1923.

10 Ibid., 'War Debts of Allies to Great Britain', note by Phillips, enclosure in Niemeyer to Chancellor of the Exchequer, 13 March 1923.

11 See, for example, T160/114/F4399/2, Niemeyer to Chancellor of the Exchequer, 13 March 1922.

12 T172/202, 'Liquidation of Post-War Liabilities', memorandum by Blackett for the Geddes Committee, January 1922; 'Funding Pensions', memorandum by Niemeyer, 9 February 1922.

13 See, for example, the statement by the Chancellor of the Exchequer, Sir Robert Horne, on 3 August 1922. According to Horne, British taxation was more than £17 per head compared with £9 per head in France: *HC*, vol. 157, col. 1744. (Also Cab 24/104, CP 1156, 'Inter-Allied Debts', memorandum by Churchill, 23 April 1920). Poincaré challenged Horne's claim about higher British taxation at a conference of 7 August 1922, pointing out the difficulty of making a fair comparison in view of the different social structures of Britain and France and the various local taxes that the French paid in addition to income tax: *Documents on British Foreign Policy* [hereafter *DBFP*], 1st Series, XX, no. 51, British Secretary's Note of an Allied Conference held at 10 Downing St on Monday 7 August 1922 at 11a.m.

14 FO 371/9682, Selby to Treasury, 14 November 1923; Foreign Office memorandum respecting the attitude of HMG towards Allied War Debts, 10 January 1924; Crewe to Curzon, 14 January 1924; T160/185/F7029, Treasury memorandum, enclosure in Niemeyer to Under-Secretary of State, FO, 4 January 1924.

15 Cab 23/21, 31(20)166, Cabinet minutes of 2 June 1922.

16 T160/114/F4399/2, 'War Debt of Allies to Great Britain', note by Phillips, enclosure in Niemeyer to Chancellor of the Exchequer, 13 March 1923.

17 T160/185/F7029, Treasury memorandum, enclosure in Niemeyer to Under-Secretary of State, FO, 4 January 1924.

18 *Punch*, 9 January 1924; *The New Leader*, 11 January 1924.

19 Michael Howard, *The Continental Commitment: The dilemma of British defence policy in the era of two world wars* (London, 1972), p. 78.

20 Diary of Thomas Jones, 22 November 1921: Keith Middlemas (ed.), *Thomas Jones: Whitehall Diary*, 3 vols (London, 1969–71), I, 178. See also *DBFP*, 1st Series, XVI, nos 439, 442, 443, 452, 517.

21 See Lloyd George's comments to the Cabinet when discussing whether or not to

send the Balfour Note in July 1922: Cab 23/30, 42(22)362, Cabinet minutes of 25 July 1922.

22 For a brief account of the run-down in British military forces in the postwar period see Basil Collier, *The Defence of the United Kingdom* (London, 1957), pp. 1–20.

23 Hankey to Tom Jones, 11 October 1928: Middlemas (ed.), *Whitehall Diary*, II, 148–9. See also Cab 4/13, CID Paper no. 625–B, Chiefs of Staff Sub-Committee, 'The Bearings of the recent Enquiries on Diversion of Shipping in Time of War and Air Raid Precautions', 3 July 1925; Austen Chamberlain Papers, FO 800/257, memorandum by Hankey, 23 January 1925.

24 *DBFP*, 1st Series, XIV, no. 442, Curzon to Balfour, 23 November 1921; no. 443, Curzon to Balfour, 23 November 1921.

25 Collier, *The Defence of the United Kingdom*, pp. 3–5; Robert W. Krauskopf, *French Air Policy, 1919–1939*, unpublished Ph.D. thesis (University of Georgetown, 1965), pp. 9–15.

26 Air 9/20, folio 4, 'The Retaliatory Measures which could be immediately directed against a continental attacking power by the Navy and Air Force', memorandum by the Air Ministry, March 1922; folio 2, 'French Air Forces in their relation to the security of the United Kingdom', memorandum by the Air Staff, 10 November 1921; *DBFP*, 1st Series, XIV, nos 442–3, Curzon to Balfour, 23 November 1923. For information on the doctrine of strategic bombing see Sir Charles Webster and Noble Frankland, *The Strategic Air Offensive against Germany* (London, 1961), I, 6–64, 71–83.

27 Cab 23/29, 18(22)282, Cabinet minutes of 15 March 1922.

28 Collier, *The Defence of the United Kingdom*, pp. 11–15; Howard, *The Continental Commitment*, pp. 82–4; M.M. Postan, *British War Production* (London, 1952), pp. 4–5; *HC*, vol. 165, col. 2142, 26 June 1923.

29 Howard, *The Continental Commitment*, pp. 81–4.

30 *DBFP*, 1st Series, XX, no. 53, Minutes of a meeting held at 10 Downing St on Monday 7 August 1922. See also T160/114/F4399/2, 'War Debt of Allies to Great Britain', note by Phillips, enclosure in Niemeyer to Chancellor of Exchequer, 13 March 1923.

31 Cab 23/20, 72(20)256–57, Cabinet minutes of 17 December 1920.

32 This point was stressed in the Balfour Note of 1 August 1922. See also T160/646/F10685/1, 'Great Britain and War Debts', Treasury memorandum, December 1927; Keynes, 'The Inter-Allied Debts', *The Nation and Athenaeum*, 9 January 1925; Lloyd George, *The Truth About Reparations and War Debts*, pp. 97–8.

33 *DBFP*, 1st Series, VIII, no. 27, British Secretary's Notes of a Conference held at Lympne, 20 June 1920.

34 Artaud, *La Question des dettes interalliées*, I,63; Moulton and Lewis, *The French Debt Problem*, pp. 18–20, 26–7.

35 For French policy on reconstruction of the devastated regions see Artaud, *La Question des dettes interalliées*, I, 71–8.

36 Melvyn P. Leffler, *The Elusive Quest: America's Pursuit of European Stability and French Security, 1919–1933* (Chapel Hill, NC, 1979), p. 25.

37 Artaud, *La Question des dettes interalliés*, I, vi. For a useful basic discussion of the problems involved in international debt repayment see Moulton and Pasvolsky, *World War Debt Settlements*, pp. 1–9.

38 Artaud, *La Question des dettes interalliées*, I, 2, 104.

39 Silverman, *Reconstructing Europe*, p. 133.

40 Moulton and Lewis, *The French Debt Problem*, p. 24.

41 A table of French Budget deficits during the early 1920s is contained in Moulton and

Lewis, *The French Debt Problem*, p. 85. Budget deficits for the years 1918–22 totalled 130bn francs. See Silverman, *Reconstructing Europe*, p. 63; Schuker, *The End of French Predominance*, p. 38; Haig, *Public Finances of Post-War France*, p. 432.

42 Jacques Néré, *The Foreign Policy of France from 1914 to 1945* (London, 1975), p. 50.
43 Silverman, *Reconstructing Europe*, pp. 94–5.
44 Ibid., p. 133.
45 Ibid., p. 17.
46 For information on the parlous state of French finances in the early 1920s see Haig, *Public Finances of Post-War France*, chs 3–6; Moulton and Lewis, *The French Debt Problem*.
47 For French attitudes see Artaud, *La Question des dettes interalliées*, I, 392–403.
48 Cited in Artaud, *La Question des dettes interalliées*, I, 384.
49 *DBFP*, 1st Series, VIII, no. 27, British Secretary's Notes of a Conference held at Lympne, 20 June 1920.
50 See, for example, T172/1278, 'Liquidation of Post-War Liabilities', memorandum by Blackett for the Geddes Committee, January 1922; 'Funding Pensions', memorandum by Niemeyer, 9 February 1922.
51 See comments by Austen Chamberlain at Cabinet meeting of 21 May 1920: Cab 23/21, 30(20)162. See also the views of Churchill in his memorandum 'Inter-Allied and Anglo-American Debts', 15 May 1920: Cab 24/106, CP 1316.
52 For the views of Lloyd George and Austen Chamberlain, the Chancellor of the Exhequer, on this see *DBFP*, 1st Series, VIII, no. 27, British Secretary's Notes of a Conference held at Lympne, 20 June 1920. See also the comments of Horne, Chamberlain's successor as Chancellor: *HC*, vol. 157, col. 175, 3 August 1922.
53 T160/365/F557/1, memorandum by Blackett, 2 February 1920.
54 Artaud, *La Question des dettes interalliées*, I, 231.
55 *DBFP*, 1st Series, VIII, no. 27, British Secretary's Notes of a Conference held at Lympne, 20 June 1920.
56 Lloyd George, *The Truth About Reparations and War Debts*, p. 104; Artaud, *La Question des dettes interalliées*, I, 105; Moulton and Pasvolsky, *War Debts and World Prosperity*, pp. 53–4..
57 Ibid., I, 107–8. For official American attitudes on cancellation of war debts at the peace conference and during the early 1920s see Schrecker, *The Hired Money*, pp. 57–68, 95–128.
58 Cab 24/97, CP 584, 'Inter-Allied Indebtedness', memorandum by Blackett, 2 February 1920.
59 Cab 24/97, CP 584, Treasury to Rathbone, 19 December 1920, in memorandum by Fisher.
60 Artaud, *La Question des dettes interalliées*, I, 237–8.
61 FO 371/4563, Lindsay to Curzon, 26 February and 6 March 1920; Artaud, *La Question des dettes interalliées*, I, 238; Moulton and Pasvolsky, *War Debts and World Prosperity*, pp. 61–5; Schrecker, *The Hired Money*, p. 101.
62 Lloyd George Papers, F7/2/27, Chamberlain to Lloyd George, 17 April 1919; F/2/34, Lloyd George to Wilson, 23 April 1919; *CW Keynes*, XVI, 429–36; Lloyd George, *The Truth About Reparations and War Debts*, pp. 105–6; Artaud, *La Question des dettes interalliées*, I, 123–35. For Wilson's rejection of Keynes' scheme see Lloyd George Papers, F60/1/14, Wilson to Lloyd George, 3 May 1919; *CW Keynes*, XVI, 440–1; R.S. Baker, *Woodrow Wilson and World Settlement*, 3 vols (New York, 1923), III, 329–30; Lloyd George, *The Truth About Reparations and War Debts*, pp. 106–7; Schrecker, *The Hired Money*, pp. 69–71; Skidelsky, *John Maynard Keynes*, I, 369–70.
63 Cab 23/21, 30(20)150, Cabinet minutes of 21 May 1920; Lloyd George Papers,

F60/1/28, Lloyd George to Wilson, 5 August 1920: Lloyd George, *The Truth About Reparations and War Debts*, p. 109.

64 Cab 24/105, CP 1297, 'The Conversations at Hythe', note by the Secretary (Hankey), 17 May 1920.

65 Lloyd George Papers, F60/1/28, Lloyd George to Wilson, 5 August 1920; Moulton and Pasvolsky, *War Debts and World Prosperity*, pp. 65–7.

66 Cab 23/23, 59(20)5, Cabinet minutes of 3 November 1920; FO 371/4563, Curzon to Geddes, 5 November.

67 Lloyd George Papers, F60/1/31, Wilson to Lloyd George, 3 November 1920; Lloyd George, *The Truth About Reparations and War Debts*, p. 110; Moulton and Pasvolsky, *War Debts and World Prosperity*, pp. 67–70; Schrecker, *The Hired Money*, pp. 135–6.

68 Orde, *British policy and European reconstruction*, pp. 77–107, 148–60, 208–26.

69 Cab 24/98, CP 621, 'Inter-Allied Indebtedness', memorandum by A. Geddes, 12 February 1920.

70 Cab 24/138, CP 4149, 'Inter-Allied Debts', memorandum by Secretary of State for the Colonies, 3 August 1922.

71 Cab 23/23, 72(20)258, Cabinet minutes of 17 December 1920; Cab 24/103, CP 1093, 'Foreign Policy and Inter-Allied Debts', memorandum by Curzon, 17 April 1920; Cab 24/116, CP 2214, 'Our American Debt', memorandum by Chancellor of the Exchequer, 30 November 1920.

72 Cab 24/105, CP1202, 'Proposed remission of Debts owing by European Allies', memorandum by Horne, 1 May 1920.

73 FO 371/4563, Geddes to Curzon, 2 December 1920; Artaud, *La Question des dettes interalliées*, I, 208–9.

74 Cab 23/23, 72(20)72, Cabinet minutes of 17 December 1920; Cab 23/24, 5(21), Cabinet minutes of 7 February 1921.

75 FO 371/7282, Geddes to Foreign Office, 17 May and 6 June 1922. Parmentier was the *Directeur du Mouvement Général des Fonds*. For his unsuccessful mission see Schrecker, *The Hired Money*, pp. 151–5.

76 FO 371/7282, minute by Sperling, 19 May 1922; minute by N. Law, 7 June 1922; Leffler, *The Elusive Quest*, p. 66.

77 T194/4, Blackett to Bradbury, 10 December 1919; Cab 24/97, CP584, memorandum by Blackett, 2 February 1920.

78 Wartime friction between members of the British Treasury mission to the United States and representatives of the United States Treasury is dealt with in Burk, *Britain, America and the Sinews of War*, chs 5–9.

79 For the Blackett-Rathbone conversations see Cab 23/21, 30(20), 159–62, Cabinet minutes of 21 May 1920, Annex, Summary of a Statement by the Chancellor of the Exchequer on the Subject of Inter-Allied Indebtedness; Artaud, *La Question des dettes interalliées*, I, 222–56; Orde, *British policy and European reconstruction*, pp. 81–2, 84, 86, 90–4, 102–3, 153, 158.

80 Cab 24/97, CP 584, memorandum by Blackett, 2 February 1920.

81 Cab 24/97, CP 584, 'Inter Allied Indebtedness', note by the Chancellor of the Exchequer, 6 February 1920.

82 Orde, *British policy and European reconstruction*, p. 89.

83 Cab 24/97, CP 584, 'Inter Allied Indebtedness', note by the Chancellor of the Exchequer, 6 February 1920.

84 FO 371/4563, minute by Sperling, 11 February 1920.

85 Ibid., minutes by Waterlow and O' Malley, 17 February 1920.

86 Ibid., minute by Sperling, 13 February 1920.

87 Ibid., Foreign Office to Lindsay, 24 February 1920; Lindsay to Foreign Office, 26

February 1920.

88 Cab 24/98, CP 621, 'Inter-Allied Indebtedness', memorandum by A. Geddes, 12 February 1920.

89 FO 371/4563, Sperling to Lindsay, 4 March 1920.

90 Cab 24/103, CP 1093, 'Foreign Policy and Inter-Allied Debts', memorandum by Curzon, 17 April 1920.

91 Idem.

92 Cab 24/104, CP 1156, 'Inter-Allied Debts', memorandum by Churchill, 23 April 1920.

93 Cab 24/106, CP 1316, 'Inter-Allied and Anglo-American Debts', memorandum by Churchill, 15 May 1920.

94 Cab 24/105, CP 1202, 'Proposed remission of Debts owing by European Allies', memorandum by Horne, 1 May 1920.

95 Cab 24/105, CP 1259, 'British Government's Debt to the United States Government', memorandum by Blackett, 11 May 1920; note by Chancellor of the Exchequer covering a memorandum by the Controller of Finance, 12 May 1920.

96 Ibid., note by Chancellor of the Exchequer covering a memorandum by the Controller of Finance, 12 May 1920; Cab 23/21, 30(20)149, 159–64, Cabinet minutes of 21 May 1920.

97 Cab 23/21, 30(20)161, Cabinet minutes of 21 May 1920.

98 Cab 24/105, CP1259, 'British Government's Debt to the United States Government', memorandum by Blackett, 11 May 1920; note by Chancellor of the Exchequer covering a memorandum by the Controller of Finance, 12 May 1920.

99 Cab 23/21, 29(20)132–33, Cabinet minutes of 19 May 1920.

100 Cab 23/21, 29(20)133, Cabinet minutes of 19 May 1920; Cab 23/21, 30(20)150, Cabinet minutes of 21 May 1920.

101 FO 371/4563, Geddes to Foreign Office, 18 June 1920; Lloyd George, *The Truth About Reparations and War Debts*, p. 110.

102 FO 371/4563, Geddes to Curzon, 22 and 23 October 1920; Cab 24/114, CP 2029, note by Hankey covering telegram from Sir Auckland Geddes; Cab 23/23, 59(20)3, Cabinet minutes of 3 November 1920.

103 Cab 24/116, CP 2214, 'Our American Debt', memorandum by the Chancellor of the Exchequer, 30 November 1920.

104 FO 371/4563, Geddes to Foreign Office, 2 December 1920; Cab 24/116, CP 2214A, 'Our American Debt', supplementary note by the Chancellor of the Exchequer, 3 December 1920.

105 Cab 24/116, CP 2214A, 'Our American Debt', supplementary note by the Chancellor of the Exchequer, 3 December 1920.

106 FO 371/4563, Geddes to Foreign Office, 15 December 1920.

107 Cab 23/23, 72(20)256–8, Cabinet minutes of 17 December 1920.

108 Idem.

109 For a history of reparations until May 1921 see Carl Bergmann, *The History of Reparations* (London, 1927), chs 1–7; Kent, *Spoils of War*, chs 1–3; Trachtenberg, *Reparation in World Politics*, chs 1–6. Trachtenberg takes the view that Germany could have made the payments required if the political will had existed. Kent takes the opposite view.

110 Bergmann, *History of Reparations*, p. 99; Sir Frederick Leith-Ross, *Money Talks: Fifty Years of International Finance* (London, 1968), p. 80.

111 Sir Henry Clay, *Lord Norman* (London, 1957), p. 198.

112 Ibid., pp. 101–2; Kent, *Spoils of War*, pp. 157–8; Orde, *British policy and European reconstruction*, pp. 169–70; Trachtenberg, *Reparation in World Politics*, p. 216. For

Rathenau's account of his visit to London see Hartmut Pogge von Strandmann (ed.), *Walther Rathenau, Industrialist, Banker, Intellectual and Politician: Notes and Diaries 1907–1922* (Oxford, 1985), pp. 273–83.

113 *DBFP*, 1st Series, XVI, no. 741, Letter from Blackett to Crowe, 22 November 1921. See also ibid., no. 744, Memorandum by Wigram on the reparation situation, 25 November 1921.

114 Cab 24/131, CP 3556, 16 November 1921.

115 BE, OV 34/100, 'Draft for the Cabinet', 28 November 1921; Cab 24/131, CP 3512, 28 November 1921; Cab 27/71, FC 36th and 37th conclusions, 1 and 6 December 1921.

116 BE OV 34/100, memorandum by Norman, 24 November 1921; G 8/54, meeting of Committee of Treasury, 30 November 1921; Clay, *Lord Norman*, p. 200.

117 BE, OV 31/5, Norman to Strong, 1 December 1921.

118 Bergmann, *History of Reparations*, p. 110.

119 Artaud, *La Question des dettes interalliées*, I, 372. Artaud describes Norman's plan as being 'd'une extrême insolence'. See also Clay, *Lord Norman*, p. 198; Orde, *British policy and European reconstruction*, p. 168.

120 Artaud, *La Question des dettes interalliées*, I, 371–2. The importance that the Foreign Office attached to good relations with France was reflected in a minute by Eyre Crowe of 30 November 1921: 'From a general viewpoint, the maintenance of the Entente with France is of capital importance. There is at the Treasury and Downing Street a tendency to substitute an Entente with Germany for the Entente with France, but it is a chimera and will remain so for a long time; for what we want is peace, and that presupposes execution of the treaty, which will not survive a rupture between France and Great Britain': FO 371/6039. For Curzon's objection to a suggestion from Horne that pressure could be put on France to accept a moratorium on reparation payments see Cab 27/71, FC 36th and 37th conclusions, 1 and 6 December 1921.

121 *DBFP*, 1st Series, XVI, no. 752, Curzon to Hardinge, 5 December 1921; Artaud, *La Question des dettes interalliées*, I, 373.

122 For the proposals put forward by Seydoux and Aron see Artaud, *La Question des dettes interalliées*, I, 374–7, 378–9; Orde, *British policy and European reconstruction*, pp. 170–1.

123 Artaud, *La Question des dettes interalliées*, pp. 378–9; Orde, *British policy and European reconstruction*, p. 171.

124 Cab 23/27, 93(21), Cabinet minutes of 16 December 1921; *DBFP*, 1st Series, XV, no. 107. See also Martin Gilbert, *Winston S. Churchill*, IV, Companion Volume, Part III (London, 1977), 166–8.

125 Louis Loucheur, *Carnets secrets* (Brussels and Paris, 1962), pp. 185–8.

126 Hankey Papers, 8/22, Hankey to Lloyd George, 29 November 1921.

127 Cab 23/27, 93(21)274, Cabinet minutes of 16 December 1921.

128 BE, OV 31/5, Norman to Strong, 17 December 1921.

129 Middlemas (ed.) *Whitehall Diary*, I, 184–5.

130 Cab 23/27, 93(21)270–71, Cabinet minutes of 16 December 1921.

131 *DBFP*, 1st Series, XV, nos 105, 107; Etienne Weill-Raynaud, *Les Réparations allemandes et la France*, 3 vols (Paris, 1947), II, 85–95.

132 *DBFP*, Ist Series, XIX, no. 101, Notes of a Meeting between the Prime Minister and M. Barthou at the Hotel Miramare, Genoa, 29 April 1922.

133 Cab 23/23, 72(20)257, Cabinet minutes of 17 December 1920; Cab 23/24, 5(21)56, Cabinet minutes of 7 February 1921.

134 Cab 23/25, 37(21)253, Cabinet minutes of 10 May 1921.

135 Cab 23/27, 93(21)274, Cabinet minutes of 16 December 1921.
136 For the Harding Administration's policy on reparations and war debts and the establishment of the World War Foreign Debt Commission see Artaud, *La Question des dettes interalliées*, I, 329–65; Leffler, *The Elusive Quest*, pp. 64–70; Moulton and Pasvolsky, *World War Debt Settlements*, pp. 110–12: Schrecker, *The Hired Money*, pp. 103–5, 119–26. For the text of the act setting up the WDC see Moulton and Pasvolsky, *op. cit*, pp. 221–3.
137 *Papers Relating to the Foreign Relations of the United States* [hereafter *FRUS*], (Kraus Reprint, N.Y., 1971–2), 1922, I, 397–9.
138 FO 371/7282, minute by Eyre Crowe, 7 June 1922.
139 Ibid., minute by Sperling, 6 June 1922. See also *FRUS*, 1922, I, 402, The Secretary of State to the Ambassador in Great Britain, 15 June 1922.
140 FO 371/7282, minute by Sperling, 24 May 1922.
141 Ibid., Geddes to Foreign Office, 16 May 1922.
142 Ibid., Geddes to Foreign Office, 17 May and 6 June 1922.
143 Ibid., minutes by Sperling 19, 24 and 25 May 1922; minute by Sir Arthur Willert, 25 June 1922; minute by N. Law, 7 June 1922.
144 Ibid., FO to Treasury, 18 May 1922; Blackett to Under-Secretary of State, FO, 23 May 1922; minute by Sperling, 24 May 1922.
145 Ibid., minute by Eyre Crowe, 7 June 1922.
146 Cab 23/30, 29(22)96, Cabinet minutes of 23 May 1922.
147 Cab 24/137, CP 4020, 'British debt to the United States Government', memorandum by the Chancellor of the Exchequer, 8 June 1920.
148 Cab 23/30, 35(22)216–17, Cabinet minutes of 16 June 1922.
149 Ibid., 217–20.
150 Ibid., 220.
151 *DBFP*, 1st Series, XX, no. 30, British Secretary's Notes of a Meeting between Mr Lloyd George and M. Poincaré, held at 10, Downing St, London, on Monday, June 19, at 2.45 p.m.
152 Cab 23/30, 36(22), Cabinet minutes of 30 June 1922.
153 Cab 23/30, 38(22), Cabinet minutes of 7 July 1922; FO 371/4563, Hankey to Balfour, 7 July 1922. The American government was informed a week later: FO 371/7282, Balfour to Harvey, 14 July 1922; *FRUS*, 1922, I, 404, The Ambassador in Great Britain to the Secretary of State, 17 July 1922.
154 FO 371/7282, memorandum by Grigg, 5 July 1922; Orde, *British policy and European reconstruction*, p. 213.
155 Skidelsky, *John Maynard Keynes*, II, 117.
156 Niemeyer Papers, T176/8, note for Chancellor of the Exchequer by Blackett, 12 July 1922.
157 Idem.
158 Cab 23/30, 42(22)350–52, Cabinet minutes of 25 July 1922.
159 Ibid., 355–6.
160 Ibid., 353.
161 Ibid., 358–9.
162 Ibid., 357.
163 Ibid., 354.
164 Ibid., 361–3.
165 Cab 27/71, FC, 40th conclusions, 31 July 1922; Cmd 1737 (1922), *Despatch to the representatives of France, Italy, Serb-Croat-Slovene State, Roumania, Portugal and Greece at London respecting War Debts*; *DBFP*, 1st Series, XX, no. 45, The Earl of Balfour to the Count of Saint-Aulaire, 1 August 1922; *The Times*, 2 August 1922;

Moulton and Pasvolsky, *World War Debt Settlements*, Appendix C, pp. 413–18. According to Lloyd George, the Balfour Note was drafted by him: Lloyd George, *The Truth About Reparations and War Debts*, p. 111.

Chapter 3   *The Balfour Note and the London Conference of August 1922*

1 Cmd 1737 (1922).
2 Idem.
3 By 1928 the difference between British debt payments to the United States and receipts from Germany and allied debtors had grown to £180m: *DBFP*, Series 1A, V, no. 187, memorandum by the Chancellor of the Exchequer on his conversation in Paris, 19 October 1928, enclosure in Tyrrell to Cushendun, 20 October 1928.
4 For details of the Anglo-American debt settlement of 19 June 1923 see Moulton and Pasvolsky, *World War Debt Settlements*, Appendix B, pp. 225–40.
5 FO 371/9682, memorandum respecting the Attitude of HMG towards Allied War Debts, 10 January 1924.
6 Idem. The amount originally borrowed by France was £453m compared to £362m in the case of Italy. By January 1923 the respective figures, with accrued interest, were £541m and £495.5m: T160/114/F4399/2, 'War Debts of Allies to Great Britain', note by Phillips, enclosure in Niemeyer to Chancellor of the Exchequer, 13 March 1923.
7 FO 371/8295, Chilton to Balfour, 3 August 1922; *The Times*, articles by Washington correspondent, 3 and 4 August 1922; Artaud, *La Question des dettes interalliées*, I, 462; Schrecker, *The Hired Money*, p. 147.
8 *The Times*, 3 August 1922. There was some dispute as to whether the main target of the Note was France or the United States. Keynes, for example, was in no doubt that it was aimed principally at France rather than the United States: *Westminster Gazette*, 'A Moratorium for War Debts', 5 August 1922; *CW Keynes*, XVIII, 12.
9 *The Times*, Washington correspondent, 4 August 1922.
10 T160/114/F4399/1, Cheetham to Foreign Office, 2 August 1922; *Le Temps*, *L'Echo de Paris*, 2 August 1922; *The Times*, articles by Paris correspondent, 2, 3 and 4 August 1922; Artaud, *La Question des dettes interalliées*, I, 438–41; Néré, *The Foreign Policy of France*, pp. 49–50.
11 See Poincaré's shocked reaction at the London conference of August 1922 when he said that the Balfour Note was 'couched in lofty and courteous terms, but indicated without possibility of doubt that Great Britain proposed to insist some day on payment. The result, so far as France was concerned, was very cruel': *DBFP*, 1st Series, XX, no. 51, British Secretary's Notes of an Allied Conference held at 10 Downing St, Monday 7 August 1922 (11 am).
12 FO 371/7282, minute by Sperling, 6 June 1922.
13 FO 371/8295, Avenol to the Secretary of the Treasury, 12 August 1922.
14 *The Times*, 25 August 1922, p. 7; FO 371/8295, Chilton to Curzon, 25 August 1922; T160/114/F4399/1, statement by Andrew Mellon, Secretary of the Treasury, 24 August 1922.
15 *The Daily Telegraph*, 25 August 1922. For Horne's statement in the Commons see *HC*, vol. 147, col. 284, 2 October 1921.
16 T160/114/F4399/1, Avenol to the Secretary of the Treasury, 26 August 1922.
17 Ibid., Waley to Niemeyer, 28 August 1922; minute by Niemeyer, 29 August 1922.
18 Harvey's remarks were made during a Pilgrims dinner in honour of the Chancellor of the Exchequer, Baldwin: *The Times*, 1 March 1923.
19 *Parliamentary Debates, Official Report*, 5th series, House of Lords [hereafter *HL*],

vol. 53, cols. 338–9, 8 March 1923.

20 The official Treasury view is set out in T160/207/7768/2, Treasury Memorandum on the relation between the Anglo-American Debt and Allied Debts to Great Britain, 12 January 1925.

21 *HC*, vol. 147, col. 284, 20 October 1921; T160/207/7768/2, Treasury Memorandum on the relation between the Anglo-American Debt and Allied Debts to Great Britain, 12 January 1925. See also Keynes, 'The War Debts', *The Nation and Athenaeum*, 5 May 1928; *CW Keynes*, IX, 49.

22 Austen Chamberlain, the Chancellor of the Exchequer, said in 1920 that 'But for the assistance we gave to the Allies and notably France we should have no American debt': T172/1123, Chamberlain to Duncannon, 4 June 1920. See also his comments to the Cabinet on 20 May 1921: Cab 23/21, 29(20)163, Appendix, Summary of a Statement by the Chancellor of the Exchequer on the Subject of Inter-Allied Indebtedness'. Chamberlain repeated such views when Foreign Secretary, saying: 'We are paying our debt in full [to the US] tho' we should not have had to borrow a cent from the USA Government if we had not used up our credit in financing the less well situated allies': FO 371/9684, minute by Chamberlain on telegram from Howard, 3 January 1925. For a similar line from Horne (Chancellor), Churchill (Chancellor) and Lloyd George respectively see *HC*, vol. 147, col. 284, 20 October 1921; *HC*, vol. 179, col. 261, 10 December 1924; Lloyd George, *The Truth About Reparations and War Debts*. p. 97. Keynes likewise argued that 'the loans she [America] made to us were for the purpose of financing our Allies rather than for ourselves': 'The War Debts', *The Nation and Athenaeum*, 5 May 1928.

23 *Le Temps*, 22 August 1922; *DBFP*, 1st Series, XX, no. 70, Hardinge to Curzon, 22 August 1922; Bergmann, *History of Reparations*, p. 148; Trachtenberg, *Reparation in World Politics*, p. 258.

24 *DBFP*, Ist Series, XX, no. 70, Hardinge to Curzon, 22 August 1922.

25 Lloyd George, *The Truth About Reparations and War Debts*, p. 116.

26 FO 371/8295, Poincaré to Hardinge, 1 September 1922, enclosure in Hardinge to Curzon, 2 September 1922.

27 Idem.

28 *The Economist*, leading article, 'The Debt Problem Once More', 9 September 1922.

29 Cab 23/30, 48(22)10, Cabinet minutes of 7 September 1922.

30 Ibid., 10–11; FO 371/8295, Tom Jones to Curzon, 7 September 1922.

31 FO 371/8295, minute by Tyrrell, 11 September 1922. For the Treasury reaction to Poincaré's allegation of overcharging see T160/114/F4399/1, memorandum by C.W. Pocock, 5 September 1922.

32 FO 371/8295, enclosure in Fergusson to Leeper, 8 September 1922.

33 Ibid., minutes by Lampson and Villiers, 11 September 1922.

34 Ibid., minutes by Tyrrell and Curzon, 11 September 1922.

35 For developments in Turkey after the Treaty of Sèvres and Anglo-French differences on the question see Harold Nicolson, *Curzon, the Last Phase, 1919–1921: A Study in Post-War Diplomacy* (London, 1934), chs 4, 9–11.

36 FO 371/8295, minute by Tyrrell, 16 September 1922; minute by Curzon, 17 September 1922.

37 Ibid., minute by Curzon, 17 September 1922.

38 *HC*, vol. 157, cols. 1746–53, 3 August 1922.

39 For Keynes' critical comments on the Balfour Note at the first Liberal 'summer school' in Oxford on 4 August 1922 see *CW Keynes*, XVIII, 11–17; Skidelsky, *John Maynard Keynes*, II, 117.

40 *The Times*, leading article, 'The Balfour Note', 2 August 1922; leading article, 'The

Wrong End', 3 August 1922; *The Economist*, 'A Lost Opportunity', 5 August 1922.

41 *The Times*, leading article, 'The Balfour Note', 2 August 1922; leading article, 'The Wrong End', 3 August 1922.

42 *The Economist*, leading article, 'Beating About the Bush', 12 August 1922.

43 *HC*, vol. 157, cols. 1745–6, 1784–5, 3 August 1922.

44 *The Economist*, leading article, 'A Lost Opportunity', 5 August 1922.

45 *The Nation and Athenaeum*, 'The Balfour Note and Inter-Allied Debts', 24 January 1925; *CW Keynes*, IX, 46.

46 *CW Keynes*, IX, 46.

47 Alan Sharp, 'Lloyd George and Foreign Policy, 1918–1922. The "And yet" Factor', Judith Loades (ed.), *The Life and Times of Lloyd George* (Bangor, 1991), p. 139.

48 Artaud, *La Question des dettes interalliées* I, 418.

49 For a typical criticism of the Balfour Note see Schrecker, *The Hired Money*, pp. 147–8.

50 Orde, *British policy and European reconstruction*, pp. 215–16.

51 Trachtenberg, *Reparation in World Politics*, p. 258.

52 Kent, *Spoils of War*, pp. 186–9.

53 See p. 35.

54 *The Times*, Paris correspondent, 29 July 1922. The plan first appeared officially in public in the *Temps* of 27 August 1922. See *DBFP*, 1st Series, XX, no. 77, n. 4.

55 See Poincaré's comments: *DBFP*, 1st Series, XX, no. 51, British Secretary's Notes of an Allied Conference held at 10 Downing St, 7 August 1922. Also Cab 23/30, 44(22)398, Cabinet minutes of 10 August 1922; Cab 23/30, 46(22),445, Cabinet minutes of 14 August 1922; Cmd 1812 (1922), no. 2, p. 22, Notes of a Conversation held at 10 Downing St on 9 December 1922 at 11.30am; Trachtenberg, *Reparation in World Politics*, p. 258.

56 Cab 23/30, 46(22)445, Cabinet minutes of 14 August 1922. The C bonds, which were non interest-bearing and were only to be issued when the Reparation Commission thought Germany's financial position allowed, were described as 'a quite worthless security'.

57 *DBFP*, 1st Series, XX, no. 77, Hardinge to Curzon, 28 August 1922. See *The Times*, Paris correspondent, 2 August 1922.

58 Cab 23/30, 46(22)445, Cabinet minutes of 14 August 1922.

59 Bergmann, *History of Reparations*, pp. 139–40.

60 *DBFP*, 1st Series, XIX, no. 25: XX, no. 1; Bergmann, *History of Reparations*, pp. 115–19; Trachtenberg, *Reparation in World Politics*, p. 240.

61 *DBFP*, 1st Series, XX, no. 3, n. 7, Bradbury to Blackett, 27 January 1922.

62 Ibid., no. 1, memorandum by Wigram on the position of the reparations negotiations at the close of the Cannes Conference, 19 January 1921. See also *DBFP*, 1st Series, XIX, no. 25; Bergmann, *History of Reparations*, pp. 115–16.

63 *DBFP*, 1st Series, XX, no. 12 n. 4; no. 19; Bergmann, *History of Reparations*, pp. 119–32; Trachtenberg, *Reparation in World Politics*, pp. 242–7.

64 Delacroix was the First Belgian Delegate on the Reparation Commission. The other members of the Bankers' Committee were d'Amelio (Italy), the vice-chairman; Vissering (Holland); J. Pierrepoint Morgan (US); Sir Robert Kindersley (Britain); Sergent (France); Bergmann (Germany).

65 *DBFP*, 1st Series, XX, no. 19; Bergmann, *History of Reparations*, pp. 125–38; Trachtenberg, *Reparation in World Politics*, p. 248; Weill-Raynal, *Les Réparations allemandes et la France*, II, 166–82.

66 Bergmann, *History of Reparations*, pp. 139, 144, 155.

67 *DBFP*, 1st Series, XX, no. 38, Bradbury to Blackett, 12 July 1922. For the text of

the German request see Bergmann, *History of Reparations*, pp. 139–40.
68 *The Times*, 14 July 1922.
69 See, for example, *DBFP*, 1st Series, XX, no. 31, Note of an interview between Blackett and Ernst von Simson on 30 June and 1 July 1922, 3 July 1922; no. 36, note by Wigram, 10 July 1922.
70 Trachtenberg, *Reparation in World Politics*, p. 159.
71 *DBFP*, 1st Series, XX, no. 61, British Secretary's Notes of a Conversation at 10 Downing St, 11 August 1922.
72 Ibid., no. 51, British Secretary's Notes of an Allied Conference held at 10 Downing St, 7 August 1922; no. 54, British Secretary's Notes of an Allied Conference held at 10 Downing St, 7 August 1922.
73 Ibid., no. 51, British Secretary's Notes of an Allied Conference held at 10 Downing St, 7 August 1922.
74 Ibid., no. 30, British Secretary's Notes of a meeting between Lloyd George and Poincaré, 19 June 1922.
75 Ibid., no. 51, British Secretary's Notes of an Allied Conference held at 10 Downing St, 7 August 1922.
76 Cmd 1812 (1923), *Inter-Allied Conferences on Reparations and Inter-Allied Debts. Held in London and Paris, December 1922 and January 1923. Reports and Secretaries' Notes of Conservations*, no. 2, Notes of a Conversation held at 10 Downing St on 9 December 1922 at 11.30 a.m.
77 *DBFP*, 1st Series, XX, no. 30, British Secretary's Notes of a meeting between Lloyd George and Poincaré, 19 June 1922.
78 Ibid., no. 30, British Secretary's Notes of a meeting between Lloyd George and Poincaré, 19 June 1922; no. 51, British Secretary's Notes of an Allied Conference held at 10 Downing St, 7 August 1922.
79 Davidson Papers, file 132, memorandum on a conversation between Bonar Law, the French ambassador and Eyre Crowe, enclosure in Curzon to Phipps, 27 December 1922.
80 Trachtenberg, *Reparation in World Politics*, p. 252.
81 For the proposals see *DBFP*, 1st Series, XX, no. 51.
82 Idem.
83 Idem.
84 Idem; Cmd 1812 (1923), no. 2, Notes of a Conversation held at 10 Downing St on 9 December 1922 at 11.30am; Artaud, *La Question des dettes interalliées*, I, 419.
85 Davidson Papers, file 132, memorandum on a conversation between Bonar Law, the French ambassador and Eyre Crowe on 24 December 1922, enclosure in Curzon to Phipps, 27 December 1922.
86 *DBFP*, 1st Series, XX, no. 94, Bradbury to Horne, 22 September 1922.
87 Cab 23/30, 29(22), Cabinet minutes of 23 May 1922; *DBFP*, 1st Series, XX, no. 30, British Secretary's Notes of a meeting between Lloyd George and Poincaré, 19 June 1922; Trachtenberg, *Reparation in World Politics*, p. 244.
88 *DBFP*, 1st Series, XX, no. 49, Bradbury to Treasury, 4 August 1922.
89 Ibid., no. 30, British Secretary's Notes of a meeting between Lloyd George and Poincaré, 19 June 1922.
90 Ibid., no. 13, Bradbury to Treasury, 24 March 1922; no. 30, British Secretary's Notes of a meeting between Lloyd George and Poincaré, 19 June 1922.
91 Ibid., no. 49, Bradbury to Treasury, 4 August 1922.
92 Ibid., no. 54, British Secretary's Notes of an Allied Conference held at 10 Downing St, 7 August 1922.
93 Ibid., no. 52, minutes of a Conference of Minister held at 10 Downing St, 7 August

1922.

94 Ibid., no. 57, Notes taken during a conversation at the French Embassy at London on 9 August 1922 between Poincaré, Lloyd George and Theunis.

95 Ibid., no. 49, Bradbury to Treasury, 4 August 1922; no. 52, minutes of a Conference of Ministers held at 10 Downing St, 7 August 1922.

96 Bonar Law Papers, box 111, folder 51, record of a conversation between the PM, the French ambassador and Eyre Crowe on 24 December 1922, enclosure in Curzon to Phipps, 27 December 1922.

97 Cmd 1812 (1923), no. 6, p. 76.

98 *DBFP*, 1st Series, XX, no. 54, British Secretary's Notes of an Allied Conference held at 10 Downing St, 7 August 1922.

99 Davidson Papers, file 132, memorandum by L. C. M. Troughton (Economic Adviser to the British Section of the Rhineland High Commission) on the proposed occupation of the Ruhr District, 10 December 1922.

100 Ibid., Grahame to Curzon, 22 November 1922.

101 *DBFP*, 1st Series, XX, no. 55, 'The relation of the Proposed French "Guarantees" to the French policy in the Rhineland', Foreign Office memorandum, 8 August 1922; no. 60, n. 1, minute by Lampson, 10 August 1922.

102 Ibid., no. 49, Bradbury to Treasury, 4 August 1922.

103 *Le Temps*, 25 April 1922; *DBFP*, 1st Series, XX, no. 19; Trachtenberg, *Reparation in World Politics*, p. 243.

104 *DBFP*, 1st Series, XX, no. 24, Hardinge to Balfour, 29 May 1922;

105 Ibid., no. 28, Bradbury to Horne, 14 June 1922.

106 Cab 23/30, 44(22)406–7, Cabinet minutes of 10 August 1922.

107 *DBFP*, 1st Series, XX,, no. 41, Grahame to Balfour, 24 July 1922, n. 3; no. 71, Grahame to Curzon, 22 August 1922.

108 Cab 23/30, 44(22)405–6, Cabinet minutes of 10 August 1922.

109 Trachtenberg, *Reparation in World Politics*, pp. 277–8.

110 Davidson Papers, file 134, Niemeyer to Chancellor of the Exchequer, 6 December 1922.

111 Idem;

112 Ibid., file 138, Bradbury to Bonar Law, 18 December 1922.

113 Bonar Law Papers, box 111, folder 39, Curzon to Bonar Law, 4 December 1922.

114 Davidson Papers, file 134, Niemeyer to Chancellor of the Exchequer, 6 December 1922.

115 Ibid., note for Chancellor of the Exchequer by Blackett, 8 December 1922.

116 *DBFP*, 1st Series, XX, no. 28, Bradbury to Horne, 14 June 1922.

117 See, for example, Davidson Papers, file 134, Niemeyer to Chancellor of Exchequer, 6 December 1922.

118 *DBFP*, 1st Series, no. 83, Grahame to Tyrrell, 12 September 1922.

119 Cab 23/36. Part I, p 161, notes of a meeting at 10 Downing St, 15 July 1922. See also *DBFP*, 1st Series, XX, no. 54, British Secretary's Notes of an Allied Conference at 10 Downing St, 7 August 1922.

120 Cmd 1812 (1923), no. 3, pp. 34–5, Notes of a Conference held at 10 Downing St on 9 December 1922 at 4 p.m.

121 Bonar Law Papers, box 111, folder 7, Bradbury to Bonar Law, 23 October 1922.

122 *DBFP*, 1st Series, XX, no. 78, Hardinge to Curzon, 1 September 1922.

123 Ibid., no. 94, Bradbury to Horne, 22 September 1922; Cab 23/32, 69(22), Cabinet minutes of 7 December 1922; Bergmann, *History of Reparations*, p. 155.

124 *DBFP*, 1st Series, XX, no. 109, Bradbury to Baldwin, 11 November 1922.

125 Davidson Papers, file 132, Curzon to Hardinge, 11 November 1922.

126 Cab 23/36, Part 1, p. 161, notes of a meeting at 10 Downing St, 15 July 1922.
127 Cab 23/30, 44(22)410–11, Cabinet minutes of 10 August 1922.
128 *DBFP*, 1st Series, XX, no. 63, British Secretary's Notes of a Conversation held at 10 Downing St on 14 August 1922.
129 See, for example, Kent, *Spoils of War*, pp. 186–90.
130 *DBFP*, 1st Series, no. 19, memorandum respecting British Central European Policy in relation to Genoa, FO, 9 May 1922.
131 Idem.
132 Davidson Papers, file 134, Lloyd-Greame to Prime Minister, 2 December 1922.
133 Idem.
134 Davidson Papers, file 134, enclosure in R. T. Nugent (Director of FBI) to Davidson, 5 December 1922.
135 Ibid., file 139, Smuts to Bonar Law, 20 November 1922; telegram from the Governor General of the Union of South Africa to Colonial Secretary, 13 December 1922.
136 Bergmann, *History of Reparations*, p. 148.
137 These included Keynes, Blackett and Bergmann. See Davidson Papers, file 138, note by Keynes, 7 December 1922; ibid., note by Blackett for Chancellor of the Exchequer, 8 December 1922; Jacques Seydoux, *De Versailles au plan Young: réparations – dettes interallieés – reconstruction européenne* (Paris, 1932), p. 193. See also Middlemas (ed.), *Whitehall Diary*, I, 224–5.
138 Davidson Papers, file 138, Bradbury to Baldwin, 27 November 1922.
139 *DBFP*, 1st Series, XX, no. 51, British Secretary's Note of an Allied Conference held at 10, Downing St, on Monday, August 7, 1922. at 11a.m.
140 Idem.
141 Kent, *Spoils of War*, p. 190. Hardinge reported that Poincaré was 'biased by his personal animosity to the British Prime Minister which it is beyond his power to suppress': *DBFP*, 1st Series, XX, no. 70, Hardinge to Curzon, 22 August 1922.
142 Paul Cambon, *Correspondence, 1870–1924*, 3 vols (Paris, 1940–46), III, 413–15.
143 *DBFP*, 1st Series, XX, no. 51, British Secretary's Notes of an Allied Conference held at 10 Downing St, 7 August 1922.
144 Ibid., no. 52, minutes of a Conference of Ministers held at 10 Downing St, 7 August 1922. See also ibid., nos 54, 57; Cab 23/30, 44(20)398–99, Cabinet minutes of 10 August 1922.
145 Cab 23/30, 44(20)403, Cabinet minutes of 10 August 1922.
146 *DBFP*, 1st Series, no. 59, Conclusions of a Conference of Ministers held at 10 Downing St, 9 August 1922. For the British counter-proposals see Cab 23/30, 44(22)412–15, appendix.
147 Cab 23/30, 44(22)411, Cabinet minutes of 10 August 1922.
148 Ibid., 407–9.
149 Ibid., 408–9.
150 *DBFP*, 1st Series, XX, no. 59, Conclusions of a conference of Ministers held at 10 Downing St, 9 August 1922.
151 Cab 23/30, 44(22)410–11, Cabinet minutes of 10 August 1922.
152 Bergmann, *History of Reparations*, p. 142.
153 Cab 23/30, 45(22)418, Cabinet minutes of 12 August 1922; *DBFP*, 1st Series, XX, no. 61, British Secretary's Notes of a conversation at 10 Downing St, 11 August 1922.
154 Cab 23/30, 45(22)418–19, Cabinet minutes of 12 August 1922.
155 Ibid., 419–20.
156 Ibid., 420.
157 Cab 23/30, 46(22)440, Cabinet minutes of 14 August 1922.
158 Ibid., 439; *DBFP*, 1st Series, XX, no. 63, British Secretary's Notes of a Conversation

held at 10 Downing St, 14 August 1922.

159 *DBFP*, 1st Series, XX, no. 63, British Secretary's Notes of a Conversation held at 10 Downing St, 14 August 1922.

160 Bergmann, *History of Reparations*, p. 142; Artaud, *La Question des dettes interaliées*, I, 436.

161 Cab 23/30, 46(22)438–41, Cabinet minutes of 14 August 1922.

162 Ibid., 441.

163 Ibid., 442.

164 Ibid., 442–4.

Chapter 4   *From the London Conference to the Occupation of the Ruhr: August 1922–January 1923*

1   *DBFP*, 1st Series, XX, no. 63, British Secretary's Notes of a Conversation held at 10 Downing St, 14 August 1922.

2   Ibid., no. 78, Hardinge to Curzon, 1 September 1922; Davidson Papers, file 134, telegram from Secretary of State for Colonies to Governor General of Canada, 5 December 1922; Bergmann, *History of Reparations*, pp. 144–5; Kent, *Spoils of War*, p. 192.

3   Davidson Papers, file 134, Niemeyer to Chancellor of the Exchequer, 6 December 1922.

4   FO 371/8295, Poincaré to Hardinge, 1 September, enclosure in Hardinge to Curzon, 2 September 1922.

5   FO 371/8633, 'History of the negotiations with regard to the Payment of Reparation and of the Inter-Allied Debts since the despatch of the Allied ultimatum to the German Government of May 5', memorandum by Wigram, not dated.

6   Idem.; *DBFP*, 1st Series, XX, no. 103, n. 5.

7   *DBFP*, 1st Series, XX, no. 94, Bradbury to Horne, 22 September 1922; 109, Bradbury to Baldwin, 11 November 1922.

8   Bergmann, *History of Reparations*, p. 142.

9   Bonar Law Papers, box 111, folder 7, Bradbury to Bonar Law, 23 October 1922.

10   Artaud, *La Question des dettes interalliées*, I, 443–4; Trachtenberg, *Reparation in World Politics*, p. 280.

11   Robert Blake, *The Unknown Prime Minister: The Life and Times of Andrew Bonar Law* (London, 1955), p. 485; Trachtenberg, *Reparation in World Politics*, p. 278.

12   Cmd 1812 (1923), no. 5, Notes of a Conversation held at 10 Downing St on 11 December 1922 at 4.15 p.m.

13   FO 371/7491, memorandum by Crowe on Saint-Aulaire's interview with Bonar Law, 22 December 1922, enclosure in Curzon to Phipps, 27 December 1922.

14   Harold Nicolson said Curzon's 'interest in finance was confined to his own income': cited in Blake, *The Unknown Prime Minister*, p. 483.

15   Davidson Papers, file 139, Crowe to Prime Minister, 20 December 1922.

16   Sir Frederick Leith-Ross, who served under Bradbury on the Reparation Commission from 1920–25, held Bradbury in very high esteem. According to Leith-Ross, he had 'the most inventive and creative mind' of all the men he met at the Treasury: Leith-Ross, *Money Talks*, p. 22.

17   *DBFP*, 1st Series, XX, no. 94, n. 1.

18   Bonar Law Papers, box 111, folder 7, Bradbury to Bonar Law, 23 October 1922; *DBFP*, 1st Series, XX, no. 109, Bradbury to Baldwin, 11 November 1922.

19   *DBFP*, 1st Series, XX, no. 114, Note by Mr Wigram on a discussion between the Prime Minister and Sir John Bradbury, held on November 22, 1922.

20 Ibid., no. 114, n. 3, memorandum by Wigram, 14 November 1922; minute by Lampson, 18 November 1922; minute by Crowe, 20 November 1922.

21 Bonar Law Papers, box 111, folder 56, Curzon to Bonar Law, 6 January 1923. Curzon had voiced a similar complaint on 12 October 1922 when he said of Bradbury: 'He acts as though he were an independent state': *DBFP*, 1st Series, XX, 98, n. 4, minute by Curzon on minutes by Tyrrell and Crowe.

22 Bonar Law Papers, box 111, folder 56, Curzon to Bonar Law, 6 January 1923.

23 Wigram, a Second Clerk, was in the Central Department of the Foreign Office.

24 *DBFP*, 1st Series, XX, no. 114, note by Mr Wigram on a discussion between the Prime Minister and Sir John Bradbury, held on November 22, 1922.

25 Idem.

26 For inter-departmental tensions between the Foreign Office and Treasury in the early 1920s see Ephraim Maisel, *The Foreign Office and Foreign Policy 1919–1926* (Brighton, 1994), pp. 199–203.

27 Idem.

28 Davidson Papers, file 134, Niemeyer to Chancellor of the Exchequer, 6 December 1922.

29 For the text of the Bonar Law Plan see Cmd 1812 1923), no. 6, Annex IV, pp. 112–19.

30 *DBFP*, 1st Series, XX, no. 94, Bradbury to Horne, 22 September 1922; no. 97, Bradbury to Treasury, 6 October 1922.

31 Ibid., no. 97, Memorandum on the Future of Reparations, enclosure in Bradbury to Treasury, 6 October 1922; Bergmann, *History of Reparations*, pp. 150–1; Trachtenberg, *Reparation in World Politics*, p. 277.

32 *DBFP*, 1st Series, XX, no. 97, Memorandum on the Future of Reparations, enclosure in Bradbury to Treasury, 6 October 1922.

33 *DBFP*, 1st Series, XX, no. 100, Hardinge to Curzon, 15 October 1922; Artaud, *La Question des dettes interalliées*, I, 443–4; Trachtenberg, *Reparation in World Politics*, p. 277.

34 *DBFP*, 1st Series, XX, no. 99, Bradbury to Blackett, 13 Ooctober 1922. For the text of the French counter-proposals see ibid., no. 1, enclosure in Hardinge to Curzon, 21 October 1922.

35 Davidson Papers, file 138, Bradbury to Baldwin, 27 November 1922.

36 *DBFP*, 1st Series, XX, no. 104, Curzon to Grahame, 1 November 1922.

37 FO 371/8633, 'History of the negotiations with regard to the Payment of Reparations and of the Inter-Allied Debts since the despatch of the Allied ultimatum to the German Government of May 5, 1921', memorandum by Wigram, not dated (1923); *DBFP*, 1st Series, XX, no. 120, memorandum by Mr Bonar Law of an interview with the French Ambassador, held on November 28, 1922.

38 *DBFP*, 1st Series, XX, nos 121, 122.

39 Bonar Law Papers, box 111, folder 40, Bonar Law to Curzon, 7 December 1922.

40 Davidson Papers, file 138, note for Chancellor of the Exchequer and Prime Minister by Bradbury 1922.

41 Ibid., Bradbury to Baldwin, 27 November 1922; note for Chancellor of Exchequer and Prime Minister by Bradbury, 11 December 1922.

42 Ibid., file 138, Bradbury to Baldwin, 27 November 1922.

43 Idem.

44 For Keynes' relations with the Treasury after his resignation see Harrod, *The Life of John Maynard Keynes*, pp. 206–7, 280–3, 294, 305–6; Skidelsky, *John Maynard Keynes*, II, 18–22, 38–9; Arthur Turner, 'Keynes, the Treasury and French War Debts in the 1920s', *European History Quarterly*, vol 26, no. 4, October 1997, 510–13.

45 Davidson Papers, file 138, note by Keynes, 7 December 1922.

46 Blackett complained that the plan was 'almost too complicated': Davidson Papers, file 138, note for Chancellor of the Exchequer by Blackett, 8 December 1922. For other examples of bafflement see Seydoux, *De Versailles au plan Young*, p. 193; Middlemas (ed.), Whitehall Diary, I, 224–5.

47 *CW Keynes*, XVIII, Keynes to Geoffrey Dawson, 3 January 1923. For Keynes' own plan, dated 23 December 1923, see ibid., 97–9.

48 Davidson Papers, file 134, Niemeyer to Chancellor of the Exchequer, 6 December 1922.

49 Idem.

50 Davidson Papers, file 134, note for Chancellor of the Exchequer by Blackett, 30 November 1922.

51 Idem; ibid., file 138, note by Blackett for Chancellor of Exchequer, 8 December 1922.

52 *DBFP*, 1st Series, XX, no. 142, Bradbury to Chancellor of Exchequer, 15 December 1922.

53 Bonar Law Papers, box 111, folder 40, Bonar Law to Curzon, 7 December 1922; folder 42, Bonar Law to Curzon, 8 December 1922; Hankey Diary, 12 December 1922, cited in Stephen Roskill, *Hankey: Man of Secrets* 3 vols (London, 1970–4), II, 326–7.

54 Bonar Law Papers, box 111, folder 39, Curzon to Bonar Law, 4 December 1922.

55 Ibid., box 111, folder 40, Bonar Law to Curzon, 7 December 1922; folder 42, Bonar Law to Curzon, 8 December 1922.

56 *DBFP*, 1st Series, XX, no. 126, summary of a statement made by M. Poincaré to English press correspondents, 4 December 1922, enclosure in Hardinge to Curzon, 4 December 1922; Artaud, *La Question des dettes interalliées*, I, 447–8.

57 Davidson Papers, file 134, Bradbury to Baldwin, 5 December 1922.

58 Cited in Artaud, *La Question des dettes interalliées*, I, 448.

59 For the British Secretary's minutes of the London conference see Cmd 1812 (1923), nos 2–5, pp. 18–66. For a summary of the proceedings see *DBFP*, 1st Series, XX, no. 133, Crowe to Curzon, 10 December 1922.

60 Cmd 1812 (1923), no. 3, pp. 32–43, Notes of a Conversation held at 10, Downing St, S.W., on Saturday, December 9, 1922, at 4 p.m.

61 Ibid., p. 38.

62 For the German plan see Cmd 1812 (1923), pp. 57–9; Bergmann, *History of Reparations*, p. 159.

63 Cmd 1812 (1923), pp. 28–31.

64 Ibid., no. 8, p. 193, Notes of a Conversation held at the Quai d'Orsay on Thursday 4 January at 3 p.m.

65 Ibid., no. 5., pp. 60–5, Notes of a Conversation held at 10, Downing St, S.W., on Monday, December 11, 1922, at 4.15 p.m.

66 Davidson Papers, file 138, Bradbury to Chancellor of Exchequer, 15 December 1922. The draft plan is enclosed.

67 Cited in Seydoux, *De Versailles au plan Young*, p. 193. See also Middlemas (ed.), *Whitehall Diary*, I, 224–5.

68 Davidson Papers, file 138, enclosure in Bradbury to Chancellor of the Exchequer, 15 December 1922.

69 Idem.

70 Bergmann, *History of Reparations*, p. 160.

71 Davidson Papers, file 138, Bradbury to Niemeyer, 19 December 1922.

72 Ibid., file 139, Bradbury to Prime Minister, 21 December 1922.

73 Idem.

74 Idem.

75 Bonar Law Papers, box 111, folder 54, Bonar Law to Curzon, 28 December 1922.

76 Ibid., box 111, folder 50, Bonar Law to Curzon, 26 December 1922. Tom Jones felt that Law was too pessimistic. He told him that 'the country at home would agree to any terms provided that they were final, and that the view on the train [taking the British delegation to the Paris conference] was that he was too pessimistic about the outlook': diary entry for 1 January 1923, cited in Middlemas (ed.), *Whitehall Diary*, I, 224.

77 Bonar Law Papers, box 111, folder 11, Crowe to Prime Minister, 25 December 1922. The ambassador, Hardinge, was more pessimistic. See Davidson Papers, file 139, Hardinge to PM, 19 December 1922: 'I am afraid that your task on 2nd [January] is almost hopeless . . . '.

78 Davidson Papers, file 139, Bonar Law to Smuts, 26 December 1922.

79 Bonar Law Papers, box 111, folder 48, Bonar Law to Curzon, 21 December 1922.

80 Davidson Papers, file 139, Bonar Law to Smuts, 18 December 1922; *FRUS*, 1922, II, 187–95, memorandum by Hughes of an interview with Geddes, 18 December 1922; FO 371/7490, Curzon to Geddes, 16 December 1922; Geddes to Curzon, 18 December 1922; *DBFP*, Ist Series, XX, no. 145.

81 *FRUS*, 1922, II, 199–202; *DBFP*, 1st Series, XX, no. 157, Geddes to Curzon, 29 December 1922.

82 Diary entry of 1 January 1923, cited in Middlemas (ed.), *Whitehall Diary*, I, 224; Davidson Papers, file 138, Bonar Law to Bradbury, 19 December 1922; Bradbury to Niemeyer, 19 December 1922; Cab 23/32, 72(22), Cabinet minutes of 29 December 1922.

83 Cab 23/32, 72(22), Cabinet minutes of 29 December 1922; *DBFP*, 1st Series, XX, no. 155, n. 3; Bergmann, *History of Reparations*, p. 167; Trachtenberg, *Reparation in World History*, p. 287.

84 *DBFP*, 1st Series, XXI, no. 9, Sir George Grahame to Crowe, 9 January 1923; no. 26, Sir R. Graham to Curzon, 15 January 1923. For the text of the Bonar Law Plan see Cmd 1812 (1923), no. 6, annex IV, pp. 112–19.

85 Cmd 1812 (1923), no. 7, p. 134; *DBFP*, 1st Series, XXI, no. 3, telegram from PM for Cabinet, enclosure in Crewe to Curzon, 3 January 1922; no. 13, Grahame to Curzon, 10 January 1923.

86 Cmd 1812 (1923), no. 8, p. 159; *DBFP*, 1st Series, XXI, no. 26, Sir R. Graham to Curzon, 15 January 1923.

87 Bonar Law Papers, box 111, folder 56, Curzon to Bonar Law, 6 January 1923. In response to Curzon's complaint, Bonar Law replied that as a matter of fact the British plan was only handed to the conference simultaneously with the French plan and they were both published together: Blake, *The Unknown Prime Minister*, p. 490.

88 Cmd 1812 (1923), no. 7, p. 120, Notes of a conversation held at the Quai d'Orsay on Wednesday, January 3, 1923, at 3pm; *DBFP*, 1st Series, XXI, no. 3, PM to Cabinet, enclosure in Crewe to Curzon, 3 January 1923; Davidson Papers, file 145, Colonial Secretary to Governor General of Canada etc, 5 January 1923. For the hostile reaction of the French press on 3 January see *L'Oeuvre. L'Echo de Paris, Le Matin, Le Figaro, Le Petit Parisien, Petit Journal.*

89 Poincaré's initial reaction was set out in a written reply: Cmd 1812 (1923), annex to no. 7, pp. 148–57.

90 Cmd 1812 (1923), no. 7, p. 120, Notes of a Conversation held at the Quai d'Orsay on Wednesday, January 3, 1923, at 3 p.m.

91 Ibid., no. 7, pp. 122–3.

92 Ibid., pp. 131–2, 152–3.

93 Ibid., pp. 162, 176–7.

94 Ibid., no. 7, p. 139.
95 For the French plan see Cmd 1812 (1923), pp. 101–8.
96 Ibid., no. 7, pp. 140–2.
97 Ibid., no. 8, p. 163.
98 Ibid., no. 8, pp. 193–5.
99 See, for example, Kent, *Spoils of War*, pp. 205–10.
100 Sally Marks, *The Illusion of Peace: International relations in Europe 1918–1933* (London, 1976), p. 47.
101 Artaud, *La Question des dettes interalliées*, I, 456.
102 Ibid., 453–6.
103 *HC*, vol. 159, col. 3233, 14 December 1922.
104 Cmd 1812 (1923), no. 7, p. 140, Notes of a Conversation held at the Quai d'Orsay on Wednesday 3 January 1922 at 3 p.m.

Chapter 5   *From the Occupation of the Ruhr to the Advent of the Second Baldwin Government: January 1923–November 1924*

1 For a detailed account of the negotiations for the Anglo-American debt settlement see Orde, *British policy and European reconstruction*, pp. 227–37.
2 Blake, *The Unknown Prime Minister*, pp. 492, 495; T. Jones, biography of Bonar Law in the *Dictionary of National Biography, 1922–1930* (Oxford, 1937), p. 489; Keith Middlemas and John Barnes, *Baldwin: A Biography* (London, 1969), p. 136.
3 FO 371/8503, Geddes to Foreign Office, 13 January 1923; Grigg, *Prejudice and Judgement*, p. 100: Middlemas (ed.), *Whitehall Diary*, pp. 225–7.
4 Bonar Law to Baldwin, 15 January 1923, cited in Middlemas (ed.), *Whitehall Diary*, I, 227.
5 FO 371/8503, Foreign Office to Geddes, 15 January 1923; Middlemas and Barnes, *Baldwin*, p. 142; Grigg, *Prejudice and Judgement*, p. 101.
6 Cab 23/45, 4(23), Cabinet minutes of 30 January 1923; Cab 23/45, 5(23), Cabinet minutes of 31 January 1923; Blake, *The Unknown Prime Minister*, pp. 493–5; Randolph Churchill, *Lord Derby, 'King of Lancashire'* (London, 1959), pp. 494–7; J. C. C. Davidson, *Memoirs of a Conservative*, ed. Robert Rhodes James (London, 1969), pp. 142–3; Middlemas and Barnes, *Baldwin*, pp. 144–7.
7 For the text of the 1923 Anglo-American debts settlement see Cmd 1912 (1923), *American Debt. Arrangements for the Funding of the British Debt to the United States of America*. The text is also to be found in Moulton and Pasvolsky, *World War Debt Settlements*, Appendix B, pp. 225–40.
8 Schuker, *The End of French Predominance*, p. 156.
9 For an assessment of the relative weight of the American debt settlements with Great Britain, France, Italy and the other debtors of the United States see Moulton and Pasvolsky, *World War Debt Settlements*, Appendix B, pp. 388–409, statement by Andrew Mellon to the Ways and Means Committee of the House of Representatives, January 4 1926. See also, Keynes, 'The War Debts', *The Nation and Athenaeum*, 5 May 1928; *CW Keynes*, IX, 47–53. Keynes calculated that the American settlement with Britain was equivalent to charging an interest rate of 3.3 per cent on the whole amount due compared with I.6 per cent and 0.4 per cent respectively in the case of the American settlements with France and Italy.
10 *The Nation and Athenaeum*, 'The American Debt', 4 August 1923.
11 *The Times*, 27 January 1923; Sir Evelyn Wrench, *Geoffrey Dawson and Our Times* (London, 1955), p. 215; Davidson, *Memoirs of a Conservative*, p. 143.
12 According to Lloyd George, the last time he saw Bonar Law the latter told him how

much he regretted not having resigned rather than approve the terms of the settlement: Lloyd George, *The Truth About Reparations and War Debts*, p. 118.

13 Not everybody in official circles regarded the Anglo-American debt settlement as unduly onerous. The Principal Private Secretary of the Chancellor of the Exchequer, P. J. Grigg, considered it quite moderate: Grigg, *Prejudice and Judgement*, pp. 103–5.

14 For information on the occupation of the Ruhr see Kent, *Spoils of War*, ch. 6; Orde, *British policy and European reconstruction*, pp. 237–45; Trachtenberg, *Reparation in World Politics*, ch. 8.

15 Orde, *British policy and European reconstruction*, pp. 239–40.

16 T160/114/F4399/2, Niemeyer to Chancellor of the Exchequer, 13 March 1922.

17 Ibid., 'War Debt of Allies to Great Britain', note by Phillips, enclosure in Niemeyer to Chancellor of the Exchequer, 13 March 1923.

18 Ibid., minute by Phillips, 11 January 1923.

19 Idem.

20 T160/114/F4399/2, 'War Debts of Allies to Great Britain', note by Phillips, enclosure in Niemeyer to Chancellor of the Exchequer, 13 March 1923.

21 Ibid., notes on bills falling due in February 1923, 10 January 1923; Niemeyer to Prime Minister, 10 January 1923; minute by J. R. Chambers, 27 March 1923.

22 Ibid., 'War Debt of Allies to Great Britain', note by Phillips, enclosure in Niemeyer to Chancellor of the Exchequer, 13 March 1923.

23 Ibid., Niemeyer to Chancellor of the Exchequer, 13 March 1923.

24 Idem.

25 *DBFP*, 1st Series, XXI, no. 194, Bradbury to Chancellor of the Exchequer, 25 April 1923, enclosure 1 in Niemeyer to Lampson, 27 April 1923.

26 Ibid., no. 194, enclosure 2 in Niemeyer to Lampson, 27 April 1923.

27 Idem.

28 *DBFP*, 1st Series, XXI, no. 194, Bradbury to Chancellor of the Exchequer, 25 April 1923, enclosure 1 in Niemeyer to Chancellor of the Exchequer, 27 April 1923.

29 Ibid., no. 194, enclosure 2 in Niemeyer to Lampson, 27 April 1923.

30 Ibid., no. 194, n. 10, minute by Lampson, 1 May 1923.

31 Ibid., no. 237, Crewe to Curzon, 19 May 1923.

32 Idem.

33 *DBFP*, 1st Series, XXI, no. 237, n. 9, minute by Crowe, 24 May 1923.

34 Ibid., Niemeyer to Lampson, 7 June 1923.

35 T160/185/F7029, 'The Reparation Problem', memorandum by Bradbury, 1 June 1923.

36 Idem.

37 Idem.

38 *DBFP*, 1st Series, XXI, no. 328, D'Abernon to Curzon, 8 August 1923.

39 *HL*, vol. 53, cols. 797–80, 20 April 1923.

40 For a summary of the German proposals see *DBFP*, 1st Series, XXI, no. 201, no. 2.

41 *HC*, vol. 163, cols. 2161–3, 8 May 1923; *HL*, vol 54, cols. 2–4, 8 May 1923; *DBFP*, 1st Series, XXI, nos 206, 210, 211, 218, 224.

42 *DBFP*, 1st Series, XXI, nos 220, 224, 226.

43 *DBFP*, 1st Series, XXI, no. 218, Curzon to Crewe, 5 May 1923.

44 Ibid., no. 220, Crewe to Graham, 6 May 1923; nos 226 and 227, Curzon to Graham, 6 and 7 May 1923; FO 371/8653, Curzon to Sthamer, 13 May 1923.

45 *The Times*, 8 June 1923; *DBFP*, 1st Series, XXI, no. 254, Curzon to Addison, 7 June 1923; Kent, *Spoils of War*, pp. 216–17.

46 *DBFP*, 1st Series, XXI, no. 257, Record by Sir Eyre Crowe of conversation with French, Belgian and Italian representatives, 8 June 1923; no. 261, Curzon to Crewe,

11 June 1923.

47 Ibid., no. 261, Curzon to Crewe, 11 June 1923; no. 266, Curzon to Crewe, 15 June 1923. See also the statements made in the House of Commons and the House of Lords by Baldwin and Curzon: *HC*, vol. 166, col. 1588, 12 July 1923; vol. 167, col. 1769, 2 August 1923; *HL*, vol. 54, cols. 992–6, 12 July 1923; col. 1526, 2 August 1923.

48 *DBFP*, 1st Series, XXI, nos 239 and 240, Crewe to Curzon, 25 May 1923; Kent, *Spoils of War*, p. 216.

49 *DBFP*, 1st Series, XXI, no. 261, Curzon to Crewe, 11 June 1923; no. 266, Curzon to Crewe, 15 June 1923.

50 Ibid., no. 264, Curzon to Count de Saint-Aulaire, 13 June 1923.

51 Ibid., no. 292, Curzon to Crewe, 6 July 1923. See also no. 293.

52 Ibid., no. 306, Draft Identic Reply to the German Government, enclosure in Curzon to French Ambassador, 20 July 1923; *HC*, vol. 167, col. 1770, 2 August 1923; *HL*, vol. 54, col. 1528, 2 August 1923.

53 *DBFP*, 1st Series, XXI, no. 307, Phipps to Curzon, 22 July 1923; no. 315, Curzon to Kennard, 30 July 1923; Chilton to Curzon, 25 July 1923.

54 Ibid., no. 318, Curzon to Phipps, 30 July 1923. Also no. 316, Curzon to Grahame, 30 July 1923.

55 Ibid., no. 316, Curzon to Grahame, 30 July 1923; no. 318, Curzon to Phipps, 30 July 1923.

56 Cab 23/46, 44(23), Cabinet minutes of 1 August 1923; *HC*, vol. 167, cols. 1771–2, 2 August 1923; *HL*, vol. 54, col. 1529, 2 August 1923.

57 Cab 23/46, 44(23), Cabinet minutes of 9 August 1923.

58 *DBFP*, 1st Series, XXI, no. 330, Curzon to the Count de Saint-Aulaire and Baron Moncheur, 11 August 1923.

59 Idem.

60 *DBFP*, 1st Series, XXI, no. 332, Phipps to Curzon, 13 August 1923.

61 Ibid., no. 332, n. 1, Treasury note, 14 August 1923.

62 Ibid., nos 337, 362.

63 Schuker, *The End of French Predominance*, p. 245.

64 *DBFP*, 1st Series, XXI, no. 352, 'Reparations and Inter-Allied Debts', memorandum by Bradbury, 4 September 1923, enclosure in Phillips to Lampson, 5 September 1923.

65 Idem.

66 *HC*, vol. 166, cols. 1584–9, 12 July 1923.

67 Middlemas and Barnes, *Baldwin*, p. 196.

68 *DBFP*, 1st Series, XXI, no. 367, Note on a Conversation of September 19, 1923, between Mr Baldwin and M. Poincaré; Middlemas and Barnes, *Baldwin*, pp. 197–201.

69 For the full text of the communiqué see *The Times*, Paris correspondent, 20 September 1923; Grigg, *Prejudice and Judgement*, p. 165.

70 *DBFP*, 1st Series, XXI, no. 373, D'Abernon to Curzon, 27 September 1923; Bergmann, *History of Reparations*, pp. 211–12; Grigg, *Prejudice and Judgement*, p. 165; Kent, *Spoils of War*, p. 224.

71 Tom Jones Diary, 22 October 1923, cited in Middlemas (ed.), *Whitehall Diary*, I, 249.

72 See passage in Curzon's speech quoted in Tom Jones' diary: Middlemas (ed.), *Whitehall Diary*, I, 247–8.

73 *DBFP*, 1st Series, XXI, no. 386, n. 1.

74 Ibid., no. 387, Crewe to Curzon, 6 October 1923.

75 *The Times*, 11 October 1923.

76 *DBFP*, 1st Series, XXI, nos 392, 393, 399, 402, 402, 415; *FRUS*, 1923, II, 68–74; Cab 23/46, 48(23), Cabinet minutes of 15 October 1923.

77 *DBFP*, 1st Series, XXI, no. 415, record by Sir E. Crowe of a conversation with the French Chargé d'Affaires, 26 October 1923; no. 460, Chilton to Crowe, 9 November 1921; Grigg, *Prejudice and Judgement*, pp. 166–7.

78 *The Times*, 10 November 1923; *FRUS*, 1923, II, 94–5, The Secretary of State to the Ambassador in France, 9 November 1923; *DBFP*, 1st Series, XXI, no. 460, Chilton to Curzon, 9 November 1923.

79 FO 371/9682, Selby to Secretary of the Treasury, 14 November 1923.

80 *DBFP*, 1st Series, XXI, no. 212; FO371/8636, Treasury to Foreign Office, 12 May 1923; FO 371/8639, Board of Trade to Foreign Office, 12 May 1923; Baldwin Papers, vol. 125, minute by Crowe, 31 May 1923.

81 FO 371/9682, Selby to Secretary of the Treasury, 14 November 1923.

82 T160/185/F7029, Bradbury to Phillips, 15 November 1923; Niemeyer to Norman, 28 November 1923.

83 Ibid., minute by Phillips, 23 November 1923.

84 Idem.

85 T160/185/F7029, Treasury memorandum of 1 January 1924, enclosure in Niemeyer to Under-Secretary of State, FO, 4 January 1924.

86 Idem.

87 T160/185/F7029, Niemeyer to Crowe, 3 December 1923.

88 Schuker, *The End of French Predominance*, p. 99.

89 T160/185/F7029, minute by Phillips, 23 November 1923.

90 FO 371/9683, minute by Lampson, 8 January 1924.

91 Idem.

92 FO 371/9683, minute by Curzon, 8 January 1924.

93 Ibid., minute by Crowe, 8 January 1924.

94 FO 371/9682, Rose Rosenberg to Foreign Office, 28 January 1924.

95 Ibid., minute by Lampson, 29 January 1924.

96 Ibid., minutes by Crowe and MacDonald, 30 January 1924.

97 *FRUS*, 1923, II, 105–6, The Secretary of State to the Ambassador in France (for Logan), 11 December 1923.

98 For the negotiations leading up to the publication of the Dawes Plan see Bergmann, *History of Reparations*, pp. 222–56; Kent, *Spoils of War*, pp. 224–61; Orde, *British policy and European reconstruction*, pp. 245–53; Schuker, *The End of French Predominance*, ch. 6.

99 Schuker, *The End of French Predominance*, pp. 183–5.

100 For the French financial crisis in the spring of 1924 and its political implications see Schuker, *The End of French Predominance*, chs 3–5.

101 Kent, *Spoils of War*, p. 252.

102 Orde, *British policy and European reconstruction*, pp. 248–9.

103 Walter A. McDougall, *France's Rhineland Diplomacy 1914–1924* (Princeton, 1978), pp. 262–3, 323–8; Kent, *Spoils of War*, p. 251; Schuker, *The End of French Predominance*, p. 201.

104 Bergmann, *History of Reparations*, pp. 213–15; Schuker, *The End of French Predominance*, pp. 27, 52–3, 90, 201; Trachtenberg, *Reparation in World Politics*, pp. 328–9. By the MICUM agreements individual mining and industrial enterprises in the Ruhr undertook to pay the German Coal Tax directly to the *Mission Interalliée de Contrôle des Usines et des Mines*. MICUM was also given control of the distribution of Ruhr coal.

105 Kent, *Spoils of War*, pp. 232–3.

106 Grigg, *Prejudice and Judgement*, p. 168.
107 *DBFP*, 1st Series, XXVI, no. 391, Phipps to MacDonald, 17 March 1924; FO 371/9825, Phipps to Crowe, 18 March 1924; minute by Crowe, 19 March 1924.
108 *DBFP*, 1st Series, XXVI, no. 398, MacDonald to Crewe, 24 March 1924; Comte Auguste Félix de Saint-Aulaire, *Confessions d'un vieux diplomate* (Paris, 1953), p. 694.
109 FO 371/9740, 'The Reparation Experts' Report', memorandum by Niemeyer, 14 April 1924. See also *DBFP*, 1st Series, XXVI, no. 387, Bradbury to Snowden, 12 March 1924.
110 *DBFP*, 1st Series, XXI, no. 254, Curzon to Addison, 7 June 1923.
111 Ibid., no. 318, Curzon to Phipps, 3 July 1923.
112 *DBFP*, 1st Series, XXVI, no. 398, MacDonald to Crewe, 24 March 1924.
113 Cab 23/48, 26(24), Cabinet minutes of 9 April 1924; *DBFP*, 1st Series, XXVI, no. 419, MacDonald to Crewe, 10 April 1924; *HC*, vol. 172, col. 449, 9 April 1924; FO 371/9740, 'The Reparation Experts' Report', memorandum by Niemeyer, 14 April 1924; 'Rough Notes on the Experts' Report', memorandum by Lampson, 9 April 1924; Schuker, *The End of French Predominance*, p. 194.
114 *DBFP*, 1st Series, XXI, no. 238, Treasury to Foreign Office, 22 May 1923.
115 T160/207/F7768/1, Howard Smith to Secretary of the Treasury, 12 July 1924; Niemeyer to Under-Secretary of State, FO, 21 July 1924.
116 Ibid., Niemeyer to Under-Secretary of State, FO, 4 July 1924.
117 Idem.
118 MacDonald Papers, FO 800/218, MacDonald to Poincaré, 26 January and 21 February 1924; *DBFP*, 1st Series, XXVI, no. 369; David Marquand, *Ramsay MacDonald* (London, 1977), pp. 333–4. The texts of both of MacDonald's letters and the replies from Poincaré were printed in *The Times*, 4 February and 3 March 1924.
119 MacDonald Papers, FO 800/218, Poincaré to MacDonald, 25 February 1924. Poincaré's reply in French is given in *DBFP*, 1st Series, XXVI, no. 371.
120 *HC*, vol. 173, col. 1339, 14 May 1924.
121 Saint-Aulaire, *Confessions d'un vieux diplomate*, p. 690.
122 MacDonald Papers, FO 800/218, MacDonald to Poincaré, 21 February 1924.
123 For this incident and MacDonald's statement see T160/114/F4399/2.
124 *DBFP*, 1st Series, XXVI, no. 436, MacDonald to Grahame, 17 April 1924.
125 Schuker, *The End of French Predominance*, ch. 5.
126 Ibid., pp. 140–50.
127 For an analysis of the discussions at Chequers and the London conference see Schuker, *The End of French Predominance*, chs 7 and 8. For Herriot's account of the Chequers talks see Edouard Herriot, *Jadis*, II (Paris, 1952), 138–45. See also Weill-Reynaud, *Les Réparations allemandes et la France*, III, 331–47.
128 Schuker, *The End of French Predominance*, pp. 235–6.
129 Hankey Papers, Diary, 11 October 1924. For the critical verdict of Phipps see FO 371/10534, Phipps to Crowe, 15 June 1924.
130 FO 371/9843, Crewe to MacDonald, 1 June 1924.
131 Schuker, *The End of French Predominance*, pp. 237–8.
132 FO 371/9749, Notes taken during a conversation between M. Edouard Herriot and Mr Ramsay MacDonald, at Chequers on June 21, 1924, at 10 p.m.
133 Ibid., Notes of meeting on 22 June 1924.
134 Idem.
135 Idem.
136 For the text of the Draft Treaty see Cmd 2200 (1924), *Correspondence between His Majesty's Government and the League of Nations respecting the Proposed Treaty of*

Mutual Assistance, pp. 4–9.
137 Marquand, *MacDonald*, p. 339.
138 Ibid. pp. 339–40.
139 Ibid., p. 340.
140 FO 371/9749, Lampson to Niemeyer, 30 June 1924.
141 Ibid., minute by Sterndale Bennett, 30 June 1924; Lampson to Niemeyer, 30 June 1924.
142 T160/207/F7768/1, Niemeyer to Under-Secretary of State, FO, 4 July 1924.
143 FO 371/9683, Niemeyer to Nicolson, 23 August 1924.
144 Cmd 2184 (1924), *Correspondence concerning the Conference Which It Is Proposed to Hold in London on July 16 1924 to Consider the Measures Necessary to Bring the Dawes Plan into Operation.*
145 *DBFP*, 1st Series, XXVI, no. 503, n. 3; Kent, *Spoils of War*, p. 257; Schuker, *The End of French Predominance*, pp. 257–8.
146 *HC*, vol. 175, col. 2143, 23 June 1924; col 2310, 26 June 1924.
147 FO 371/9849, Phipps to Prime Minister, 6 July 1924; *DBFP*, 1st Series, XXVI, no. 503.
148 FO 371/9849, M. de Montille to Foreign Office, 6 July 1924; Crewe to MacDonald, 7 July 1924.
149 FO 371/9849, Notes taken during a meeting at the British Embassy, 8 July 1924, 10pm; *DBFP*, 1st Series, XXVI, nos 508–9.
150 Cmd 2191 (1924), *Franco-British Memorandum of 9 July 1924, concerning the Application of the Dawes Scheme*, p. 5. This is also to be found in FO 371/9683.
151 For accounts of the London conference see Orde, *British policy and European reconstruction*, pp. 253–65; Schuker, *The End of French Predominance*, ch. 8.
152 Marquand, *MacDonald*, p. 342.
153 FO 371/9863, Phipps to Foreign Office, 24 and 25 July 1924; Phipps to MacDonald, 27 and 31 July 1924.
154 Ibid., minute by Sterndale Bennett, 28 July 1924.
155 Ibid., minute by MacDonald, 13 August 1924.
156 Cab 29/105, 88th conf., 28 July 1924, MacDonald's report to the British Empire Delegation; Cab 23/48, 44(24), Cabinet minutes of 30 July 1924.
157 FO 371/9683, Note by the French Delegation on the Settlement of Inter-Allied Debts, submitted by Clémentel, 4 August 1924.
158 Ibid., Niemeyer to Crowe, 14 August 1924.
159 Ibid., minutes by Crowe and MacDonald, 8 August 1924.
160 FO 371/9749, Lampson to Niemeyer, 30 June 1924.
161 On 8 August 1924 MacDonald minuted 'I have almost brought things to a point where the Americans may come in but nothing must be done as yet as I may not in the end succeed': FO 371/9683.
162 T160/207/F7768/1, Niemeyer to Crowe, 14 August 1924.
163 Ibid., Treasury note on Clémentel's Aide Memoire, enclosure in Niemeyer to Crowe, 14 August 1924.
164 *Le Matin*, 10 August 1924.
165 FO 371/9863, Phipps to Foreign Office, 10 August 1924.
166 Idem.
167 T160/207/F7768/1, minute by Niemeyer on Phipps to Foreign Office, 10 August 1924, 11 August 1924.
168 FO 371/9863, minutes by Lampson and Sterndale Bennet, 11 August 1924.
169 T160/207/F7768/1, Lampson to Phipps, 20 August 1924.
170 FO 371/9761, Auriol to MacDonald, 6 August 1924.

171 The Treasury suggested that the letter should be ignored, but the Foreign Office eventually drafted a non-committal reply: FO 371/9761, minute by Lampson, 4 September 1924; MacDonald to Auriol, 15 September 1924.
172 T160/207/F7768/1, Crowe to Niemeyer, 14 August 1924; Niemeyer to Crowe, 14 August 1924.
173 For Snowden's conduct at the London conference see Colin Cross, *Philip Snowden* (London, 1966), p. 211; Marquand, *MacDonald*, pp. 346–50; Schuker, *The End of French Predominance*, pp. 296–7, 302–3, 315–16.
174 FO 371/9683, Hankey to Lampson, 16 August 1924.
175 Cmd 2270 (1924), p. 96.
176 *DBFP*, Series 1A, I, no. 1, Foreign Office memorandum respecting the Locarno Treaties; Marquand, *MacDonald*, pp. 352–5.
177 Marquand, *MacDonald*, pp. 364–7.
178 Ibid., pp. 378–88.

Chapter 6 *Negotiations for the Churchill–Caillaux Provisional Debt Agreement of August 1925*

1 T160/382/F8348/1, memorandum for Niemeyer by Leith-Ross, 28 March 1925.
2 Austen Chamberlain Papers, AC 53/161, Crewe to Chamberlain, 16 April 1926.
3 For varying assessments of Churchill as Chancellor of the Exchequer see Paul Addison, *Churchill on the Home Front 1900–1955* (London, 1992), chs 7 and 8; Gilbert, *Churchill*, V, chs 4–8; Middlemas and Barnes, *Baldwin*, pp. 281–2, 289–91, 302–7; Henry Pelling, *Winston Churchill* (London, 1974), pp. 298–310, 322–5; Grigg, *Prejudice and Judgement*, ch. 5.
4 T172/239, Churchill to Hopkins, 14 December 1924; Neville Chamberlain diary, 26 November 1924, cited in Gilbert, *Churchill*, Companion Volume V, Part I, 263–4.
5 *HC*, vol. 179, cols. 259–65, 10 December 1924.
6 Baldwin to King George V, cited in Gilbert, *Churchill*, Companion Volume V, Part 1, 259–60.
7 Although eager to engage in discussions about a general settlement of reparations and war debts, successive French governments had so far been unwilling to enter bilateral negotiations about their obligations to Britain and the United States.
8 FO 371/10680, Crewe to Foreign Office, 21 January 1925; Schrecker, *The Hired Money*, pp. 194–5.
9 FO 371/10680, Phipps to Crowe, 23 January 1925.
10 Ibid., Crewe to Chamberlain, 23 January 1925.
11 Churchill Papers, 18/3, Churchill to Niemeyer, 25 November 1924.
12 Ibid., 18/21, draft memorandum by Churchill for the Cabinet, 1 December 1924.
13 Ibid., 18/3, Churchill to Niemeyer, 25 November 1924.
14 Idem.
15 FO 371/10680, 'French Budgetary Position and National Income', Treasury memorandum, 2 January 1925.
16 Ibid., Bradbury to Churchill, 13 December 1924.
17 FO 371/9683, Churchill to Chamberlain, 1 December 1924.
18 Idem.
19 FO 371/9683, minute by Lampson, 2 December 1924; minute by Tyrrell, 1 December 1924; minute by Crowe, 1 December 1924.
20 Frederick Leith-Ross joined the Treasury in 1909 and was assigned to the Finance Division. From 1920 to February 1925 he served on the Finance Board of the Reparation Commission, before being recalled to London to act as Deputy

Controller of Finance under Sir Otto Niemeyer. In this capacity he served as the principal adviser to the Chancellor of the Exchequer on reparations and war debts. In March 1932 he was appointed Chief Economic Adviser to the government, in which post he continued to deal with questions relating to reparations and war debts.

21 See below p. 186.

22 Churchill Papers, 18/21, draft memorandum by Churchill for the Cabinet, 1 December 1924.

23 Ibid., Churchill to Niemeyer, 25 November 1924.

24 Ibid., draft memorandum by Churchill for the Cabinet, 1 December 1924.

25 Idem.

26 BE, G30/13/4039/4, Rechnitzer to Norman, 8 December 1924; Austen Chamberlain to Churchill, 15 December 1924, cited in Gilbert, *Churchill*, Companion Volume V, Part I, 302.

27 BE, G30/13/4039/4, memorandum by Norman, 1 December 1924.

28 Ibid., Rechnitzer to Norman, 17 November 1924.

29 Ibid., memorandum by Norman, 1 December 1924.

30 Ibid., Norman to Rechnitzer, 18 November 1924; memorandum by Norman, 1 December 1924; Churchill to Chamberlain, 16 December 1924; Sir Richard Hopkins Papers [hereafter Hopkins Papers], T175/4, Niemeyer to Grigg, 29 November 1924; Churchill to Chamberlain, 1 December 1924; Norman to Niemeyer, 2 December 1924.

31 Hopkins Papers, T175/4, Clémentel to Churchill, 13 December 1924.

32 Ibid., Churchill to Chamberlain, 16 December 1924.

33 Idem.

34 *FRUS*, 1925, I, 133–4, 140–3, 145–50; Artaud. *La Question des dettes interalliées*, II, 699–720; Leffler, *The Elusive Quest*, pp. 124–5; Orde, *British policy and European reconstruction*, pp. 292–3; Schrecker, *The Hired Money*, pp. 186–90.

35 *HC*, vol. 179, cols. 264–5, 10 December 1925.

36 Notes by Churchill on the Paris talks, cited Gilbert, *Churchill*, Companion Volume V, Part I, 332.

37 Cited in Gilbert, *Churchill*, Companion Volume V, Part I, 336–7.

38 Churchill Papers, 18/21, memorandum by Churchill, 12 January 1925.

39 Idem.

40 See above p. 151.

41 T160/207/7768/03/1, Clémentel to Churchill, 10 January 1925.

42 FO 371/10680, Churchill to Clémentel, 13 January 1925; minute by Chamberlain, 11 January 1925; minute by Sterndale Bennett, 11 January 1925; Duff to Sterndale Bennett, 11 January 1925.

43 Grigg, *Prejudice and Judgement*, p. 206.

44 For negotiations on evacuation of the Cologne zone and the lead-up to the Treaty of Locarno see *DBFP*, Series 1A, I, no. 1, Foreign office memorandum regarding the Locarno Treaties, 10 January 1926; David Dutton, *Austen Chamberlain: Gentleman in Politics* (Bolton, 1985), pp. 238–48; Jon Jacobson, *Locarno Diplomacy: Germany and the West 1925–1929* (Princeton, 1972), pp. 3–59; Middlemas and Barnes, *Baldwin*, pp. 349–58.

45 Austen Chamberlain Papers, FO 371/257, Crowe to Chamberlain, 3 February 1925.

46 FO 371/10680, record of conversation between the French ambassador and Crowe, 9 February 1925.

47 Leith-Ross, *Money Talks*, p. 95.

48 Grigg, *Prejudice and Judgement*, p. 208.

49 Austen Chamberlain Papers, FO 371/257, Crowe to Chamberlain, 3 February 1925.

50   Leith-Ross Papers, T188/273, Niemeyer to Leith-Ross, 31 January 1925.
51   Idem.
52   Idem.
53   FO 371/10680, Treasury draft memorandum sent to Foreign Office, 27 January 1925.
54   Ibid., minute by Sterndale Bennett, 28 January 1925.
55   Ibid., minute by Lampson, 29 January 1925.
56   CP 46(25), enclosure in Cab 23/49, 5(25).
57   Cab 23/49, 6(25)217, Cabinet minutes of 4 February 1925; T160/382/F8348/1, Churchill to Clémentel, 6 February 1925. On 3 February 1925 Leopold Amery, the Colonial Secretary, noted in his diary: 'Cabinet meeting on Allied Debts & adopted Winston's scheme with a modification suggested by myself.' Cited in Gilbert, *Churchill*, Companion Volume V, Part I, 370, n. 1.
58   T160/382/F8348/1, Churchill to Clémentel, 6 February 1925.
59   FO 371/10680, Crewe to Crowe, 8 and 9 February 1925.
60   Ibid., record of a conversation between the French ambassador and Crowe, 9 February 1925. See also T160/382/F8348/1, minute by Lampson, 9 February 1925.
61   T160/382/F8348/1, Lampson to Secretary of the Treasury, 11 February 1925; FO 371/10680, Niemeyer to Under-Secretary of State, FO, 16 February 1925.
62   T160/382/F8348/1, minute by Niemeyer, 13 February 1925.
63   Ibid., minute by Waley, 12 February 1925.
64   Ibid., minute by Niemeyer, 13 February 1925.
65   Ibid., Niemeyer to Under-Secretary of State, FO, 16 February 1925.
66   FO 371/10680, Chamberlain to de Fleuriau, 19 February 1925; record of a conversation between Crowe and the French ambassador, 24 February 1925.
67   T160/382/F8348/1, Niemeyer to Churchill, 4 March 1925; minute by Churchill, 5 March 1925.
68   FO 371/10680, Howard Smith to Secretary of the Treasury, 2 March 1925; Niemeyer to Under-Secretary of State, FO, 6 March 1925; Clémentel to Churchill, 28 February 1925.
69   See, for example, the article by the Paris correspondent of *The Times* on 3 April 1925.
70   T160/382/F8348/1, Niemeyer to de Rinquensen, 3 April 1925.
71   Ibid., memorandum by Niemeyer, 3 April 1925.
72   Ibid., memoranda by Niemeyer, 3 and 7 April 1925.
73   Cab 23/49, 20(25)415, Cabinet minutes of 8 April 1925; T160/382/F8348/1, memorandum for Chancellor of the Exchequer by Niemeyer, 7 April 1925.
74   T160/382/F8348/1, memorandum by Niemeyer, 7 April 1925.
75   Cab 23/49, 20(25)415, Cabinet minutes of 8 April 1925.
76   Churchill Papers, 18/12B, minute for Niemeyer by Churchill, 7 April 1925.
77   FO 371/10680, minute by Lampson, 14 April 1925.
78   *The Times*, article by the Paris correspondent, 4 April 1925; 11 April 1925.
79   Ibid., article by the Paris correspondent, 3 April 1925.
80   *The Times*, 6, 11 and 17 April 1925.
81   For information on Caillaux's life before he became Finance Minister in 1925 see Rudolph Binion, *Defeated Leaders: The Political Fate of Caillaux, Jouvenel and Tardieu* (New York, 1960), pp. 1–94.
82   FO 371/10681, Chamberlain to Crewe, 30 April 1925.
83   Haig, *Public Finances of Post-War France*, p. 120; Leffler, *The Elusive Quest*, p. 130.
84   Leffler, *The Elusive Quest*, pp. 128–30; Schrecker, *The Hired Money*, pp 176–80.
85   *Le Temps*, 19 May 1925; T160/207/F7768/03/1, Crewe to Chamberlain, 19 May 1925.

86 FO 371/10681, Phipps to Tyrrell, 20 May 1925.

87 Idem.

88 FO 371/10681, minutes by Lampson, Tyrrell (both 23 May 1925) and Chamberlain, undated.

89 Ibid., Niemeyer to Churchill, 26 May 1925.

90 Ibid., Phipps to Tyrrell, 21 May 1925.

91 Idem.

92 FO 371/10681, Churchill to Chamberlain, 27 May 1925.

93 His name had been changed under the terms of a will.

94 FO 371/10681, Churchill to Chamberlain, 27 May 1925.

95 Ibid., Chamberlain to Churchill, 31 May 1925.

96 Ibid., Chamberlain to Tyrrell, 8 June 1925.

97 *The Manchester Guardian*, 1 September 1927.

98 The central part which the Entente played in Chamberlain's political strategy is not open to question and is brought out clearly in Jacobson, *Locarno Diplomacy* and Dutton, *Austen Chamberlain*. See also Douglas Johnson, 'The Locarno Treaties', in Neville Waites (ed.), *Troubled Neighbours: Franco-British Relations in the Twentieth Century* (London, 1971), pp. 105–6.

99 FO 371/10681, Tyrrell to Phipps, 2 June 1925; Phipps to Tyrrell, 4 June 1925.

100 Ibid., Phipps to Tyrrell, 10 June 1925; Tyrrell to Niemeyer, 15 June 1925.

101 Ibid., enclosure in Pelletier to Phipps, 10 June 1925.

102 Ibid., Treasury memorandum, enclosure in Niemeyer to Tyrrell, 20 June 1925.

103 T160/382/F8348/1, note for Churchill by Leith-Ross, 6 June 1925.

104 Idem.

105 Idem.

106 Idem.

107 T160/382/F8348/1, note for Churchill by Niemeyer, 15 June 1925. Churchill commented in the margin: 'We can explore this later'. In the event, however, nothing came of the proposal.

108 FO 371/10681, enclosure in Niemeyer to Tyrrell, 20 June 1925.

109 Idem.

110 T160/382/F8348/1, Niemeyer to Tyrrell, 20 June 1925; Tyrrell to Phipps, 25 June 1925.

111 FO 371/10681, minute by Lampson, 25 June 1925; minute by Tyrrell, 24 June 1925.

112 Ibid., minute by Chamberlain, 25 June 1925; Lampson to Niemeyer, 25 June 1925; Chamberlain to de Fleuriau, 25 June 1925.

113 Ibid., Chamberlain to de Fleuriau, 25 June 1925.

114 Ibid., de Fleuriau to Chamberlain, 2 July 1925.

115 T160/382/F8348/1, note by Leith-Ross, 4 July 1925; FO 371/10681, Niemeyer to Under-Secretary of State, FO, 7 July 1925; minutes by Troutbeck (8 July 1925), Tyrrell and Chamberlain (both 9 July 1925).

116 FO 371/10681, Niemeyer to Under-Secretary of State, FO, 7 July 1925.

117 Idem.

118 FO 371/10681, Chamberlain to Crewe, 7 July 1925.

119 T160/382/F8348/1, Churchill to Chamberlain, 7 July 1925.

120 T172/1504, note of a conversation between the Chancellor of the Exchequer and the French ambassador, 9 July 1925.

121 Ibid., note of a conversation between the Chancellor of the Exchequer and the French ambassador on 17 July, 21 July 1925.

122 Leith-Ross spoke of the terms of the Balfour Note becoming 'a mere excuse for pettifogging debate': T160/382/F8348/1, note for Chancellor of the Exchequer by

Leith-Ross, 6 June 1925. For details of the wrangle triggered off by the Churchill-de Fleuriau talks see FO 371/10681, note by Harold Nicolson, 20 July 1925; de Fleuriau to Chamberlain, 20 July 1925; minute by Lampson, 22 July 1925; Niemeyer to Under-Secretary of State, FO, undated.

123 Foreign Office officials were bewildered by de Fleuriau's arguments. See FO 371/10681, note by Nicolson, 20 July 1925; minute by Lampson, 22 July 1925.

124 FO 371/10682, Phipps to Tyrrell, 16 July 1925.

125 Ibid., de Fleuriau to Chamberlain, 22 July 1925.

126 T172/1504, Churchill to de Fleuriau, 25 July 1925.

127 The composition of the French Treasury team was somewhat different from that originally envisaged which had been Moreau-Néret, Barnaud, Pelletier and Professor Guyot of the Sorbonne who was a member of Caillaux's *Cabinet*: FO 371/10681, Phipps to Tyrrell, 16 July 1925.

128 T160/382/F8348/2, notes of first meeting of British and French Treasury experts, 3 p.m. 27 July 1925.

129 Idem.

130 FO 371/10682, memorandum by Wigram, 28 July 1925.

131 Ibid., minute by Lampson, 29 July 1925.

132 Ibid., minute by Chamberlain, 29 July 1925.

133 Baldwin Papers, vol. 3, p. 162, Fisher to Baldwin, 28 July 1925.

134 T160/382/F8348/2, notes of second meeting of British and French Treasury experts, 11.30 a.m., 29 July 1925.

135 Idem. For the position of British holders of French war bonds see Arthur Turner, 'British Holdings of French war bonds: an aspect of Anglo-French relations during the 1920s', *Financial History Review*, vol. 3, Part 2, October 1996, 153–74.

136 T160/382/F8348/2, notes of second meeing of British and French Treasury experts, 11.30 a.m., 28 July 1925.

137 Cab 23/50, 41(25)275–6, Cabinet minutes of 29 July 1925.

138 T160/382/F8348/2, notes of third meeting of British and French Treasury experts, 4 p.m., 29 July 1925.

139 Idem.

140 T172/1498, British proposals regarding French war debt sent to French experts on 30 July 1925.

141 FO 371/10682, minute by Lampson, 30 July 1925; Cab 23/50, 45(25)356, statement by Churchill at Cabinet meeting of 26 August 1925; FO 371/10682, note by Sterndale Bennett, 15 August 1925.

142 Phipps Papers, 1/4, Phipps to Chamberlain, 23 August 1925; T172/1498, Phipps to Foreign Office, 22 August 1922.

143 T172/1498, Leith-Ross to Churchill, 22 August 1925; Niemeyer to Churchill, 25 August 1925.

144 FO 371/10682, 'The Comparative Capacity of Germany, France and Great Britain to Effect Payments Abroad', memorandum by Leith-Ross, 5 August 1925, enclosure in Niemeyer to Selby, 7 August 1925.

145 Ibid., Niemeyer to Selby, 7 August 1925.

146 Baldwin Papers, vol. 115, p. 110, Austen Chamberlain to Baldwin, 27 August 1925.

147 T172/1498, Hankey to Baldwin, 26 August 1925.

148 Ibid., Niemeyer to Churchill, 25 August 1925.

149 Baldwin Papers, vol. 115, p. 110, Churchill to Baldwin, 26 August 1925.

150 *The Times*, leading article, 'The French Debt', 3 August 1925. *The Times'* flattering comments on Caillaux formed a strong contrast with its usual attacks on French unwillingness to accept the sacrifices necessary to restore sound finances. See, for

example, *The Times*, leading article, 'A Crisis in France', 4 April 1925; 'City Notes', 1 August 1925.

151 T172/1498, Hankey to Baldwin, 26 August 1926.

152 Baldwin Papers, vol. 115, p. 93, Chamberlain to Baldwin, 27 August 1925. Chamberlain was impressed by Caillaux's grasp of economics. As he commented in June 1925, 'M. Caillaux shows a considerable appreciation of the facts. Unlike most of the French Finance Ministers with whom I have had to deal he knows what he is talking about': FO 371/11829, minute by Chamberlain on a telegram by Phipps, 25 June 1925.

153 T172/1504, Churchill to Caillaux, 30 October 1925; T160/382/F8348/3, Churchill to Painlevé, 2 November 1925.

154 For a summary of the discussions see T172/1499A, '1925. The Present Position of the French Debt Negotiations', Treasury memorandum, August 1925.

155 T160/382/F8348/3, memorandum respecting Caillaux's visit to London regarding the French War Debt, August 24–26 1925. Prepared by the Foreign Office, 8 October 1925, Annex C.

156 Ibid., Annex B.

157 Cab 23/50, 45(25)357, Cabinet minutes of 26 August 1925.

158 T172/1498, Hankey to Baldwin, 26 August 1925.

159 T160/382/F8348/3, memorandum respecting Caillaux's visit to London regarding the French War Debt, August 24–26 1925. Prepared by the Foreign Office, 8 October 1925, Annex C.

160 Cab 23/50, 45(25)356–7, Cabinet minutes of 26 August 1925.

161 Baldwin Papers, vol. 115, p. 93, Chamberlain to Baldwin, 27 August 1925.

162 Idem.

163 T160/382/F8348/3, memorandum respecting Caillaux's visit to London, August 24–26. Prepared by the Foreign Office, 8 October 1925, Annex D.

164 Cab 23/50, 45(25)358, Cabinet minutes of 26 August 1925.

165 Idem.

166 T172/1498, Hankey to Baldwin, 26 August 1925.

167 Baldwin Papers, vol. 115, p. 92, Chamberlain to Baldwin, 26 August 1925.

168 T172/1498, Hankey to Baldwin, 26 August 1925.

169 Idem.

170 Idem.

171 Idem.

172 Cab 23/50, 45(25)358, Cabinet minutes of 26 August 1925.

173 Cab 23/50, 45(25)360, Cabinet minutes of 26 August 1925; T172/1498, Grigg to Tom Jones, 27 August 1925; *The Times*, 27 August 1925.

174 *The Times*, 27 August 1927.

175 Chamberlain to Churchill, 2 September 1925, cited in Gilbert, *Churchill*, Companion Volume V, Part I, 357.

176 T160/382/F8348/3, memorandum respecting M. Caillaux's visit to London regarding the French War Debt, August 24–26. Prepared by the Foreign Office, 8 October 1925. Annex G, Caillaux to Chancellor of the Exchequer, 4 September 1925; Annex H, Churchill to Caillaux, 14 September 1925; Annex I, Caillaux to Churchill, 15 September. See also T172/1499A, '1925. The Present Position of the French Debt Negotiations.', Treasury memorandum, undated (1925).

177 T160/382/F8348/3, memorandum respecting Caillaux's visit to London regarding the French War Debt, August 24–26. Prepared by the Foreign Office, 8 October 1925.

178 *The Times*, 17 September 1925.

179 *The Times*, 27 August 1925; *The Morning Post*, 21 and 29 August 1925; *The Observer*, 30 August 1925; *The Daily Mail*, 28 August 1925; *The Daily News*, 27 and 29 August 1925.

180 *The Daily Express*, leading article, 'A Very Bad Bargain', 27 August 1925; *The Evening Standard*, 27 August 1925; *The New Statesman*, 29 August 1925; *The Manchester Guardian*, 28 August 1925.

181 *The Daily Express*, leading article, 'The Tangle of War Debts', 26 August 1925.

182 Alan Wood, *The True History of Lord Beaverbrook* (London, 1965), pp. 177–8. It was in Beaverbrook's *Evening Standard* that Keynes wrote the series of articles attacking the return to the the Gold Standard which were later published as *The Economic Consequences of Mr Churchill*.

183 The editor of *The Daily Express*, Ralph D. Blumenfeld, had strong doubts about the ability of the French to pay their debts. He did not approve of Beaverbrook's 'persecution' of Churchill and 'watered it down – whenever he could and whenever he was in charge': Churchill Papers, 18/9, F.E. Guest to Churchill, 27 August 1925.

184 *The Daily Express*, 27 August 1925.

Chapter 7 *Towards a Final Settlement*

1 For the debate amongst French policymakers about whether priority should be given to a settlement with Britain or the United States see Schrecker, *The Hired Money*, p. 207.

2 Churchill to Chamberlain 7 September 1925, cited in Gilbert, *Churchill*, Companion Volume V, Part I, 539.

3 The text of the Mellon–Bérenger agreement is to be found in Moulton and Pasvolsky, *World War Debt Settlements*, pp. 363–71. The terms of the settlement are analysed by Artaud, *La Question des dettes interalliées*, II, 785–807; Moulton and Pasvolsky, *World War Debt Settlements*, pp. 363–74; Schrecker, *The Hired Money*, pp. 224–34. For Caillaux's unsuccessful mission to Washington in September 1925 see Artaud, *La Question des dettes interalliées*, II, 755–73; Leffler, *The Elusive Quest*, pp. 134–5; Schrecker, *The Hired Money*, pp. 211–18.

4 Cmd 2580 (1926), *Agreement for the Settlement of the War Debt of Italy to Great Britain*; Moulton and Pasvolsky, *World War Debt Settlements*, pp. 427–32.

5 For an assessment of the Anglo-Italian settlement and a comparison with that between Italy and the United States (signed 14 November 1925) see Moulton and Pasvolsky, *World War Debt Settlements*, pp. 53–5.

6 T172/1499A, note for Churchill by Niemeyer, 2 February 1926.

7 For the French financial crisis of April–July 1926 see Artaud, *La Question des dettes interalliées*, II, 821–34.

8 T172/1504, Churchill to Caillaux, 15 October 1925.

9 Painlevé was Minister of Finance from 29 October to 28 November 1925. He was succeeded by Loucheur who held the office from 28 November until 16 December 1925 when he was replaced by Paul Doumer (16 December 1925 to 9 March 1926). For a list of French governments and finance ministers for the inter-war period as a whole see Wolfe, *The French Franc between the Wars*, appendix 4, pp 219–20.

10 *HC*, vol. 193, col. 466, 17 March 1926.

11 T172/1504, Churchill to Caillaux, 15 October 1925; Churchill to Caillaux, 30 October 1925; Churchill to Painlevé, 2 November 1925; Churchill to Loucheur, 16 December 1925; Churchill to Doumer, 24 December 1925; T172/1505, Churchill to Péret, 12 March 1925.

12 T160/382/F8348/3, Churchill to Painlevé, 2 November 1925.

13 T172/1504, Chamberlain to Churchill, 13 November 1925; Lampson to Grigg, 11 November 1925.

14 See, for example, Austen Chamberlain Papers, FO 800/258, Chamberlain to D'Abernon, 30 September 1925. For Chamberlain's affection and regard for 'large-hearted, generous Briand', as he called the French Foreign Minister, see Sir Austen Chamberlain, *Down the Years* (London, 1935), pp. 179–88; Dutton, *Austen Chamberlain*, pp. 246–9, 259–60, 264–5; Keith Feiling, *Life of Neville Chamberlain* (London, 1946), p. 152; Jacobson, *Locarno Diplomacy*, pp. 25, 59, 63, 72, 75, 114, 125, 128, 378–9; Johnson, 'The Locarno Treaties, in Waites (ed.), *Troubled Neighbours*, pp. 116–17; Sir Charles Petrie, *The Life and Letters of the Right Hon. Sir Austen Chamberlain*, 2 vols (London, 1939–40), II, 275–6, 290.

15 Chamberlain had a deep distrust of the French Right, as personified by Poincaré: Petrie, *Life and Letters of Sir Austen Chamberlain*, I, 86–7; II, 155.

16 T172/1504, Chamberlain to Churchill, 13 November 1925.

17 Ibid., Churchill to Chamberlain, 14 November 1925.

18 Ibid., Lampson to Grigg, 11 November 1925.

19 Ibid., minute by Churchill, 12 November 1925.

20 T172/1505, note for Chancellor of the Exchequer by Grigg, 30 January 1926.

21 Ibid., minute by Churchill, 30 January 1926; Churchill Papers, 18/29, Churchill to Doumer, 1 February 1926.

22 T172/1504, Churchill to Doumer, 24 December 1925; Doumer to Churchill, 5 January 1926.

23 T172/1505, note for Churchill by Niemeyer, January 1926; Churchill to Doumer, 11 January 1926.

24 T172/1499A, Doumer to Churchill, 11 February 1926.

25 Ibid., Doumer to Churchill, 18 February 1926; Grigg to Selby, 25 February 1926; Doumer to Crewe, 2 March 1926; Crewe to Chamberlain, 3 March 1926.

26 T172/1505, Doumer to Churchill, 7 March 1926; Churchill to Doumer, 17 March 1926.

27 See, for example, *The Times*, 3 February 1926; *The Manchester Guardian*, 3 February 1926.

28 *The Manchester Guardian*, 4 February 1926.

29 See, for example, *The Financial Times*, 'France and her War Debt', 4 March 1926.

30 *The Times*, 19 March 1926. For a similar letter signed by a Sir Daniel Stevens see *The Times*, 19 May 1926.

31 FO 371/12633, Annual Report on France for 1926, enclosure in Crewe to Chamberlain, 18 March 1927.

32 T160/382/F8348, memorandum by Phipps, 12 February 1926. See also Artaud, *La Qestion des dettes interalliées*, II, 798.

33 *The Financial Times*, 'France and its Debts: A Statistical Extravaganza', 4 February 1926.

34 FO 371/11826, Mendl to Tyrrell, 8 February 1926. Sir Charles Mendl, press attaché at the Paris embassy, claimed that the speeches were only intended for domestic consumption and that they would not have had much publicity if they had not been reported in *The Times*, *The Daily Express* and *The Sunday Express*. For an account of the meeting by a member of the British embassy staff who attended it see T160/F8348/3, memorandum by R. F. Wigram, 2 February 1926.

35 *The Times*, 'A French View of Debts', 3 February 1926.

36 *The Financial Times*, 'France and its Debts. A Statistical Extravaganza', 4 February 1926; *The Times*, 'A French View of Debts', 3 February 1926; *The Manchester Guardian*, 'France Owes Us Nothing. A Great Discovery', 3 February 1926.

37   *The Financial Times*, 4 February 1926.
38   *The Financial Times*, 'France and Her War Debt. M. Doumer's Visit', 4 March 1926.
39   T172/1499A, undated minute by Leith-Ross.
40   See, for example, the views of Colonel Willey, the President of the FBI, above p. 208.
     See also T172/1499A, R. T. Nugent (Direcor of FBI) to Churchill, 17 May 1926;
     T. D. Harrison (Albion Ironworks, Leigh) to J. R. Remer MP; Remer to Churchill,
     13 March 1926.
41   *HC*, vol. 192, col. 2617, 21 February 1926.
42   Ibid., vol. 192, col. 2597, 11 March 1926.
43   Ibid., vol. 193, cols. 1272–6, 24 March 1924.
44   Ibid., vol. 193, col. 1267, 24 March 1926.
45   Ibid., vol. 193, cols. 1236–44, 24 March 1926.
46   T172/1505, J. R. Remer to Churchill, 13 March 1926.
47   Ibid., Churchill to J. R. Remer, 19 March 1926.
48   Churchill Papers, 18/29, Churchill to Doumer, 1 February 1926.
49   T172/1499A, note for Churchill by Niemeyer, 2 February 1926; note for Churchill
     by Niemeyer, 4 February 1926.
50   Ibid., Notes on Outstanding Points by Leith-Ross, enclosure in Niemeyer to
     Churchill, 2 April 1926.
51   T172/1499A, note by Leith-Ross on outstanding points in the French debt negoti-
     ations, enclosure in Niemeyer to Churchill, 2 April 1926.
52   Ibid., note for Churchill by Niemeyer, 2 February 1926.
53   Idem.
54   T172/1499A, note for Churchill by Niemeyer, 2 February 1926.
55   Idem.
56   Idem.
57   *The Times*, 18 May 1926.
58   T160/382/F8348/4, note for Churchill by Niemeyer, 20 May 1926.
59   T160/382/F8348/3, minute by Niemeyer on a minute by Phipps of 12 February
     1926.
60   T172/1499A, note by Leith-Ross on outstanding points in the French debt negoti-
     ations, enclosure in Niemeyer to Churchill, 2 April 1926.
61   Idem.
62   T160/207/F7768/03/1, undated minute by Leith-Ross.
63   Churchill Papers, 18/29, Churchill to Péret, 12 March 1926.
64   T172/1505, Péret to Churchill, 28 March 1926.
65   Ibid., Churchill to Péret, 1 April 1926.
66   Ibid., note by F. Maxse, 5 April 1926.
67   Ibid., Foreign Office to Crewe, 7 April 1926.
68   T160/3b3/F8348/3, enclosure in Crewe to Chamberlain, 8 April 1926; T172/1505,
     Péret to Churchill, 9 April 1926.
69   T172/1499A, Crewe to Chamberlain, 18 April 1926.
70   FO 371/12633, Annual Report on France for 1926, enclosure in Crewe to
     Chamberlain, 18 March 1927.
71   *HC*, vol. 194, cols. 1716–17, 26 April 1926; T160/383/F8348/4, Churchill to Péret,
     4 May 1926.
72   T160/383/F8348/4, Churchill to Péret, 4 May 1926.
73   Ibid., Leith-Ross to Niemeyer, 5 May 1926; Niemeyer to Leith-Ross, 7 May 1926.
     For Churchill's role in the General Strike see Gilbert, *Churchill*, V, chs 9–11.
74   *The Times*, articles by Paris correspondent, 30 April 1926; 18, 19, 20, 22 May 1926.
75   *The Times*, 17 May 1926.

76 Ibid., Paris correspondent, 18 May 1926.
77 Idem.
78 BE, Strong–Norman Correspondence, G1/42/3658/2, Strong to Norman, 11 June 1926.
79 T172/1499A, note for Chancellor of the Exchequer by Niemeyer, 15 May 1926.
80 For French anger against the Mellon–Bérenger agreement see Artaud, *La Question des dettes interalliées*, II, 811–21; Kent, *Spoils of War*, pp. 268–9.
81 T172/1499A, note for Chancellor of the Exchequer by Niemeyer, 15 May 1926.
82 Ibid., 'Settlement of French Debt to USA and outstanding points as regards Debt to Great Britain', note by Leith-Ross, 15 May 1926; note for Chancellor of the Exchequer by Niemeyer, 15 May 1926.
83 *The Times*, 17 May 1926.
84 BE, ADM 20/15, Norman Diary, 17 May 1926.
85 Ibid., Norman Diary, 18 May 1926.
86 BE, Strong–Norman Correspondence, G1/421/3658/2, Norman to Strong, 19 May 1926.
87 Idem.
88 T160/383/F8348/4, Churchill to Péret, 18 May 1926.
89 T172/1499A, Péret to Churchill, 18 May 1926.
90 *The Times*, Paris correspondent, 19 May 1926. On 19 May the franc lost 10 points in one day, finishing at 172 to the pound: ibid., Paris correspondent, 20 May 1926.
91 *The Times*, Paris correspondent, 19 May 1926.
92 T160/383/F8348/4, Churchill to Péret, 18 May 1926.
93 T172/1499A, Churchill to Péret, 18 May 1926; FO 371/12633, Annual Report on France for 1926, enclosure in Crewe to Chamberlain, 18 March 1927.
94 T172/1499A, Churchill to Péret, 18 May 1926.
95 *The Times*, Paris correspondent, 21, 22, 24 May 1926.
96 T172/1499A, note for Chancellor of the Exchequer by Leith-Ross, 4 June 1926.
97 Idem.
98 Idem.
99 T160/383/F8348/4, Crewe to Chamberlain, 4 June 1926.
100 Ibid., Phipps to Foreign Office, 27 June 1926.
101 Ibid., Leith-Ross to Churchill, 7 June 1926.
102 Ibid., Niemeyer to Churchill, 20 May 1926.
103 Idem.
104 Idem.
105 Idem.
106 T172/1499A, note for Chancellor of the Exchequer by Niemeyer, 21 May 1926.
107 Idem.
108 T160/383/F8348/4, Crewe to Chamberlain, 4 June 1926.
109 T172/1499A, Péret to Churchill, 12 June 1926.
110 FO 371/12633, Annual Report on France for 1926, enclosure in Crewe to Chamberlain, 18 March 1927.
111 T172/1499A, note for Chancellor of the Exchequer by Leith-Ross, 4 June 1926.
112 Ibid., Mendl to Tyrrell, 22 June 1926.
113 *The Times*, Paris correspondent, 5 July 1926; FO 371/12633, Annual Report on France for 1926, enclosure in Crewe to Chamberlain, 18 March 1927; Artaud, *La Question des dettes interalliées*, II, 826. More specifically the expert committee's report concluded that stabilisation of the franc would require an American loan of $150m, which would only be available after ratification of the Mellon–Bérenger agreement.
114 T172/1499A, Dunn to Birkenhead, 29 June 1926.

115 Idem.
116 T172/1499A, note for Niemeyer by Leith-Ross, 30 June 1926.
117 T172/1499A, Dunn to Birkenhead, 29 June 1926.
118 Idem.
119 T172/1499A, note for Niemeyer by Leith-Ross, 30 June 1926.
120 Ibid., minute for Chancellor of the Exchequer by Niemeyer, 30 June 1926.
121 Ibid., minute by Churchill, 1 July 1926.
122 T172/1499A, note for Niemeyer by Leith-Ross, 30 June 1926.
123 Idem.
124 Idem.
125 Idem.
126 Idem.
127 Idem.
128 Idem.
129 T172/1499A, Churchill to Caillaux, 5 July 1926; T160/383/F8348/5, note by Leith-Ross, 5 July 1926.
130 T172/1499A, Churchill to Caillaux, July 1926.
131 Ibid., note for Chancellor of the Exchequer by Niemeyer, 5 July 1926; undated note for Chancellor of the Exchequer by Leith-Ross; T160/383/F8348/5, Leith-Ross to Churchill, 10 July 1926; 'Final Negotiations for the French Debt', note by Leith-Ross, 14 July 1926.
132 This was the first time he had ever travelled by air: *The Daily Herald*, 14 July 1926.
133 T160/383/F8348/5, 'Final Negotiations for the French Debt', note by Leith-Ross, 14 July 1926.

Chapter 8   *The 1926 Settlement and its Aftermath*

1   For the text of the Churchill–Caillaux setlement see Cmd 2692 (1926), *French War Debt. Agreement for the Settlement of the War Debt of France to Great Britain with an Exchange of Letters between the Chancellor of the Exchequer and the French Minister of Finance.* The text can also be found in Moulton and Pasvolsky, *World War Debt Settlements*, Appendix C, pp. 432–5.
2   *The Economist*, 'The Debt Settlement with France', 17 July 1926.
3   T160/646/F10685/1, 'Great Britain and War Debts', Treasury memorandum, December 1927, Appendix A.
4   The text of the supplementary letters not included in the White Paper can be found in T160/383/F8348/5.
5   BE, G1/302/2528/3, Niemeyer to Norman, 23 July 1926.
6   Andrew Boyle, *Montagu Norman: a Biography* (London, 1967), p. 203; Clay, *Lord Norman*, p. 228.
7   Leith-Ross, *Money Talks*, p. 94.
8   *HC.*, vol. 198, cols. 233–4, 13 July 1926.
9   *The Manchester Guardian*, 15 July 1926.
10 *The Times*, leading article, 'The French Debt', 14 July 1926. See also *The Economist*, which argued that it was far more important for a trading nation like Britain to 'assist France towards monetary stability' than to gain a little extra in the amount to be paid over a long period: 'The Crisis in France', 24 July 1926.
11 *The New Statesman*, leading article, 'Those Confounded War Debts', 24 July 1926; *The Manchester Guardian*, leading article, 'M. Caillaux's Success', 13 July 1926; *The Nation and Athenaeum*, leading article, 'The Franc Once More', 17 July 1926.
12 *HC*, vol. 198, col. 955, 19 July 1926.

13 Ibid., cols. 968–9.
14 Ibid., col. 961.
15 Ibid., col. 920.
16 Ibid., cols. 919–24.
17 Ibid., cols. 914–19.
18 Between 1907 and 1916 Runciman had been successively Financial Secretary to the Treasury, President of the Board of Education, President of the Board of Agriculture and President of the Board of Trade.
19 *HC*, vol. 198, cols. 939–42, 19 July 1926.
20 Ibid., col. 987.
21 Ibid., cols. 930–6.
22 Ibid., cols. 991–2. For similar remarks by Wallhead and David Kirkwood see *HC*, vol. 213, col. 335, 9 February 1928; vol. 215, col. 845, 26 March 1926.
23 See *HC*, vol. 193, col. 1267, 24 March 1926; vol. 230, col. 1686, 26 July 1929.
24 See Arthur Turner, 'British holdings of French war bonds: an aspect of Anglo-French relations during the 1920s', *Financial History Review*, vol. 3, Part 2, (October 1996), 153–74.
25 Aldcroft, *The British Economy Between the Wars*, p. 15.
26 Ibid., pp. 15–16. For information on the state of the British economy during the 1920s see Aldcroft, *From Versailles to Wall St*, pp. 202–4; Aldcroft, *The Inter-War Economy*, pp. 133–6; A. J. Youngson, *Britain's Economic Growth 1920–1966* (London, 1967), pp. 23–74.
27 Aldcroft, *From Versailles to Wall St*, pp.205–7; Tom Kemp, *The French Economy 1913–1929: The History of a Decline* (London, 1977), ch. 7; W. Arthur Lewis, *Economic Survey 1919–1939* (London, 1949), pp. 32–3; Clay, *Lord Norman*, pp. 226–7; George Peel, *The Economic Policy of France* (London, 1937), pp. 119–27.
28 Grigg, *Prejudice and Judgement*, p. 208.
29 See, for example, Churchill Papers, 18/45B, minute for Niemeyer and Leith-Ross by Churchill, 19 June 1927. Churchill wrote: 'In order to obtain a settlement we made immense concessions on the [French] debt, concessions which we may think in the light of current events exceeded what was right.'
30 Baldwin Papers, vol. 115, p. 317, Churchill to Baldwin, 26 September 1928.
31 Leith-Ross, *Money Talks*, p. 95.
32 T160/153/F5904, Norman to Robineau, 21 March 1923; Clay, *Lord Norman*, pp. 227–8.
33 Emile Moreau, *Souvenirs d'un gouverneur de la Banque de France: Histoire de la stabilisation du franc (1926–1928)* (Paris, 1954), pp. 1–2. According to his deputy Pierre Quesnay, Moreau was 'profoundly shocked' when he first learned of the terms of the 1923 agreement: BE, G1/302/2528/3, note on miscellaneous points which arose in Paris, 26th and 27th February 1927, 2 March 1927.
34 See Arthur Turner, 'Anglo-French Financial Relations in the 1920s', *European History Quarterly*, vol. 26, no. 1 (January 1996), 31–55.
35 *The Nation and Athenaeum*, 'Is there Enough Gold? The League of Nations Inquiry', 19 January 1929. Benjamin Strong had expressed similar views a year earlier when he wrote that 'London was absolutely dependent on the good-will of the Bank of France for protection against a raid on its gold': cited in Clay, *Lord Norman*, p. 263.
36 In May 1927 Moreau noted with some satisfaction the distress and fear caused at the Bank of England by the 'révélation brutale de la puissance de la Banque de France sur le marché de Londres': *Souvenirs*, pp. 317–18.
37 The French financial crisis is discussed in Artaud, *La Question des dettes interalliées*, II, 821–34. See also Wolfe, *The French Franc Between the Wars*, ch. 2; R. G. Hawtry,

The Art of Central Banking (London, 1932), pp. 4–8

38 Moreau, *Souvenirs*, p. vi, preface by Jacques Rueff.
39 Ibid., pp. 48–9. See also Boyle, *Montagu Norman*, pp. 198–200.
40 S. V. O. Clarke, *Central Bank Cooperation 124–1931* (NY, 1967), pp. 115–16.
41 According to Miles Lampson of the Foreign Office, Norman was 'certainly not over-inclined to take the French point of view into consideration – to judge by our experience of him during recent months'.: FO 371/9751, Lampson to Crowe, 22 July 1924.
42 Boyle, *Montagu Norman*, p. 194.
43 Ibid., p. 212.
44 Ibid., p. 173; Edward W. Bennett, *Germany and the Diplomacy of the Financial Crisis, 1931* (Cambridge, Mass., 1962), p. 172; Lord Vansittart, *The Mist Procession* (London, 1958), p. 301. According to Vansittart, Norman was 'infatuated' by Schacht.
45 T160/430/F12317/1, 'The Position of the Franc', memorandum by Leith-Ross, December 1926; Moreau, *Souvenirs*, p. 212.
46 *The Nation and Athenaeum*, 'The Stabilisation of the Franc', 30 June 1928.
47 BE, OV9/379, memorandum for Sir Austen Chamberlain by Norman, 4 February 1928.
48 For details of the Austrian stabilisation project and the discord which it caused between the Bank of England and the Bank of France see Clay, *Lord Norman*, pp. 183–5; Orde, *British policy and European reconstruction after the First World War*, pp.130–8.
49 BE, OV9/379, memorandum for Sir Austen Chamberlain by Norman, 4 February 1928.
50 Moreau, *Souvenirs*, pp. 273, 484, 488–9, 504.
51 Sir Arthur Salter was from 1919 Director of the Economic and Finance Section of the League. Sir Henry Strakosch was a member of the Financial Committee of the League from 1920 to 1937. Niemeyer was also a member of the Financial Committee, becoming its chairman in 1927. In addition, Norman was, in the words of one of his biographers, 'virtually an important though unofficial member': Clay, *Lord Norman*, p. 181. See also Orde, *British policy and European reconstruction after the First World War*, pp. 310–11.
52 It is clear from Moreau's memoirs that his attitude on the question of financial assistance to Poland, Romania and Yugoslavia was determined largely by political considerations. See, for example, *Souvenirs*, pp. 483–4.
53 BE, OV9/379, memorandum for Sir Austen Chamberlain by Norman, 4 Feb. 1928.
54 For detailed accounts of the negotiations for stabilisation of the Polish and Romanian currencies see Clay, *Lord Norman*, pp. 258–66; Orde, *British policy and European reconstruction after the First World War*, pp. 303–10.
55 Moreau, *Souvenirs*, pp. 48–9.
56 Boyle, *Montagu Norman*, p. 199.
57 Moreau, *Souvenirs*, p. 49.
58 Norman had given Caillaux a lecture on the same subject the previous August: BE, ADM 20/14, Norman Diary, 26 August 1925.
59 Moreau, *Souvenirs*, p. 52.
60 BE, G1/302/2528/3, Note of the conversation between the Governor and M. Moreau in Paris on Saturday 26 February 1927.
61 Siepmann was Head of the Central Banking Section of the Bank of England from 1926 to 1936. Before joining the Bank of England he was a senior official at the Treasury.

62 Quesnay was the *Directeur des Etudes économiques de la Banque de France*.
63 BE, G1/302/2528/3, Norman to Leith-Ross, 8 March 1927; Moreau, *Souvenirs*, pp. 242–4.
64 Moreau, *Souvenirs*, p. 251.
65 BE, G1/302/2528/3, Norman to Leith-Ross, 8 March 1927; Note of the conversation between the Governor and M. Moreau in Paris on Saturday 26 February 1927; T160/153/F5904, Norman to Leith-Ross, 11 March 1927.
66 BE, G1/302/2528/3, Miscellaneous points which arose in Paris, 26 and 27 February, 3 March 1927.
67 Ibid., Note of the conversation between the Governor and M. Moreau in Paris on Saturday 26 February 1927.
68 Ibid., Norman to Leith-Ross, 8 March 1927. For Moreau's scheme see T160/153/F5904, enclosure in Norman to Leith-Ross, 8 March 1927
69 Ibid., Norman to Leith-Ross, 8 March 1923; Leith-Ross to Norman, 11 March 1927, with enclosed Treasury note on 'Origin of French proposal for modification'.
70 Moreau, *Souvenirs*, pp. 252–3.
71 Ibid., p. 40.
72 Boyce, *British Capitalism at the Crossroads*, p. 144; Clarke, *Central Bank Cooperation*, pp. 108–11; Clay, *Lord Norman*, pp. 227, 235–6. By 10 May 1927 the Bank of France had acquired almost £100m sterling: Moreau, *Souvenirs*, p. 306.
73 BE, G1/302/2528/3, Moreau to Norman, 19 March 1927; Norman to Moreau, 21 March 1927; Norman to Moreau, 22 March 1927.
74 Moreau, *Souvenirs*, pp. 263–4; BE, G1/302/2528/3, Notes of a conversation between the Governor and M. Moreau, together with Mr Siepmann and M. Quesnay, on 24 March 1927.
75 BE, G1/302/2528/3, Notes of a conversation between the Governor and M. Moreau, together with Mr Siepmann and M. Quesnay, on 24 March 1927.
76 Idem.
77 Idem.
78 BE, G1/302/2528/3, Norman to Moreau, 31 March 1927; L. Lefaux to Moreau, 31 March 1927.
79 Moreau, *Souvenirs*, pp. 274–5.
80 BE G1/302/2528/3, Note of a Conversation of Governor with M. Moreau and M. Rist in Calais, 3 April 1927.
81 Idem; Moreau, *Souvenirs*, p. 281.
82 BE, G1/302/2528/3, Niemeyer to Norman, 12 April 1927; Norman to Niemeyer, 13 April 1927.
83 *The Economist*, Paris correspondent, 24 July 1926; Artaud, *La Question des dettes interalliées*. II, 830–4.
84 T172/1499A, Mendl to Tyrrell, 22 June 1926. Mendl's report was read by both Churchill and Austen Chamberlain.
85 T160/383/F8348/6, Niemeyer to Churchill, 28 July 1926; T172/1499A, note for Chancellor of the Exchequer by Niemeyer, 28 July 1926.
86 T160/383/F8348/6, Niemeyer to Pouyanne, 30 July 1926; Leith-Ross to Niemeyer, 25 October 1926; *HC*, vol. 198, col. 2805, 3 August 1926. Churchill told Wedgwood Benn that Poincaré would ask the Chamber to ratify the debt settlement 'as soon as possible and at the latest as soon as the Chamber meets in the autumn'.
87 T160/207/F7768/03/2, Crewe to Chamberlain, 5 October 1926.
88 T160/383/F8348/6, Leith-Ross to Niemeyer, 25 October 1926.
89 Ibid., Niemeyer to Churchill, 27 October 1926. For French hostility to the Mellon-Bérenger accord in the summer of 1926 see Artaud, *La Question des dettes interalliées*,

II, 811–20; Schrecker, *The Hired Money*, pp. 235–43.

90 T160/207/F7768/03/2, Niemeyer to Churchill, 27 October 1926.
91 Ibid., Niemeyer to Churchill, 9 November 1926.
92 Ibid., Grigg to Niemeyer, 12 November 1926.
93 Ibid., enclosure in Niemeyer to Churchill, undated, November 1926.
94 Ibid., Niemeyer to Churchill, undated, November 1926.
95 Ibid., minute by Churchill, 17 November 1926.
96 Ibid., note for Niemeyer and Chancellor of Exchequer by Leith-Ross, 11 December.
97 Moreau, *Souvenirs*, p. 190.
98 T160/382/F6348/6, Niemeyer to Churchill, 27 July 1926.
99 BE,G1/349/2526/6.
100 The decision to lift the ban was announced by Churchill in a speech at Sheffield on 3 November 1925: *The Times*, 4 November 1925.
101 BE, G1/349/2526/6, R. H. Trotter to Sir Eric Hambro, 12 November 1926.
102 Leffler, *The Elusive Quest*, pp. 174–7; Schrecker, *The Hired Money*, pp. 249–50.
103 Hopkins Papers, T175/4, Norman to Niemeyer, 21 February 1927.
104 Idem.
105 BE, G1/349/2526/1, d'Erlanger to Norman, 1 and 2 March 1927.
106 Ibid., Tiarks to Norman, 11 April 1927.
107 Ibid., Norman to Niemeyer, 7 March and 13 April 1927.
108 BE, G1/349/2526/6, Norman to d'Erlanger, 8 March 1927.
109 *The Financial News*, 16 January 1928; *The Times*, 17 January 1928; Kent, *The Spoils of War*, pp. 269, 272; Leffler, *The Elusive Quest*, pp. 127–30, 174–7; Schrecker, *The Hired Money*, pp. 298–318. See also BE, G1/349/2526/6, Dudley Ward to Norman, 17 January 1928; Siepmann to Dudley Ward, 17 January 1928.
110 In late 1927 Sir Richard Hopkins moved to the Treasury from the Inland Revenue Board where he had served as chairman since 1922. Niemeyer's departure to the Bank of England was followed by an administrative reorganisation at the Treasury and Hopkins became Controller of Finance and Supply Services. He later became Permanent Secretary (1942–45).
111 BE, G1/349/2526/6, Norman to Hopkins, 4 February 1928.
112 Ibid., Norman to Leith-Ross, 26 September 1928.
113 Hopkins Papers, T175/4, Wilkinson to Norman, 28 September 1928.
114 Idem.
115 BE,G1/349/2526/6, Norman to Fisher, 2 October 1928.
116 Hopkins Papers, T175/4, Leith-Ross to Churchill, 6 October 1928.
117 Ibid., minute by Hopkins, 7 October 1928.
118 Hopkins Papers, T175/4, Note for the Chancellor of the Exchequer by Leith-Ross, 6 October 1928.
119 Ibid., minute by Churchill, 9 October 1928.
120 Ibid., Hopkins to Norman, 10 October 1928.
121 T160/383/F8348/7, Poincaré to Churchill, 15 February 1927; note for Sir Richard Hopkins and Chancellor of the Exchequer by Leith-Ross, 5 January 1928; Poincaré to Churchill, 4 February 1928.
122 T160/383/F8348/6, 'Interview with Monsieur Pouyanne of 28 January 1928', note by Leith-Ross, 28 January 1928; 'Interview with Monsieur Pouyanne of 1 February 1928', note by Leith-Ross, 1 February 1928; Leith-Ross to Sargent, 4 February 1928; note by Leith-Ross of interview with Pouyanne, 7 February 1928.
123 For Snowden's question see *HC*, vol. 202, col.1105, 17 February 1927.
124 Idem.
125 Churchill Papers, 18/43, Churchill to Poincaré, 17 February 1927.

126 Ibid., 18/73, Churchill to Poincaré, 11 February 1928; Churchill to Selby, 11 February 1928.
127 The reasons why Poincaré remained unwilling to seek ratification of the British and American debt settlements after the elections of April 1928 are discussed in Artaud, *La Question des dettes interalliées*, II, 908–10.
128 *The Times*, 22 June 1928, p. 16; T160/207/F7768/03/2, note for Sir Richard Hopkins and Chancellor of the Exchequer by Leith-Ross, 27 June 1928.
129 *DBFP*, Series 1A, no. 88, Chamberlain to Crewe, 12 July 1928.
130 T160/207/F7768/03/2, note for Sir Richard Hopkins and Chancellor of the Exchequer by Leith-Ross, 27 June 1928.
131 Idem; ibid., Churchill to Chamberlain, 2 July 1928.
132 *DBFP*, Series 1A, V, no. 88, Chamberlain to Crewe, 12 July 1928. see also ibid. no. 93, Crewe to Chamberlain, 19 July 1928.
133 For this celebrated incident in September 1922 see Hardinge of Penshurst, *Old Diplomacy* (London, 1947), pp. 272–3; Sir Harold Nicolson, *Curzon: The Last Phase, 1919–1925* (New York, 1925), pp. 273–4.
134 For Parker Gilbert's diplomatic activity during 1928 see Artaud, *La Question des dettes interalliées*, II, 891–8; Jacobson, *Locarno Diplomacy*, pp. 143–5, 156–63, 215–20; Kent, *Spoils of War*, pp. 272–86; Leffler, *The Elusive Quest*, pp. 182–7; Leith-Ross, *Money Talks*, 103–5.
135 For the negotiations leading up to the decision to establish a committee of experts see Baldwin Papers, vol. 112, 104–10, Cushendun to Lindsay, 19 September 1928; Jacobson, *Locarno Diplomacy*, pp. 195–200; Kent, *Spoils of War*, pp. 276–80.
136 For Poincaré's efforts to settle the question of the French war debt in the context of a broader agreement involving reparations see Schrecker, *The Hired Money*, pp. 319–44.
137 For Churchill's account of his talk with Poincaré see Baldwin Papers, vol. 230, memorandum by Churchill, 19 October 1928; *DBFP*, Series 1A, no. 187.
138 *DBFP*, Series 1A, V, no. 187, Memorandum by the Chancellor of the Exchequer on his conversation in Paris, 19 October 1928. For the legal and political implications of ratification by decree see Schrecker, *The Hired Money*, pp. 352–6.
139 *DBFP*, Series 1A, V, no. 187.
140 Idem. Churchill's private secretary described Poincaré as being 'unusually amiable' during the meeting: Grigg, *Prejudice and Judgement*, pp. 208–9.
141 For the deliberations of the Young committee see Artaud, *La Question des dettes interalliées*, II, 901–8; Kent, *Spoils of War*, pp. 286–303: Hjalmar Schacht, *My First Seventy-Six Years: The Autobiography of Hjalmar Schacht*, translated by Diana Pyke (London, 1955), pp. 236–47.
142 *The Daily Herald*, 9 May 1929; *The Nation and Athenaeum*, 11 May 1929; *HC*, vol. 127, col. 2311, 9 May 1929; Snowden, *An Autobiography*, 2 vols (London, 1934), II, 782.
143 *HC*, vol. 227, col. 121, 16 April 1929. Snowden followed up his parliamentary comments with a newspaper article in *The Sunday Express*, again arguing that France's failure to ratify the 1926 settlement meant that the British government was 'perfectly free to have this tentative agreement reconsidered'. There was some support for this argument at the Treasury where Leith-Ross expressed the view that Snowden was substantially correct, even if his language was somewhat incautious. According to Leith-Ross, since Britain had so far paid the United States £200m in excess of what she had received on account of inter-alled debts and reparations, it would be possible to negotiate a new settlement with France without repudiating the Balfour Note principle. Moreover, the British government would be in a strong posi-

tion to get better terms than in 1926 because 'at that time France was on the verge of ruin whereas now she loses no opportunity of asserting her financial power'. See *The Sunday Express*, 21 April 1929; Leith-Ross Papers, T188/7, Leith-Ross to Grigg, undated, April 1929.

144 *The Daily Herald*, leading article, 'Debts and Debtors', 18 April 1929; ibid., 22 April 1929; Snowden, *An Autobiography*, II, 755.

145 *HC*, vol. 227, cols. 359–65, 17 April 1929.

146 Artaud, *La Question des dettes interalliées*, II, 868–9; Jacobson, *Locarno Diplomacy*, pp. 159–60; Kent, *Spoils of War*, pp. 269, 277; Leffler, *The Elusive Quest*, p. 180. See also Petit, *Le Règlement Des Dettes Interalliées, 1919–1929*, pp. 217–18; Schrecker, *The Hired Money*, p. 296.

147 Kent, *Spoils of War*, p. 269.

148 The following account of the German financial crisis of 1931 and its wider repercussions is based mainly upon: Bennett, *Germany and the Diplomacy of the Financial Crisis*, chs 1, 3, 5; David Burner, *Herbert Hoover: A Public Life* (New York, 1979), ch. 7; Kent, *Spoils of War*, ch. 9; Leffler, *The Elusive Quest*, chs 6 and 7.

149 Leith-Ross, *Money Talks*, pp. 133–4.

150 Ibid., p. 135; Kent, *Spoils of War*, p. 341.

151 Kent, *Spoils of War*, pp. 341–2: Leffler, *The Elusive Quest*, pp. 236, 238.

152 For the text of Hoover's proposal see *FRUS*, 1931, I, 33–5. It can also be found in Arnold J. Toynbee (ed.), *Survey of International Affairs 1932* (London, 1933), pp. 99–100. For Hoover's motivation in proposing a moratorium see Bennett, *Germany and the Diplomacy of the Financial Crisis*, p. 165; Burner, *Herbert Hoover*, pp. 300–301; R. H. Ferrell, *American Diplomacy in the Great Depression: Hoover-Stimson Foreign Policy, 1929–33* (New Haven, 1957), ch. 7; Herbert Hoover, *The Memoirs of Herbert Hoover*, vol. 3, *The Great Depression, 1929–1941* (London, 1954), 63–71; Kent, *Spoils of War*, pp. 322, 343–5; Leffler, *The Elusive Quest*, pp. 234–9; P. Lochner, *Herbert Hoover and Germany* (New York, 1960), ch. 6.

153 For the hostile French reaction to the Hoover moratorium see *DBFP*, 2nd Series, II, 107–8. 166–7; *FRUS*, 1931, I, 44, 47, 57–8, 61, 80, 96, 105–8, 133–5, 142–3, 150–59; Bennett, *Germany and the Diplomacy of the Financial Crisis*, pp. 167–78; Burner, *Herbert Hoover*, pp. 301–2; David Carlton, *MacDonald versus Henderson: The Foreign Policy of the Second labour Government* (London, 1970), pp. 198–9; Walter E. Edge, *A Journeyman's Journal: Fifty Years of American Business and Politics* (Princeton, 1948), pp. 191–7; Ferrell, *American Diplomacy in the Great Depression*, pp. 113–15; *The Memoirs of Herbert Hoover*, III, 71–2; Leffler, *The Elusive Quest*, pp. 241–5; Leith-Ross, *Money Talks*, p. 136; Marquand, *MacDonald*, p. 605; *Survey of International Affairs 1932* [hereafter *SIA 1932*], pp. 100–102; Geoffrey Warner, *Pierre Laval and the Eclipse of France* (London, 1968), pp. 31–3.

154 Carlton, *MacDonald versus Henderson*, p. 198; Marquand, *MacDonald*, pp. 604–5. For the warm British response to the Hoover moratorium see *DBFP*, 2nd Series, II, nos 69, 74; *HC*, vol. 254, cols. 36, 414–16, 22 and 24 June 931.

155 For British efforts to organise an early conference at Lausanne see *DBFP*, 2nd Series, II, no. 314, Simon to Tyrrell, 16 December 1931; no. 318, Tyrrell to Simon, 19 December 1931; III, no. 1, Campbell to Simon, 28 December 1931; no. 2, Lindsay to Simon, 28 December 1931. A detailed discussion of British diplomatic activity prior to the Lausanne conference is to be found in Kent, *Spoils of War*, pp. 362–6.

156 *DBFP*, 2nd Series, II, no. 319, Notes of a Conversation of December 19 between Sir F. Leith-Ross and M. Flandin regarding German Reparations and War Debts; III, no. 13, Tyrrell to Simon, 10 January 1932; no. 19, Simon to Rumbold, 12 January 1932; Cab 23/70, 1(32), Cabinet minutes of 11 January 1932; Leith-Ross, *Money*

Talks, p. 143.

157 Congress was adamantly opposed to concessions over debts. On 22 December, while reluctantly giving retrospective approval to the Hoover moratorium, it resolved that it was 'against the policy of Congress that any of the indebtedness of foreign countries to the United States should in any manner be cancelled or reduced': *FRUS*, 1931, I, 248–9; *SIA 1932.*, p. 108. Influenced by the mood of Congress, Secretary of State Stimson was equally unyielding in a conversation with the French chargé in Washington on 29 December 1931: Kent, *Spoils of War*, p. 363; Leffler, *The Elusive Quest*, p. 289.

158 Burner, *Herbert Hoover*, p. 304; *SIA 1932*, pp. 105–6, 108.

159 Leffler, *The Elusive Quest*, pp. 159–69.

160 *DBFP*, 2nd Series, III, no. 134, Notes of a Meeting held at the British Embassy, Paris, on June 11, 1932, at 6.30 p.m.

161 *SIA 1932*, p. 110.

162 Ibid., p. 111. For Herriot's opening speech at the Lausanne conference see *DBFP*, 2nd Series, III, Stenographic Notes of the Second Plenary Session of the Conference, Friday, June 17, 1932, 10 a.m. Also pp. 237–40, 257–9, 267–9. For discusssions at conference see *DBFP*, 2nd Series, III, nos 137–92.

163 *DBFP*, 2nd Series, XXI, Annex to no. 165; *FRUS*, 1932, I, 684. For the text of the 'Gentleman's Agreement' see *DBFP*, 2nd Series, enclosure in no. 186; Cmd. 4129 (1932), *Further Documents relating to the Settlement reached at the Lausanne Conference (Lausanne June 16–July 9, 1932)*, No. 1; *FRUS*, 1932, I, 688. See also John Wheeler-Bennett, *The Wreck of Reparations* (London, 1933), pp. 272–3.

164 For details of the German reparation agreement reached at Lausanne see Cmd. 4126 (1932), *Final Act of the Lausanne Conference Lausanne, July 9, 1932*, pp. 5–12; Moulton and Pasvolsky, *War Debts and World Prosperity*, pp. 354–66. See also Leffler, *The Elusive Quest*, p. 291; Leith-Ross, *Money Talks*, pp. 150–2.

165 *SIA 1932*, pp. 114–15.

166 *HC*, vol. 268, cols. 1180–81, 83–4, 12 July 1932; *FRUS*, 1932, I, 686–7, The Ambassador in Great Britain to the Secretary of State, 12 July 1932; *SIA 1932*, pp. 114–15.

167. *FRUS*, 1932, I, 691, President Hoover to Senator William E. Borah, 14 July 1932; John W. Wheeler Bennett (ed.), *Documents on International Affairs 1932* (London, 1933), No. 1, pp. 35–6. On 14 July 1932 the Treasury issued an official statement making it clear that Chamberlain had not intended to suggest US representatives had approved what had been done at Lausanne: *FRUS*, 1932, I, 690.

168 *FRUS*, 1932, I, 754–6, The British Ambassador to the Secretary of State, 10 November 1932; 727–7, The French Embassy to the Department of State, 10 November 1932; Leith-Ross, *Money Talks*, p. 154.

169 Leith-Ross, *Money Talks*, pp. 154–5. All the British notes were drafted by Leith-Ross and Sir David Waley, on the directions of the Chancellor of the Exchequer.

170 Kent, *Spoils of War*, pp. 354–5; Leffler, *The Elusive Quest*, pp. 306–7; Leith-Ross, *Money Talks*, p. 157; *SIA 1932*, pp. 107–8, 128.

171 *SIA 1932*, pp. 129–31. For Hoover's difficulties as a 'lame duck' President see Jordan A. Schwarz, *The Interregnum of Despair: Hoover, Congress and the Depression* (Urbana, 1970), chs 8 and 9. Hoover's public views on debt cancellation were expressed in messages to Congress on 6 and 19 December 1932: *Documents on International Affairs*, No. 10, pp. 66–7; *FRUS*, 1932, I, xxii–xxv.

172 *FRUS*, 1932, I, The Secretary of State to the British Ambassador, 23 November 1932; *Documents on International Affairs*, No. 6, pp. 45–7; Leith-Ross, *Money Talks*, p. 154.

173 T172/1506, 'War Debts: The Next Step', note for Sir Warren Fisher and Chancellor of the Exchequer by Leith-Ross, 5 December 1931.

174 *FRUS*, 1932, I, 758–70, The British Embassy to the Department of State, 1 December 1932; *Documents on International Affairs 1932*, No. 8, pp. 49–61; *SIA 1932*, pp. 122–3; Leith-Ross, *Money Talks*, p. 155.

175 *FRUS*, 1932, I, 771–5, The Secretary of State to the British Ambassador, 7 December 1932; 776–8, The British Embassy to the Department of State, 11 December 1932; *Documents on International Affairs*, No. 15, pp. 77–8; *SIA 1932*, pp. 126–7; Leith-Ross, *Money Talks*, p. 155.

176 For the note which the French government sent to Washington on 1 December 1932 see *FRUS*, 1932, I, The French Embassy to the Department of State, 1 December 1932; *Le Temps*, 3 December 1932; *Documents on International Affairs 1932*, No. 9, pp. 62–4.

177 The text of the communiqué issued after these talks is to be found in *The Times*, 9 December 1932.

178 *FRUS*, I, 741–2, The Ambassador in France to the Secretary of State, 9 December 1932.

179 Herriot, *Jadis*, II, 335–7; *Documents Diplomatiques Français 1932–39*, Ire Série (Paris, 1964–), II, 191–201; Leith-Ross, *Money Talks*, p. 155. The text of Herriot's speeches setting out his policy in the Chamber on 12, 13 and 14 December 1932 is to be found in *Documents on International Affairs 1932*, No. 20, pp. 82–129. For the resolution adopted by the Chamber on 14 December see ibid., No. 19, pp. 80–2. See also *FRUS*, 1932, I, 743–7.

180 Leith-Ross, *Money Talks*, pp. 158–9.

181 For the evolution of Roosevelt's policy on foreign war debts see Leffler, *The Elusive Quest*, ch. 9. See also Leith-Ross, *Money Talks*, pp. 171–2, 178.

182 Leith-Ross, *Money Talks*, pp. 159–63; *SIA 1933* (London, 1934), pp. 81–3.

183 Leith-Ross, *Money Talks*, pp. 170–1.

184 *SIA 1933*, p. 83.

185 Leith-Ross, *Money Talks*, pp. 178–9.

186 Ibid., p. 179.

187 Cmd. 4129 (1932), No. 5, Letters from the Chancellor of the Exchequer to the French and Italian Ministers of Finance regarding French and Italian Debts to the United Kingdom, 8 July 1932; *FRUS*, 1932, I, 689; *SIA 1932*, p. 114.

Bibliography

1 Unpublished Primary Sources

Government Archives, Public Record Office, London (Kew)
Cabinet Papers
Cab 23   Cabinet Minutes
Cab 24   Cabinet Memoranda
Cab 27   Cabinet Committees: General Series
Cab 29   Proceedings of the London Reparations Conference

Foreign Office Papers
FO 371   General Correspondence: Political
FO 800   Private Collections
    FO 800/147–58   Curzon Papers
    FO 800/220   Correspondence between Sir William Tyrrell and Sir Charles Charles Mendl
    FO 800/226   Reading Papers
    FO 800/243   Sir Eyre Crowe Papers
    FO 800/256–63   Sir Austen Chamberlain Papers
    FO 800/280–84   Arthur Henderson Papers
    FO 800/292   Lectures on British Foreign Policy by R. F. Wigram
    FO 800/330   Reports from Sir Charles Mendl, Press Attaché to the Paris embassy

Treasury Papers
T160   Finance Files
T172   Chancellor of the Exchequer's Office
T175   Sir Richard Hopkins Papers
T176   Sir Otto Niemeyer Papers
T188   Sir Frederick Leith-Ross Papers

Bank of England Archives
ADM 20   Montagu Norman Diaries (Photocopy)
ADM 25   H. A. Siepmann Papers
C44/268   Investments, Bank of France Credit
G1   Governors' Files
G30   Governors' Miscellaneous Correspondence
OV 9   Sir Otto Niemeyer Papers
OV 179   British War Debts

Private Collections and Personal Papers
Baldwin Papers, Cambridge University Library
Bonar Law Papers, House of Lords Record Office
Cecil of Chelwood Papers, British Library
Sir Austen Chamberlain Papers, Birmingham University Library
Churchill Papers, Churchill College, Cambridge
Hugh Dalton Papers, British Library of Political amd Economic Science
J. C. C. Davidson Papers, House of Lords Record Office
Hankey Papers, Churchill College, Cambridge
Lloyd George Papers, House of Lords Record Office
James Ramsay MacDonald Papers, Public Record Office
Sir Eric Phipps Papers, Churchill College, Cambridge

2 Published Primary Sources

Official Publications
E. L. Woodward, Rohan Butler *et al.*, *Documents on British Foreign Policy 1919–1939*,
 First Series, vols VIII, XIV, XV, XVI, XIX, XX, XXI, XXVI (London, 1958–85).
 Series 1A, vols I, V, VI, VII (London, 1966–77).
 Second Series, vols II, III (London, 1947–8).
Ministère des Affaires Etrangères, *Documents Diplomatiques Français 1932–1939*, Ire Série
 (Paris, 1964–), II.
Department of State, *Papers Relating to the Foreign Relations of the United States 1920–32*
 (Kraus Reprint, N.Y., 1971–2)
Parliamentary Debates, Official Report, 5th series, House of Commons.
Parliamentary Debates, Official Report, 5th series, House of Lords.

Parliamentary Papers:
Cmd 1737 (1922) *Despatch to the Representatives of France, Italy, Serb-Croat-Slovene
 State, Roumania, Portugal and Greece at London respecting War Debts*
Cmd 1812 (1923) *Inter-Allied Conferences on Reparations and Inter-Allied Debts. Held in
 London and Paris, December 1922 and January 1923. Reports and
 Secretaries' Notes of Conversations*
Cmd 1912 (1923) *American Debt. Arrangements for the Funding of the British Debt to the
 United States of America*
Cmd 2184 (1924) *Correspondence concerning the Conference Which It Is Proposed to Hold
 in London on July 16 1924 to Consider the means Necessary to Bring the
 Dawes Plan into Operation*
Cmd 2191 (1924), *Franco-British Memorandum of 9 July 1924, concerning the Application
 of the Dawes Scheme*
Cmd 2200 (1924) *Correspondence between His Majesty's Government and the League of
 Nations respecting the proposed Treaty of Mutual Assistance*
Cmd 2270 (1924) *Proceedings of the London Reparation Conference July and August 1924*
Cmd 2580 (1926) *Agreement for the Settlement of the War Debt of Italy to Great Britain*
Cmd 2692 (1926) *Agreement for the Settlement of the War Debt of France to Great Britain,
 with an Exchange of letters between the Chancellor of the Exchequer and
 the French Minister of Finance*
Cmd 3779 (1931) *Correspondence respecting Position of British Holders of French Rentes
 issued in the United Kingdom in 1915–1918*
Cmd 4126 (1932) *Final Act of the Lausanne Conference Lausanne, 9 July 1932*

Cmd 4129 (1932) *Further Documents relating to the Settlement reached at the Lausanne Conference (Lausanne, June 16–July 9, 1932)*

Autobiographies, Diaries and Memoirs
Brand, Hon. R.H., *War and National Finance*, (London, 1921).
Caillaux, Joseph, *Mes Mémoires*, 3 vols, vol.3, *Clairvoyance et force d'âme dans les épreuves, 1912–1930* (Paris, 1947).
Cambon, Paul, *Correspondence, 1870–1924*, 3 vols (Paris, 1940–6).
Chamberlain, Sir Austen, *Down The Years* (London, 1935).
Clémentel, Etienne, *La France et la politique économique interalliée* (Paris, 1931).
Cole, Margaret, (ed.), *Diaries of Beatrice Webb, 1924–32* (London, 1956).
Dalton, Hugh, *Call Back Yesterday: Memoirs 1887–1931* (London, 1953).
Edge, Walter E., *A Journeyman's Journal: Fifty Years of American Business and Politics* (Princeton, 1948).
Grigg, P. J., *Prejudice and Judgement* (London, 1948).
Herriot, Edouard, *Jadis*, 2 vols, vol.2, *D'une guerre à l'autre, 1914–1936* (Paris, 1952).
Hoover, Herbert, *The Memoirs of Herbert Hoover*, vol. 3, *The Great Depression, 1929–1941* (London, 1954).
James, Robert Rhodes (ed.), *J. C. C. Davidson: Memoirs of a Conservative* (London, 1969).
Jones, Thomas, *A Diary with Letters 1931–50* (London, 1954).
Klotz, Louis, *De la guerre à la paix: Souvenirs et documents* (Paris, 1924).
Leith-Ross, Sir Frederick, *Money Talks: Fifty Years of International Finance* (London, 1968).
Loucheur, Louis, *Carnets secrets 1908–1932* (ed. Jacques De Launay, Paris, 1962).
Middlemas, Keith, (ed.), *Thomas Jones: Whitehall Diary* (London, 1969).
McAdoo, W. G. *Crowded Years* (London, 1932).
Moreau, Emile, *Souvenirs d'un Gouverneur de la Banque de France: Histoire de la Stabilisation du Franc 1926–1928* (Paris, 1954).
Schacht, Hjalmar, *My First Seventy-Six Years* (London, 1935).
Snowden, Viscount, *An Autobiography*, 2 vols (London, 1934).

Newspapers
The Daily Herald   *The Manchester Guardian*   *The Nation and Athenaeum*
The Times

Use has also been made of selected newspaper articles on Anglo-French relations available at Chatham House. The selection includes extracts from both British and French newspapers, including *The Daily Telegraph*, *The Manchester Guardian*, *The Observer*, *The Times*, the *Echo de Paris*, the *Figaro* and the *Temps*.

3   Secondary Sources

Addison, Paul, *Churchill and the Home Front 1900–1955* (London, 1992).
Aldcroft, Derek H., *The Inter-War Economy: Britain 1919–1939* (London, 1970).
——, *The European Economy 1914–1980* (London, 1980).
——, *From Versailles to Wall Street, 1919–1929* (London, 1977).
Artaud, Denise, *La Question des dettes interalliées et la reconstruction de l'Europe 1917–1929*, 2 vols (Lille and Paris, 1978).
Baker, Ray Stannard, *Woodrow Wilson, Life and Letters*, vols 6–8 (New York, 1937–9).
——, *Woodrow Wilson and World Settlement*, 3 vols (New York, 1922).

Balogh, Thomas, 'The Import of Gold into France', *The Economic Journal*, XL (1930), pp. 442–60.

Bennett, Edward W., *Germany and the Diplomacy of the Financial Crisis, 1931* (Cambridge, Mass., 1962).

Bérenger, Henry, *La Question des dettes* (Paris, 1933).

Bergmann, Carl, *The History of Reparations* (London, 1927).

Binion, Rudolph, *Defeated Leaders: The Political Fate of Caillaux, Jouvenel and Tardieu* (New York, 1960).

Blake, Robert, *The Unknown Prime Minister: The Life and Times of Andrew Bonar Law* (London, 1955).

Bogart, Ernest Ludlow, *War Costs and Their Financing: A Study of the Financing of the War and the After-War Problems of Debt and Taxation* (New York, 1921).

Boyce, Robert W., *British Capitalism at the Crossroads, 1919–1932: A study in politics, economics, and international relations* (Cambridge, 1987).

Boyle, Andrew, *Montagu Norman: a Biography* (London, 1967).

Bunselmeyer, Robert E., *The Cost of the War 1914–1919: British Economic War Aims and the Origins of Reparation* (Hamden, Conn., 1975).

Burk, Kathleen, *Britain, America and the Sinews of War 1914–1918* (London, 1985).

Burner, David, *Herbert Hoover: A Public Life* (New York, 1979).

Carlton, David, *MacDonald versus Henderson: The Foreign Policy of the Second Labour Government* (London, 1970).

Chandler, Lester V., *Benjamin Strong, Central Banker* (Washington, 1958).

Clarke, Steven V. O., *Central Bank Cooperation 1924–1931* (New York, 1967).

Clay, Sir Henry, *Montagu Norman* (London, 1957).

Cross, Colin, *Philip Snowden* (London, 1966).

Dulles, Eleanor Lansing, *The French Franc 1914–1928: The Facts and their Interpretation* (New York, 1929).

——, *The Dollar, The Franc and Inflation* (New York, 1932).

Dutton, David, *Austen Chamberlain: Gentleman in Politics* (Bolton, 1985).

Einzig, Paul, *Finance and Politics* (London, 1932).

——, *The Fight for Financial Supremacy* (London, 1932).

——, *International Gold Movements*, 2nd edn (London, 1931).

——, *Behind the Scenes of International Finance* (London, 1931).

——, 'Some New Features of Gold Movements', *The Economic Journal*, XL (1930), pp. 56–63.

——, 'Fine Gold v. Standard Gold', *The Economic Journal*, XL (1930), pp. 461–5.

Fabre-Luce, Alfred, *Caillaux* (Paris, 1933).

Ferrell, R. H., *American Diplomacy in the Great Depression: Hoover-Stimson Foreign Policy, 1929–33* (New Haven 1957).

Fisk, Harvey E., *The Inter-Ally Debts: An Analysis of War and Post-War Public Finance 1914–23* (New York and Paris, 1924).

Fowler, W. B., *British-American Relations 1917–1918: The Role of Sir William Wiseman* (Princeton, 1969).

Gilbert, Martin, *World in Torment: Winston S. Churchill*, vol. 4: 1917–1922 (London, 1975).

——, *Prophet of Truth: Winston S. Churchill*, vol. 5: 1922–1939 (London, 1976).

——, *Winston S. Churchill*, Companion Volume, part 2, vol.5 (London, 1977).

——, *Winston Churchill, a Life* (London, 1992).

Gregory, Sir Theodore, 'Lord Norman: A New Interpretation', *Lloyds Bank Review* (April 1968), pp. 31–51.

Haig, Robert M., *The Public Finances of Post-War France* (New York, 1929).

Hamilton, Mary Agnes, *Arthur Henderson: A Biography* (London, 1938).

Hirsch, Fred, *Money International* (London, 1967).

Harrod, R. F., *The Life of John Maynard Keynes* (London, 1951).

Hemery, J. A., 'The Emergence of Treasury Influence in British Foreign Policy, 1914–1921' Unpublished Ph.D. Thesis (University of Cambridge, 1988).

Jacobson, Jon, *Locarno Diplomacy: Germany and the West 1925–1929* (Princeton, 1972).

James, Robert Rhodes, *Churchill: A Study in Failure, 1900–1939* (London, 1970).

Jenkins, Roy, *Baldwin* (London, 1988).

Jèze, Gaston, and Truchy, Henri, *The War Finance of France: The War Expenditure of France* and *How France met Her War Expenditure* (New Haven, 1927).

Kemp, Tom, *The French Economy 1913–1979: The history of a decline* (London, 1972).

Kent, Bruce, *The Spoils of War: The Politics, Economics and Diplomacy of Reparations 1918–1932* (Oxford, 1989).

Keynes, J. M., *Collected Writings*, vols IX, XVI, XVII, XVII, XIX (London, 1971–81).

Kirkcaldy, A. W., *British Finance During and After the War* (London, 1971).

Kooker, Judith L., 'French financial diplomacy in the interwar years', in Benjamin M. Rowland (ed.), *Balance of Power or Hegemony: The Interwar Monetary System* (New York, 1976).

Kuisel, Richard F., *Capitalism and the State in Modern France: Renovation and Economic Management in the Twentieth Century* (Cambridge, 1981).

Leffler, Melvyn P., *The Elusive Quest: America's Pursuit of European Stability and French Security, 1919–1923* (Chapel Hill, 1979).

Lloyd George, David, *The Truth About Reparations and War Debts* (London, 1932).

Lochner, P., *Herbert Hoover and Germany* (New York, 1960).

McDougall, Walter A., *France's Rhineland Diplomacy 1914–1924* (Princeton, 1978).

Maier, Charles S., *Recasting Bourgeois Europe: Stabilisation in France, Germany and Italy in the Decade after World War I* (Princeton, 1975).

Maisel, Ephraim, *The Foreign Office and Foreign Policy, 1919–1926* (Brighton, 1994).

Marks, Sally, *The Illusion of Peace: International Relations in Europe 1918–1933* (London, 1976).

Marquand, David, *Ramsay MacDonald* (London, 1977).

Meyer, Richard, *Bankers' Diplomacy: Monetary Stabilisation in the Twenties* (New York, 1970).

Middlemas, Keith, and Barnes, John, *Baldwin: A Biography* (London, 1969).

Miquel, Pierre, *Poincaré* (Paris, 1961).

Moggridge, D. E., *British Monetary Policy 1924–1931: The Norman Conquest of $4.86* (Cambridge, 1972).

——, *The Return to Gold: The Formulation of Economic Policy and its tactics* (Cambridge, 1969).

Morgan, Austen, *James Ramsay MacDonald* (Manchester, 1987).

Morgan, E. Victor, *Studies in British Financial Policy 1914–25* (London, 1952).

Moulton, Harold G., and Lewis, Cleona, *The French Debt Problem* (New York, 1923).

Moulton, Harold G., and Pasvolsky, Leo., *War Debts and World Prosperity* (Washington, 1932).

——, *World War Debt Settlements* (New York, 1926).

Mouré, Kenneth, *Managing the Franc Poincaré: Economic Understanding and Political Constraint in French Monetary Policy, 1928–1936* (Cambridge, 1991).

Myers, Margaret G., *Paris as a Financial Centre* (London, 1936).

Néré Jacques, *The Foreign Policy of France from 1914 to 1945* (London, 1975).

Nicolson, Harold, *Curzon, the Last Phase 1919–1925: A Study in Post-War Diplomacy* (London, 1934).

Orde, Anne, *British policy and European reconstruction after the First World War* (Cambridge, 1992).

Peel, George, *The Economic Policy of France* (London, 1937).

Petit, Lucien., *Histoire Des Finances Extérieures De La France Pendant La Guerre (1914–1919)* (Paris, 1929).

——, *Histoire Des Finances Extérieures De La Guerre: Le Règlement Des Dettes Interalliées (1919–1929)* (Paris, 1932).

Petrie, Sir Charles, *The Life and Letters of the Right Hon. Sir Austen Chamberlain, K.C., P.C., M.P.*, 2 vols (London, 1939–40).

Pollard, Sydney, *The Development of the British Economy 1914–1967*, 2nd edn (London, 1969).

Rhodes, Benjamin D., 'Reassessing Uncle Shylock: The US and the French War Debt 1917–29', *Journal of American History*, vol. 55 (March 1969), 787–803.

Roskill, Stephen, *Hankey, Man of Secrets*, 3 vols (London, 1970–4).

Rueff, Jacques, and Hirsch, Fred, 'The Role and The Rule of Gold', *Princeton Essays in International Finance*, XLVII (June 1966), pp. 1–18.

Rupieper, Hermann J., *The Cuno Government and Reparations 1922–1923: Politics and Economics* (The Hague, 1979).

Sauvy, Alfred, *Histoire économique de la France entre les deux guerres*, 2nd edn, 3 vols (Paris, 1984).

Schrecker, Ellen, *The Hired Money: The French Debt to the United States 1917–1929* (New York, 1978).

Schuker, Stephen A., *The End of French Predominance in Europe: The Financial Crisis of 1924 and the Adoption of the Dawes Plan* (Chapel Hill, 1976).

Schwarz, Jordan A., *The Interregnum of Despair: Hoover, Congress and Depression* (Urbana, 1970).

Seydoux, Jacques, *De Versailles au plan Young: réparations – dettes interalliées – reconstruction européenne* (Paris, 1932).

Silverman, Dan P., *Reconstructing Europe after the Great War* (Cambridge, Mass., 1982).

Skidelsky, Robert, *John Maynard Keynes*, 2 vols (London, 1983, 1992).

Suarez, Georges, *Briand: sa vie-son oeuvre avec son journal et de nombreux documents inédits*, vols 5–6 (Paris, 1941–1952).

Tillman, S. P., *Anglo-American Relations at the Paris Peace Conference* (New York, 1972).

Trachtenberg, Marc, *Reparation in World Politics: France and European Economic Diplomacy 1916–1923* (New York, 1980).

Turner, Arthur, 'Anglo-French Financial Relations in the 1920s', *European History Quarterly*, vol. 26, no. 1 (January 1996), 31–55.

——, 'British holdings of French war bonds: an aspect of Anglo-French relations during the 1920s', *Financial History Review*, vol. 3, part 2 (October 1996), 153–74.

——, 'Keynes, the Treasury and French War Debts in the 1920s', *European History Quarterly*, vol. 27, no. 4 (October 1997), 505–30.

Vineberg, Philip F. *The French Franc and the Gold Standard 1926–1936* (Montreal, 1936).

Waites, Neville (ed.), *Troubled Neighbours: Franco-British Relations in the Twentieth Century* (London, 1971).

Warner, Geoffrey, *Pierre Laval and the Eclipse of France* (London, 1968).

Weill-Raynal, Etienne, *Les Réparations allemandes et la France*, 3 vols (Paris, 1947).

Wheeler-Bennett, J. W., *The Wreck of Reparations* (London, 1933).

Wolfe, Martin, *The French Franc Between the Wars* (New York, 1951).

Wolfers, Arnold, *Britain and France between Two Wars* (Hamden, Conn., 1963).

Wrench, Sir Evelyn, *Geoffrey Dawson and Our Times* (London, 1955).

Young, G. M., *Stanley Baldwin* (London, 1952).

Youngson, A. J., *Britain's Economic Growth 1920–1966* (London, 1967).

Index